Ex Líbrís

GREENPEACE III

Journey into the Bomb

DAVID McTAGGART
with
ROBERT HUNTER

COLLINS
St James's Place, London
1978

William Collins Sons & Co Ltd
London · Glasgow · Sydney · Auckland
Toronto · Johannesburg

First published 1978
© David McTaggart 1978
ISBN 0 211885 8

Set in Monotype Garamond
Made and Printed in Great Britain by
Butler & Tanner Ltd, Frome and London

Contents

Contents

To Lisa, Kerin and Tamra

Acknowledgements

Thanks to Nigel's perseverance, steadiness and guts; Ann-Marie's love and ingenuity, Grant's humour and open friendliness and Mary's sensible warm companionship the voyages were successful.

Thanks to Jack Cunningham's understanding, Thierry Garby's enthusiasm and faith there was follow through.

Thanks to Brice Lelond's friendship and support, Paris was made available.

Thanks to my brother Drew's calm guidance I was able to keep a reasonable presence of mind. My mother's and father's unfailing support and steadying influence gave the much-needed backbone to all involved. And it was Ben Metcalfe who triggered the event.

This is their story – my deepest gratitude to them all.

There were so many others who helped – six years through thirteen countries, it would be impossible to name all those who helped and supported us – but I can only mention a few.

Mrs Mabel Hetherington, Honorary Secretary, CND – a beautiful, humble young lady in her seventies who stood as the symbol of my voyages. Harry Pope, Gene and Pat Horne; Richard Northey, Birdie Mann, Don McLeod, Bob Mann and all the others of CND (New Zealand) for their calm and realistic approach; R. B. Moss, Mr Francis M. Auburn, John Litgaard, Erl Pleasants, Charles Blackie, Mike Montague, Peter Dodge, Dr Auburn, Sandy Heraldson, Ernie Seagar, Terry Gillespie, Wally Stuhlman, Peter Randal, David Exel, and many others.

ONE

The subject of our discussions is the Ocean,
which was described in older times as
immense, infinite, the father of created things,
and bounded only by the heavens; the Ocean
whose never failing waters feed not only upon
the springs and rivers and seas, according to
the ancient belief, but upon the clouds,
also, and in certain measure upon the stars
themselves; in fine, that Ocean which encom-
passes the terrestrial home of mankind with the
ebb and flow of its tides, and which cannot
be held or enclosed, being itself the possessor
rather than the possessed.

Hugo Grotius, 1603

ONE

Soon I would be forty years old – if I lived that long. The candle that might yet mark my birthday would be a nuclear bomb, ten megatons, two hundred and fifty times as deadly as the bomb that laid waste Hiroshima.

Ahead lay Mururoa Atoll, le Centre d'Experimentations Nucléaires du Pacifique. Ahead lay the warships of the French Navy. Ahead lay reefs and shoals. Ahead lay further storms. Ahead lay the loom of a military base ringed by steel and guns, enough to turn back whole armies. Ahead lay a forbidden zone where, soon, a mass of Uranium 235 would go critical, instantaneously vaporizing everything within four cubic miles, putting everything within seven miles to the torch.

Not for the first or last time I wondered, as my aching arms clung to the tiller of *Vega*, now wrenching this way, now wrenching that: how the hell did I get into *this* one? The swell was immense. Hissing and thrusting high overhead, it seemed impossible that tiny *Vega* had not yet been engulfed. Yet she hadn't. And within days we would cross the invisible line of the cordon the Republic of France had thrown around Mururoa defying anyone in the world to enter. And, again, the answer that came back to my question was: *Why* is not something you can ever hope to know. Some balance, some process that went beyond my knowing, was being struck.

The barometer had dropped from 1014 to 1007 that day and I knew there was extremely bad weather ahead. It was towards dusk now and a black weather front had passed over us. Twenty-five-foot waves were stacking themselves up. The wind was force eleven – over sixty miles an hour. I sniffed the hot animal odours coming like whiffs from a bellows through the vent of my collar, felt the itch, licked the salt away from

3

my lips. *Vega* was still being driven to her hull speed by the wind in the masts and rigging, under bare poles. Astern, green mountains lifted over my head. Both Nigel and Grant were below, either asleep or lost in that tossing hallucinatory world where your body rolls in its bunk like a wet bag. *Vega*'s bow buried itself like a blunt sword into the heel of the next green barrier and shuddered. The rigging hummed. Above, a silver sky was racing. My head pounded. My bones cried out.

It was not a new feeling, and I secretly exulted for it was much like coming to the end of a long, ferocious set against a formidable player. No player could be quite so formidable as the sea, yet there were parallels that rang themselves through my memory. My head was spinning, had been spinning for weeks, and I found myself again close to laughing. Each time the feeling came up, I suppressed it. A full-blown laugh this minute might lead to a numbing sense of depression the next. Better to pace yourself. The real test lay ahead, once we had crossed the line of the forbidden zone around Mururoa. I thought of the bottle of champagne we had saved. It might be the last bottle of champagne we would ever drink, and we would have to split it three ways, but no matter, it would beat the flat taste of instant coffee, of water that had been in the tanks since New Zealand.

Champagne made me think of victory parties. Briefly, again, I tried to struggle with the question of *why*. It seemed that if only for an instant *Vega* would stop moving, the sea would stop moving, and Mururoa would stop coming ever closer, I might have that blessed moment where I could think about the big question instead of the thousand vital little questions. It would be like a breathing spell, and there had not been many breathing spells in the last few months.

Earlier, clinging to my seat while Nigel was on watch, I had written in my log:

I have maintained in the past that it is not the adventure or the "romance" but the cause that has forced me on, but is that true? Could it be competitiveness that forces me on? Or is it just the romance? I wonder if it matters what the

4

reasons are. Is it not the act and the benefits of the act that are the important factor and not the reasons for entering into the act?

A laugh – more harsh than I expected – did come to my lips then. I wondered, briefly, if I wasn't slightly mad. Images swirled in the back of my mind, some of them so clear that for several moments I did not see the waves and *Vega* vanished entirely from my senses, along with my own stink and the throbbing of my muscles, all thoughts of the Bomb and the possible awful death that lay just ahead, a death I had invited and could not at this stage of the game avoid facing.

I was back instead at the corner of 16th and Granville, fifteen years old, 128 pounds, waiting for the bus to take me home, clutching five silver cups in my arms. An unknown, I had walked into the Vancouver Lawn and Tennis Club and entered all six championship events, the under 16 and under 18 mixed doubles. I had won five of the six junior championships and there was no joy that night in the Vancouver and district world of badminton. No one had cheered. That part of Vancouver, at least, had been very British in those days. It was not just the game that counted. One was supposed to have manners. It was terribly crude to try too hard, and I had tried much too hard.

Three years later, still a junior, I shattered Canadian badminton statistics by taking on the senior champion and beating him. A junior beating the Canadian champion? Unheard of. But then, so was it unheard of five years later when I took on Joe Alston, the US national badminton champion, who had just been featured on the cover of *Sports Illustrated*, took him on and managed to beat him in the third set. A Canadian beating the American champ? The Americans would come back and trounce the upstart. After all, the Thomas Cup itself was at stake. And, to make it even more irritating, I was a smoker and drinker. In badminton you don't smoke and drink and still win. But the next day America went down again in three sets. And soon after that I finally met, and beat, the world champion. In badminton, I felt I had done all I wanted to do.

And now, three thousand miles out from New Zealand, bearing rapidly down on the French cordon around Mururoa, here I was still trying to do something that even the most experienced Kiwi sailors had dismissed as impossible. Just getting to Mururoa was the equivalent of sailing across the entire Atlantic Ocean. And once at Mururoa, there would be no welcome except from a hostile French navy which had declared 100,000 square miles around the atoll as off-limits to everyone.

Assuming they didn't blow *Vega* out of the water or sink her, the very best I could hope for was to be left undisturbed until the moment the Bomb went off. Assuming that by some miracle we were to survive the blast and avoid the fall-out, we had nothing further to look forward to except another blast, and then another, and if by a multitude of miracles we survived all that, then we would have to sail back through the Roaring Forties with no chance for rest or recovery.

I remembered saying, when I first heard of the crazy plan to send a boat into the French test zone to protest against the blast: "The Roaring Forties in winds seventy to eighty knots, that's the last place to be. It's impossible, just bloody impossible!"

Vega shuddered again, her fat kauri pine hull spreading plumes of spray. Braced in the cockpit, arms around the tiller, I found myself talking to her half-audibly: "Atta girl, you just keep it up, you beautiful old bitch." I talked to her lovingly, as you would to a prize horse.

My first thought about her, when I had seen her at anchor two and a half years before in the bay at Picton, had been that she was a tender beast. No worms, tight as a drum, she had been built twenty-four years before by Alan Orams, one of New Zealand's greatest craftsmen from a design based on the famous Colin Archer pilot boats of Norway. Orams had taken two years to build her entirely by hand, not using any power tools, and while she would not arouse any envy in the chrome and polish yacht club set, I knew that she was one of the best sailing boats in existence.

In her, I had vested and focussed much of the feeling that I

6

no longer dared – was no longer able – to put into other human beings. Neglected and ragged when I had bought her with the last of my capital, she was trim now, and I knew that if any sailing vessel in the world could make this impossible voyage, it was *Vega*, sweet lively *Vega*, squat – twelve-and-a-half-foot beam – and solid as though carved from a single giant tree. In the way of all skippers, I had come to know her with an almost carnal knowledge, and I *did* love her. That love was as real now, if not more real, than any love I had ever known – except for my daughters.

Briefly – ever so briefly – I allowed myself to picture them for a moment. They were beauties, but I had lost them in a California divorce. Enough, I thought, bringing my attention back to the present. Enough. Even a few seconds thinking about my daughters released the torment I had no desire to let flood through me.

In the turbulence of the thought of the three girls, I dimly sensed that there was a connection with my decision to try to go out and stop the Bomb. Yes, I had fled to the South Seas after my business collapsed. Yes, I was less than a part-time father, but I was still their father, and in the search for the *why* I had my feelings about the children. Still. Even after three years without seeing them.

As *Vega* rode closer and closer to the Bomb, some primeval anger, father-anger, grew stronger in me. In fact, now that I thought about it, I realized that back in New Zealand, when I had been contemplating the voyage to Mururoa, I had had only feelings of helplessness. They had barely been offset by my sailor's indignation that the French, or anybody else, should dare to cordon off a huge slab of the high seas in defiance of every known maritime law.

Now, approaching Mururoa, I was aware that my indignation had ripened into a clawing gut anger that went beyond mere questions of legality. Anger approaching rage was what I felt.

Anger approaching rage. A lot of people had felt that – in Polynesia, in Australia, in New Zealand. But the feelings all

7

remained impotent. For seven years, France had been testing atomic bombs in the sky over Mururoa atoll, less than a thousand miles from Tahiti, ignoring the Atmospheric Test Ban Treaty, which had been signed by the United States, Russia and Great Britain.

The French had been content to test bombs in the Sahara Desert until fall-out began to drift towards Europe. That and the political changes in Africa had forced them to pack it in. But they still had colonies in the South Pacific. No matter if radioactive fall-out swept across the Southern Hemisphere, dusting Peru, dusting the islands of a paradise now irrevocably lost, dusting whole subcontinents and archipelagos, General Charles de Gaulle had declared that France would have its *force de frappe* and the *force de frappe* would be nuclear. That was all there was to it. If there was a shape to be perceived in the phallic clouds that towered over Mururoa, it was the outline of the ghost of Napoleon.

But I had had little or no sense of this at all. French imperialism was not a subject that interested me. All my life, I had avoided "politics", except to the extent that I would have called myself a conservative. Certainly my Scottish parents were conservative, my family had been conservative, and, at the most, a few of my friends might have been liberals. At one point in my life I had been worth close to a million dollars, most of it made in the construction industry, both in the United States and Canada. I had been obsessed by work, had worked for seventeen years with scarcely three weeks off, and had hardly noticed as my marriages and life slipped by. Sex and work and sports, booze and cigarettes. French imperialism? Radiation levels? They had not been subjects I had had time or inclination to study. I had been a voracious reader but had quit during high school and had not looked back. Ecology? In California, where I had built a ski resort, I had learned a little bit about it – had even won awards. But my concern had been with land development and protection of the land. I had known this much—that it only makes good business sense to protect the land. If you wipe it out, it's gone, and that's stupid. You lose your whole investment. To me, ecology had meant aesthetics, and that was tied to continuing profits. Just plain, hard-driving good business sense.

So I had not been much affected by the ecology fad of the late sixties. Back in April, in Hamilton, New Zealand, when Gene Horne had put down his newspaper and asked: "D'you read about that Canadian group planning to protest the French nuclear tests this year?" my reply had been: "No, what group is that?"

"Oh, they call themselves Green something. Greenpeace!"

"Never heard of them," I had replied.

"Well, 'twas in the paper. I thought you'd know about them because they have their headquarters in Vancouver – and that's where you come from."

I had known nothing about them. It had been fifteen years since I'd lived in Vancouver.

"Seems they're looking for a yacht to sail into the test zone at Mururoa atoll," Gene had said. I had immediately dismissed the notion as being nothing less than bizarre. My only interest lay in the fact that this "Greenpeace" group was based in Vancouver. Seldom did I hear news from "home". I had heard nothing of the quixotic voyage of two vessels from Vancouver which had attempted to sail to the Aleutian island of Amchitka in 1971 – a year before –trying to reach the site of the US Atomic Energy Commission nuclear tests. Although neither vessel – first, the *Phyllis Cormack*, an 80-foot halibut seiner, and second, the *Edgewater Fortune*, a 150-foot converted minesweeper – had succeeded in reaching the remote Aleutian island, the protests had struck a deep responsive chord. Before they were over, some 20,000 Canadians had been roused to move down to the US–Canada border and plug it with their bodies, the first time the world's longest undefended border had been closed since the War of 1812. Badly shaken, Canadian politicians, from prime minister Pierre Elliott Trudeau down, had been forced to take a stand on the issue, and, in the end, although the bomb test at Amchitka had gone ahead, the US government had been forced to abandon its Aleutian test site and turn the island back into a game sanctuary. But I knew nothing about this. At the time, I couldn't have cared less.

9

Protests were generally something that involved political types. At worst, anarchists.

Only briefly, at first, was my curiosity aroused. Gene Horne, a muscular one-armed Kiwi, a house builder, electrician, cat operator, mechanic, businessman and a good sailor to boot – but no less conservative than my own father – had displayed a hint of annoyance at the thought of the French bomb tests. "It's a bit much," Gene had said. "I don't think it's right!"

I had gone to the bookshelf and brought out a large Atlas. Laying it on the table, I had thumbed through to a map of the South Pacific. "There it is," I said, pointing to an insignificant dot in the vastness of the Pacific. "It's at the south-eastern end of the Tuamotu Archipelago. That would be about eight hundred miles south of Tahiti and well over three thousand miles from New Zealand." I broke into a smile then, a sardonic smile, and said: "Do you think they have any idea what they're asking?" Gene shook his head.

"It would mean a round trip of over seven thousand miles and laying off Mururoa and protesting – whatever that is – an atomic bomb." I laughed. "How you do that, I just don't know. That would mean that the whole venture would take between three and four months at sea, and you'd never once see land!"

"How about the boat?" asked Gene.

"Well," I said, unknowingly taking the first small step, "it would have to be one hell of a boat. Something like *Vega*. Capable of taking every kind of sea. The next problem would be crew ... four months at sea. Who knows what stresses you'd come up against, knowing you could be going halfway to South America and maybe never be seen or heard of again?" There was silence between us.

"Today is April 12th," I had said, clinching the point. "And you say the tests begin June 1st? That's six weeks – just over. If anyone was crazy enough to try it, they would first have to find a crew, then check the boat completely from stem to stern, secure provisions for at least six months, do a million other things, and it would have to be done in two weeks, because it's at least a six-week voyage. Impossible! Bloody impossible!"

Still unknowing, I had already taken the second small step – actually thinking about what would have to be done. So far as I knew, my plans were still to fix up *Vega* and sail on to Australia, past the Great Barrier Reef, through Torres Strait, across the Indian Ocean, through the southern Atlantic to the Mediterranean. But now it was time to go to the hospital to see Gene Horne's daughter, Ann-Marie, who was in for a minor leg operation, the girl whom I planned to take with me.

In sex, the most powerful players are young women. Next come successful older men. Although I did not know this either, with the crumbling of the family unit and the onslaught of "liberation", North America and Europe were going through a revolution aimed, on the surface, at defining new limits of equality and freedom. My own situation was hardly unique. It was not strange – given the times – that myself, age thirty-nine, and Ann-Marie Horne, nineteen, should be lovers.

Arriving at the hospital, I handed her some yellow and white marguerite daisies, hugged her, and sat on the edge of the bed. Ann-Marie had perfect bright white teeth, long blonde hair, a perfect body. She was then studying English at the University of Waikato. It had been two weeks since we had been together, and any thoughts I might have had earlier about bombs quickly vanished. "I'll be out in a few days," Ann-Marie said. "Quickly, tell me all you've been doing."

That wasn't what I wanted to talk about, but within minutes I found myself mentioning the discussion with Gene about the Canadian group wanting to protest the French tests at Mururoa. Ann-Marie's moods, I knew, could change from a normal feather-light radiance to intense seriousness at the drop of a single phrase and now, much to my discomfort, I saw her leaning forward, looking at me closely as I described the project. Quickly, as with Gene, I pointed out the flaws in the plan. "People don't realize the Pacific is five times the size of the Atlantic," I said. "The voyage alone is a big enough challenge to anyone, let alone everything else that would be involved."

Challenge? I wished I hadn't used that word.

Ann-Marie looked at me directly. Her arms were wrapped

around her knees under the sheets. Although I knew little about what thoughts occupied the back of a nineteen-year-old Kiwi woman's mind, I still had not expected her to take the whole damn thing so seriously, so quickly.

"Any cause, David, no matter what it is, cannot be successful until you first of all believe in it – and they obviously believe in it."

I had wanted to talk about what we would do when she got out of hospital, where we would go sailing. I thought of swimming, loving, playing.

"Someone should protest," she said emphatically. "Someone's got to do something." Her look was intense, direct, embarrassing.

I looked back uneasily. Actually all I wanted to do was to climb into bed with her immediately. And then get back out to *Vega*. And then take off for a holiday, and be free, goddamn it. This is paradise, you're an angel. My head felt vaguely squeezed. All this talk about French bombs! Irritably, I got up and went to the window. Shaking off my uncomfortable feelings, I made one last try to dismiss the whole subject. "You're right," I said lightly, and tried to joke: "But protests are for the young, not old guys like me."

She shook her head, penetrating blue eyes fixed on me. "You can't just dismiss it that way, David! It is *not* the responsibility of the young. It's everyone's responsibility." Her voice rose slightly. Then she began to talk about rights, about apathy, even about children. I tried to keep my distance, wishing that the visit had not taken this turn. Then, finally, a nurse pushed a surgical trolley into the room, signalling that it was time to go.

Ann-Marie had one of the warmest, most guileless smiles I had ever known. It made me want badly to stay with her. "I'll be back tomorrow," I said, glad that the talk about abstract stuff had ended.

By the time I was back on the street, in the early dusk of downtown Hamilton, I found, however, that the conversation was continuing in my head. When thoughts begin to move in a given direction, objects in the outside world have a way of

12

falling neatly into place as though drawn by the thoughts. Within a few blocks' walk, I found myself confronted by a travel poster advertising Canada, and that made me think harder about the Canadian protest group back in Vancouver. A block later, I spotted a handbill taped to the window of a store, the sort of handbill I would normally never have noticed. It urged readers to demand that the New Zealand government join other countries trying to stop the French atomic tests. It was signed by Mrs Mabel Hetherington, honorary secretary of the Campaign for Nuclear Disarmament. Before I quite realized what I was doing, I had written down the telephone number, gone to a phone booth, and called Mrs Hetherington. She wasn't in, so I left Gene Horne's number and asked that someone call me back.

I had not done anything more than make a phone call, but I was the only person in New Zealand with a boat – a boat capable of getting to Mururoa – who had made that call. I left the phone booth, whistling. Nothing was for certain yet. Nothing at all. But I felt good. I sauntered through the dusk, sniffing the mixture of carbon monoxide and salt air, aware of the play of my muscles. I knew myself to be in excellent shape, still an athlete, even though my hair had receded a third of the way back on my head, and my sideburns had traces of white. No decision had been made, so far as I was aware. Yet I felt a slight exhilarating shiver go through me, a special feeling which I had not felt for a long long time. For years now, I had had a sense of being a survivor, of having to force myself to stay on my feet in the midst of the ruins of my life. Just for a moment, I felt buoyant. The weight was gone. There was no jumble of thoughts, just a good light feeling of walking through the rich South Pacific dusk. Ah, yes. Good.

My introduction to the world of *realpolitik* came swiftly. After talking the matter over with Gene Horne, I had agreed that nobody – not the French government, not any government – could possibly have the right to cordon off 100,000 square miles of the ocean, denying the right of free passage to sailors, in clear defiance of the international law of the sea. Although

13

it had only been hours since Gene had first mentioned the Mururoa protest plan, I now found myself already speaking of the beauty of it: "If I sailed into the danger zone and ignored the French cordon line, I could sit in international waters entirely within my rights! If I sat just outside the legal twelve-mile limit, they'd be forced to board me and tow the yacht out of the zone before they could carry on with their tests."

Gene had added the rest: "As they would be doing that in international waters, which the law clearly says it is, then they would be committing an act of piracy ... unless they decided to detonate the bomb over you, and then it would be murder."

After talking to Mabel Hetherington of the Campaign for Nuclear Disarmament, and getting the number for the Greenpeace Foundation in Vancouver, I had called the Greenpeace chairman, Ben Metcalfe, who assured me: "We are a group of ordinary people dedicated to stopping nuclear testing. We are completely non-political." Metcalfe promised that Greenpeace would pay the cost of provisions, fuel, extra equipment, any damage sustained by the boat, medical treatment in case of injuries and legal repercussions. It did not occur to me then that "stopping nuclear testing" was a political act in itself because it pitted you automatically against a military establishment, with a government – whatever its political leaning – looming behind it. My only concern – innocently enough – was whether or not the Greenpeace Foundation was composed only of militants and anarchists. "What kind of support do you have?" I had asked Metcalfe.

"Plenty," had been the reply. "We have the support of people such as Linus Pauling, Jean Paul Sartre, Jacques Cousteau, Simone de Beauvoir, Buckminster Fuller, and we have the endorsement of the World Council of Churches, the Sierra Club, Les Amis de la Terre, the Canadian government, and many others throughout the world."

I had said I would call back in the morning if I decided to go, and had put the phone down.

Gene and Mrs Horne had long since gone to bed and the early hours of the morning were quiet and peaceful except for the creaking of the easy chair that niggled at my fidgeting as I rolled another cigarette. It was just twelve hours ago that Gene had casually mentioned the Greenpeace article in the newspaper, and as soon as it was mentioned I felt a finger pointing at me just as assuredly as a needle points on a compass. Twelve hours ago my life was quiet, orderly, peaceful and free, as it had been for the last three years since turning my back on the competitive and capitalistic world in which I had been a very eager and successful participant. I could never go back. I was happy for the first time in my life, and I was free! But that finger still pointed, just like a signpost.

I had sailed close to those waters the French intended to cordon and it irritated my mind thinking about having to sail around cordons when the reason I went to sea in the first place was because it was the last free place on earth. I am a Canadian, the finger pointed out, and I have one of the best cruising yachts that could meet the challenge of such a voyage, in a city that is the closest taking-off point to Mururoa. It is a Canadian group from my own city that plans to go. Something inside of me said that if I didn't go, I would be making a mistake. I wouldn't be doing something that I was supposed to be doing. Rebalancing the scales. Putting back something after taking out so much. "I'll go," I said to myself," and confirm with Vancouver in the morning."

I was not given to mystical thoughts. Even to acknowledge that a "finger" pointed to me was about as far down that line of thinking as I wished to go, and perhaps it was simply coincidence that both Greenpeace and myself should have had their homes in Vancouver, that Greenpeace was looking for a boat from New Zealand, that I happened to be in New Zealand, that I just happened to have the right boat, that Mururoa just happened to be the Greenpeace Foundation's next target after Amchitka Island. It was Ann-Marie who said later, after I'd told her my decision: "It was almost as though the situation was just waiting there especially for David to get involved in." Karma? Whatever it was, from the moment I made up my mind, events began to move rapidly, like pieces falling eagerly into place, almost as though preordained. The game had begun, a game quite unlike any other that I had ever played. A brutal game, with enormous stakes – as I was quickly to learn.

There was a formidable amount of work to be done before I could get away from the dock. The diesel engine had to be serviced because I would be depending on it to charge the batteries – apart from anything else. The injectors would have to be taken out and inspected and the oil filters cleaned. The stern gland needed tightening and a new propeller fitted. The existing fuel tanks had to be examined and auxiliary ones installed. The water tanks also had to be cleaned. I had, too, to get plugs to seal the air vents against fall-out. There was a lot of checking to be done: tool kits, foul-weather gear, safety flares and flashlights, rigging and all the fittings including the radar reflector; the self-draining cockpit and the bilge pumps; also the medical supplies. Other things that had either to be bought or inspected were: charts of French Polynesia, a new barometer, a spare sextant, spare warps and a nylon one for the sea anchor, spare rigging wire, the life raft, a portable twelve-volt generator for emergency standby, binoculars, cameras and film and a portable tape recorder for keeping the log. And I had to victual the ship for six months. Finally, *Vega* would have to be slipped and given a new coat of anti-fouling. I estimated I had fifteen days to get all this done if I were to leave in time to reach Mururoa before the tests began.

And then, of course, there was the question of a crew. Who was I going to find to go into Mururoa with me? One crew member was immediately decided on. When I phoned Ben Metcalfe in Vancouver to confirm my intentions of sailing, Metcalfe insisted on coming, even though he was fifty-one years old. "I'm as fit as a thirty-five-year-old," he said. He also claimed to be a radio expert, had handled the radio on the first Greenpeace expedition to Amchitka island. More to the point, he hinted that since Greenpeace was footing part of the bill, he wanted to come along as the "representative of the Foundation".

As for the next crew member, I immediately thought of a twenty-six-year-old British navigator I had met only days before, Nigel Ingram. While taking a job painting a ketch – broke at the time – I had encountered Nigel on the docks. Dark-haired and paint-splattered from similar work, Nigel had spent the last couple of years skippering racing boats about in the South Pacific. He had much more sea experience than I, having raced and cruised in England and the Caribbean, the United States, Australia and Japan. He had graduated from Oxford in mathematics and philosophy. He had been a lieutenant in the Royal Navy. More important, I had taken an instant liking to him. Nigel would be perfect. He was strong, calm – and experienced.

At first, he balked. "I'm sorry, David, but I've tentatively accepted a job to deliver a large yacht to the Caribbean." It wasn't until a day later that Nigel sat down with me for a beer and a discussion of the problems of the voyage. At the end of it, the young Englishman got up and said: "I will have to break the news to my girlfriend. She was looking forward to a trip to the Caribbean. I'll see you on *Vega* in the morning." So now I had a navigator and a radio operator. Enough to start with.

The next morning Ann-Marie showed up at the boat, which was moored in Auckland. She was followed soon afterwards by Nigel and his girlfriend, Mary Lornie, a legal executive, medium height, well-set, another Kiwi. The four of us set to work making up lists of things to be done. The word had not yet gone out that *Vega* would be sailing into the blast zone, so we worked undisturbed, unaware that we had stepped into the web of an immense political spider, or that the spider would soon be rushing down on us. At that stage, we were just four people working hard, readying for an unusual voyage, but still not all that different from any four people hurrying to ready a boat for sea. The web had not yet tingled. The spider had not yet pounced and, fretting over my lists, I was still blissfully unaware that I was about to set forces in motion in several world capitals – Wellington, Paris and Ottawa among them – that would move swiftly, ferociously, in an effort to destroy me. My time of innocence was coming to an end.

At that stage, I was still so naive that I fully expected the Canadian government to come out in support of what I was doing, because the Canadian government, I had read, was "opposed to nuclear testing". It never occurred to me that my own government would betray me, would literally throw me to the sharks. I knew nothing about uranium deals between Canada and France, about pay-offs between Wellington and Paris – I simply had no idea of the tiger-tails upon which I was already treading, by virtue of the simple, private decision I had reached – to sail into the Mururoa cordon. Neither Nigel nor Ann-Marie had any idea either, and so there were no warnings.

It wasn't until the third day after I had made the decision that I agreed, at the insistence of an old Canadian friend, David Exel, now a prominent journalist with New Zealand Television, to do an interview about my plans. I was reluctant to appear on television, but Exel had insisted. There would be no hassles, he promised. I had finally agreed, warning that I knew nothing about pollution, fall-out, balance of power, or any of the other things I expected to be asked. "I'm not a pro-tester in the usual sense," I had protested. "My reasons are personal. I'm not going to make a spectacle of myself."

The interview went well, I thought afterwards. Relaxed. Polite. There were no arguments. My personal views were respected. I felt relieved.

After the interview, I went to visit Richard Northey, head of the Campaign for Nuclear Disarmament. I had not had much to do with ban-the-bombers before, but had been advised by Exel that they were "very legitimate, honest, hardworking and solid". Northey and the other CND people were all of that. I felt better. A joint CND-Greenpeace fund was established to channel the money coming from Vancouver and New Zealand. Northey promised to arrange an office at the university and a phone, with students to run it in shifts. Volunteers would be organized through the office. I went back to *Vega* that night feeling content. The voyage had got nationwide coverage, help was starting to materialize, the beginnings of an organized effort. The people I had met so far had seemed serious and intelligent. It was going well. I had to admit I felt slightly moved, even though still embarrassed, by their warmth. It was Monday, April 17, 1972.

The next morning the cops arrived.

I was below when I heard the thump of heavy feet on the deck. *Vega* began to wobble as more feet landed on her. Five plainclothes Kiwi cops were pushing in a rush down through the galley into the cabin. "We have a search warrant," snapped the one in charge.

"Let me see it," I demanded. The cop waved it at me. When I reached forward to take it, the cop pulled it away. "You can't touch it!" he spat. The other four arrayed themselves, ready to move. Helplessly, I stepped aside. The five immediately swarmed through the boat, throwing cushions on the floor, yanking open lockers, pulling drawers out and turning them upside-down. Within seconds, the cabin was a shambles. I was dumbfounded. I had never experienced a bust before. My belongings were flying in every direction. After a few minutes of pandemonium, the Kiwis settled wherever they could in the mess and started picking through the debris. The top man helped himself to my private letters. Another dug in Nigel's mail. A third started tearing books from the shelf and whipping through the pages. There was an excited yell from the side cabin and a cop emerged with my revolver. The top man took it and put it in his pocket.

Still in a state of shock, I tried to explain: "All cruising yachts carry a gun. It's simply for protection. It was issued through your department and it's properly registered." Top Man looked at me coldly, said nothing, and went back to reading my personal mail. Another cop came out carrying a number of old money bags with the names of various New Zealand banks on them. I had been using them to store loose shackles and bits and pieces of hardware. They were confiscated with a nod. Then the cop who had found the revolver appeared with a watch in his hand, with the guarantee still wrapped around the strap.

"Did you claim this when you came through customs?" Top Man demanded.

"No! nor a hundred other things on this boat!" My temper was starting to cloud my head. "I didn't claim my sextant, my camera, my barometer – "

"Okay!" Top Man shouted to one of the others. "Get

19

customs down here!" Just as the flunky started to hustle out of the boat, Nigel stepped from the dock into the cockpit. Two cops rushed and grabbed him by the arms. Another jumped forward and frisked him. Blood rushed to Nigel's face. His jaw muscles began to work.

"Empty your pockets on the table!" Top Man yelled.

"Go screw yourselves!" Nigel yelled back, with a rasp in his voice that would have done a petty officer justice, refusing to budge. The three cops who were holding him, faces only inches from his, tried to stare him down. He glowered back, then noticed his private correspondence open on the table, with another cop reading it. Nigel's face tightened visibly. He coiled and was about to leap when I shouted: "Nigel! Put your stuff on the table!" And then, more quietly: "They're just about finished. Let them get the hell out of here." The furious young Englishman thrust past the cops, forcibly bumping two of them aside, and slammed the contents of his pockets on the table – coins, bills, a cigarette lighter, the stub of a pencil and a half pack of smokes. Immediately, Top Man picked up the cigarette package and checked through it carefully. He tossed it back on the table. "Anybody find any dope?" Top Man demanded. The others shook their heads, disappointed. Top Man kicked at one of the cushions on the floor. "Okay, okay, all outside!" he ordered. Wading through the mess they had made, the cops started to retreat, only to stop when two customs officers in uniform appeared at the entrance.

Top Man looked at them and said: "You've been told what to do?" Nigel and myself were ordered out onto the deck, with the pack of five cops following us, while the customs men – obvious looks of disgust on their faces at the mess the plainclothesmen had made – went methodically through the boat, even checking the fuel and water tanks. In pointed contrast to the gangster style employed by Top Man and his boys, the customs men replaced every single thing they removed. When they had done, it was as though they had never carried out an inspection, while the rest of the cabin was a shambles.

Shaking slightly from anger, I stood with Nigel on the deck. The cops shuffled to the forward deck, heavy black shoes scraping the paintwork, muttering to one another. When a young man came sauntering across the dock and started to climb on *Vega*, a can of paint in one hand – obviously a student volunteer – two of the cops grabbed him by the arms. The whistle on his lips died. His mouth dropped. They seized the paint can and an old valise he was carrying and began a quick, harsh frisk. "Hold it!" I almost screamed. "He's not with us!" Top Man whirled and waved his finger in my face.

"One more sound out of you and I'll take you in."

"For what?"

"Interference, that's what!"

"Interference in what? Your *duty*? You call what you've done down there your –" It was Nigel's turn to do the restraining. He put his hand on my arm. Top Man turned back to his newest prisoner.

"Open the bag and empty his pockets," he yelled violently at his men. The valise was opened and the contents spewed on top of the cabin – a pair of overalls, a small can of thinner, a couple of brushes and a pack of sandwiches. Top Man poked angrily through the stuff, then wheeled and clambered back onto the dock, followed quickly by his pack. The five of them marched away without looking back. The young volunteer stared at them, still stunned.

I was just about to unlease a stream of obscenities when the customs officers climbed stiffly onto the deck. Speaking evenly, with no attempt to intimidate, the older officer held out seven watches, each with its guarantee still attached to the strap. "Are these your watches?" the officer asked.

Taking a deep breath, I said: "Yes, they're mine."

"Then will you come down to the office tomorrow morning and explain them? Not to me, to the superintendent."

Bleakly: "Yes. I'll be down."

"Thank you." The two officers turned and left.

Nigel, myself and the still-dumbfounded young volunteer painter stared at each other. Finally, recovering his composure, Nigel observed: "Someone pushed the panic button when they saw that TV interview."

I nodded, but my mind was elsewhere. Now I *was* in trouble.

21

Taking Nigel aside, I lowered my voice and said: "I'd better explain the watches to you, Nigel."

"You don't have to," Nigel answered quickly. "You don't owe me any explanation."

I shook my head uneasily. "Well, I'd like to, because there's a helluva lot more than seven watches involved . . ."

I had been in Fiji the previous summer when the American dollar was suddenly frozen. All I had with me was twenty-five hundred dollars, *American* dollars. I had tried to open a bank account in Suva, but three banks in a row had turned me down. None of the hotels would even look at American money. So I had gone to one of the Indian shops in Suva – it was reasonably well-known that the Indians would trade when others wouldn't. At the first shop I approached, I was offered fifty cents on the dollar. Beginning to feel desperate, I tried another, and this time I was offered seventy-five cents on the dollar, *if* I bought something. Well, I thought to myself, it's better than a kick in the ass with a frozen toe. The shopkeeper recommended I purchase watches. They were at least compact.

I had left the shop with a sackful of duty-free Seiko watches hoping that I might be able to sell them in the Mediterranean, at least cutting my losses. I had planned to go from Fiji to Australia, but changed my mind and went to New Zealand instead. Entering New Zealand, I had not declared the watches, knowing that smuggling was something of a national sport among yachtees, and that enthusiastic Customs men might seize them, leaving me with no assets at all.

Instead, I had placed them – roughly one hundred watches – in a safety deposit vault at one of the Auckland banks. At the time, I had not planned to remain long in New Zealand. That was before I met Ann-Marie. With no thought in mind of smuggling, I had purchased the watches in my own name, and had kept the guarantees with the name of the Indian shop in Fiji. The seven which the customs officers had found were those I had removed from the vault to send to Vancouver as Christmas presents for my nieces, only to realize that they

22

were men's watches. I had stuffed them in a drawer on *Vega*, and forgotten them. In the raid, either the cops or the customs officers must have found the guarantees, along with the address of the Fiji shopkeeper. It would just be a matter of time before they called Fiji, and then – then what?

I had always prided myself on being hard-nosed. The business jungle had made me cautious. More than that, it had taught me to think out every move in advance, to cover my flank, to keep my eyes open, hawklike, scanning for weaknesses, possibilities, opportunities, to move fast and keep my ass to the wall. Years of bidding on large construction projects, years of promotional deals, of red herrings, board meetings, profit and loss statements, learning to fire and hire – by now I considered myself to be a fairly tough operator. The last thing I considered myself to be was naive.

Yet now I wondered. My confidence seemed to be ebbing away. Oddly, the thing that worried me most wasn't simply that if customs confiscated all my watches I would lose every penny I had left in the world, or even that *Vega* might never clear the dock for Mururoa – it was the thought of the mortification my parents would feel if their son was branded a smuggler. They were old now; it would just about break their hearts.

"Well," said Nigel. "You could always throw them over the dock."

I looked at him sharply, still furious about the raid.

"No! No! The watches! Not the customs!"

I laughed, and we both relaxed.

There was no point in spending time worrying – there was enough to worry about, so we went below to start cleaning up the mess and get back to work. That afternoon, I went with Richard Northey to the student building at the University of Auckland. Northey, although only thirty, was a professor of law. He showed me the office that had been set up in the common room, the walls covered with notice boards and photographs of past alumni. Thirty written replies from people willing to sail to Mururoa had been received, and there had been forty phone calls from others either willing to sail or willing to help prepare the boat, donate supplies and equipment or money. Two lists had been drawn up – the possibles and the improbables. Two students were going through the lists. By suppertime, I had picked my fourth crew member, an artificer who had served with the Royal Navy. His name was Roger Haddleton, and he had had nearly six years' sea experience before being discharged as a leading hand. Over the phone, he said: "I'm available immediately."

Getting back to *Vega* late that night, I found packages and stores beginning to pile up in the cabin. Ann-Marie and Nigel and Mary were bleary-eyed, but a dent had been made in the long list of things to be done which had been posted on the bulkhead. Before going to sleep, I drafted a cable to be sent to prime minister Pierre Trudeau. It read: SAILING IN A WEEK FOR MURUROA AS NUCLEAR PROTEST AND ASSUMING RIGHTS TO BE FREE IN INTERNATIONAL WATERS STOP AS A CANADIAN CITIZEN I APPEAL FOR YOUR PERSONAL SUPPORT FOR ME AND MY CREW STOP DAVID F MCTAGGART WESTHAVEN BOAT HARBOUR AUCKLAND NEW ZEALAND.

No reply was ever to come. Scribbling away under the yellow-orange lamp on *Vega*, in my first attempt at sending diplomatic notes, it did not, of course, so much as cross my mind that there might be Canadian cabinet ministers who held directorships and owned shares in multinational corporations that were even now vying for the rights to sell uranium to France, uranium which was the key to the bombs at Mururoa. Instead, I went to my bunk thinking that it would only be logical that the Canadian government, which was on record as being "opposed to nuclear testing", and, moreover, which was my own government, would quite naturally support me. It was a comforting illusion.

Shortly after breakfast, the new crew member, Roger Haddleton, arrived at the boat with his duffel bags. Nearly six feet tall, Roger was powerfully built. His muscles had been acquired on English rugger and soccer fields. Large scarred hands were hooked by the thumbs to his pants pockets. "Your immediate responsibility will be the diesel," I explained.

"Then I'll get to work!" said Roger.

Leaving him to start checking over the engine, I set out

to a phone and called Gene Horne. "How would you like another job?" I asked.

"What is it?"

"A trip to Mururoa. I'll make you an offer you can refuse. It'll take about three months. There's no pay. The weather will be lousy. The quarters are cramped. But we could sure use you if you'd like to come."

There was a silence, then Gene said, calmly: "Yes, I'm interested. But wait by the phone for a few minutes and I'll call you back."

When the phone rang moments later, it was Gene. "Yes, I'll join you. There are a few things I would like to talk about, but I will come down early tomorrow. I'll see you on board." The older man's voice was steady.

I had a moment when my eyes almost misted. I felt relieved. I had a full crew, and a damn fine bunch too. Then I took a deep breath. Okay, now to the customs department. Deliberately I kept my mind blank. Wait and see. Wait and see. But I felt vulnerable. This was going to be a pisscutter.

The office of the inspector of customs was square, with plain walls and a window overlooking the harbour. His desk was bare except for a blotter pad, a telephone and an empty metal tray. One piece of paper, face down, was lying on the desk to one side. The inspector was thin, with thin hair. His eyes were deep set with hollow cheeks. White shirt. Black tie. Like some kind of Dickens character, he leaned forward on his elbows, tapping his fingertips together. He had the air of a man who had been waiting. He made no attempt to smile. When I stepped into the office, the inspector stared at me for a full minute, before saying, in a voice as thin as his face and hair:

"McTaggart?"

"Yes."

"Sit down!"

The Inspector eyed me stonily for several minutes before reaching abruptly into a drawer and tossing the seven watches on to his desk.

"These your watches?"

"Yes."

"All of them?"

"Yes."

"You admit these watches are yours?"

"Yes."

"Did you declare them when you came to New Zealand?"

"No."

"Why not?"

"When I came here, I had no intention of staying. Just long enough to get myself organized to sail to the Mediterranean."

"And what did you intend to do with the watches?"

"Take them with me."

"You were going to smuggle them into the Mediterranean?"

"I had no intention of smuggling. I was going to take them with me and sell them to recover my cost."

"Just recover your cost?" The inspector smirked. His mouth curled with contempt. "You weren't going to make a profit? Then why did you buy them?"

I explained.

The inspector stared at me blankly while I talked, then snorted. "Why didn't you declare them?"

"I've just told you. I didn't intend staying."

"But you stayed."

"Yes. My plan changed."

"Okay! Where are the rest of the watches?"

It was hopeless, I could see. So I said nothing. Just stared back at the inspector.

"We know how many watches you bought! Where are the rest of the watches?"

I continued to stare.

Enjoying himself, the inspector flipped over the piece of paper and pushed it across the table. "Fill out this form and tell me where the watches are!"

"I'm not filling out this form."

"Welllllll. Then you are going to sit here until you do." He slouched lazily back in his chair, still tapping his fingertips together.

26

"I don't think I am," I said. "You have seven watches. Charge me."

The inspector jerked forward, leaning halfway across the desk, his eyes narrow. "Look! No watches – no Mururoa!" The words had come out too fast. Flinching, as though he regretted what he had said, he pulled back into his chair, tapping his fingertips excitedly.

I glared at him, thinking, you sonofabitch, so the whole thing is a setup. You don't give a shit about the watches. Mururoa, eh? Abruptly, I stood up.

"Where are you going?" demanded the inspector, surprised.

"I'm leaving." I allowed my own lips to curl with contempt.

"You can't leave!" spluttered the inspector.

"Do you have a warrant?"

The inspector was silent. I turned, grabbed for the door handle, and walked out. No one tried to stop me.

Forcing myself to walk evenly, I left the building and went out into the sun. My hands were shaking and I was sweaty. I took several long deep breaths, told myself to cool down, and then went to a telephone booth. What I needed was a lawyer.

I called Mary Lornie. She told me to come over to her office right away and she would put me in touch with the head of the firm.

At the office, Mary met me and led me to a large library-like room with thick carpets, a large polished oaken desk, and crimson leather chairs. Behind the desk sat a thin white-haired old man with twinkling blue eyes, as mellow and pleasant as the inspector had been flinty and bitter. The old man's name proved to be, of all things, Mr Pleasants. I relaxed immediately. Ah, life. In fact, I wanted to laugh with relief.

"I have always found it best to start at the very beginning and let it all out," said Mr Pleasants – pleasantly, of course. I could not help but trust him implicitly. I told the whole story. At the end, Mr Pleasants thought for a moment.

"Do you want to go to Mururoa?"

"Yes! I'm going."

"Then it's up to you," said the old man softly. "I know what those watches mean to you, but you can sit here and not

27

give them up and they will never let you away from the dock. You can sit here for six months and they will let you go and they will have nothing on you except seven watches. You might get a couple of months in jail, but when you come out, you will still have your watches."

I repeated that I had every intention of going to Mururoa. "I'll do whatever is necessary to ensure that."

"Well," said Mr Pleasants, "you are going to have to turn the watches over to them. We can do this. I'll try to make an arrangement with the Customs Department – an agreement to surrender the watches, which are, and have been, in the bank vault all the time, in return for them letting you off."

Within an hour we were back in the inspector's office.

"I cannot do that!" protested the inspector, pacing back and forth behind his desk. "I'm in no position to do that!"

"But you can make such a recommendation," argued Mr Pleasants.

The inspector thought about it for a few minutes more. "All right, I will agree to recommend to the magistrate that McTaggart be let off when all the watches have been produced."

"We have your word?"

"Yes! Where are the watches now?"

Mr Pleasants told him. The inspector strode out of the office immediately. He called two young officers. "I want you to go with McTaggart here" – he jerked his thumb over his shoulder. "He has a bunch of watches in a safe deposit box downtown. Make sure you get all of them. Understand?"

The two officers nodded. The inspector stepped back into the office. "These two officers will go with you."

When the watches had been neatly stacked up on his desk, all one hundred and four of them, the inspector busied himself signing papers. He handed them over to Mr Pleasants, who stood up to leave, holding the papers in his heavily-veined hand. I followed him outside. On the steps, the old lawyer paused and unfolded one of the papers, read it, and passed it to me.

"Well," he said, "you are indicted under the Customs Act for unlawfully importing into New Zealand one hundred and four watches without paying lawful duty. You are summoned to appear before the magistrate next Monday."

For the rest of the week and over the weekend, *Vega* wobbled like a sleek contented queen bee while a steady stream of volunteers jumped from her deck to the jetty and back again, working until dawn and then, in relays, all through the day. I met more people in those few days than I had in the last three years.

I was impressed. They included people like Mabel Hetherington from CND, an elderly dignified woman with the ability to spread a glow of warmth around her. Promptly, Mrs Hetherington set to work showing Ann-Marie and Mary how to cover eggs with wax so they would last for three months at sea. Student volunteers showed up by the score, each of them seizing on any task and applying themselves vigorously. I had not worked with any volunteer groups before and I was astonished at their discipline and the amount of work they got done – for nothing but the honour of helping.

Gene Horne arrived and set to work immediately with Roger, getting the diesel into shape. Radio Hauraki, which had been collecting signatures petitioning against the French tests, regularly broadcast appeals for assistance. In steadily increasing numbers, New Zealanders began to find their way down to the jetty, bringing food and other provisions – including, in one case, a brand-new portable generator. Sailors, students, housewives, whole families, couples, many of them bringing their children just to look at the boat that would go out to face the Bomb on their behalf.

In the midst of the steady hum of activity, I paused often during those days, astonished by how much *love* I felt around me. I was used to groups that were competitive, raucous, defiant, proud. But here was something different. Here was something that I didn't want to even try to put into words. There was an almost religious atmosphere – not a revival, no sermons. It was quiet, whatever it was.

The hard core of workers came down to perhaps twenty who plugged at it steadily, and these were mostly people channelled through CND, who were adamantly opposed to the Bomb, and yachtsmen and sailors who opposed the cordoning of 100,000 square miles of international water. Almost all of them were Kiwis who were ashamed that their own Conservative government in Wellington was more concerned with selling butter and cheese in France than it was with possible genetic damage to the next generation, or the illegal grabbing of a huge chunk of the South Pacific.

Sunday was a fine warm day with gentle breezes. The hum of activity had increased over the weekend, and I was just beginning to feel confident that everything would be ready in time. I had talked with Mr Pleasants again, and a defence had been worked out for my case in court the following day. After talking to Mr Pleasants' assistant at length, I had put the matter out of my mind. Early in the evening, to my surprise, my old friend David Exel, from New Zealand Television, showed up on the jetty. Exel's face was unsmiling. Without comment, he handed me a newspaper, pointing to a headline:

PARIS BUYING PERU'S SILENCE ON TESTING?

The story said:

The French government appears to have initiated a shrewd economic initiative to mute Peruvian protests against the planned nuclear tests in the Pacific in June.

Monetary credits of sixty million US dollars will be made available to the Lima Government under arrangments made in Paris just four days after the French announced their intention last month to hold the tests. There is concern that the credits will be cut should Peru protest at the tests in a manner considered offensive by Paris.

I laid down the paper, suddenly crushed under a feeling of utter powerlessness. My God! I had not had time to think clearly about just what I was up against. If France could buy off a whole country just like that, what chance did little *Vega* have to make even a dent?

Exel looked at me closely.

30

"Look, David," my old friend said, "I know the law is exact, and it's generally fair, but the politics of this issue is a dragon with many heads. It could destroy you. If they can persuade the press that it's a stunt, they'll cut you into little pieces." Exel was speaking intensely. "I guess what I'm saying is that you've got the dragon in front and the sharks behind!"

I blew air out through my mouth, rubbed my chin nervously, and stared at the water.

"I didn't realize it was going to be so heavy," I said tiredly.

"You're not alone, David. For one thing, you have right on your side. I believe in what you're doing. So do a lot of other people – more than you realize. But, David, be careful! You are going to have some very powerful enemies. And you'll be discredited, abused and abandoned. The way I see it, you're sailing into a storm that you may not be able to survive!"

For the first time I felt truly frightened.

I trusted Exel, both as a friend and for his judgement. A part of me wanted badly to forget the whole damn mess, to take Ann-Marie, and split. I didn't owe anybody anything. What the hell? But then I heard Ann-Marie below, laughing.

I found myself talking rapidly, almost harshly:

"Look, I don't know what's going to happen out there. I do know it's going to take all I can do just to keep us alive in that ocean, but I'm *going*! And no one is going to stop me!"

"David, I'm asking you as a friend. *Change your mind.*"

"No way! We're going and that's it!"

"Well, I tried. I felt I owed that to you." Exel put out his hand. "I wish you all the luck in the world. You know that."

We shook firmly, and Exel walked away down the jetty.

Savagely slamming my new feeling of fear out of my mind, I went below and joined the others. Ann-Marie was radiant.

It was three-thirty in the morning when I woke with a start from an uneasy sleep. My dreams had been lousy. I shook them off. There was no time to waste before the rising tide peaked. *Vega* had to be moved if we were to apply a badly-needed coat of anti-fouling and replace the propeller. Both Nigel and I, stiff and miserable in the clammy cold, climbed into the dinghy and began to row, towing the heavy old ketch towards the grid where she would be nursed into position against the pilings. With her diesel stripped down, awaiting the replacement of reconditioned injectors, she was a dead weight in the water. Oarlocks creaked. There was phosphorescence and black whirlpools. It took an hour to get her into position, firmly lashed so that when the tide receded she would rest on her keel. By first light, I was already covered with sweat and my muscles ached, but I still had to hurry to the airport to pick up Ben Metcalfe, from the Greenpeace Foundation in Vancouver, and after that, I had to face the magistrate. I wondered, briefly, how much longer I could keep this up. And I had not forgotten the fear in David Exel's voice. Shut it all out, I told myself. One thing at a time . . .

The news-stand at the Auckland International Airport was piled high with wads of newspapers and magazines. While waiting for Metcalfe, I looked through them and spotted a headline that said:

THEY SAIL AT OWN RISK – SAYS PRIME MINISTER
. . . The arrest of people who sail into the French nuclear test zone was a "hypothetical situation at this point," the Prime Minister, Mr Marshall, said today. He said any person who sailed into international waters was free to do so but, if anyone sailed into the French test area, he would do so at some risk . . .

Nigel and Roger were still reading the article when the announcement came over the public address system that the jet bearing Ben Metcalfe had arrived.

It was only because I'd been away from Vancouver for fifteen years that I hadn't heard of Metcalfe, who was, at that time, the West Coast theatre critic for the Canadian Broadcasting Corporation. In addition, Metcalfe's caustic opinion pieces were a regular part of breakfast listening for thousands of British Columbians.

My first reaction to Metcalfe was disbelief. In contrast to the tattered jeans and sandals worn by Nigel, Roger and myself, Ben Metcalfe was expensively tailored, exactly like a successful P.R. man, with a meticulously etched continental beard. He was almost six feet tall, and probably over two hundred pounds, certainly not looking, in my view, to be even remotely in the condition of a thirty-five-year-old. Nigel and I looked at each other with dismay. In the cramped space of *Vega*, Metcalfe's size alone was going to be a problem. His voice was a deep baritone.

"David McTaggart? Of course! I'm very glad to meet you." He shook hands vigorously all around. He had an air of confidence, but I was still taken aback, mainly because Metcalfe seemed to bear no similarity at all to the quiet sincere kind of people I had been meeting during the past week. Where the CND people like Richard Northey and Mabel Hetherington had been low-key, and at times almost saintly in their calm dedication, Ben Metcalfe was almost boisterous, very urbane, but very North American. My intuition told me there were going to be problems. I did not feel overjoyed.

As we drove from the airport to the harbour, Metcalfe talked in generalities, and inquired about the fishing. "I'm quite a fisherman and love to have a rod in my hands." Glancing at the rear view mirror, I could see that Nigel was seething. What with all the work yet to be done, this bloke wanted to go fishing!

"What publicity have you had from the press?" Metcalfe wanted to know.

I hesitated, then said: "Not very much."

"Then we'll soon change that!"

I could see Nigel cringing visibly.

Neither one of us had much taste for publicity. My own feeling was that you did your job first, then answered questions. To put yourself out on a limb in the press, and then fail to pull it off, was to risk looking like an ass later. Metcalfe, I was soon to learn, had a philosophy that was completely different. His art had been, for years, in his own words, "to apply airbrush-strokes to reality". Media came first. Reality was a distant second.

Dropping Nigel and Roger at the harbour, I drove on to a

motel where I had booked Metcalfe a room. As soon as we were alone, I said: "Ben, there's something you should know. I have to appear in court this afternoon to answer a customs charge of smuggling some watches. I thought you should know about it." Confessing this, I felt embarrassed, and half-expected Metcalfe to react with horror, especially since he was so obviously interested in good publicity.

But Ben Metcalfe only shrugged.

"Don't worry about it, it doesn't sound all that serious. It'll make for good press coverage."

I was stunned.

Good or bad, one thing was certain – there was going to be plenty of press coverage. The press enclosure in the courtroom was packed.

There was the smell of polished woodwork and oiled block floors. Everyone spoke in low tones. I tried to force myself to be calm, but my palms were damp. I had never been charged with anything in my life, but now I was standing in the witness box, and the lawyer for the customs department was saying, in a loud clear voice that filled the courtroom:

"David Fraser McTaggart! You are charged with unlawfully smuggling into New Zealand, on or before April, nineteen hundred and seventy two, goods subject to duty under Section 242 of the Customs and Excise Act, specifically, one hundred and four watches, with bracelets or leather wrist straps. You are further charged with failing to declare said watches upon your entry into New Zealand on the seventh of November, nineteen hundred and seventy one, contrary to Section 245 of the Customs Act of New Zealand. How do you plead?"

As instructed, I answered: "Guilty."

When the time came, Mr Pleasants rose, pointing out that I had been "a victim, along with many many others, of finding that his currency, specifically United States dollars, was unacceptable due to a monetary crisis that suddenly set itself upon the world and over which he, or others, had absolutely no control. All this man was able to do was to trade his

34

unacceptable currency for something that was acceptable, namely the watches ... If he had wanted to smuggle them, as the term suggests, make some gain on them, he has had ample time to sell them here, but he has not ... this man cannot be considered a smuggler!"

The magistrate's face remained impassive. He flipped through the pages of a report in front of him, then cleared his throat and looked directly at me.

"You are fined seven hundred dollars on the first charge and one hundred dollars for the second. Or one hundred and twenty days in prison. The fine must be paid immediately."

The lawyer for the customs department jumped to his feet. "Your honour, we did not intend for you to put him in jail immediately! Will you give him until Wednesday to raise the money?"

"Denied!"

Mr Pleasants, obviously shocked, took a couple of moments to compose himself. "Your honour, I am sure your honour is acquainted with the trip Mr McTaggart is about to venture on, and I am sure you, as I, believe in the principle of what he is going to do. Would your honour instruct the press not to report this?"

"Denied!" The gavel came down hard. "Next case!"

This isn't real, I thought. Uncertain, I half-turned and started to walk out of the witness box towards Mr Pleasants. But the court officer opened a side door. It swung outward blocking my way. The officer nodded to the open doorway. Numbly, I turned and went through the doorway, down the steps, into a small grey room. The door clanged shut behind me. It was as though a boulder had come down on a narrow mountain trail, and all my friends were on the other side. The path back to *Vega* was blocked. The path to Mururoa was blocked. Just like that, I had been cut from the herd, isolated, locked in a pen. What David Exel had said came back to me: *They'll cut you into little pieces ... you'll be discredited, abused and abandoned.* Well, I felt that I was in little uncoordinated pieces, quite unable to pull my thoughts together. I knew I had been discredited. I felt, yes, definitely abused. And with the

35

jail door shut behind me, it was impossible not to feel abandoned. There were no windows, no clocks. I might be a thousand feet underground. I experienced a disjointed sensation that I might be anywhere on earth, even on another planet, swallowed up, with no route back.

There were makeshift benches along the walls, with four other prisoners sitting as far apart from each other as possible. They glanced at me, disinterested. I found myself moving to the end of the room and sitting down on the wooden stairs, fumbling for my cigarettes. With a shock, I realized I only had four left. One of the other prisoners looked at me enviously, and I almost started to offer a smoke, then stopped, thinking of the one hundred and twenty days I had ahead of me. Four cigarettes! How the hell do you get cigarettes in a place like this? Embarrassed, I puffed on my smoke for a few minutes, then butted it, only one-third done, and slipped it carefully back into the package. I felt no urge to talk to the others. Silence.

Hours later – I wasn't sure how much time had passed – three guards entered and beckoned everyone out. We were escorted down corridors and stairways to an outer gate where the paddy wagon was waiting. The motion of the vehicle made me think of *Vega* at sea. My mind continued to churn without direction, and I kept hoping the news would somehow not reach my parents, but I knew it was bound to. I thought of Ann-Marie and how inaccessible she now was. When the paddy wagon stopped, we were at Mount Eden, New Zealand's largest prison, a castle-like structure, every window barred, and it occurred to me briefly that only a sadist could have dreamed up such a name for such a place.

We were herded out of the wagon, through an open metal door that clanged shut with an echo behind us. Down one corridor after another. Everything was metal, the stairs, the walls, as though we were in a vast warship. Bars everywhere. More steel corridors. More cage doors. Each one creaking open, clanging shut. The deeper we were taken into iron Mount Eden, the deeper my depression grew. I had a wild urge to push at the walls but knew that in a hundred years I would never be able to force my way out, not even with cutting tools or blowtorches. Four months in here! The thought overwhelmed me. When, finally, I was led into a cell, and the cage swung shut behind me, I slumped onto my army bunk and stared blankly at the light green wall. There was a single light and a pottie under the bed. An old man sat on the other bed, saying nothing. He glanced at me briefly, as though I was an intruder, then looked away. I laid down and tried staring at the ceiling, feeling immensely tired. Four months! I wondered if I would go just a little bit crazy, and at that thought, my emotions became jangled, like an itch in the middle of my brain.

Late that night, the cell door clanged open.

"David McTaggart!" said the guard. "Pack up everything. Fold your blankets and sheets and bring them with you." Groggily, I swung out of the bunk and did as I was told. The guard held the door open for me, then led the way through the corridors, down the metal stairway.

"It's long after closing," said the guard. "But we got you out. Go get 'em, lad, and good luck!"

Another door swung open, and one of Mr Pleasants' assistants stepped through. He handed me a cheque and a note guaranteeing I would pay the money back to the lawyers. I numbly signed the note, gave it to the lawyer, then gave the cheque to the guard.

Suddenly, I realized what was happening. I was free. The fine had been paid. Not only that, but I was free because the guards themselves had bent all the rules to make it possible. In my earlier state of shock, I hadn't appreciated the things that were being said to me, but I realized now that the guards – even the guards! – had wanted to see me free, back on *Vega* and on my way to Mururoa. According to their own regulations, they were forbidden to let anyone out after eight at night. It was past eleven. Probably for the first time, the iron gates of Mount Eden had voluntarily swung open to disgorge a prisoner into the night. I recalled now how dinner had been delayed, how the departure from the courthouse had been delayed, how the guards had stalled every inch of the way, bidding for time, and realized that it had all been happening because they did not want to hold me, they wanted me loose.

Go get 'em, lad, the guard had said.

God! Even the guards!

From the time I had left for court, Nigel had taken command. The work on *Vega* had not slowed down. The diesel was almost reassembled, the propeller and glands were ready, extra fuel tanks and water tanks had been installed and the underside and keel had been given their coating of anti-fouling. An inflatable life raft had been purchased.

The following day was Anzac Day, a national holiday. Nigel was just finishing painting the name *Greenpeace III* – this would be the third Greenpeace expedition – on *Vega*'s side, when a lean square-faced man in a business suit appeared on the jetty. Stepping down through the hatchway, he cleared his throat and offered me a card.

"Good morning," he said, "my name is Turner, from the marine department."

Turner's dark hair was brushed flatly across his head. He had sharp features, small eyes. He looked furtive. What now? The card indicated Turner was the head of the marine department. What was he doing here on a public holiday?

"Yes, Mr Turner, what can I do for you? Can I offer you some tea?"

Turner tried to smile but failed. He cleared his throat again.

"Your yacht will have to be surveyed before it can leave New Zealand." His lips hardly moved.

There were several people in the cabin. They all looked puzzled, except for Nigel, who immediately understood what was happening. All New Zealand yachts have to pass a safety inspection which has to be carried out by two marine surveyors approved by the marine department. The boat is checked structurally, which means taking it out of the water and examining every piece of safety equipment – life rafts, flares, life preservers. Such a survey would take the better part of a week. If *Vega* was not at sea within two days, the chances of reaching

38

Mururoa before the beginning of the tests would be reduced to zero.

"Mr Turner," I said, "would you tell me why I have to be surveyed. *Vega* is not a New Zealand yacht."

Turner looked surprised. "Yes it is!"

"No it's not!"

I almost smiled then. So this was their latest ploy. Quickly I rapped out the story. I'd bought *Vega* in New Zealand in 1970 and had decided to have her registered so I could prove she was mine if ever I decided to sell. I put her through the marine department survey, passed, and was given my registration number.

"There it is up there, Mr Turner." I pointed to the roof of the cabin where the number was carved into a beam.

A year later, wanting to leave for Fiji, I'd asked customs for clearance and also asked them if they wanted an M1434 form, an application for a certificate for a pleasure yacht departing for a port beyond New Zealand. Customs had told me it was unnecessary because *Vega* was a Canadian-owned boat and the form only applied to New Zealand boats. "Just in case there were any misunderstanding between customs and the marine department, I asked them! They told me that they had no jurisdiction over me because *Vega* is a Canadian boat since I am a Canadian citizen. When I returned to New Zealand in 1971, I put *Vega* on the slip at Allan Oram's shipyard. The customs inspector wrote on the bottom of my clearance papers that if this boat is sold in New Zealand it shall be considered a Canadian boat and shall pay all necessary import duties, et cetera, et cetera."

Pleased at having turned back this attack so easily, I made no effort to keep the scorn out of my voice. "Why has your department changed its mind, Mr Turner?"

The official could only shake his head.

"If you want me to have her surveyed, I'll certainly do so," I finished, "but tell me now!"

"I don't think that will be necessary," Turner mumbled. He got up and quickly left the cabin.

The others looked pleased, but both Nigel and I knew that

this was only the beginning. If the marine department was being trundled into play against us, there was plenty to worry about. The department could fall back on a whole battery of technical tricks to delay us, could lasso us with enough red tape to keep *Vega* tethered to the dock for years. Turner's visit had just been a tentative probe, clumsy at that. The next assault would undoubtedly be more efficient.

I decided we needed help. The person who came immediately to mind was a tough salt named Harry Pope, who was both a marine surveyor, and in many people's eyes, one of the finest skippers in the world. It was Harry Pope who had pointed me to *Vega*, and then had given me my heaviest lesson in foul-weather sailing.

"I have to deliver this small plywood racing yacht to Melbourne," Harry had said. "Two thousand miles across the most dangerous ocean in the world, the Lower Tasman, and it's the middle of winter. Two others tried in similar yachts. Both were lost. If we make it, we'll be the first. Do you want to crew with me?" I had jumped at the chance. I knew Harry's reputation, and knew that I would never find a better teacher.

We made it – only just. The yacht was forty feet. It had a sleek thin chine hull, with a fragile fin keel, and a hull speed of nine knots. With a crew of four we set out from Auckland, headed around New Zealand's North Cape, and then were promptly hit by two fierce winter storms that drove us directly down into the Lower Tasman. The second storm was the worst Harry Pope had ever experienced in all his years of sailing. For nine days and nights, under bare poles, we surfed down the flanks of sixty-foot waves, like mountains that had chosen to get up and move. The wind blew steadily between sixty and seventy knots, with the waves piling higher and higher until we were flying blind. The needle slammed against the topmark of the speedometer, 22 knots, but we knew we had in fact passed 22 and were probably doing 25. The hull hummed like a tuning fork, like a drumskin about to explode. More than surfing, we shooshed down one wave after another, the bow burying itself like a torpedo at the bottom, and the whole grey mountain collapsing on top of us.

One of the crewmen broke a finger. The second, an older man, collapsed from exhaustion. That left Harry and myself, two hours on, two hours off, having to lash ourselves into our bunks. It took three-quarters of an hour to change watch. There was no way to prepare food so we all went without, our flesh melting rapidly away, as though sandblasted by the wind. So much as an eighth of an inch deviation in the tiller as we zipped down the flank of a wave and the boat would have instantly turned turtle or broached – rolling and disintegrating like a Chinese lantern.

Towards the end, I had the first hallucinations of my life. A similar thin-hulled boat had hit a whale in those waters the year before. The boat had exploded. Lashed in my bunk, with only a sheet of plywood between me and the sea, I had seen a single giant multicoloured whale-eye hovering in the air. But for Harry Pope's untrembling hand, we would never have made it. When we finally pulled into Melbourne, our survival was considered such a miracle that a crowd turned out to greet us. I had had truly a solid schooling in the art of survival at sea.

Now, faced with a different menace, I called Harry. Within an hour, the short wiry skipper was jumping catlike onto *Vega*'s deck, vigorously pumping my hand. With his hair parted precisely in the middle, he had an almost comical appearance, but he buzzed with energy. "McTaggart, you bugger, what's all the fuss about? You're outside their jurisdiction, that's all there is to it! They can't touch you. But what I'll do is ask around, talk to another surveyor and come back to you."

With Harry Pope covering my flank, I felt much better. If the marine department was going to try to throw its tentacles around *Vega*, they'd have to contend with Harry, and if anybody could chop them up, it was the man who could take on the Lower Tasman itself.

There was a press conference at the university that evening. The whole crew – Nigel, Gene Horne, Roger Haddleton, Ben Metcalfe and myself – attended, along with Richard Northey and several CND people. I had half expected to be badgered over the business of the watches, but the reporters proved to be solidly in favour of the voyage to Mururoa, and angry at their own government for failing to take any action against France.

Harry Pope was waiting on the deck of *Vega* when we got back. Hard on our heels came Turner of the marine department.

He got straight to the point.

"You have changed the name of your boat from *Vega* to *Greenpeace III*! You realize you cannot do that!"

"Mr Turner," I said as calmly as I could, "I haven't changed the name. I know *Greenpeace III* is painted on the side, but if you'll come with me aft, I'll show you where *Vega* is painted on the stern." I took him along the jetty and pointed. "*Greenpeace III* is not the yacht's name," I added. "It is the code name for our voyage and identifies us with the Greenpeace Foundation in Canada."

Turner ground his teeth together, turned smartly, and marched away across the jetty.

"If he'd spoken to me like that, I'd have smashed him in the mouth," snarled Harry Pope.

"What did the others say?"

"They agree with me. You being Canadian makes *Vega* a Canadian boat, no question about it. They can't order you to have a survey."

I thought quickly, still wary of the marine department octopus. The matter had better be brought to a head. "Will you come down with me to the marine department first thing in the morning and get this settled?"

"You bet I will," said Harry.

Faced the next morning with Harry's expert opinion and my insistence, the marine department boss could do no more than fling his pencil down on his desk, disgusted. When we left his office, Harry said with a grin: "He was beaten. He knew it. Don't worry. I'll see you before you leave."

Thinking everything was finally under control, I hurried back to the dock. It was high tide and time to slip *Vega* into the water. The last of the supplies and food was being loaded. Although everybody had been working flat-out for almost two weeks, there was no slackening. Instead, the tempo had quickened. Cut out of black cloth, the name *Greenpeace III* had been stitched to the sail, along with the peace and ecology symbols (the familiar upside down Y used by the CND, and the Greek letter Omega). One of the few major outstanding problems was the installation of the radio, which was Ben Metcalfe's responsibility. Other than that, everything was clicking into place. Gene Horne was off to town, getting his passport. I found myself starting to think ahead to the sea. *Vega* had never looked better. For the first time since finding myself in jail, I began to feel that I was once again in control of events.

Just then, Ann-Marie came up quickly, looking worried.

"David! There's a policeman to see you." I closed my eyes for a moment and rubbed my hands over my face. Oh well.

The cop was waiting on the jetty.

"Are you David McTaggart?"

I was beginning to wish I wasn't.

"You're the owner of the revolver that was found on your yacht a few days ago?"

"Yes."

"You are wanted down at the station tomorrow morning at eleven o'clock."

"Why?"

"We want to talk to you."

Undoubtably just a coincidence that I had stated at the press conference that we would be away by eleven.

"*Why* do you want to talk to me?"

"We want to talk to you about some forms you didn't fill out."

"*What* forms?"

"When you left New Zealand a year ago, you forgot to fill out a form."

I said: "Yes."

The cop waited. We stared at each other.

"Well! Are you coming to the station tomorrow morning?"

"What for?"

"I don't know. They just want to see you."

"I'm leaving tomorrow."

"I've been told to get you to the station tomorrow morning at eleven o'clock."

"Do you have a warrant for my arrest?"

"No, I do not."

Another silence. I could think of nothing to say or do.

"Are you coming to the station tomorrow?"

I was silent for another moment. Then, abruptly, I made up my mind what to do. There was only one move left to make. If I waited to fill out one more form, there would be another form after that, and another after that.

"Yes," I lied. "I'll be in." I turned my back on the cop and climbed back on board *Vega*.

A few minutes later, the lines were cleared and the boat floated free of the grid. Roger started the diesel and we motored back to the other dock to load the last supplies. A group of supporters had gathered along with several reporters. Everyone set to work.

Then Gene Horne came striding down the jetty, his face stricken.

"I can't go on the trip," he said, disgusted. "The department of immigration won't give me a passport." Tears welled into Ann-Marie's eyes and she went and put her arms around him.

I sagged. I had been counting on his skill and steadiness. "Did they give a reason?"

"They said I was at the bottom of the list and there were nine hundred applications ahead of me. They would not be able to get it out in time. I would have to wait my turn."

"It's bloody obvious they don't want any New Zealanders on board," said Ann-Marie.

I had already made up my mind to leave that day but had not planned to tell anyone until the last minute. Now I was short of a crewman. That didn't make things easier. I thought quickly, then remembered a cheerful young man named Grant Davidson, who had wanted badly to come, and who claimed to be a good cook, even though he had no sea experience. I remembered one other detail. The young man had said he had dual Australian and New Zealand citizenship. That would

44

technically give us four nationalities on board, four governments France would have to answer to if anything went wrong. I slipped away, made several phone calls, leaving messages for Grant Davidson to come down to the boat immediately. Then I threw myself into the work, pushing everyone to hurry, but trying not to look concerned. The last-minute activity had attracted close to a half-dozen newsmen. They kept demanding to know the exact departure time.

"Tomorrow," I kept repeating. "Tomorrow."

The last whip of the octopus came at one o'clock when two officials from the marine radio department arrived. "We have orders to check over your radio," one of them said. I was beginning to get the feeling that I was in quicksand. I'd barely get one foot out of the goo when the other would sink in deeper. I knew there were no regulations requiring a "radio inspection", but also sensed it was useless to argue. Numbly, I showed them the radio.

They wrote down the call signal and switched it on. For several minutes they fiddled with the dials but nothing happened. The radio didn't work.

"Get Ben Metcalfe down here!" I screamed through the hatch.

Metcalfe clambered down the stairs.

"The radio isn't working," I said, straining to sound casual. Metcalfe grunted, fiddled about, and then said lamely:

"Well, it seemed to be a few days ago."

The marine radio men left. I glared at Ben, started to say what was on my mind, then decided against it. Now a radio repairman would have to be found, and quickly.

He arrived within half an hour. As he was leaving, with the radio under his arm, I whispered to him: "We're trying to get away in a couple of hours. It's urgent." The repairman nodded and hustled away. Grant Davidson arrived.

"Grant, do you still want to come?"

"Fair dinkum!"

"Can you be ready in an hour? Whatever you do, don't tell anyone that we are trying to get away in the next few hours. Anyone! Remember!"

I waited until the cigarettes had arrived and been stowed with the rest of the bonded stores, then took the crew aside and told them we'd be leaving at five o'clock. Nigel sagged. He obviously had his last night all arranged. "I'm sorry," I said, "but it's too big a risk to stay any longer." I explained about the police. "We'll all leave the boat now. We'll lock her up as though we're just leaving for the day. Just be careful that none of the newspaper men follow. We'll meet at the pub."

Nonchalantly, we sealed the boat and headed to our cars. A short while later, we reassembled at a nearby pub. Richard Northey and a few others had been alerted. I told them the plan. Ann-Marie was shattered. She had been preparing herself for a farewell tomorrow, not today. Mary Lornie and Nigel held hands dejectedly. So much for the last night together. A round of drinks was ordered. While we drank – solemnly, no one had enough energy left to be boisterous – I slipped away and made two calls. One to the repairman to make sure the radio would arrive on time. The other to customs, asking that someone be sent down to clear us.

Within half an hour, everything was ready, the radio installed, the bonded goods checked and cleared. I returned to the pub, allowing myself to settle in beside Ann-Marie. Her mood was dark. She had lost eight pounds in the last two weeks and had been repeatedly staggered by her government's behaviour, the police, the courts, the hassles with customs. She was exhausted, disappointed because we had not been able to get any time privately. She was afraid of what would happen to the boat and upset at the thought of the long separation that lay ahead.

Much later, she was to write about that last evening at the dock at Westhaven:

I think everyone was just anxious for them to be able to leave, and right then we were not thinking so much of what would happen when they were actually on their way. Still, David was afraid and nervous and I felt that way for him. I know he wasn't as cool as most people saw him because when he hugged me goodbye in the galley he was crying, so much

46

tension, sadness, worry, everything was in his eyes. It's the only time I have ever seen him cry like that.

It was just starting to darken. The sky was wintery, overcast. *Vega* was riding heavily in the water, weighed down by all the extra supplies. With the mooring ropes away, a breeze took the sail. The figures on the jetty shrank from sight.

Nigel called from below: "Course east northeast."

The lights of the harbour winked. We headed directly for Matiamatia Bay, fifteen miles from Auckland, each too tired and emotionally drained to talk much. Having cleared customs, we could not legally set foot in New Zealand again without placing ourselves back within reach of the octopus. Two hours later, we dropped anchor. *Vega* was still a shambles of stores, supplies and equipment which had been thrown on board but not properly stowed. Grant cooked supper and we cracked open a bottle of wine. Radio Hauraki was playing quietly in the background when lights from the shore began to sweep across the portholes. There was distant shouting. The announcer on the radio broke in with the news that *Greenpeace III* was anchored in the bay and several dozen young people had gone down to the shore to wish the crew a safe voyage. People began phoning in to the station, asking for messages of good luck to be relayed.

Climbing out on deck, the five of us waved. Headlights of cars flashed on and off. Horns honked. It was to be the last contact with friends for months. I fell into my bunk, feeling only dullness. *Vega* rolled gently, the last night she would sit like this before entering the storms of winter.

Far away around the curve of the planet, planes and warships were gathering at Mururoa.

TWO

Whenever I find myself growing grim
about the mouth; whenever it is damp,
drizzly November in my soul; whenever I
find myself involuntarily pausing before
coffin warehouses, and bringing up the rear
of every funeral I meet; and especially
whenever my hypos get such an upper hand
of me that it requires a strong moral
principle to prevent me from
deliberately stepping into the street, and
methodically knocking people's hats off –
then, I account it high time to get to sea as
soon as I can. This is my substitute for
pistol and ball.

Herman Melville
Moby Dick

Word of the clandestine launching of *Greenpeace III* moved swiftly on the wire services. The headlines were small, initially, but they appeared in many countries. In Wellington, there was anger because, despite every effort to thwart the voyage, New Zealand butter sales might be at stake. In Canada, there was disbelief, because news editors could still not accept the idea that anything "Canadian" could possibly have any impact on the world outside. In Australia and Great Britain, there was grudging acceptance that a "story" might be in the works, but little willingness to consider that the strategy might actually work. At best, the trip was still viewed as quixotic. In Paris and Tahiti, memos were flying back and forth. Ironically, the only people who were taking the launching really seriously were the French military.

On board *Vega*, the problems were of a different order. They centred quickly on Ben Metcalfe and the radios. Before leaving the shelter of Matiamatia Bay, I decided we'd better have a lesson in how to operate our new Ham radio, in case of emergency. It was a Swan 500 cx single side band Ham transceiver and it had a vital role. We had three radios, the large Ham set for long-distance transmitting, my smaller marine radio with a range of 700 miles at best, and our portable radio for listening to ordinary short-wave news broadcasts. Without the Ham set, we'd be unable to let the outside world know what was happening.

With Nigel and myself looking on, Metcalfe turned dials and knobs for several minutes. There was no response. Metcalfe's brow furrowed and he bent to the task, flicking more switches. Still nothing.

It was Nigel who said, with elaborate politeness:

"Ben, I don't think she's turned on."

His face reddening, the older man continued to play with the dials, but by now Nigel and I had both come to the conclusion that he didn't know how to operate it. He had, indeed, operated the radio on the first Greenpeace voyage to Amchitka, but it was a different unit.

Furiously, I stalked out of the cabin. On deck, Nigel and I decided to get on my old original marine radio and call the repairman. But when I went to turn on the old set, it wasn't working either. That left us with no choice but to row ashore, illegally, and call customs for permission to bring the radio man on board. Another delay. Another chance for the octopus to snare us. Fortunately, the man I got hold of at customs was a sympathetic friend. Permission was granted. Then I called the radio technician, who caught the first hydrofoil out of Auckland. He quickly repaired the marine radio, but when the time came to tackle the big new Ham set, a new problem developed. The diesel had to be started to provide the power, but the moment the Ham set was switched on, the pitch of the engine changed. The technician shook his head.

The Ham set pulled so much power that it would drain the batteries in minutes. "It will require a major electrical re-arrangement to generate enough power to operate it properly," said the technician. Our vital link with the outside world was gone already. I sat on the deck, weighing the odds. I knew that the risks had suddenly increased enormously . . . but . . . there could be no turning back.

We saw the repairman off, finished stowing the loose gear, and hauled up the anchor. Magnificent Barrier Island passed to port as *Vega* moved out into the swells. Despite my anger at Metcalfe, despite my anxiety about the lack of long-range radio communication, I found myself grinning. We were finally at sea.

Winter was coming in the southern latitudes. The steady force four southwesterly at our backs bellied *Vega*'s sails and pushed us 178 miles outward the first day, 157 miles the next, but there was a deep chill in the wind. At the helm, warm clothes and oil skins had to be worn. With the extra supplies and fuel crammed, crowded and strapped into every corner, the boat seemed to be bludgeoning her way through the dark green water. The head – about the size of a lavatory on a modern jet–was packed from floor to ceiling with potatoes, onions, canned food and sails, so the only way to relieve yourself was over the side, hanging on to the safety rail – a cold and lonely business.

Vega moved with such unexpected swiftness the first two days, as though catapulted forward, that I had no time to break in the three greenhorn crewmen on the tiller. The sea was hissing by. Nigel and I took all the watches, two hours on, two hours off. Hard work, but Nigel's eyes danced, even as the boat was dancing, in the first exultant rush of arriving in the amphitheatre of the open sea. To log even eighty miles a day is not bad. Despite her burden, *Vega* was doing twice that. From time to time at the helm, spray glistening his face, Nigel would let out a whoop.

We had entered that vast archless cathedral, waves marching in white-flecked rows like pews, shafts of light breaking from the clouds as through stained-glass windows. On land, inevitably surrounded by trees or buildings or hills, it is easy to forget the *size* of the world, but at sea, impossible to ignore. Once out in the ocean, the scale of everything changes as though you had entered a new dimension, a dominion of gigantic beings.

In theory, the plan for the voyage was simple. We would run with the prevailing southwesterlies in the cold southern latitudes. With good sailing and no mishaps, we should be twenty-five hundred miles out from Auckland in fifteen or twenty days. Then we would turn north, eventually picking up the southeasterly tradewinds and head for Mururoa. On the return trip, circumstances and the French permitting, we would have the tradewinds behind us.

I worked out a precise set of rules for survival. There was one parallel between life in the mountains where I had spent my youth and life at sea. A single slip and you're finished and no one can come to save you. To avoid losing someone overboard – where the odds are a hundred to one that he can ever be recovered – the rule was that the man on night watch could not leave the cockpit under any circumstances and must at all times wear a safety harness clipped to the nearest available stay. The harness was also to be worn while working on the foredeck or dumping off the side.

Under the crowded conditions on *Vega*, it was important, I knew, that minor irritations be avoided. To prevent any disagreement, the watch had to be changed promptly, especially at night, when a cold and tired helmsman notices every moment's delay before his replacement arrives.

Three days out, I had hoped to start lessons in manning the helm and night navigation, but the wind rose to force seven – about thirty knots – and the sea heaped up into fifteen-foot crested waves. There were gusts up to force nine, forty-five knots. The wind took on a dervish wail. Still heavy, *Vega* wallowed in the troughs like a great white sea turtle, mast bending to the task. The water had lost its green colour. Blue pyramids erupted, with the wind skimming the foam in blizzard-like plumes. *Vega* was rolling now, her bow crashing down into the waves and coming up slowly, decks awash, like the horn of a squat sea-beast. By noon the next day, my arms felt as though they were ten feet long, but we had logged 183 miles, the equivalent of racing a car at eighty miles an hour for twenty-four hours from Paris to Athens. Nigel was delighted. "That's moving, man!"

Grant Davidson was adjusting rapidly to his first experience of the sea. Quickly, he had learned to protect his shins from the heavy gimballed table, had discovered, through bumping his head, where all the beams were, and had learned the critical art of waiting for the boat to roll before straining to grasp for anything. He and Ben Metcalfe, both outgoing, spent the evenings perched in their corners around the table, swapping stories. Grant's father had made a fortune manufacturing pinball machines, but Grant himself couldn't care less about money. He was a life-lover, out front, willing to work hard, and had always wanted to go to sea. Everything about the sea fascinated him. He had taken a firm grip on himself from the first day, after the abysmal discovery that if it was blowing, it might take two hours to cook a single meal, and you could only cook for one person at a time. Curly brown hair, a drooping moustache, and an Aussie joke or curse non-stop all the time, he revelled in his new environment. He was twenty-six, one of those people who would quite literally never hurt a fly. At nights, spinning yarns, he'd scream with gut laughter, hollering with joy when *Vega* pitched violently, completely trusting.

Metcalfe had a deep throaty laughter of his own. Years an making pronouncements into a microphone had given him of unconscious sense of theatre and he was, after all, a theatre critic. Quite quickly, a gap had opened between himself and Nigel and myself, partly because he had not attended to his job with the radios, partly because he had wanted to go fishing while we were straining to get the boat away from the docks. Accordingly, he spent most of his time out of his bunk with Grant, unravelling one anecdote after another, enjoying the young Aussie's howls of laughter.

At the end of four days at sea, I distinctly did not like Ben Metcalfe and I wished I'd never agreed to bring him along. On a small sailing yacht, togetherness is not only essential, it can quickly become a matter of life or death. Squeezed together in a space smaller than the average bedroom, a single individual idiosyncrasy – like, perhaps, not brushing your teeth – can drive another individual, at a critical moment, wild with rage. Already the damage had been done.

On the fourth day, things went from bad to worse. I tried to teach Metcalfe night navigation. The compass light had failed, so we had to sail by the stars – sighting a star, lining it up with the rigging, keeping it fixed in place and checking the compass by flashlight every fifteen minutes or so. Also, we were still in the shipping lanes, so an alert watch had to be maintained. Metcalfe repeatedly failed to keep the boat lined up with a star, and after several experiments, I decided that the older man simply could not see well enough to manage. Yet he refused to admit he couldn't see the star properly. And he was also spending more and more time in his bunk.

Four days out, Metcalfe demanded to see the charts. Looking them over, he asked, curtly: "Why aren't we heading straight for Mururoa?"

I had already explained to everybody that our only hope of picking up favourable sou'westerlies was to remain in the lower colder latitudes until the right moment. I explained again. Metcalfe's response was:

"Yes, but I think I have the right to make some of the decisions on this voyage."

"Look, Ben, you're not the skipper! This boat is my responsibility."

"Well I'm going to make some of the decisions!"

There is, and always has been, an immutable rule at sea – there can only be one skipper. It is not so much a matter of territory or turf, it has evolved as a law for pure reasons of survival. A squabble at the helm in a time of crisis invariably spells doom for the whole crew. History has seen plenty of skippers with poor judgement who have taken their crews to their deaths, but the law remains, because there is no other way. A ship can respond only to the will of one man at a time. My reservations about Metcalfe deepened into alarm.

In the haste to ready *Vega*, it had not been possible for me to test the crew or get to know them. I realized now that this was the greatest weakness of the venture.

By the fifth day, even though the weather had settled down, my mind had begun to churn. On the surface, everything was still cordial on board, yet I could see that the unrelenting worry about what lay ahead had not given anyone a chance to catch a second wind. Nigel and I had enjoyed our first few days of wild careening across the water, but the effort to hang on to the tiller during the gale had sapped our strength.

We logged an impressive 172 miles that day. But as May 5 dawned, the wind died. We logged only 47 miles. Calm days at sea are normal enough, and yachtsmen learn to take advantage of them, to rest themselves. Near nightfall, though, a restless Ben Metcalfe demanded:

"Why aren't we motoring to keep up speed?"

As patiently as I could, I replied:

56

"It would be impracticable to use the engine, because we have to conserve our fuel supply for charging the batteries later."

Metcalfe wasn't satisfied. "But we're wasting time! When we haven't got the wind, we should be running on the engine."

"We certainly can't motor 2,000 miles to Mururoa because there's no wind! We'll just have to wait. It'll come up soon enough."

"I don't agree. Switch on the engine and let's get going!" Metcalfe was getting angry.

"Look, Ben, why don't you relax? Enjoy the break. The wind'll be up soon."

"But we should be running on the engine!"

"Ben, I'm not going to argue with you. That's it!"

That settled it in my mind. I could see there was no hope now of holding this particular crew together. The others had all overheard the argument and I could see their private thoughts going off in four different directions. These first few days had been the easiest part of the voyage. If we were divided already, it would be hopeless later.

In the evening, I called everybody together and laid out a chart on the table.

"Our position at the moment is here," I said, making a mark on the chart. "About twenty-three hundred miles from Mururoa and we've been making excellent time up to this point. But I'm going to change course." They all looked up from the chart, surprised. Knowing there was no point in recrimination, I gave a reason that was plausible: "We're all tired and we need a rest for a few days. So we'll head for Rarotonga to the northwest. It'll give us a chance to renew our supplies and maybe we can find a way to get the Ham radio working properly."

Rarotonga was the nearest island. Located in the Cook Islands, it was 1400 miles northwest. To reach it, we would have to sail toward the Equator, and then, later, beat into the headwinds for 1500 miles to Mururoa, which would make the voyage twice as difficult. But the alternative was prolonged confinement, with ever-increasing stress levels, crisis piled on crisis, and I knew intuitively that long before we reached Mururoa, the crew would have disintegrated with one man at another's throat. *Vega*, I was confident, could handle just about any kind of weather. The psychological storms were the real danger now.

A brief golden period followed.

During the night of May 11, I was awakened in my cabin by a "green one" sloshing down the vent, soaking me. *Vega* was creaking and straining. Up on deck, Nigel was grinning exultantly again. "Steady eight and a half knots!" he shouted with delight. Although the wind had come up, he'd chosen not to reef the sails, instead letting the boat's toerail bury itself, spray flying, racing now with the sails stretched taut like great upflung wings.

At dawn on the 13th of May, Rarotonga came up over the horizon. After the monochromatic blue of the sea, the green of the jungle was as sweet as it was unreal. Crashing surf on the reef hung a necklace of spray across the water, with drifts of ghostly rainbows moving in the soft morning light. We could hear the distant screech of thousands of birds. Easy, coming in from sea, to understand why Polynesians thought of each and every one of their islands as the home of a particular god.

Rarotonga proved to be anything but restful.

We had only been ashore a few hours when the wind came up so that the palm trees began to clatter like monstrous insects and sand began to drift like spray up from the beaches. *Vega* was almost lost as the gale drove ugly swells against the breakwater, banging the handful of yachts moored inside the harbour against the pilings. The boats were sucked downward, then lifted and hurtled against the wharf. By the time I got back down to the harbour, *Vega* had chafed through all but one of her lines. The harbour offered almost no protection against a northerly. The waves came surging heavily and easily over the outer reef. It was already too late to try to motor out through the narrow channel to the safety of the open water. We were trapped. That first night, we had to maintain a double watch all night, hearts thumping each time *Vega*'s sixteen tons came crashing sickeningly against the wharf. No one got any sleep.

Radiophone calls to Auckland had proved dispiriting. First, we had had to wait three hours, perspiring in the island's only radio station. Then, when we got through we could only talk one direction at a time, and talk rapidly because the moment you stopped talking you were cut off and the line opened at the other end. The voices coming from New Zealand were distant and tinny, difficult to hear because of the chattering of the dozen mothers with babies who were in the room, waiting their turn to call off-island. Teletypes rattled noisily in the background and the room vibrated with the spastic sound of telegraph keys.

The news was bad. It seemed that the press had turned against us. One headline had said: PEACE BOAT BOMBS OUT! A French official had been quoted as saying "We have too much concern for people's lives to place them in jeopardy ... as Mururoa is being used for a nuclear explosion, I do not see that the yacht will be allowed to reach the area." This had prompted the newspaper to write that *"Greenpeace III* appears to be sailing on an abortive mission." There was other bad news too. In Wellington, the finance minister had announced that arrangements were being made through a consortium of international banks for a loan to New Zealand of seventy-five million French francs, about twelve million dollars. It was the first loan New Zealand had raised in France, and so it looked as though the pay-off gambit the French government had used in Peru was also being applied to New Zealand. On the positive side, the New Zealand Federation of Labour had voted to refuse to service any French planes or ships, but even then only while the bomb tests were actually being conducted.

After the long agonizing night of smashing against the wharf, Nigel, Grant, Roger and myself staggered over to the hotel where Ben Metcalfe had taken a room. He had spent much of the previous day at the radio station, making calls to New Zealand and Canada. He was looking tense and strained and was evasive about what he had learned.

Later in the day, Nigel put through a call to Mary Lornie in

59

Auckland. I was sitting on the verandah of the hotel when I saw the young Englishman come storming back from the radio station, his face flushed with anger.

"We're a bloody hoax!" he snapped. "A cover for some other bloody boat from Peru or somewhere! The Sunday paper carried an article claiming that we were a hoax, a front to distract the French while another boat sneaks into Mururoa. They're right pissed off with us, our friends, the people from CND, everybody! They're all wondering why the hell we didn't tell them we were only a cover. The article's by Ben Metcalfe himself."

Nigel was furious and confused. "Jesus, I really don't mind us being a part of a sensible plan, but why the hell didn't Ben tell us about it? And why did he leave Richard Northey in the dark? The CND did a lot of hard work for us."

We found Metcalfe in his hotel room.

"What the hell is going on, Ben?" I demanded.

"You keep your minds on handling the yacht," Metcalfe rumbled. "I'll take care of the publicity. There's nothing to be concerned about."

I almost exploded then. "What d'you mean, nothing to be concerned about! We've deceived all those people in Auckland and the CND! They're madder than hell and I want an explanation!"

"I told you there's nothing to be concerned about. I'm a professional newspaperman and I know what I'm doing."

"Look! I've got no objection to being a decoy if that's what the plan called for but surely to Christ we could be trusted with the truth! I'm risking my yacht and all of us our lives, and I want to know what is going on!"

"Well I can't tell you," Metcalfe insisted. "It's secret and it's got to remain that way."

"What do you mean you can't tell us?"

"It's secret! And I'm *not* going to tell you!" Metcalfe turned away, ignoring us, his hands shaking slightly.

Both Nigel and I were flabbergasted. And confused. It was the craziest thing we had ever heard. The whole thing was unreal – this bizarre melodrama in a sparsely-furnished hotel room, warm gusts of wind coming through the open French doors, the sound of motorbikes out in the streets, clattering palm tree leaves and the whoosh of the surf. Unable to stand the insanity of it any longer, I turned on my heel and strode out of the room, Nigel following. We both needed a drink.

Later, the wind strengthened, and we had to hurry back down to the harbour to keep an eye on *Vega*. Two of the other yachts were already badly damaged. By the time we reached the jetty, the wind was tearing at our clothes and we had to bend into it to reach the boat. The waves surging over the reef were gigantic. *Vega* was throwing herself around like a wounded animal in a pen. While the wind tore at us, we fought to position her safely. It took eleven lines strung back and forth across the harbour and three anchors thrown into the bay before she could be considered reasonably secure.

By nightfall, all four of us were beginning to suffer from tropical fever. After another sleepless nightmare night, we arose with the shakes and chills. A minor cut on my finger had become infected and I had to stagger up to the hospital for penicillin shots. The winds were gusting to sixty knots. There was still no way we could get *Vega* out of the harbour without being smashed on the reef, not while the huge surges of water were still exploding through the narrow channel.

The fourth night in Rarotonga, I had to go back to the hospital, this time to have the infected finger lanced – not once, but three times. What worried me most was that this was the sort of thing that could become extremely serious when we were a thousand miles out to sea. I was not the only one with medical problems. Roger Haddleton's tropical fever was hitting him hard. He had a drawn sickly look to him and was shuddering and sweating in his bunk.

Early the following morning, Metcalfe arrived by taxi at the dock. Conspiratorially, he beckoned me to follow him some distance down the jetty. There was something about his manner that reminded me of old spy movies, Humphrey Bogart and panama hats. Metcalfe waited until we were out of earshot of the taxi driver, and then he spoke in hushed urgent tones.

"I have to leave for Peru at once," he said. "Our Greenpeace man there, the one in charge of the protest boat, has been thrown into jail. I have to fly over there and get him out right away. I've booked a seat out tomorrow morning on the weekly plane for Fiji."

I stared at him blankly. I had already told the others the night before that I was going to put Metcalfe off the boat because I didn't think the older man was up to the trip. But that hadn't been the real reason. The real reason was that the man was a divisive influence, whatever his newspaper skills. Now, exhausted and racked with pain from my finger, I felt nothing except a sense of relief that I wouldn't have to fight to get rid of him. There were things that still needed clearing up, though.

"All right," I said. "Then we'll have a meeting in your room this afternoon."

The meeting was short and bitter. And nothing got cleared up. It just got messier.

Metcalfe insisted that there was nothing more he could say about the boat from Peru, he didn't know what radio frequencies the mystery boat would be using, there was nothing more he could say "because that side of the project must remain secret for reasons that I can't explain to you". He assured us repeatedly, in response to direct questions, that the Greenpeace Foundation would stand behind us regardless of what happened. When the others got up to leave the room, Metcalfe asked: "When you leave Rarotonga, will you maintain radio silence on the voyage?"

"Ben, you bloody well have to be kidding!" I said. By now, I was convinced the whole scene was a charade. That night, Grant admitted that Metcalfe had asked him to forward all of his tapes and photographs to Vancouver immediately after returning from Mururoa. Point-blank, I told him that if he was going to do that, he, too, was off the boat. After all that Metcalfe had put us through, I had no intention of letting the newspaperman get away with that one. I no longer trusted Metcalfe, and although I didn't quite know what to think about the story of the Peruvian protest boat, I sensed it was a fabrication. Much later, I was to learn that no one else in the Greenpeace organization had known anything about it either, and no one was ever able to find out anything about the "Greenpeace man in Peru" whom Metcalfe was supposed to be flying off to rescue.

The next morning, after seeing Metcalfe to the airport we returned to a still wildly-lurching *Vega*. The twin-engined weekly plane to Fiji dipped over the bay, gleaming in the tropical sun, then climbed out over the ocean and was gone.

Grant was sent to stock up the boat with lemons, limes and a sack of avocadoes. Friendly Cook Islanders came down to the jetty with huge sacks of oranges picked in their own gardens. A good rack of green bananas was picked up in the local market and hung in the rigging.

We were stowed again and the sea had calmed down enough for us to make it through the channel, but Roger was still pale and drawn, barely able to eat. The fever had not left him, as it had the others. My finger was still throbbing. I decided to delay for another day to give us both a chance to recover.

The following morning broke clear. The sea was still running heavily, with spray drifting from the crests of the waves, but nothing that would trouble *Vega* deeply. My finger was better, but Roger was still weak. If anything, he looked worse than ever. While we were clearing Customs, I finally forced myself to face the fact that I couldn't risk taking him. It was a painful scene. "I'm game," Roger said, and there could be no doubt that he was more than willing to press on. Despite his stiff upper lip and his bulldog determination, I knew it would be irresponsible to take him, at this stage, far beyond the reach of medical aid. The only choice was to arrange through the CND people in Auckland to have money sent to Rarotonga so Roger could be flown back to New Zealand.

We set the log at zero and slipped past the reef out of the harbour. Looking back, I could see Roger, pale, head bent, with his duffel bags beside him, looking very alone on the dock. On the foredeck, Nigel and Grant paused in their work with the sails and waved at him. He waved back listlessly. For a moment, I had an urge to bring *Vega* about and go back for him. With only three of us left on board, the boat seemed strangely empty. But I held our course. Ahead, the Pacific rose and fell with piston-like regularity as though great machines were working beneath the surface, indifferent to our hopes, indifferent to politicians and clowns, warriors, fools and saints.

It seemed the three of us would soon be alone in that purifying immensity. But, of course, we were not. Even as we left Rarotonga for Mururoa, the French Pacific fleet was making its preparations to head for the same destination.

French military sources who contacted me later described the following scene that took place in Papeete on May 20.

The naval and military shipyard that dominates the harbour was clangorous with the noise of massive cranes swinging over storage sheds. Work crews caught hold of steel cables, hooking pallets loaded with equipment and hoisting them onto grey black-numbered transport and supply ships.

There were over twenty ships berthed along the concrete docks, the South Pacific fleet of the French navy for the Centre des Expérimentations Nucléaires du Pacifique. At one of the quays the sharp-edged lines of the command cruiser *De Grasse* towered over nearby escort vessels, a tall communications tower thrusting over the entire dockyard. Close by, swarming with workmen and sailors, sat the *Medoc*, A612, a converted liner fitted out as a barracks and accommodation ship. Moored aft of *Medoc* was the *Garonne*, A617, a maintenance and repair ship with three 40-mm anti-aircraft guns sheathed on her gun platforms and two Alouette helicopters on her stern pad. Across the dock, having just arrived from New Caledonia, sat the minesweepers *La Paimpolaise*, M729, and *La Bayonnaise*, M728, alongside their sister ship *La Dunkerquoise*. Nearby was *Hippopotame*, A660, and the *Scorpion*, A728, together with *Courageux*, A760, a fleet tug. Supply and support ships and tankers of the fleet were deployed at bunkers and supply establishments. The last of the equipment and provisions were in the process of being loaded, and there was an unmistakable sense of urgency that signalled that these were indeed the final preparations for the move to Mururoa.

In the officers' wardroom of the flagship *De Grasse*, a briefing was taking place. The captains of the fleet had all been assembled.

Admiral Claverie was just finishing the regular part of the briefing.

"... and each vessel will take its assigned positions according to the schedules of deployment, as dictated by your sailing orders." He looked around the room.

"Are there any questions?"

There were no questions from the officers.

"There is one other matter," continued the admiral. "Captain Rochebrochard of *La Paimpolaise*!"

"Sir!" A young officer with a crewcut that came to a birdlike point low in the middle of his forehead snapped to his feet.

"And the captain of *La Bayonnaise* . . ."

"Sir!" The second officer rose smartly.

The admiral looked at them both.

"You are to be congratulated on your quick passage from New Caledonia." Admiral Claverie gave a quick nod to both. They sat down.

"Your attachment to the fleet is for a special assignment," the admiral said. "The reason your ships have been brought here is so that they can be used to track and watch a Canadian protest ship that, according to intelligence information, has left from Rarotonga heading for Mururoa. We have had a radio fix on them for some time, plotted between our bases at Tahiti and New Caledonia.

"We shall continue cross-plotting them through to Mururoa. Then it is up to the radar. It is a wooden ship, but radar could lose it very easily during stormy weather. We must keep track of it. For two reasons."

Both captains listened closely.

"One is, depending on where they position themselves, we may not be able to detonate without injuring the crew, and therefore cause international repercussions."

The admiral paused for a moment.

"We are friendly with the Canadian government, and the British government – the navigation is British – and there is a man on board with dual citizenship for Australia and New Zealand."

The admiral started pacing slowly behind the head table.

"We shall have to play it by ear at the beginning, but I don't think they will be able to last too long, hove-to around Mururoa. Another reason we will have to keep a close watch is because they will have great difficulty keeping a fixed position. If they unknowingly float into our twelve-mile limit, they will be boarded and taken away."

"Sir!" interjected another captain, standing up. He was older, with the look of a longtime man of the sea, weather-beaten and hard. Admiral Claverie looked at him and nodded.

"Why don't we just run them down at night? Nobody would know the difference."

A commander also rose to his feet – much younger, with sharp features. He spoke enthusiastically.

"Respectfully, sir, it is a good suggestion. I would like to volunteer."

The admiral looked at both of the officers. There was just the slightest pause. Then:

"Definitely no! I don't want harm to come to them." The two officers sat down. The admiral continued his pacing.

"From my experience of sailing, they'll end up tired and fighting between themselves after a few days hove-to . . . But . . ." He hesitated, stopping for a moment and looking at Captain Rochebrochard. ". . . their English navigator does have a lot of sailing experience." The admiral looked around the room and continued pacing.

"The best thing is to leave them alone and pay no attention to them. The weather is their worst enemy and the long-range forecast is poor. That should take care of them." The admiral turned and went back to his chair. Before sitting down, he said:

"In any case, I have a contingency plan. But we will discuss that after it is seen how they conduct themselves."

He looked once more around the room.

"As we sail at 0700 hours tomorrow, the 21st, I will leave you to your duties. That will be all."

Unaware that we were being monitored by powerful tracking stations in Tahiti and New Caledonia, and had, in fact, been

66

monitored since before our arrival in Rarotonga, Nigel and I
began working out false positions and broadcasting them
nightly. Each day we increased the deviation between our
actual position and the positions we reported, hoping that, this
way, we might succeed in slipping across the cordon at a time
when the French thought us to be still two hundred miles
away. It was a good strategy, but it made no allowance for the
space age electronic technology that was being employed to
give the warlords of Mururoa precise daily fixes on the whereabouts of one small sailing boat in the lonely reaches of the
Pacific.

During the first four days out of Rarotonga, southeasterly
winds pushed *Vega* far to the north, at least forty degrees off
course for the atoll. The wind was almost on the nose, forcing
us to tack. She was a stiff boat, fat-bellied, with six tons of lead
ballast, so she did not heel over as far as a more tender boat
would have done, but under these conditions the job at the
tiller required greater strength than ever. The helmsman could
not let up his concentration for even a moment.

I had known that this would be the toughest leg of the journey
and it was the price we had to pay for having detoured to
Rarotonga, but that didn't lessen my exhaustion at the end of
my watch. Grant was now taking his turn at the helm. Our
muscles were hardening rapidly, but at the same time, each of
us was sinking further and further into depression.

With only three of us on board, alternating watches, collapsing at the end of our watch into our bunks, exchanging only a
few mumbled words, each of us found himself spending long
hours alone in the cockpit. Nigel still had a touch of tropical
fever. I continued to take penicillin pills for my finger until I
realized they were making me even more sleepy than I already
felt. Grant's normally healthy appetite had not recovered from
his own illness in Rarotonga. With the many wind changes,
the sails had to be changed frequently, which meant that no
one got an uninterrupted sleep. *Vega*'s heavy tiller was like the
wrist of an inexhaustible sixteen-ton man with only one purpose in life – to arm-wrestle all through the day, all through the
night, never letting up, forcing the helmsman to curl himself

67

into a near foetal ball, knees braced, both hands wrapped tightly around the straining wooden wrist, wrestling, wrestling, wrestling.

But it was not just fatigue setting in. It was also an oppressive sense of isolation. Every morning we listened eagerly to Radio Australia on our portable radio, hoping for some word about the French tests, about how the other protests were developing, wordlessly hoping that there might be some mention of our own venture – any indication that the world out there might still know, or care, that we existed. There was nothing. After the unearthly nerve-sawing static would come "Waltzing Matilda" and then the announcer's voice wishing good morning to all the islanders of the South Pacific, his voice fading in and out as though someone were repeatedly putting a pail over his head and taking it off. On those days when Radio Australia didn't come through, our only other contact was the Pacific area time signal from Hawaii, a special frequency that provided a twenty-four-hour time check. *Beep* . . . *beep* . . . *beep* . . . and a throaty female voice, so seductive it made you want to cry, giving the Greenwich Mean Time.

At 1945 hours every day, I would climb down into my cabin and try to get through on the old marine radio. We broadcast on 2182, the normal ship frequency and also the frequency used for distress calls, which everyone listens to for five minutes after each half hour. Our powerful Ham set simply pulled too much power and we therefore used it infrequently. Calling over a ship radio is as different from calling over a telephone as climbing a mountain is to taking an escalator. You are shouting into an electromagnetic maelstrom swept by clutter from sunspots and distant blooms of lightning, auroras and magnetic disturbances, crossfires of impulses from other transmitters, ghostly echoing voices shouting through bottomless caverns. "This is *Greenpeace Three, Greenpeace Three, Greenpeace Three* calling Rarotonga. Do you receive? Do you receive? Over." Crackles. Squeals. Manic shrieks and whistles. For three quarters of an hour every night, we would hunch our shoulders eyes squeezed shut, me trying to will my voice outward, Nigel listening like a bat.

On the rare night when we managed to get through to Rarotonga, the reception was always poor, the message garbled and incomprehensible, only exhausting us further. Whether we got through or not, we would still go ahead broadcasting our false position report, thinking that at least the French might pick it up, and the torture of broadcasting would have served a purpose. In Tahiti and New Caledonia, we were, indeed, being picked up, but it was our actual position that was being calculated, with the French paying no attention to the phoney reports themselves.

"Rough as guts," said Grant, glad that the agony was over with for another night.

Heavy seas were not making navigation easy, either. Shortly after picking up the time-check signal from Hawaii, Nigel would climb onto the deck with his sextant, handing me the Seiko chronograph watch, which he had set precisely, along with a pad and paper. Accurate use of a sextant on a yacht in rolling water requires the combined skills of an acrobat and a hawk. The height of the eye above the horizon is only six feet. In the seas we were encountering, the waves were continually blocking the distant line between sea and sky. A sextant requires an unobstructed simultaneous view of both the horizon and the sun. It was necessary to judge the movement of the waves carefully and take the sight in the brief instant that *Vega* rose over the top of a wave. The lurching of the boat, the possibility of clouds crossing the sun, the chance of sails blocking vision, a haze on the horizon making it difficult to sight accurately at the critical instant, the dash of spray that might at any time obstruct vision or mist the mirror and the lens of the sextant, all combined to turn the task of taking a sun sight into yet another irritant.

Spreading his legs and hooking an arm around a stay, Nigel leaned sunward with the device to his eye. Depending on conditions, he took from three to six shots.

"Stand by!" he called.

I fixed my eye on the second hand of the watch, scribbling down the precise time and the angle of the sun as Nigel read quickly from the sextant.

69

Finally satisfied that he had an accurate sight, Nigel made his way below and hunched into what had become his most characteristic pose, bent over the saloon table with a pencil in his mouth, working out our first position line of the day. Ideally, three shots would be taken each day, one in the morning, one at noon when the sun was at its zenith, and another at mid-afternoon. These provided three position lines that intersected on the chart to show exactly where *Vega* had arrived.

In practice, the three lines rarely intersect at one point, but form a triangle known as the *cocked hat*. The smaller the triangle, the more accurate the position fix. On a cloudy or stormy day when no sight is possible, then the position is worked out by dead reckoning – estimating the position by relating the speed of the boat, the time travelled, and compass direction. An endless number of factors, such as ocean currents causing drift or a helmsman's lapse in maintaining a steady course, can introduce errors and complications. Nigel had his work cut out for him.

When not at the tiller or working at the sails or cooking, Grant stayed in his bunk, smoking his pipe and reading. In my few moments of spare time, when I was not too exhausted to stay awake, I kept meticulous logs. I also wrote down as many of my thoughts and impressions as I could, even though my handwriting was rendered near to incomprehensible by the pitching of the boat.

With round-the-clock watches, taking four hours apiece during the day and three hours at night, we have to stagger our sleeping hours and so can rarely sit together and talk. It is this profound sense of loneliness that is beginning to displace our sense of togetherness. At first we were happy to be under sail again and with two less crew members we were no longer falling over one another so that it is much easier to keep the old girl in order. But outside of the few housekeeping chores, our most constant companion is the deserted sea and the unhappy thought of the bomb at the end of our voyage.

It is difficult to describe the magnitude of the South Pacific to anyone accustomed to living on land. Looking

over the charts, ordered and subdivided with lines of latitude
and longitude, the great blanks of the Pacific covered with
islands and atolls and peppered with depth soundings, it all
appears so reassuringly organized and tamed. On the surface
of the ocean, you can see no more than ten miles to the
horizon in any direction. The hull of *Vega* pulses, as if alive,
with the repeated angry concussions of the sea, and everything is in constant motion. Beneath the hull, perhaps two
and a half miles down, mountains and canyons sit in still
darkness, while above your head the skies seem to stretch
forever.

Through the lonely hours at the helm, we each had to cope
with the frustration of knowing that the southeasterly winds
gusting in our faces meant a much longer voyage. It was no
longer possible to head directly for Mururoa. Tacking, we
were zig-zagging our way forward and perhaps doubling the
distance we had to travel.

I found myself beginning to wonder if there might not be
some force – above, below, *out there* – that was trying to turn us
away from our destination. At night, with the stars of the
Southern Cross laid like silver shrapnel across the dark of the
universe, I had moments when my skin prickled. I caught myself twitching and looking nervously out over the black water
with its phosphorescent tracings, unable to avoid the distinct
feeling of being watched. No one knows enough about what is
loosely called human nature to say with finality that some
primeval instinct had not sniffed out the vibrations coming
from the tracking stations, or even, with any more certainty,
that we were *not* being watched from Above. A more primitive
man might easily have perceived that the signs pointed the
other way. The winds bent against us, as surely as a great
shoulder butting a running player away from approaching goal-
posts. And a more primitive man might well have known much
that I didn't know. No man, no matter how "modern", stays out
on the ocean for long without coming up, sooner or later,
however uneasily or begrudgingly, against the thought of God
– or Allah or Jehovah or Buddha. There is a universe above,

another universe below, and only a fragment of tooled ordinary reality between, solid, touchable, a small floating shelter that keeps him alive for the moment, but a hull is not much more than a bubble. And any moment it can burst. If nothing else there is always the tidal wave that might lift the horizon without notice, swallowing every bubble, leaving nothing behind but bits of wood and machinery and flesh to be re-cycled immediately by lice and crabs and the patient albatross.

Nobody had ever made it into a nuclear test zone before. Perhaps no man was intended to. Any man who did might be turned to salt. The wind pushed against us, and seemed – in those awful eerie moments – to be saying clearly: GO BACK. IT IS FORBIDDEN. Shaking off the goosebumps, I told myself I was just tired. And besides, if there was a God – and I supposed that there had to be one, in some form or other, or non-form, whatever – surely He or It could not possibly want to see the world laid to waste by radiation. But then, when I thought about that one – thought about the things I had seen done in the world by human beings in my own lifetime – I had to wonder. It could just as easily be that God *did* want the world, the goddamned world and the goddamned people, laid completely to waste, and it could just as easily be that God's wind was blowing against us to tell us that we had no business interfering with His vengeance. *You're just tired boy*, I yelled at myself.

But even in my bunk, I could hear *Vega* straining and thrashing against a sea that was driving her ever further off course, shouldering her – heavy blue shoulder after heavy blue shoulder – further and further away from the goal. And, after a while, *Vega*'s groans were a voice rumbling through my sleep. IT IS FORBIDDEN. IT IS FORBIDDEN.

The night of the 23rd was bad, with unsteady winds varying anywhere from force four to force eight. Sleep had been reduced even more savagely because of changing and re-setting the sails. Grant knocked at the bulkhead of my cabin. It was my turn again for the watch, already. My body tried to ignore the command of my will to move. I knew, from long years of athletic training, that you would hit a slump period where your heart was ready to burst, rather than carrying on any further. If, by sheer will, you could get through the slump, you would come out of it, would find yourself doing almost effortlessly what had seemed all but impossible before. I forced myself up, my limbs feeling like clumps of kelp.

The heavy seas slopping over the toerail had forced me to keep the vent in my cabin closed. The temperature was up to ninety-five degrees. Everything was clammy. Beads of sweat dripped down the walls. Outside, the wind was squalling. Rain hissed into the cockpit. Clinging to the tiller, his hair hanging in limp coils, Grant was a pathetic sight. His eyes were red, his hands almost pure white and wrinkled, pickled-looking. There were bluish hollows under his cheeks. He had had to do two difficult watches that night with no more than three hours' sleep between them, if he had been lucky to get that much.

"Good morning," he said weakly. "Jesus, this is really rubbishing a cobber when he's down."

On May 25, five hundred miles out from Rarotonga, with the wind still lashing pitilessly out of the east, our heading was north of Tahiti toward the island of Bora-Bora. Nigel and I were slumped over the charts, our hair matted, our bodies itching from the humidity.

"We should start our return tack this afternoon," I said, rubbing my eyes. "If conditions stay like this, with the wind head-on, it's going to be a long one. Five or six hundred miles." Both of us knew that if we did not get favourable winds very soon, we would not reach Mururoa in time. We were still nearly a thousand miles away.

Briefly, after we changed course, our spirits rose. It seemed that despite everything we were making headway. But we were unable to raise either Rarotonga or Tahiti on the radio that night and the wind dropped, forcing us to use the engine for several hours. The heat in the cabin increased to the point where it had literally become a sauna. The following day, the 26th, the wind picked up, but it was still on the nose. In the evening, the wind slackened again. By now, the day of the first scheduled tests was approaching fast. *Vega* had a deadline.

73

On the morning of May 28, we saw the enormous fang of Tahiti's Tairapu Mountain rising over the edge of the horizon seventy-five miles off the port beam. The urge to put into port was overwhelming . . .

I sat on the deck for hours, staring at Tairapu, with the feeling that my life had somehow come full circle. It was like watching a lodestone go by. It worked magnetically on my memory, stirring chips of recollection, drawing them like bits of broken glass to the surface of my mind, hurtful, chaotic, leaving me with a dull sense of wonder that so much could change in so little time.

Tairapu stood Stonehenge-like in the ruins of what seemed now to be a previous lifetime, yet it had only been seven years ago that Betty and I had honeymooned beneath that great green rock. Thinking about it, I could not escape a feeling of tremendous dislocation, as though the man I had been then had been another person entirely, somebody I might have read about somewhere. Money. Money had been the thing. Around it, everything else had pivoted. But, God, the *work*! I had worked every bit as hard to get the money as I had worked to take championships, except it was like a training session that never ended. If I had had to learn to run sometimes ten miles in a single badminton set, to acquire my fortune I had had to learn to *keep* running. It had been a long run. By the time Betty and I arrived in Tahiti, it had taken me to a plateau where I was the general manager and vice-president of Bear Valley Development Corporation, in charge of a 400-acre ski resort in the High Sierras east of San Francisco. The world was open to me. I could jet where I wanted. I had my Mercedes 280SL, my bride was achingly beautiful . . . and then:

The explosion was a single ground-shuddering concussion that sent debris whirling over the other buildings and out to the highway, a hundred yards in every direction. I had been in the main office, going through the books. I knew immediately where the sound had come from – my own propane-heated lodge, a lodge which could hold up to forty-eight guests. My first thought was: *God, how many?* Then I was out of the door, scrambling wildly through the snow. Wreckage was still settling like black petals out of the sky and the first smoke had begun to arise from the crater where the lodge had been. I could hear screams. *How many? How many?* The snow was so deep I floundered, cursing and coming as close as I ever had to panic. I was the first one to reach the wreckage, with a young marine close behind. Blowtorch bursts of flame were starting up.

The loudest, most agonizing screams, were directly ahead, coming from the maintenance man, half-buried in collapsed timbers. The marine and I clawed his arms free and yanked, but he was caught tight. More bursts of flame. Another explosion might come any second. The marine was powerfully built. "We've gotta get him out of here!" I screamed. "*Pull!*" We pulled furiously, ruthlessly, and he came free slowly, like a rusted nail coming out of wood – leaving one leg behind. He was a big man, well over six feet. He was a friend. As we crashed back through the snow, expecting another explosion any second, I rasped at him: "The others? Any others?" Fading in and out of consciousness, the man managed to gasp the name of another friend, the woman who served as cook at the lodge. Leaving the burly marine to carry him away. I whirled and launched myself back through the heaped white powder. I found her just outside where the entrance had been. Only a finger was sticking up through the snow. I pawed for her. Flames were erupting everywhere and I knew that all the gas lines were broken. I dug out her head. She was in a shock but alive. One arm was thoroughly mangled. The marine got back to us then. We hoisted her between us and ran.

By a stroke of vast good fortune, the dozen-odd guests who had been staying at the lodge had been up on the slopes skiing that afternoon. Except for the two employees, no one was in the building. The maintenance man had been near the centre of the explosion and had been driven through three walls. He was to remain in hospital for a year. The cook's arm was permanently damaged, which meant that she would never again be able to do that kind of work.

My drive for upward mobility had ended there that afternoon in the High Sierras.

No one ever blamed me for what happened. The gas company had installed the propane equipment, had supplied the gas, and had even sent repairmen the day before the explosion because someone had smelled a leak. After working eight hours, they had informed my manager that there was nothing wrong and so everything had gone back to normal. Less than twelve hours later, there was nothing left of the lodge. Had the blast occurred six days afterwards, the whole US Olympic team would have been staying there.

No one blamed me. There was no suggestion of negligence. Yet I couldn't put the sight of those mutilated bodies out of my mind. It was I who had given them their jobs. The explosion left more than a crater in Bear Valley. It left a parallel smouldering socket where my drive and ambition had been. When the initial shock wore off, I found a strange new thought lying bare in my mind: If this is what making money involves . . . It was irrational, my associates told me. Don't take it personally. Don't let it get to you. But it *had* got to me. And I couldn't shove it away. My stride had been broken and everything I had been doing automatically for years, without questioning, without pause, now came up for examination. Assembling my goals in my mind, I looked at them and they no longer quite fitted together.

I was responsible, no matter what the laws said. It was my fault. I knew it.

But it was not something I could explain, or saw any purpose in trying to explain. Outwardly, after a few days of walking around in a state close to shock, habit took over, and I set to work trying to pull the shattered threads of my life back together. My career was anything but over. I had dropped a couple of hundred thousand dollars, and had shareholders to deal with, but it was generally assumed that it was just a matter of time before I won the court case that was quickly set in motion and the settlement would put me back on my feet. I had interests elsewhere, and it was only a short time later that I got an offer of fifty-thousand dollars a year plus a substantial stock option from a New York group to move into venture capital. I flew to New York, accepted, and found myself set up

76

as president of a company that was now backed up by some of the biggest capital interests in the world.

It was heady stuff for a Canadian who was still in his mid-thirties, and there lay my strength. In most corporations, the men at the top are at least well into their forties. It takes that long to accumulate the experience. But by then the elemental drive has worn down. I had by-passed university, set to work in construction while still in my teens, and had formed my first company by the time I was twenty-one. In terms of experience, it had given me a ten-year start on most of the other rising young executives, and it was this combination of experience and youth that was working so well now for me. I knew the stock market and I knew the construction industry backwards and forwards. I had built high-rises, low-rises, hotels, tract houses, warehouses, offices. I had done foundation work and piledriving, had become an early expert at developing high-mountain resorts, and understood how to nurture the second-home market with both summer and winter use, giving a return over a ten-month period instead of the usual four-month period when bad weather could ruin an investment. Chrysler Reality had ranked me as one of the two top consultants in the field in the United States. Despite the explosion at Bear Valley, I was still firmly on a trajectory taking me up into the big leagues. Already a fledgling millionaire, the door had opened for me onto multi-millionaire status. All I had to do was keep rolling along, two phones ringing all the time, eating on the run, mind locked with crystalline focus on the nexus of problems and possibilities served up each day from the moment I awoke.

It was the roughest year of my life. The door was ajar, but I still owed a lot of money, not only to the bank, but to share-holders, creditors, lawyers. Many of them were uneasy. Not a few of them started to close in, scenting that I might be in serious trouble. Everything hinged on the outcome of the court case, with some three hundred thousand dollars at stake – non-tax-able, which made it the equivalent of a million and a half. It wasn't just that I had creditors to fend off. My marriage was starting to break down. I had turned inward, was concentrating

77

so hard on work that I spent almost no time at all with Betty, despite the love I felt for her.

The court case was a disaster. I was unable to get the trial moved out of the county, where it turned out that every single member of the jury was a longstanding friend of the owner of the propane company. They threw the case out.

I was suddenly all but broke.

I could, of course, appeal and have the venue shifted to San Francisco where the lawyers were positive they would win. I could do many things. I could borrow, I could hustle, I could keep on doing all the things I had been doing for years. I had plenty of good contacts. There were powerful backers I could go to. But a kind of numbness came over me. During the year between the explosion and the court case, I had found myself increasingly disinterested in what was happening to me, as though I was just a half-dimension removed from my life. Events had been sweeping me along, and to all outward appearances I had been moving as swiftly and aggressively as ever, if not more so. Yet it was all done on accumulated momentum.

I had been so long in the world of money that the sudden loss of it left me feeling like a man who has lost his limbs. It had become so much a part of my sense of myself that I fell into an assumption that would seem only slightly short of insane to other men, but which, in my particular environment, seemed perfectly logical: I assumed that my wife would not love me without money. It seemed to me at that point in my life that the only "decent" thing to do was to break our relationship off then and there, to set her free. Lying, I told her I didn't love her, that I didn't want to see her any more. Masking my sense of amputation, I methodically set to work arranging to pay off all the small people to whom I owed money, then flew to Aspen, Colorado, to straighten out my remaining business affairs, and then drove to San Francisco, gave my Mercedes to a friend, stumbled onto an airplane – as wooden as a man committing *hari-kari* – and flew to Tahiti. For the next six months I lived with an artist friend on the nearby island of Moorea, drinking myself hopefully into oblivion. It was as far down the road to suicide as I could go. I felt my body getting more and more wasted, my mind becoming less and less clear. The goals I had begun to question after the explosion at Bear Valley dissolved steadily into smoke, I had reached limbo.

And then one morning I woke up to find myself still intact, tired of limbo. I found, to my amazement, that I had at least one urge left, perhaps the oldest urge of all – to go to sea. And so from Moorea I had gone to New Zealand, where I heard that boats were cheap. And had found *Vega*. And met Ann-Marie.

And now the outline of Tairapu had sunk back over the horizon to our port and Mururoa lay only seven hundred miles ahead.

We were coming to the most critical part of the voyage. Ahead and to our port lay the Tuamotu Archipelago, a crescent-shaped chain of atolls that spread across thousands of miles of the South Pacific, like teeth just on or below the surface of the water. Unlike islands, the razor-sharp coral atolls give no shelter on their lee side, yet any ship driven into them is torn to shreds.

To head into one of the lagoons for shelter would be akin to going into a shark's mouth to keep warm. Once inside, you are at the mercy of the wind and swell. We had planned on sailing within thirty miles of the first atolls. The skies lay like cereal on the horizon. Nigel had to double and triple-check his calculations, for a single error in his dead reckoning, coupled with a westerly gale of any size, would lead to us being pushed into the heart of the atolls.

Around midnight, when I was in my cabin trying unsuccessfully to make radio contact with anyone, the storm hit us. It howled through the night at force nine, blowing at forty-five knots. Still out of the east – IT IS FORBIDDEN – the wind was pushing us even further off course away from Mururoa. By morning, the blow had settled to force seven and we decided to head for the open sea, skirting south around the Duke of Gloucester atolls, which would put more space between us and the Tuamotus.

In heavy seas, with swells rising up to twenty feet, we could

79

not risk running the diesel to charge the batteries because the water intake for the cooling system was out of the water and sucking air too often. When, finally, we had to luff into the wind to slow *Vega* down so we could run the engine in neutral, Nigel tried the big 500-watt Ham radio. A few moments after he started it up, there was an explosion in my cabin. I rushed below, only to find Nigel sitting, staring into space, in front of a smoking Ham set. It was no surprise that with the condensation and moisture the radio had shorted out. We tried to make contact on the 2182 frequency on the smaller marine radio but were answered only by electromagnetic screeching.

The wind blew to force nine again the following night. We had gained an extra day when we had crossed the international dateline, and despite the wind had been making steady headway. By the evening of the 31st, Mururoa was only 320 miles away, and the cordon itself was less than 200 miles. It was our last night before entering the forbidden zone.

The wind had been easing all day. By sunset it was gone, and a silence descended more complete than any either Nigel or I in our combined experience of sailing had ever known. A golden eye lay upon the horizon and the sea stretched perfectly flat all around us, a burnished membrane. This was no ordinary sun. But neither, I thought, was the Bomb. Bronze burst bags of feathery clouds. A seemingly bewitched sea as tawny as a stippled desert. And a hush as though the planet had taken in her breath and was holding it. Entranced, the three of us sat on the deck, turning our heads slowly, absorbing the spectacle, letting our mutual feelings of awe claim our whole being. After nights of feeling that some elemental force was beating against us, it seemed now that the elements had changed their minds, and a switch had been thrown, giving us a glimpse of nirvana. The coincidence of the timing was more than awesome – it was disturbing and even frightening, for the three of us were rational men, and this was much too much like a sign, a blessing, a warning, a manifestation.

Grant finally said: "When I grow older and tell my children about a night like this, they'll never believe me."

Softly, Nigel said: "Children?"

We were silent after that.

The next evening, at 2245 hours, we crossed the cordon into the forbidden zone. The arbitrary line had not been drawn in a circle around Mururoa. Rather, it was a keyhole shape with a long end running east to northeast toward South America. It was in this direction that the main fallout would occur.

The line we had crossed did not, in fact, exist in any agreed legal sense. France had established the cordon unilaterally, in contravention of the international law of the sea, which clearly divided the oceans into two categories – "high seas" and "territorial waters". Territorial waters extended three nautical miles, with a contiguous defensive zone between four and twelve nautical miles. Beyond twelve miles, the oceans become part of the high seas where all vessels have the right of innocent passage unless they are suspected of being involved in piracy or slave trading.

A University of Auckland expert in international law had prepared a document for us, setting down the major points. I had read it over many times and knew that the issue was quite clear. On the high seas no nation can exercise a right of visitation or search upon the ship of another state, except in times of war. *Thus in times of peace it is illegal for a warship of one state to interfere with a foreign vessel whilst on the high seas* . . . any visit or search carried out on the high seas by a foreign country does in fact amount to a violation of the sovereignty of the state whose flag the searched or visited vessel flies. French criminal law cannot be enforced on the high seas against ships of foreign nations flying the flag of that foreign nation.

The red and white maple leaf flag flapping from *Vega's* backstay meant that the boat was a little part of Canada and, however little, as sovereign as any rock or tree or patch of Canadian soil. In terms of all existing international law, for France to violate *Vega* on the high seas would be no different from launching an invasion against Canada itself. If the Canadian armed forces existed for any purpose, it was to defend that sovereignty. So long as Vega remained outside the twelve-mile limit, she was theoretically untouchable. The cordon itself, spread out over 100,000 square miles of the high

81

seas, had no existence in any of the articles or conventions of accepted law.

After having had all this pointed out to me in Auckland, I remembered asking: "If the case for freedom of the high seas is so strong, why has France been allowed to close off such a vast area of international waters?" The answer had been: "Very simple! No one has dared to challenge France over it. You are the first! Not one nation or state has taken a stand, because it has not been politically expedient to do so."

After crossing the cordon, we broke open the bottle of champagne. We had covered thirty-five hundred miles of stormy ocean. As yachtsmen, we had much to celebrate, but the jokes we exchanged in the warm rush of the drinks were forced. The darkness around us felt too much like a vast cavern.

I had been reading *The Lord of the Rings*. I could not avoid thinking of parallels between our own little fellowship and the long journey of the Hobbits into the volcano-haunted land of Mordor, home of the Dark Lord who lived in his fortress surrounded by fierce armies, his Evil Eye scanning, scanning, scanning for intruders.

On board the flagship *De Grasse*, a French naval rating was concentrating on the revolving arm of the radar. It swept slowly around the screen, etching the outlines of the shore into phosphorescent relief. Near the bottom of the screen, a faint blip appeared. It glowed slightly, then faded.

When the arm swept around again, there was nothing.

Once more, the antennae on the upper superstructure of the cruiser revolved. The blip reappeared. The technician put a marker on the screen. Another sweep of the arm, and a barely perceptible glow registered. Enough to be certain.

The technician signalled to a nearby officer who stood beside him, watching the sweep lines pass over the mark. The blip flared faintly, faded. Another sweep. It reappeared.

The officer picked up the telephone.

"Radar contact at 256 degrees true. Range twenty-five miles. Heading zero-eight-zero degrees. Appears to be small vessel."

He studied the screen for a moment as the sweep recorded a very faint prick of light.

"Advise the radio room we now have the protest vessel on our screen."

THREE

. . . as the rage of the wind was still great,
though rather less than at first, we could
not so much as hope to have the ship hold
many minutes without breaking in pieces,
unless the winds, by a kind of miracle,
should turn immediately about. In a word,
we sat looking one upon another, and expecting
death every moment, and every man acting
accordingly as preparing for another world.

Daniel Defoe
Robinson Crusoe

We did not have long to wait for the first sign that we had entered a new domain.

We had just finished breakfast and were climbing out of the cabin when a tremendous crash of sound hit us, causing each of us to duck instinctively as a four-engined aircraft came swooping less than three hundred feet over our heads. We scrambled onto the deck just in time to see it bank and level out, heading straight back towards us exactly as though on a strafing run.

"Holy Christ!" yelled Grant. We stood there, frozen. I barely controlled an impulse to leap for the water before the bullets started tearing us apart. It seemed for a moment that the plane had every intention of diving straight into *Vega*, but at the last second, its nose lifted and it screamed over our heads like a giant albatross and headed away in the direction we soon would be following, towards Mururoa.

Our ears were still ringing.

"Well, they know we're here," I said, finding myself oddly pleased. At least *someone* knew where we were. I had awakened that morning possessed by an anxiety that the French, perhaps deceived by our phoney position reports, might not have known we were in the area and gone ahead and blown the Bomb. It was June 1st. Only minutes before the plane arrived, I had attached the radar reflector to the backstay to announce our arrival.

We had decided to take a position twenty miles from the atoll. That would leave eight miles between *Vega* and the legal territorial limit. "The best position to lay in," Nigel had said, "is the northeast end of the atoll, just within the tail of the restricted zone."

"The downwind range."

"Yes. That allows us two escape routes to the open sea if the weather turns for the worse and looks like it might drive us towards the Tuamotus. We could run to the west, back in the direction we came from, or northeast, away from them. Also, being downwind, it would be the same direction as the fallout would take if the French follow the same plan as previous years."

The three of us had sat still for several minutes. Grant chewed on his pipe.

"That would catch us with our tweeds and underchunders down, wouldn't it now?" he said.

We had discussed it back in Auckland and had agreed that the whole point of the exercise was to place ourselves directly in the path of the fallout. It was the only move we could make to prevent the bomb from being detonated.

And now *Vega* was stopped. We were three human fish-bones lodged in Mururoa's throat. The task was now to try to hold our position. It was to prove to be an even harder task than we had imagined, although we knew that we would have to allow for drift of current and the wind. No one could avoid a feeling of solemnity as we lowered the sails. Except for the slop of water against the hull, everything was silent.

That night the wind came up, not strong, but enough to start *Vega* rolling. It was a whole new kind of motion for our bodies to get used to. Under sail, a yacht favours one side or the other and the constant pressure of wind on the sails tends to hold her comparatively fixed in position. What movement there is is mostly lateral along the length of the boat. But when hove-to, she rolls from side to side.

When we tried to get to sleep, the clatter of supplies and gear became a cacophony in our ears. A can in the bilge rolled unpredictably. The gimballed stove squeaked. The blocks banged back and forth against the rigging and masts. Through the night, the waves reared up into lumps that slammed heavily against the hull. We got little sleep that first night on the edge of Mururoa. Lying in our bunks was impossible, so we stuffed sail-bags around our bodies, jammed ourselves in. Towards morning, rain began to patter on the decks.

Groggy and irritated, I crawled up the hatchway to take a leak. A twenty-five mile an hour wind was blowing, sending waves splashing over both sides of the lurching boat. I happened to look starboard – and my whole body jerked with shock. Not much more than a mile away was a neat array of yellow lights flashing dimly through the mist.

"For Christ's sake get up! We're nearly aground!"

Nigel and Grant scrambled onto the deck, while I grabbed my binoculars, waiting for *Vega* to come up out of the trough so I could get a bearing on the lights, which had vanished. We had expected to drift no more than two miles during the night. Now it looked like we had drifted right on top of Mururoa, which meant that the French could legally grab us, but it also meant that the reef around the atoll must be right in front of us.

Dawn was beginning to bleach the scud around us. Nigel ripped away at some of the canvas and the sail slapped viciously. For a brief few seconds, the haze of rain and cloud cleared, the lights re-appeared, and I could suddenly make out the silhouette of a large ship.

"It's a ship! A French warship!"

"Then let's get the hell out of here," gasped Nigel.

"I thought it was the beach. We must be right near the limit."

The ship was either a destroyer or a minesweeper, its lights stacked just like a small town. It was silent, ghostly in the mist.

"If we can hardly see her, we must be almost invisible to them," said Grant.

"Let's see how good their radar is," I said, unfastening the reflector. "It'll make it harder for them to find us again."

Nigel quickly raised the storm jib and three reefs in the main. Daylight was coming quickly, but the warship was still barely visible in the grey squall. I grabbed the helm. Slowly, *Vega* came about. Just as we started to move a greasy smudge of black smoke broke from the military ship's funnel, as though it was preparing to give chase. *Vega* began to move swiftly. The warship vanished. Soon we had lost ourselves between the furrows of the sea. But a tension gripped us now. At any moment a towering silhouette might materialize out of the mist. We had the distinct feeling for the first time of being hunted.

We tried to get a sun-sight that morning to work out how far we had drifted during the night, but the weather stayed murky. We travelled for about eleven miles, then hove-to again and began experimenting with ways to reduce the drift and cut *Vega*'s awful rolling. We tried the storm jib alone, the staysail alone, and the main alone. We had the main fully reefed, reducing it to handkerchief size. Then we tried every conceivable combination of these, with the tiller lashed in different positions. Finally, we settled on a reefed main. It at least helped a little to control the wild rolling.

We tried for several hours to get through on our only remaining transmitter, but were blocked by a solid wall of static. Long after Nigel and I had given up, Grant kept calling into the microphone. Finally, he clicked the set off, and slammed his palm on the table.

Late in the afternoon, the weather cleared enough for a sun-sight. Nigel bent to his calculations. "We are about twenty-seven miles from Mururoa," he announced. I realized that we must have been very close to the twelve-mile limit when I spotted that warship. It occurred to me that the ship had probably been waiting to pounce on us the moment we drifted across the line.

Since morning, we had not seen a trace of the other vessel.

Night was coming. "We'd better make ourselves obvious to avoid being accidentally hit in the dark," I said. We switched on the masthead light, re-attached the radar reflector, and hung our two-dollar kerosene lantern on the missen boom over the cockpit. The total effect in the middle of the Pacific, I thought, was like striking a match on a mountain range. But it did give us a feeling of security.

The sea was swept with constant rainstorms and squalls. Cascades of foam swept down the surfaces of the waves and clouds like a mass of solder pushed in an unbroken tide over *Vega*'s wildly-waving masts.

We saw no further sign of the French. For all our senses could tell us, we might be a million miles from any place called Mururoa, anywhere in the great single ocean of the world. It was a bit as though we were on a small ark, waiting for the flood to pass. It seemed obvious that with weather like this, the Bomb would not be tested – the fallout would be carried too far and high. The position we wanted to take was slightly northeast of Mururoa, but with strong winds coming out of the east, we would not be able to avoid being blown directly towards the atoll. The only choice for the moment was to hang in west of our target. Each night, we were driven away from the atoll. In the day, we hoisted the sails and tacked back to anywhere within twenty to twenty-five miles of the test site. It was like curling up to sleep near the top of a slow-motion DOWN escalator, waking up to find yourself near the bottom, and having to plod all day upward against moving steps, go to sleep at the top, wake up near the bottom again, and repeat the climb. Except that *Vega* drum-rolled furiously without stop, and our muscles cried out for a break, even a one-minute break in the ceaseless tossing and wallowing.

The days began to blur.

We played cards, read, talked, with one man always monitoring the receiver or trying to make contact on the radio. The stumbling bone-jarring lurch of the boat had made writing more difficult than ever. Increasingly, I took to using the tape recorder to keep my log:

The fifth of June, New Zealand time. It blew fairly hard all last night. We got up about 0700 hours and started the engines to build up the batteries. We sailed about due south, bringing us back around twenty-five miles from Mururoa. The idea is to sit off a fair distance from Mururoa during this bad weather, and then when it clears up, making it in a little closer. We haven't seen hide nor hair of any French boats or planes. . . . Everybody slept a little better last night, getting a little more used to the boat rolling

91

around. It's hard to imagine what it's like just lying here with the boat just rolling back and forth. It's definitely hard to live with, but, anyway, we discussed it last night and we're prepared to sit out here for at least two or three weeks and then we'll see what happens. We spend a lot of time listening to the radio. There's been nothing reported on BBC or Australia News. I think I mentioned we heard a little bit on the Indian news that the Australian and New Zealand labour people were not servicing French boats and that the French were going ahead with the tests. We had a lot of discussion about what the French are thinking and what they plan to do with us and our general opinion is that they'll just leave us until three or four days before the test, then come and warn us to get out, and then when we don't leave they'll come back and board the ship and take her far enough away ... They'll have to do this with their own crews ... Everybody's thinking of their friends. We look at my watch, which is always on New Zealand time, and we think of what our friends are doing at that time of day, and we're very lonely. I think what makes it the loneliest is that we don't think anyone knows that we're here. We really believe that the positions we gave showed us heading north and maybe a lot of people think we just kept on going, maybe up to Hawaii. Mom and Dad might think that we headed east or got into trouble. But anyway, it's hard to visualize us sitting out here, really in the middle of nowhere, sitting here, the three of us, trying to play hearts and waiting for something to happen. We heard today that the Stockholm conference on the environment has started and this leads us to believe that the French will not let off the bomb while this conference is going on, which would mean we've got at least two weeks to sit here. The main thing, that we're trying to stress between ourselves, is that we've got to be patient. And that's hard for me.

On the evening of June 6, we decided to move in closer to Mururoa than we had yet done. We were hove-to and had just finished playing another game of hearts. We decided to climb up into the cockpit for some fresh air before turning in. It was then that we saw the halo of light off our starboard bow. It was the loom of Mururoa, the lights of the atomic test site reflecting off the sky. Ever so slightly, I caught the muted distant sound of heavy machinery.

In the morning, two large aircraft passed overhead, one, a transport, flying low, the other, a military weather observer, much higher. Activity around the base at Mururoa seemed to be quickening.

Shortly before noon the gale struck. Within hours, a black weather front had passed over us and the waves were already up to twenty feet. The barometer had dropped alarmingly. Astern, I could see what looked like a small tidal wave rolling down on top of us. Then *Vega* was being lifted on a frothing crest and pitched forward. The wind hummed thunderously through the rigging.

"We must slow her down!" I yelled. "Use the nylon warp for a sea anchor."

Nigel and Grant struggled with all the warp we had, hurling it over the stern as *Vega* shot a wave top and plummeted into a cavernous trough. In the next ten hours, even with bare poles and a sea anchor, we were driven sixty miles. Sometimes gusting to seventy knots, the gale blew through the night. *Vega* rolled so steeply that we had to clutch the sides of our bunks, straining every muscle just to avoid the wall of the cabin. I would find myself looking *up* at Grant on the other side, then *down* at Grant. Sometimes we would hear a deep rumbling out in the dark, advancing steadily, becoming a roar filling the cabin, fading like the swish of gargantuan robes, and we could take a breath again, waiting for the next big one.

"Am I imagining that it's worse than it really is?" asked Grant, the strain beginning to show in his voice.

"It always seems worse," I grunted. "I know it's bad enough."

"I'll be damned glad when it's over," said Nigel quietly.

At first light, obsessed with a frantic desire to make contact with the outside world, I gave in to absurdity. I scribbled a short letter to Ann-Marie and slipped it into an empty wine bottle, along with a note asking the finder to forward the letter. Feeling giddy, I threw the bottle into the seas, and watched as it bobbed upward in an approaching wave, and vanished in an avalanche of froth. I was beginning to wonder, as Grant would put it, if I was "not the full quid" any longer. In other words, if I wasn't losing my mind. But at least it felt no more stupid than writing one's last will and testament.

June 8 brought clearer skies, but no slackening of the gale. I had known exhaustion often enough, but the feeling coming over me now was something that went further, as though a void had started to open in my marrow and it was expanding outward through my bones. The storm had been making a shambles of our plan to stay tucked in close to Mururoa, batting us wildly to the east, the northeast, the north. It *was* a bit like a badminton game, except that in this case *Vega* was the "bird".

By June 8, however, we had made a determined drive to gain some control over the situation. Even at the risk of unknowingly passing within the twelve-mile limit, we had pushed *eastward*, and were now hove-to, thirty miles east of Mururoa, directly in the path of any fallout. The wind had shifted around, so that it was now blasting, almost with the force of a bomb itself, out of the east. The game continued – the bird being blown away from Mururoa during the night, tacking doggedly back toward the test site during the day. Behind us now lay the Groupe d'îles Actéon, a half-dozen atolls, capable of shredding *Vega* like a corpse. Grimly, I realized that the situation had not really changed since back in Auckland – still the dragon ahead and the sharks behind.

That afternoon, we were, in fact, visited by a shark, an eight-footer who glided like a shadow under the surface. I rigged a handline with a lure on it, in the manner of the islanders. The shark casually took both line and lure. I tried an eighty-pound test line with sardines attached to the lure. I tossed a few sardines overboard first to whet the creature's appetite. At this

94

point, Nigel and Grant retreated nervously to the cabin, neither one of them appreciating the game. Grant felt the shark was a bad omen, and Nigel worried that I might lose a finger. Ignoring their uneasiness, I got my line in the water. Soon it was twanging. I fought the shark for half an hour before the line finally snapped. I made up another line with an eight-foot steel leader. The shark merely sniffed the lure this time, but hung around the yacht speculatively for most of the afternoon.

Another visitor arrived, a beautiful grey land bird. It circled us, then beat its way slowly across the sky towards Mururoa. I wondered what would happen to it when the Bomb went off. I wanted to shout: "Get the hell out of here!"

Over the radio we managed to pick up a weak and garbled transmission from the BBC. One piece of information was clear enough: "... even with the world pressure, the French will still go ahead with their test this summer."

June 10 was a Saturday. We were holding our position more steadily now, exactly where we had hoped to be, in the middle of the downwind range from Mururoa. The gale had eased and the sea was calming down. Activity around the invisible base was stepping up. A plane appeared to the north. Early in the afternoon, we heard two muffled explosions, like the guns of a heavy destroyer. We also became aware of a distant drone, the sound of large turbine generators, and a short time later spotted a white object floating in the water. Starting the engines we motored over to it. Grant leaned over the bowsprit and scooped it up. "Christ!" he yelled, "it's a time bomb!"

Cautiously, we examined it. Smaller than a breadbox, it proved to be some kind of portable weather forecasting device with an array of bright-coloured electronic components packed inside its polyethylene container. It did not seem to have been in the water very long, so we concluded it must have fallen from a disabled weather balloon.

By mid-day we had seen three planes in the distance. Then, just before supper a black dot hopped over the horizon and came beating towards us. It was a large helicopter, military brown with a white bottom. Making its wild chattering sound, it circled us twice, not much higher than the top of *Vega*'s masts, flattening the water in stippled patches around us. A sailboat and a helicopter and nothing else but sea all around. We were like two wholly different creatures sniffing each other suspiciously, the one with its lineage going back through millennia of human history, and the other like an alien time machine having darted in for a visit to the twentieth century. Then, lifting – no waves having been exchanged – the helicopter egg-beat its way in the direction of Tahiti.

Watching the helicopter dwindle to a fleck on the horizon, Nigel said: "It won't be long now."

The feeling that the game was coming rapidly to some sort of a head was uppermost in our minds. It was impossible, on the great table of ocean, to avoid thinking in terms of chess. *Vega* was a pawn, the helicopter might have been a bishop, the ship we had seen almost a week ago would have been a knight, and it was just possible that we had truly moved into position to block the nuclear queen. The following day, we heard over the radio that other pieces had been set in motion. Eight nations were reported to have signed a treaty in Stockholm to ban atomic tests. In New Zealand, dock workers were refusing to service French ships. Similar boycotts had started in Fiji and Tonga. The feeling of being alone diminished. In the evening, our spirits took another leap when we thought we had finally broken through to the outside world.

At 2025 hours, I sat down at the marine radio and tried again to raise Rarotonga or Pitcairn or Tahiti on the 2182 frequency. When, as usual, that got no results, I tried sending a call to "all ships", on the emergency frequency.

Faintly, ever so faintly, I heard:

"*Greenpeace ... Greenpeace ... Greenpeace.*"

Nigel and Grant jumped out of their bunks, Grant letting out a whoop. I found myself trembling with excitement.

The scene in the radio and communications room of the cruiser *De Grasse* was described to me much later by one of the men who was present. Admiral Claverie and a second senior officer had just stepped into the communications centre, a

96

perfunctory visit involving dispatches from Paris. One of the consoles was tuned to the 2182 frequency. The admiral stopped as he heard:

"All ships ... all ships ... This is *Greenpeace Three* ... *Greenpeace Three* ... *Greenpeace Three* ... All ships ... all ships ... Do you receive? Over!"

The admiral looked at the clock on the wall. Then he stepped over to the console.

"They are trying to communicate on emergency time. Do you have their frequency jammed?" he asked the operator.

"Yes, sir."

"All ships ... all ships ... This is *Greenpeace Three* ... *Greenpeace Three* ... *Greenpeace Three* ... All ships ... all ships ... Do you receive?"

The admiral was silent for a moment. Then he said:

"Answer back in English, giving our call signal. They are in difficulty."

"Yes, sir," said the operator, quickly pushing the necessary buttons and switches on the control console.

"*Greenpeace* ... *Greenpeace* ... *Greenpeace* ... This is FAYM ... Do you receive? Do you receive?"

My voice came back within minutes. I had misunderstood the call signal.

'AOYM ... AOYM ... This is *Greenpeace Three* ... this is *Greenpeace Three* ... Receive you faintly ... we have been twenty miles off Mururoa for the last ten days ... Have food enough for five weeks ... All well ... Request you advise ZLD in New Zealand. Please acknowledge with roger ... roger ... roger ... if you receive and understand."

The console operator looked at the admiral questioningly.

"Acknowledge," said the admiral.

"Roger ... roger ... roger," said the operator into the microphone. A crackle of static.

"AOYM ... AOYM ... This is *Greenpeace Three* ... This is *Greenpeace Three* ... Reception very weak ... Request you call us at 2025 hours tomorrow ... Acknowledge."

The admiral nodded.

"Roger ... roger." The transmission ended.

Admiral Claverie rubbed his chin thoughtfully.

"They have mis-read our call sign," he said to the other officer. "They think they are talking to a civilian ship." He turned back to the radio operator. "You are to continue our control over their radio, maintain your conversations with the *Greenpeace*, but bluff them in order to get as much information as possible. I want to know how much food they have, how much water. See if you can find when they expect to leave."

"Yes, sir," said the operator. "How shall I identify?"

"Continue with the false call sign AOYM, not Fox Alpha Yankee Mike. Give your name as . . . Mueller. And the name of the ship is . . . *The Astrid* . . . out of Belgium. Give your position as the island of Tubai, which is about eight hundred miles away."

"Yes, sir, I understand."

The admiral turned to the other officer. "Monitor all their communications to AOYM and have them forwarded to me. You will continue to block all their other transmissions and all incoming calls from Rarotonga, ZLD Auckland, or Pitcairn. Make arrangements to have the telex equipment turned off at the time of transmission to reduce the noise in this room. I don't want them to suspect they are talking to one of our vessels just over the horizon."

The officer nodded, stepping aside as the admiral left the room.

A short while later, another unusual event took place. All personnel in the radio room were ordered by the chief radio communications officer to sign a letter of agreement never to discuss any of the conversations that took place between *De Grasse* and *Greenpeace III*. This agreement was in addition to the regular oaths of secrecy and confidentiality to which all military personnel and officers are sworn.

That night, we went to our bunks feeling happier than we had in weeks. All we could think about was the radio call. We doubted that even our short message had got through properly, but another human voice saying "roger . . . roger . . . roger" was more than music. It was like a lifeline thrown down into a deep pit. Going up on deck just before I went to sleep, I saw the loom of Mururoa again. It only added to my new sense of happiness. I felt as though we had joined the human race again.

We spent most of the following day eagerly composing messages. There was so much that we wanted to say, so many people we wanted to contact, that it took a collective exercise in discipline to boil them down to just two planned cables, a short one if reception was poor, a longer one in case conditions were reasonable. Our entire existence had quickly come to focus on the prospect of communication that night. The day slipped by quickly.

We ran the diesel for an hour to charge up the batteries. At 2025 hours, I sat down at the radio as gingerly as a man perched on the edge of a cliff, reaching for a golden ring dangling from the sky. Blissfully, I was unaware that by this time we had a sizeable audience. Every night since we had arrived in the control zone and begun our regular broadcasts, all the short-wave radios on the atoll and in the fleet were switched on and tuned to our frequency. Officers relaxing between clean sheets listened in on our every word. Technicians and ratings stood around in groups, also eavesdropping. It was not just for the sake of entertainment. Most of them were genuinely curious about the small boat which had surfaced on the doorstep of their fortress atoll. It was something beyond their military experience.

"AOYM . . . AOYM," I called, my voice echoing through the atoll and the ships of the Pacific fleet, but going nowhere else. "This is *Greenpeace Three* . . . *Greenpeace Three* . . . *Greenpeace Three* . . . Do you receive? Over . . ."

Nigel and Grant and I huddled tensely around the radio, listening to the buzz and percolation of static. For twenty minutes, I called again and again and again. And then, very faintly, over the receiver, we heard:

"*Greenpeace Three* . . . *Greenpeace Three* . . . This is AOYM . . . This is AOYM . . . Having great difficulty receiving you . . . Over."

"AOYM . . . AOYM . . . This is *Greenpeace Three* . . . This is *Greenpeace Three* . . . Advise wire services arrived twenty miles

99

off Mururoa June first. Stop. Minimum five weeks provisions left . . . Intend staying. All well . . ."

There was no confirming reply. In despair, I assumed that the message had not got through. Reception worsened. Finally, I gave up. After the expectations that had gripped us all day, we fell numbly, miserably, into our bunks, plunging as low as we had been high during the day.

Our mood had not been helped, either, by a stocktaking operation we had carried out. We were out of cookies, flour, barley, and worst of all, rice. There are a hundred things one can do with rice to help cover the taste of canned meat. We did have countless packages of dried potatoes that tasted about as good as hot paper. We still had some figs, a few precious real potatoes, a couple of onions and a small mountain of flavourless hamburger patties. The balance of our provisions consisted of cans of bully beef, dried soup, fifty cans of beer, some hard liquor and a single bottle of wine. Our morning treat of canned peaches was a thing of the past. We were substituting canned pineapples that tasted as though they had been preserved in formaldehyde. The prospect of weeks and weeks of food of this ilk was enough, in our depressed state, to reduce us to tears.

In the morning, we found that the barometer had started falling. The wind made a high-pitched atomic sound in the rigging. There were flat explosive claps of sound as the seas kicked up again. We had just barely begun to recover our energy after the last gale, and the thought of another brutal round of being hurled from wall to wall put a look on our faces of men who have been on the rack. We found that we were talking less and less. At this rate, our language would soon be reduced to a series of grunts and grimaces. Everything seemed sticky and damp. We retreated into books. I had about finished *The Lord of the Rings*, identifying by this time very strongly with the two exhausted Hobbits who were crawling on their bellies across the last grim plain toward the Mountain of Mordor. I was also ploughing through Lawrence's *Seven Pillars of Wisdom*. Grant had buried himself in a book called *An Island to Oneself*. We tried to ignore the high keening of the wind, the shuddering impact of waves that seemed to come up under us like whales.

By June 13, we were only fifteen miles out from Mururoa. We could see the radio towers and white bunker-like buildings on the shore. That night there was a loud clear burst of voices over the 2182 frequency. It was a freighter, identifying itself as the *Lorina,* en route to Rarotonga. I dived for the microphone, but before I could say a word, the operator on the other end had switched off, leaving me calling into an immense silence. *Lorina* had sounded close enough to touch.

Reception improved briefly the next night, and we clearly heard the overseas announcer of Radio Australia reporting on the outcome of the United Nations conference on the environment at Stockholm:

"Australia supported the resolution to ban nuclear tests, which was passed fifty-six to three in favour, with twenty-nine abstentions. France, which plans to explode a nuclear device in the South Pacific this month, opposed the resolution, along with China and the African state of Gabon. The United States, England and Russia were amongst those who abstained . . ."

At 2025 hours, encouraged by the reception, I switched on the transmitter and tried again to reach our lifeline, AOYM. The static was heavy, but after several attempts, a weak message came back. I found myself holding my breath.

"*Greenpeace Three* . . . *Greenpeace Three* . . . This is AOYM . . . ZLD Auckland urgently requires your position and asks how your condition is . . . Over."

I quickly gave him our position, said that we were all well, repeated that we had food supplies for five weeks – although both Grant and Nigel grimaced at the mention of the word "food" – and said that we intended to remain where we were. Then I asked AOYM where he was located.

Back came the lie:

"*Greenpeace Three* . . . *Greenpeace Three* . . . This is AOYM . . . our position is on the island of Tubai, near Rapa . . . Am not receiving you clearly . . . Will you call again? Over."

The radio operator in the communications room of *De*

Grasse wrote down the details of what I had said and passed it to one of the officers. The message was quickly taken to Admiral Claverie's quarters, where a meeting was in progress with senior technical and scientific personnel.

The officer handed over the message.

"The protest vessel indicates that it is intending to stay in its present position," the admiral said. "They are still downwind of the site."

"We cannot afford to wait any longer," said one of the scientific officers.

"Let's get the balloon in the air," said another. "That should frighten them off."

The admiral shook his head. "I don't think they will frighten that easily. They are here to prevent us from conducting a test. I think they will only withdraw when they think the test has been completed."

He paused for a moment.

"We will raise the balloon and try to scare them off. If they do not leave, we will conduct a test, but only of the trigger device, as soon as they are a little out of position. It will not be large enough to cause them harm, but it will indicate to them that they have failed in their mission. I think then they will withdraw."

"That will be an expensive exercise, Admiral," remarked one of the officers, frowning. "The balloon and the hydrogen, plus the trigger device – a tremendous increase in overhead and support costs to withdraw the personnel . . ."

"It is expensive every day we are being delayed!" snapped the admiral. "We must get them out of there! The tests must go ahead!"

After supper on June 16, I climbed blearily to the cockpit to check the horizon. Still no sight of ships, just the lavish tropical sunset with purple and red clouds flung wildly across half the sky. Mururoa was almost due west of us, just slightly to the south of where the sun was sinking. Taking in the view, something unusual in the clouds caught my attention. A helicopter? It would be directly over the atoll. Barely perceptible, the thing hung amid the apocalypse of blinding colours just above the horizon. I quickly clambered back into the cabin for the binoculars.

"What is it?" Grant called out.

"Just a minute." I braced myself against a stay and focussed carefully, squinting against the light. Clouds. Clouds. Water. Blinding. And then the object bobbed into view in the lens, a black round silhouette. My heart jogged.

"It's a balloon! A damned bloody great balloon!"

The binoculars almost dropped from my fingers. The three of us stood for a moment, staring.

"They're getting ready to blow the goddamn bomb," I heard myself saying. "They're really going to do it."

I stepped backwards automatically, as though trying to move away from that shape, half-expecting a fireball to erupt even more blindingly than the sun. Would they fire it now, at this time of day? I didn't know.

There was silence. Grant tugged the binoculars from me. "Fuck," he said. "That's it."

Nigel stood at the hatchway, naked, his skin reddish-bronze in the last rays of light, a polka-dot handkerchief tied around his head to keep his mass of curly hair out of his eyes. He waited patiently for his turn at the binoculars, not saying anything. Finally, he let his breath out.

"The bastards," he said quietly. "The bastards."

I tried to keep my voice calm. "That Frenchman in Rarotonga, the guy who knew all about last year's tests, what did he say? They lift the bomb over the atoll with a dirigible balloon."

"Yes," said Nigel distantly, still staring. "And that scientist in Auckland said that when you can see the balloon you are too close, there's no use worrying about anything else."

Carefully, we had not looked at each other. Then, when the sun dipped below the horizon, we glanced at each other's faces, a quick glance, then looked away. Each face was completely wooden. That single glance told me everything I needed to know. *We were all scared shitless.*

Even after dark, we imagined we could see the image of the

balloon in the star patterns just above the horizon. Its presence was burned into our senses, and there was almost nothing else we could think about. We had gone over the details of our tactics a dozen times before, but now we went over them obsessively again. Making the assumption that the French would attempt to board us – probably the next day – we rehearsed our reaction. We would let the boarding take place, would present the officer in charge with a copy of the legal document which had been prepared for us by the University of Auckland, setting out the regulations of the law of the sea. Then, when the French took control of the boat, we would demonstrate how to start the engine, and turn the boat over. We would not sail it ourselves since we would be, in effect, prisoners of war. I suspected we would then be taken to some other island and held until the tests were over. Probably not Tahiti, because of the publicity.

At 1900 hours, we sighted a light aft of us. It looked like a masthead light, and we assumed it would be a French boat, probably getting ready to seize us. We decided to take turns on watch all night. We weren't going to be able to sleep anyway.

I tried desperately that night to get through to our contact at AOYM, but the reception was so poor we could barely hear the voice at the other end. I felt a rising urge to claw at the radio. Forcing myself to curb the sudden tendency for my voice to rise, I gulped several times, speaking as clearly as I could. I repeated our position a half-dozen times. But AOYM had faded, and we got no acknowledgement.

It was close to midnight before I reached my decision. "I think," I said, "that we should try to get in closer, say about fifteen or sixteen miles. We might as well try to force their hand."

It meant putting ourselves squarely beneath the place where the bomb would go off, so close, in fact, that if it were to be detonated, *Vega* would be sitting well under the umbrella of the mushroom cloud – for the few micro-seconds she would have before being utterly destroyed.

In the early hours of the morning, the ship's light we had seen aft of us disappeared over the horizon.

At dawn, we hoisted the sails. *Vega* began to slide quietly toward Mururoa. The balloon was at a bearing of 230 degrees magnetic. As we moved closer, the balloon loomed higher and higher over the horizon. Caught in the first slanting rays of the sun, it was a dazzling bone-white, looking very much like the old-time dirigibles with a huge fin on the back. Try as we might, we couldn't avoid talking in low tones, as though stealth might somehow help. There was even a tendency to step softly, as though the balloon were a sleeping monster we had no desire to awaken. I was astonished at how many irrational reactions I was having.

Nigel took a sun-sight, then checked and double-checked his calculations. There could be no room for error now. When we were sixteen miles out, we hove-to, with the balloon looming large like the single white petal of a giant flower well above the horizon. It seemed as oddly fragile as existence itself, as fragile as our own existence had become.

Our precise position at that point was 21 degrees, 41 minutes south, 138 degrees, 21 minutes west. We were east-northeast of Mururoa.

The wind was coming directly out of the west, from behind the atoll. From the point of view of the weapons-makers, it could not have been more perfect. The fallout would be carried straight down the corridor of the cordon.

Engulfing little *Vega* on the way.

As the day broke more fully, visibility improved. Now we could see the radio towers again. According to our pilot book, the radio masts were located on the southeast corner of the atoll. Nigel took a bearing on the balloon. He judged it to be seven hundred to one thousand feet in the air. The wind factor put its position directly above the lagoon that we could only see on our charts.

We photographed it several times and kept a nervous watch on it through the binoculars. As the light improved, another object became visible just below its main bulk.

"Could that be the bomb?" asked Grant, his mouth dry.

"I dunno," I said.

"Could be," said Nigel. "Could be."

The two younger men had lived all their lives with the Bomb. Its image had been imprinted on their minds since childhood. They had listened to its roar on the newsreels. It was the single most dreadful image they knew. Previous generations had trembled before visions of hellfire and brimstone, but theirs was the first generation for whom the hellfire was real. It was a hellfire that could be directed and aimed by men. No wall existed that it could not breach. No hole existed that was deep enough for escape. There was no place on earth the fire could not reach. And no father's arm could hold it at bay. Since Hiroshima, no child had been born on the planet who truly knew security.

"What do you think the French will do tomorrow, if anything?" I asked Grant.

"What I've said all along. From what we've seen of the situation so far, I think there's a good chance they won't come."

"That they won't come at all? What's your feeling about them not coming at all?"

"Well, you know, I don't know really."

I looked over at Nigel. "You've always thought that they would come to tell us first to get out of the way."

"Yes."

"And you question that now?"

"Uh-huh."

"You actually think they'd set off the bomb with us here?"

"Possible. Yes."

I waited.

"I'm saying that that is something seriously to be taken into consideration," Nigel added slowly. "I take it as a serious possibility."

"Well, let's get ready for it then," I said, heaving myself to my feet.

Moving mechanically, we placed wooden plugs beside each of the boat's vents, plugs that could be hammered quickly into place to seal the interior. We agreed that if and when the blast went off, two of us would stay below while the third would go out on deck after the initial explosion wrapped in oilskins and start motoring us out of the danger zone. The third man out would be chosen by drawing straws. *Vega* had a Honda generator that could be used to pump sea water up to wash the decks and sails down to control any fires. We would put a hose down twenty or thirty feet under the surface to pump up what we hoped would be uncontaminated water.

The effect of the preparations was to send grotesque images tumbling through our minds – of scorching walls of heat, blinding unearthly light, shock waves coming across the water like freight trains and showers of heat-cracked rocks and charred wood. I caught myself looking at my own and the other's skin, wondering how much laceration it could take.

We started wearing sunglasses – just in case. And each developed the habit of squinting automatically when we looked in the direction of the balloon, already half-consciously trying to protect our eyes in case the thing suddenly went off. Every time I climbed up on the deck, I tried to avoid looking at the balloon and its strange burden entirely. But it was like having a maniac standing behind you with a sledgehammer. No matter how hard I tried, my attention kept being drawn back to that one object that shared the sea and the sky with us.

During the afternoon, we picked up part of a radio broadcast, reporting that motions and amendments were still being made to the Stockholm treaty urging a ban on nuclear tests. We realized we were probably the only people in the world besides the French who knew that the balloon was up.

We had spaghetti for dinner and opened our last bottle of wine. It was my turn to cook. Standing over the stove seemed such an ordinary domestic thing to be doing – and it evoked so many powerful recollections – that everything began to seem enormously unreal. The porthole above the stove was open. I could clearly see the balloon, I found myself actually giddy, just standing there, whipping up a pot of good old spaghetti, with nothing less than the Sword of Damocles poised above the horizon less than sixteen miles away, just stirrin' the sauce, stirrin' the sauce, waitin' for the holocaust. Grant made a joke about the "last supper", but Nigel and I only managed to grunt.

After the meal, we composed a telegram that we would try to get out over the radio later. It said simply: BALLOON RAISED OVER MURUROA LAST NIGHT STOP GREENPEACE THREE SIXTEEN MILES NORTHEAST STOP SITUATION FRIGHTENING PLEASE PRAY AND ACT. Afterwards, I took the tape recorder and settled myself in the cockpit. As the sun began to sink, the balloon became a silhouette again. It seemed like a planet.

Well, it's about quarter to eight in the evening. Grant's reading a book, the sun is just setting, looks absolutely beautiful. I can see the sun just setting now in front of me and just to port I can see the balloon . . . This afternoon the three of us became very close and we cleaned up the cabin, cleaned up the galley, cleaned up the deck, got everything ship-shape. I guess tomorrow we're expecting something to happen. Then we all decided to have a drink and we had a couple of gins . . . We decided about an hour ago to take the can of meths – that's the methylated spirits which we are using to start the primus, and a five-gallon can of gas that we use for the Honda generator, and throw them overboard in the morning, because if they do set the bomb off, uh, they would be the first things to blow up . . . We, uh, hope to get our cable away tonight if the radio works . . . I have never been very religious, but I hope our cable gets through tonight and I hope a lot of people pray because that balloon sits there on the horizon looking at us, and we've discussed it in detail, and we've decided now that the French really aren't coming to get us . . . It's interesting that none of us have discussed or even brought up the subject of let's get outta here. Instead, we've discussed palm trees, coconuts, Tahitian girls, our friends back home, but nobody has talked about the specific thing, and that is getting out of here. Anyway, the sun has gone down now, and the wind is out of the northwest, and I'm sure the French know where the wind will go, probably southwest, and tomorrow morning, I guess, they'll either come and see us, or let the damn thing go off . . .

Morning came grey and overcast. We could barely make out

the balloon against the leaden clouds. Nobody had slept more than a couple of hours at a time, getting up repeatedly to see if the lights of any ships had appeared. We had raised AOYM only faintly and had little hope that our message had been received. Now, we weren't certain what to think. We felt as leaden as the clouds. There was a possibility that the poor weather might lead to the test being postponed, but it also condemned us to more waiting. We had only drifted about a mile eastward during the night, which still left us sitting less than eighteen miles from ground zero. So we remained where we were.

At 1600 hours, we were sitting around the saloon table playing cards when Grant glanced up through a porthole.

"A ship!" he yelled.

From the deck, we could see it clearly enough to know that it was large and military. It was about a mile off our port bow. But it was just sitting in the water. If the French had indeed moved one of their knights out onto the board, it was so far remaining passive. We studied it through the binoculars for several minutes.

"Well, what do we do now?" asked Grant.

I thought for a moment. Then, driven by the same impulse which had prompted me to move closer to the balloon – perhaps an instinct to press an opponent – I said: "Let's go check her out." The moment we began to move forward, the ship belched smoke and backed away. For an hour and fifteen minutes, we "pursued" the ship, but it easily maintained the distance between us. It was impossible – despite our overall tension – not to be slightly amused by the irony of a warship retreating before a yacht. When it became apparent that the vessel was not going to let us get close, we hove-to, and settled down to have supper. We had two companions now in the vast sweep of sea, the balloon and the ship. Whether it was justified or not, the presence of the other vessel eased our anxiety about the bomb going off immediately, although we decided to mount an all-night watch in case the French were merely waiting for dark to make their move.

In the evening, we tried without success to raise AOYM.

We did, however, catch the news from Radio Australia – and the first mention of our existence. Still fading in and out, the announcer said:

"The French government advised that it will take all necessary measures to protect anyone likely to be in the vicinity of Mururoa atoll in French Polynesia, where a projected nuclear test is to be held. This assurance was given by the government to the Australian embassy in Paris, in reply to a request. A young Australian, Grant Davidson, is believed to be in the area in the ketch *Greenpeace III*. The French foreign minister said he has noted the Australian government's concern and France would take any necessary measures to ensure that they would not be affected by the nuclear blast."

"Fair dinkum!" bubbled Grant. We all felt electrified. We immediately assumed that the report meant at least some of our messages had got through to the outside world. In fact, they had not. I was later to learn that the inquiry was not the result of any of our messages, but of phone calls by Grant's father and mother. At the time, though, the effect of the news report was close to that of a last-minute reprieve on death row. It was only now, in the warm rush of relief, that we truly realized how tense we had been since the balloon had appeared. It had been hanging like an upraised guillotine over our heads, and even though it still hung there ready to flash down and extinguish our lives, we now had two good reasons for expecting to live – the warship whose lights we could see in the distance, and the statement by the French that they would "insure that they would not be affected by the blast". It was only later, as I was crawling into my bunk, that I started to think about the other part of the statement: "France would take *any necessary measures*." The more I thought about it, the more threatening it sounded.

The wind blew twenty-five to thirty knots all night, pushing us steadily outward from the atoll. By morning, we were close to twenty-five miles out, with the other ship still maintaining a position about two miles away. At 0730 hours, we hoisted the main and yankee, and began to sail back toward Mururoa. The wind was steady at force five, the sea rough and flecked with whitecaps. In this kind of weather, if any attempt was going to be made to board us, it would be anything but easy.

From the moment we started moving, our watchdog threw plumes of smoke into the air – the image came to mind of a snorting dragon getting up to move – and came tossing over the water in our wake. One moment it would be obliterated by a ridge of water as *Vega* sliced down into a trough. But as we topped the next crest, it would still be firmly on our track, its bow chopping the waves heavily. As an experiment, I tried slowing *Vega* down, speeding her up. The warship slowed and sped up accordingly. The distinct feeling developed that we were being stalked and that the moment had simply not yet come when the stalker would pounce. It was like trotting across an open field with a bull pawing the ground and snorting behind you, matching your pace.

While Nigel took the tiller, I made a quick, nervous report into the tape recorder, just in case . . .

Our friend is following right behind us. He's coming up pretty fast on us now. That's about it for a few minutes . . . It's eight-fifty local time and the wind is still blowing about ten or fifteen knots, maybe more than that. There's no question they'd have trouble boarding us in this sea. I'm sure they're thinking the same thing. The tension here is growing quite a bit. We're heading straight for Mururoa right now. We are probably about twenty miles away, and I guess the boat is about two miles behind us . . . Every time we speed up, he speeds up. When we slow down, he slows down. I don't know what they're up to . . . I seriously think that maybe we're much more of a problem than we think we are. Maybe they're not quite sure what to do. I would think it would be the first time in modern history that an act of piracy is just about to take place and that's exactly what it is if they board us, because they have no right on this boat and we have all the right in the world to be in these waters. They're international waters and they belong to you and me . . . The time is twenty-five to twelve local

III

time now and the boat, our friend behind us, is closing in very quickly on us now . . . It's twenty to twelve now, and he's closing very very quickly. We've sighted what looks like the radio mast . . .

Smoke had bloomed from the funnels as the warship began to overtake us. Spray began to fan like gull wings from around her bow. Soon, over the hiss of water on *Vega*'s decks, we could hear the deep throb of engines. I found myself instinctively casting my eye around for a place to duck for cover, but of course there was no place to flee. We were out in the open with a warship bearing purposefully down on us. Waves hissed in a boil as they sheared off her bow.

"It's a minesweeper!" Nigel yelled.

The ship was on our starboard quarter. As she pulled up on us, we judged her to be at least one hundred and fifty feet long – a sleek light grey wedge with a slanting blade of a bow, long and narrow-beamed with a large funnel amidships. She looked built for speed. From the deck of *Vega*, a few feet above water level, she was immense.

After the long weeks of being accustomed to *Vega*'s top speed of nine knots, I was stunned at the swiftness with which the minesweeper had closed the gap between us.

"She's doing at least eighteen knots!" Nigel yelled, his voice almost lost in the roar of the bigger vessel's engines. She had pulled abeam of us, and seemed like a wall drawn across the sky. We could easily make out the large black number near the bow – M728 – and the name, in smaller letters near the stern – *La Bayonnaise*. There were at least a dozen chaps on the deck, staring down at us impassively.

"Not friendly chaps, are they?" said Grant, his face almost white.

It was like a great unequal race, *Vega*'s sails full as she pounded up one wave and down the next, now wagging her masts from side to side as the minesweeper's bow wave passed under us. The ship was less than thirty yards away, running so sleekly she might have been on a monorail mounted just under the water. I fought the urge to veer off, and instead held the tiller hard, staying on a straight course for Mururoa. Within moments, *La Bayonnaise* had swept ahead of us. In her wake, *Vega* bobbed furiously and the tiller wrenched at my arms. Suddenly, we were in the river of sizzling eddies that was the minesweeper's wake, and the ship, its speed unchecked, peeled off a few points and kept right on going. It took several more minutes before the waves fell back into their normal pattern, and the roar of the minesweeper's twin props stopped pounding in our ears.

The tension didn't ease. I half-expected the minesweeper to wheel around and take another pass at us. Instead, to our surprise, it kept moving rapidly toward the horizon. We were left with the jangled nerves of a bicycle-rider who has just been overtaken on a motorway by a transport truck.

"Well, that got the old adrenalin going, didn't it?" said Grant.

"What's she doing now?" I yelled to Nigel, who was on the foredeck.

"They're taking off," was the reply. "There's something . . . I'm not sure, it looks like another boat, it looks like a large boat . . . much larger boat with a white hull." And then: "There's the balloon!"

"Grant," I said, "go up the mast and have a look."

The minesweeper was moving directly toward the second ship which was stationary about three miles from *Vega*. The minesweeper slowed, circled, and then started heading back toward us. The other ship immediately blew smoke and began to move away.

"Let's go over there!" yelled Nigel.

The vessel was at least three times as long as the minesweeper and painted in a brilliant white. Antennae jutted above her smoke-stack. There was a huge radar dish toward the bow, with a large box-like building near the stern. I took several telescopic-lens photographs, from which I was later able to identify her as the US Victory ship *Wheeling*, T–AGM–8. Although I did not realize it at the time, this was to be my initiation into the complex world of nuclear intrigue. As a signatory to the Nuclear Test Ban Treaty, the United States was not supposed to be involved in any way with atmospheric nuclear tests. Yet here was an American instrumentation ship, well within the French cordon – obviously with the approval of French authorities – on the eve of an atomic blast. I did not know then that we had stumbled across proof that American and French officials were coordinating their activities, so that the US could collect data from atmospheric blasts that it had signed an agreement not to conduct itself.

All we knew at the time was that, after several hours of trying to move near to the big white ship, it was apparent we weren't going to be allowed to get any closer than three miles. *La Bayonnaise*, having delivered her warning to the other ship to watch out for the tiny Canadian yacht, now settled back to her behaviour of the day and night before – remaining about a mile and a half away, moving when *Vega* moved, stopping when she stopped. When all attempts to approach the bigger ship had proved futile, I turned *Vega*'s nose back toward Mururoa. We hove-to fifteen miles from the atoll, still in position in the throat of the cordon. But now our long period of isolation was definitely ended. On one horizon sat the white mystery ship. Off our starboard bow sat *La Bayonnaise*. Above the horizon hung the balloon with its payload slung like an egg beneath it. Several helicopters buzzed back and forth over the atoll. The ocean seemed to have bloomed with a deadly kind of life.

"I guess we'd better set up a watch," said Nigel tiredly. We had sailed altogether for seven hours that day, and had not had a decent sleep for so long we couldn't remember when it had been. The stress of the last two nights in particular had ground us down into a state of numbness. Our eyes were bloodshot.

"To hell with it," I said, stumbling to my bunk.

Flanked by warships, with an atomic bomb hanging over our dreams, the three of us slept soundly until dawn. *Vega*'s red and white maple leaf flag flapped fitfully in the wind.

Ottawa. June 19. There was a sleepy stirring in the House of

Commons as the honourable member for Hillsborough, Mr Heath Macquarrie, got to his feet at the beginning of the question period.

"Mr Speaker, I wish to direct a question to the secretary of state for external affairs. Can he advise whether he has definite word that the French government, in the face of world criticism, is proceeding with its scheduled nuclear test, and can he also advise whether the government has any information on the whereabouts of the *Greenpeace III* and its fine, public-spirited crew?"

The Honourable Mitchell Sharp, secretary of state for external affairs, got up.

Mr Sharp, the country's most powerful politician, spoke in a tight, high-pitched monotone.

"Mr Speaker, it is my understanding that the nuclear test is scheduled to begin in the Mururoa atoll zone at 8 pm tonight, Eastern Daylight Time. We are not quite sure whether it will take place as scheduled because meteorological conditions may not be favourable. I regret very much that this is taking place despite the representations we have made and that many other countries have made. It is our hope that the French government, notwithstanding this particular test, if it proceeds, will join with the rest of the world in trying to stop all nuclear tests both in the atmosphere and underground."

Mr Sharp resumed his seat.

Mr Macquarrie rose again.

"Would the minister direct himself to the other part of my question regarding those fine people of the *Greenpeace III*?"

The external affairs minister rose again.

"Yes, Mr Speaker. As I understand it, the *Greenpeace* is somewhere in the area."

There were sounds of sarcastic surprise from the opposition benches. A Conservative member quipped: "That's about as close as you fellows ever come."

Mr Sharp did not smile.

"This is not a Canadian ship," he said. "It is not registered here. *It does not carry our flag.* It is very difficult for us to keep track of a ship sailing under some other flag or some other ownership." He paused. "We understand there is a Canadian aboard, and of course I do hope the ship is not going to get involved in the explosion and that the necessary steps will be taken to see it is removed from the area . . ."

During the night, the wind as usual pressed us away from Mururoa. At 0845 hours, we began to sail back in again. *La Bayonnaise* maintained its one and a half mile sentry position, generally staying aft of us during the morning, but moving eventually into position abeam. At one point in the afternoon, the minesweeper had worked its way around in front of us.

On an impulse, I began to reduce our speed slowly. The waves were still tumbling in whitecaps around us. I waited for a moment when *La Bayonnaise* dropped out of sight, then Nigel pulled down the radar reflector, and I quickly brought *Vega* about, and we took off with a gust of wind on another tack. We saw a startled burst of smoke over the waves. Within minutes, the minesweeper was crashing after us at full speed.

I found myself staring at our watchdog with an odd sense of *déjà vu*, almost as though I had seen it before. That couldn't be possible, I told myself. But when I squeezed my eyes shut and thought back to all the years I had spent living on the West Coast of British Columbia, the shape of *La Bayonnaise* seemed somehow familiar. It was very much like Canadian mine-sweepers, I thought. Many months later, looking into the matter, I was to learn that the ship had, in fact, been built at the Esquimault shipyards, less than a hundred miles from my home, and that she had originally been a Canadian navy ship, the *Chignecto*. It had rather generously been donated by the Canadian government to France in April, 1956. There had only been one condition to the gift – the ship was to be restricted to NATO use only, and only in the Mediterranean and the Atlantic Ocean. More intrigue . . .

We found ourselves becoming fond of *La Bayonnaise*. None of us had studied prison psychology, so we did not know that prisoners who have been in solitary confinement often develop warm feeling toward their guards because the guards represent their only contact with the outside world.

"What the hell," Grant said. "Let's ask the skipper over for a Kiwi beer."

"Sure!" I laughed. "You can tell them some of your lousy Aussie jokes."

Nigel promptly saluted and went up on deck. It was dark. We had hove-to with our lights off and radar reflector still down. *La Bayonnaise* was laying less than a mile away, her own lights ablaze. Using *Vega*'s sail as a light reflector, Nigel sent a morse code message with his flashlight. He repeated it three times. There was no response.

"The bastards are snubbing us!" he laughed, climbing back into the cabin.

"This neighbourhood's going to rubbish," said Grant.

Reception over the radio that night was better than average, and full of news about the French tests. The cordon had been officially declared in effect as of 10 am that day. Mariners were requested to keep one hundred and twenty miles away from Mururoa. Protests were mounting in several parts of the world. There had been demonstrations in Australia. Peru had threatened to break diplomatic relations with France if the blast went ahead. Someone had attempted to bomb the French Consulate in Melbourne. Threats had been made against the French Embassy in Wellington. In Auckland, somebody had actually thrown a hand bomb into the office of a French airline. The news report ended with:

"There has been confusion over the position of the protest yacht *Greenpeace III*, which last night was reported heading near the French nuclear weapons range of Mururoa Atoll. Radio Hauraki reported in Auckland that radio signals from the vessel indicated that it was in or near the test area. In Paris, French navy officials said they have received no reports about the protest vessel ..."

"The shit's gonna hit the fan soon," said Grant. "It has to."

An unsmiling Admiral Claverie was seated at his desk in the corner of his quarters on board *De Grasse* at anchor in Mururoa

Lagoon. His forehead was furrowed as he studied the document in his hand.

The cabin door opened and an officer entered, followed by four men, three of them in civilian clothes. The other officer closed the door and the group settled quickly into chairs along the walls.

"I have just received word from Paris," the admiral said without preamble. "The tests must commence immediately! In view of the delays, we must expedite this as quickly as possible." He looked at the faces of the others. Two of them nodded vigorously.

"There are one or two problems that need to be attended to," the admiral continued. He looked directly at the senior officer, a commander. "What is the position of the protesting vessel?"

"She is fifteen miles east of sight. Downwind, sir."

"*La Bayonnaise* has her on twenty-four-hour visual contact?"

"Yes, sir."

"Even with the balloon up, they give no indication of leaving. We have been delayed long enough. We cannot wait any longer." Admiral Claverie fixes his eye on the commander.

"A message will be prepared and delivered to the captain of the *Greenpeace III*, advising withdrawal from the area to a point where safety can be guaranteed. If she withdraws, it will be acknowledged and the test will proceed immediately. If she does not withdraw, then efforts must be made to confuse her about her position, and she is to be arrested as soon as she enters territorial waters."

"Yes, sir, I understand," said the commander.

The admiral looked at one of the men in civilian clothes, an elderly scientist with wavy grey hair and horn-rimmed glasses.

"What is the immediate status?"

"We are ready to go, subject to arming the device."

The admiral switched his attention to one of the other men, a meteorologist, who said, without prompting: "The present weather is favourable."

"Then there is no time to waste," said Admiral Claverie.

Ottawa. June 20. Inside the opulent chamber of the House of Commons, the Member of Parliament for Hillsborough, the Honourable Heath Macquarrie, rose again.

"Mr Speaker, may I direct my question to the acting secretary of state for external affairs or to the parliamentary secretary? Has the government any information on the present whereabouts of the Canadian-owned and Canadian-skippered ship, *Greenpeace III*? Also, has the government of France been asked for any information on the location of this vessel and the well-being of its crew?"

The honourable member sat down.

Mr Paul St Pierre, parliamentary secretary to the secretary of state for external affairs, rose from the government seats.

"Mr Speaker, the government does not know the exact location of *Greenpeace III* at this time. If I may respond to the second part of the honourable member's question, the government of France has, we understand, publicly stated that it will not permit the occupants of *Greenpeace III* to place themselves in a position of danger."

He sat down.

Mr Macquarrie rose again.

"May I ask whether it is the view of the government of Canada that the government of France has the right to arrest ships on the high seas in these circumstances?"

Jeers and catcalls peeled from the opposition benches.

The Speaker, governor of the rules of the House, slammed his gavel down.

"Order, please! The honourable member is asking for a legal interpretation and I doubt that the question is in order."

"Greenpeace III! Greenpeace III! Greenpeace III!

A metallic voice seemed to be coming from somewhere far off in a dream. I rolled over groggily, not sure whether I was awake or asleep. My mouth was dry and my first thought was of the stale brown water which was all we had left in our two remaining tanks. I rolled my tongue around in my mouth, then heard Nigel and Grant thumping urgently out of their bunks. And then three shattering blasts from a ship's klaxon hit me, paralysing me for a second.

I leaped for the porthole. There was only a grey-white wall blotting my view out entirely. Then I was flinging myself out of bed and racing up the hatchway. *La Bayonnaise* towered over us in the weak dawn light. Having scrambled so unceremoniously up on the deck, I felt vaguely foolish and unnerved. A uniformed man with a megaphone was leaning on a rail above us. "WE HAVE A LETTER FOR YOU," his voice boomed. "WE HAVE A LETTER FOR YOU."

Cautiously, an inflatable was lowered into the swells, running at from ten to twelve feet. As the inflatable leapt and danced, bouncing off the hull of the minesweeper, a seaman lowered himself gingerly from a rope ladder amidships. As soon as he had groped his way into the rubber boat, an outboard engine was lowered on a rope, and he managed to secure the engine to the stern of his small, bouncing craft. Another sailor and an officer, obviously tense, climbed down from the side of *La Bayonnaise* and leapt into the inflatable. All three seemed nervous about being in such a rig in a sea as heavy as this one. Finally, there was a faint blue puff of smoke, the lines were cast loose, and the inflatable began its minor odyssey across the swells toward *Vega*. I could see the expressions of relief on the Frenchmen's faces when they at last made it to *Vega*'s side and threw a line that Grant quickly grasped.

As the officer groped clumsily for the rail, Nigel greeted him with controlled British understatement, considering that we had not greeted another human being in the flesh for thirty days.

"Good morning," he said.

Neither the officer nor the two seamen responded. The officer fumbled in his shirt and brought out a brown envelope which he handed to me. They hesitated for a moment, then, at a nod from the officer, Grant let go of the line, and they allowed themselves to fall astern, wheeled, and headed back to *La Bayonnaise*, where they climbed tortuously back up the side of the minesweeper. The inflatable was hauled back on deck by ropes, and *La Bayonnaise* moved away.

The contact, brief as it was, had a ceremonial quality to it, as though we were all bit actors in some kind of stage production. I had not had time even to begin to relate to the three Frenchmen as individuals. They had just bobbed over the side, gone through a few quick motions, and disappeared back over the side, dwindling away. I almost wanted to laugh, except that I knew the envelope contained the clue to the next scenario. The first page was in French:

AVURNAV

URGENT: Reférence avis aux navigateurs 72
1825 P. Les navigateurs sont informés que des
expérimentations nucléaires auront lieu dans
la zone du Pacifique Central Sud à partir de
20 Juin STOP La zone dangereuse est définie
comme suit: – Un cercle centré sur
MURUROA (21 degrés 50 minutes S – 138
degrés 47 minutes W) et de rayon milles
nautiques STOP
– Un secteur circulaire centré également sur
MURUROA (21 degrés 50 minutes S – 138
degrés 37 minutes W) entre les azimuts 045
degrés et 100 degrés en passant par l'Est
(090) et de rayon 200 milles nautique.
Les navigateurs sont instamment priés de
rester en dehors de cette zone dangereuse à
partir du Juin 20 1 TU et jusqu'à nouvel
ordre

The second page was in English:

ATTENTION

Mariners are warned that nuclear experiments
will be conducted in the South Central
Pacific area from the 20 June at 0001 TU
STOP
The following area has been declared
dangerous: – A circular area radius one

hundred and twenty nautical miles centered
on MURUROA (21 degrees 50 minutes
S – 138 degrees 47 minutes W) STOP
– A circular sector centered on
MURUROA (21 degrees 50 minutes S –
138 degrees 47 minutes W) extending 200
nautical miles eastward between azimuths 045
and 100 STOP
Mariners are instantly requested to keep off
the above area from June 20 at 0001 TU and
till further notice.

"You know," said Nigel, allowing himself a small smile,
"it was damn nice to say good morning to someone else."

We took the letter and filed back into the cabin for breakfast. *La Bayonnaise* resumed her position a mile and a half
away. We waited until we had eaten before discussing the
situation.

"There's no question of us complying," I said.

The others nodded their agreement.

A twenty-knot wind was blowing. At 1000 hours, we
hoisted the sails, each of us feeling a sense of relief. After the
prolonged period of not knowing whether we were, in fact,
near Mururoa or somewhere else in the world, after all the
buffeting in the grey void, the tension of waiting, we were
possessed by a mutual feeling that the battle had at last been
joined. The joust had started. And in the simple act of tugging
on the ropes to lift *Vega*'s sails, we were delivering our
answer. The wind gusted to thirty knots, crashing into the
sails, filling them like shallow white chalices, and, immediately,
the old girl began to move.

We had no sooner begun to move than something broke the
water directly ahead of our bow, cleaving it sweetly and
moving, as we were moving – despite *La Bayonnaise*, despite
any traffic tickets written out by weapons makers – directly
toward Mururoa. For a moment, my western rationality
disintegrated, for I knew after a second glance that the creature
twanging through the water ahead of us was a mahi mahi

122

dolphin fish, the great sacred fish whom none of the South
Sea islanders will kill, whose presence is deemed to be the
most auspicious of good luck omens. I told myself that I *knew*
it was just a coincidence, even though it was the first mahi mahi
we had seen since New Zealand, well over four thousand
miles ago, but there was a brief moment when the presence of
the fantastic creature, and the moment it had chosen to appear,
signalled some vast approval from the gods, and I had
feelings as "primitive" as those experienced by any primitive
man anywhere. All right, Bomb! Your time has gone! And
then the mahi mahi vanished back into the deep, and the feeling
faded with it, although not entirely – a feeling, there was no
other word for it, of *power*, as though the universe was indeed
on our side.

La Bayonnaise stayed on our tail, still as frightening as a
bull in an open pasture, stalking us as we slammed through the
waves toward Mururoa. But at least the game was being
played according to rules.

"There's no way they could miss the point now about us
intending to ignore the notice," I said to Nigel as we crouched
in the cockpit, watching over our shoulders as the minesweeper chopped through the water in our wake.

"The captain's probably notifying the admiral of the fleet
and getting instructions," Nigel said. "Might as well put this
thing up now." Without further comment, he raised the flag
we had decided to fly, a "K" flag, an international signal
meaning "I wish to communicate with you".

It was grand sailing. *Vega* loved a good wind. And there
was a certain joy about being in the thick of it. The French had
thrown down the gauntlet, *Vega* had shouted her defiance
with a burst of sails, and it was impossible at this stage of the
game not to feel excitement.

Shortly after noon, back in full view of the balloon, we
dropped the jib and mainsail and hove-to. I went below to get
together a package for the captain of *La Bayonnaise*. I wrote a
short covering letter to go with the document from the
University of Auckland, spelling out the international law of
the sea.

The letter read:

The Commanding Officer,
French Warship *La Bayonnaise*
20 June, 1972

Sir:
We thank you for your message this morning, requesting us
to leave this area. We have enclosed a copy of a document
prepared for us by the legal department of the University of
Auckland, New Zealand, stating our rights to sail in these
international waters and we intend to remain, as long as we
are able to maintain these rights.
    Signed – D. F. McTaggart, N. S. Ingram, G. J. Davidson

With the swell that was running before a thirty-knot wind, I
did not think the French would attempt another trip by
inflatable that day to accept our message. But shortly after
we hove-to, *La Bayonnaise* came up just off our starboard
quarter, and the uniformed man – an officer – appeared at the
rail. Wielding his megaphone, he shouted:
"HAVE YOU GOT MESSAGE? HAVE YOU GOT
MESSAGE?"
We nodded and motioned to the "K" flag. Over the side of
the minesweeper came the inflatable again. It bucked and
tossed in the swell. No less than four crewmen picked their
way down the ladder, waiting until the right moment, then
throwing themselves one at a time into the craft. By the time
they managed to make their way to *Vega*'s side, their faces
were white with anxiety, and I realized then that somebody
upstairs must have placed a lot of importance on this seemingly-
bizarre exchange of notes to order his men into a sea like this.
    No one said anything. Nigel and Grant and I just stared at
the Frenchmen and passed them the letter and document
sealed in a plastic container. One of the seamen thrust an
official-looking envelope at me, while the outboard motor of
the inflatable spluttered on air and gurgled as the swell lifted
it up and down. Then, when the notes had been exchanged,
one of the men barked something at the engine operator, the

engine increased in pitch, and they wheeled around and headed back through the swells to the minesweeper.

The brown envelope contained a letter with a personal signature. It was typed on plain white paper in capital letters:

FROM: ADMIRAL COMMANDING NUCLEAR TESTS
   FORCE
TO: GREENPEACE III
   YOU ARE STILL IN THE AREA DEFINED IN THE
   NOTICE TO MARINERS YOU RECEIVED THIS
   MORNING – STOP – YOU ARE REQUESTED TO
   KEEP OFF THE ABOVE AREA OR AT LEAST SAIL
   IMMEDIATELY AND JOIN POSITION 15 (FIFTEEN)
   NAUTICAL MILES WEST (270) OFF TURÉIA
   WHERE I WILL INSURE YOUR SAFETY AGAINST
   NUCLEAR EFFECTS.

We got out the charts and quickly located the position the admiral had indicated. It was forty miles northwest of our present position. In order to reach it, we would have to sail through the night – sunset was only an hour and a half away. If we obeyed, the position we would reach at the end of that time would be between the territorial limits of two French-held islands, Turéia and Vanavana. It would be nearly impossible to avoid drifting into their territorial waters while hove-to, which, of course, would give the French an excuse to arrest us immediately.

Nigel let out a contemptuous snort.

"That's so transparent, it's not worth talking about," he said.

"We ignore it then?" asked Grant.

"Bloody right," I said.

We agreed to remain hove-to for the night, and then, in the morning, head back in closer to Mururoa again.

"I wonder," I said, "if this part – where the admiral says 'I will ensure your safety against nuclear effects' – is a legal dodge, meaning that our refusal of his offer releases him of any responsibility?"

"Well, there seems to be no question in his mind that the

bomb is going to go off," said Nigel. "*When* is as soon as he can get us out of the way."

We knew then that the confrontation was finally just ahead of us, whatever form it would take. There was no sense of relief. We had been so far down, had had our moments of being so far up, that we had finally levelled off in a stage which could only be described as an absence of feeling. Something was going to happen. It might be a boarding. It could be anything from a ramming to guns going off in the night, or to the Bomb itself being unleashed in our faces. Events had been taking so many unexpected turns that we knew one thing at least: it would be stupid from now on to make any assumptions, any assumptions at all. It was Nigel's idea that we make sure where our passports were, and that we exchange the addresses of parents in case . . . Well, in case whatever. It did not seem to us to be a dramatic gesture, simply a genuine concern for each other. Without thinking much about it, we straightened up the cabin again, and made sure our personal belongings were stowed away. I found myself feeling, if anything . . . sad. Yes, it was a sad evening. We had no sense of bravado. No sense of anything having an epic quality. It was just too damn bad that any of us had to be out here at all. There were so many other places to be . . .

We had a drink, said "Cheers" to each other, and turned in early. I tried to read from *The Seven Pillars of Wisdom* but gave up quickly and fell into a fitful sleep.

Grant had not been able to sleep.

Just before dawn, the feeling of suffocation got so bad he clawed his way out of his sweaty bunk and groped his way up the stairs to the cockpit. There, at least, he could breath. The wind was perhaps twenty knots and the swells moved listlessly, almost tiredly.

To his surprise, the French minesweeper was gone. No sign of the other ship either, and we had drifted as usual so that the balloon had dipped below the horizon. No birds. Nothing. Just the slow heavy swish of the swells, the creaking of the boat.

The sky lightened quickly, a pale wash of golden yellow

with silver ribbons of cloud high up, but a dark grey storm-front rolling in from the west so that Grant felt like a tiny gnat perched under the edge of a giant table. It was probably going to rain before long. As the light spread through the archipelagos of flowing broken clouds, the sea lost its inky colour and assumed a gunbarrel tone.

He was just thinking about going below to fetch his pipe when his eye caught a shape against the horizon, like a small smoking pyramid. He froze, squinting against the light. Smoke, definitely. A boat, definitely. Surprisingly quickly, it took on an angular boxcar-like form, with some kind of tower, a bit like the Eiffel Tower, sticking up from the middle. Whatever it was, it wasn't anything like the minesweeper. In the few moments that he sat there, staring, it doubled and tripled in size until there could be no doubt it was coming straight toward us and coming at an awful speed. He finally found his voice:

"Christ! There's a huge bloody ship coming right at us!"

Suddenly realizing he was naked, he scrambled down the hatchway to find something to wear. Nigel and I were already stumbling about the cabin, doing the same thing.

"They're finally coming to get us," I mumbled. Yanking on his shorts, Grant stayed by the hatchway, sticking his head out every few seconds while Nigel and I tried to pull ourselves together.

"It's only two miles away . . . Big as a mountain . . . got a weird-looking tower on her . . ."

By the time I got on deck the vessel was close enough for me to see that the game had shifted to a new level.

"She's a cruiser!" exclaimed Nigel. "Probably six hundred feet! Well, they're sending out the big boys now."

"Let's get the sails up," I said. Nigel and Grant leaped for the main, which rose smartly in the morning light, shaking itself out like a bird. I grabbed the tiller, realizing that our bow was pointing outward from Mururoa, roughly in the direction of the two islands we had been advised in the admiral's note to head for. That was fine. The French might think we were just getting ready to follow instructions.

127

As the cruiser closed in, we could make out the number near the bow – c610. She had a superstructure the size of an eight-storey apartment block, with a radar dish on top that was at least as large as *Vega*. There were four tank-sized gun turrets on her foredeck. The tower near the stern must have lifted one hundred and twenty feet into the air. As the sun broke over the horizon, it turned her metal walls the colour of blinding bronze.

If the intention of the French had been to impress us with a show of brute power, they succeeded. Although I had seen plenty of large ships, I had never seen one like this – a steel seagoing fortress that could have annihilated all of ancient Rome's armies in a day – under such circumstances. It was like sending out an armour-clad knight to do battle with a naked urchin. The thunder of the cruiser's engines was now quite audible. Its bow curved like a sickle, sending rags of foam with quavering rainbows through the light of dawn.

Suddenly Grant yelled and pointed – and there, just coming over the horizon were two more warships, one well ahead of the other. The sheer inequality of the contest that I knew must be coming left me stunned. What were they doing? Sending out the whole fleet? After one lousy sailboat? For the first time, I fully understood how deep a nerve we had struck. And I had a brief moment of triumph.

Then the massive cruiser was roaring past us like a freight train about a quarter of a mile off our port side. As it swept by, I caught the name. It was *De Grasse*, the flagship itself.

For a moment, the cruiser and the sailboat were parallel. I caught a glimpse of seamen lining the decks, like spectators watching a game, and that, at least, felt familiar.

I watched as the cruiser's massive bow wave came sizzling in a line of white froth across the water towards us. By unspoken agreement, I had handed the tiller to Nigel, whose years of yacht racing made him without doubt the best helmsman. Nigel now faced the deadliest race of his life. As soon as *De Grasse* had passed, he brought *Vega* around one hundred and eighty degrees, the wind took the sails, and the yacht and her gigantic opponent were suddenly heading in opposite directions, *Vega*'s bow aimed directly toward Mururoa. It was a neat manoeuvre, leaving the two other warships coming up on our stern.

Despite the harsh pounding of my heart, I could not avoid a matador-like rush of excitement, as though we had side-stepped the horns of a great charging bull. The sensation vanished quickly when I looked back over the stern, for the bull was already turning with bone-chilling agility. It swung to the starboard, twelve thousand tons of steel spinning virtually on its heel. A torrent of smoke blasted from the funnel as though the great machine had given vent to a snarl. Within minutes, it had come completely about and was tearing back across *Vega*'s thin trickle of wake, blotting out the view of the two other ships, now less than half a mile behind.

If this was turning into a race for Mururoa, *Vega* had the lead for only a moment – open sea ahead, the cruiser pulling up rapidly on our starboard beam, and the two other vessels, one of them now clearly *La Bayonnaise*, closing shoulder to shoulder on our stern. Towering over us, *De Grasse* crashed past so swiftly that for a moment it seemed to my dis-believing sense that *Vega* was actually going backwards. Then, having pulled fifty yards ahead, the cruiser abruptly slowed and swung like a needle to port, seeming to skid to a halt. There was a tremendous boil of water at her stern. And then *Vega*, her sails full, was suddenly racing toward a solid steel cliff laid directly across her path.

"Start the engine!" I screamed, rushing for the tiller while Nigel dived through the hatchway, cranking the diesel to its full eighteen hundred revs immediately. Grant was frozen on the foredeck, clinging to the railing as we rushed towards what seemed like an inevitable collision. Above, I could see hundreds of faces peering down at us, like sightseers along the edge of a canyon. The cruiser's wall had already filled up half the sky, and still *Vega* plunged directly forward. It all seemed like a dream whose outcome I was powerless to affect in any way, except to brace myself, knowing that *Vega* would be smashed to pieces.

The onslaught of ships had been so sudden that we had

not had time to raise all the sails. The wind was off our port bow. I could see that if I tried to fall off to the starboard, our speed would only be increased, and long before we could clear the cruiser's stern, we would be hurled against its hull. The only hope was to make a hard turn to port, and with the slight extra thrust of the engine, pray that we would come about. I strained desperately against the tiller. *Vega* shuddered, her nose cleaving into the wind, and the mainsail snapping out of control, then bulging taut as she caught the wind from the other side and lurched violently, careering off on a port tack. Still – she was being carried by her forward momentum, coming around agonizingly, an inch at a time. The great wall of the cruiser was rushing toward us, closer, closer – twenty yards, fifteen, ten, *five*! There was an instant when it seemed utterly hopeless. We're gonna hit! We're gonna hit! Then, astonishingly, we were running beside *De Grasse*, so close I could have leaped across the intervening space, the faces lining the railings were looking down, directly down, at us and could have dropped coins onto our deck. Huge metal plates were rushing by. And then *Vega*'s nose was swinging back toward open water again.

"Raise the jenny! Raise the jenny!" I cried. "Fast!" Instantly, Nigel and Grant threw themselves to the task and *Vega* was swinging like a compass needle. The cruiser was to our stern, and we were facing *La Bayonnaise* and its companion, their bows rising and falling like axes.

"I'm gonna jibe!" I warned, still bearing furiously to the port, shifting my attention immediately from the near-miss with the cruiser to the job of avoiding the onrushing warships. "Haul in the starboard sheet!" *Vega* was coming rapidly about, putting us halfway between *De Grasse* and the other two ships. The mainsail slammed over and, still bearing to the port, we emerged from the manoeuvre having come full circle around the cruiser's stern – heading once again straight for Mururoa.

But there was no time even to catch our breath. No sooner had the brutal merry-go-round ride been completed than *De Grasse* swung hard over herself, putting her nose toward the atoll.

With all her sails up now, *Vega* quickly picked up speed.

Nigel took the tiller again and the strange race resumed. Mastodon-like, the cruiser swept past our port side.

"Get ready!" I yelled to Nigel.

The massive flagship swung in front of us about one hundred yards ahead. *Vega* leapt skyward as the avalanche of foam rolled like a surf outward in its wake. Then, to our surprise, instead of attempting any other manoeuvre, the cruiser maintained its speed and pulled steadily ahead. There was something imperial – Napoleonic was the word that came to mind – about the way it proceeded on its course back to Mururoa, as though it had merely emerged from its castle for the sport of drawing first blood. Looking over Nigel's head, I could see the smaller warships coming up on us fast. And I had the sudden sinking sensation that we were about to be abandoned to the hounds – that the emperor and his entourage had had their amusement but did not wish to stick around for the distasteful business of the kill.

A feeling of despair clawed at me as the cruiser pulled further and further away – and the hounds closed in.

They were about a hundred yards behind now, one on either side of our stern. To the port was *La Bayonnaise*.

"What's the other one?" I asked nervously.

Nigel peered through the binoculars.

"It's a deep-sea tug. The . . . the *Hippopotame*!

As it drew closer, we could make out its number – A660. Unlike the sleek wooden-hulled minesweeper, it was squat, with a blunt ugly bow, and entirely made of steel. We could make out a half-dozen men on its foredeck.

"Those guys are serious," Nigel said, flexing his shoulders to ease the tension.

I dug out the lifejackets, threw one to Nigel, tossed the other to Grant.

"I don't know if they're going to ram us or not, but put these on anyway." My feeling of dread had deepened almost into fatalism.

Nigel's own fear was not so much that we were being deliberately thrown to the hounds. Rather, it emerged out of his experience in the royal navy when he himself had taken part in several boardings of French fishing boats that had entered England's twelve-mile limit. His opinion of French seamen's ability was low. He sensed that the game was about to get rough, and was afraid that an excitable French helmsman might make a mistake.

The wind was blowing a steady force six out of the east. There was a good swell. *Vega* was moving at close to eight knots. Behind us, the tug and the minesweeper were pacing each other, and it suddenly struck me that they were going to try to catch *Vega* between them. They edged in quickly. Eighty yards ... Sixty ... It was madness! They were really going to do it!

Vega ran, flanked on one side by a six-hundred-and-forty-ton tugboat, on the other by a four hundred-ton minesweeper. The pounding of the warships' engines throbbing through my body seemed to set the decks vibrating beneath my bare feet. Inexorably, the French ships pulled abreast.

In the moments we had left to us before – whatever – I grabbed the tape recorder. It was no less absurd an act than throwing the bottle with the note to Ann-Marie into the ocean. My voice was hoarse, and I was gasping, and the background was filled with the fizzle of waves from the warships, the pulsating of their engines:

The *De Grasse* just tried to block us, came right in front of us. We had to start the engine up and come about very quickly. We had the other boats coming up on the other side. Oh we had to try to come about to miss the *De Grasse*! We just managed to come about. The other boats are on us, right on us, coming down on us ... We've got three boats, the *De Grasse* ahead, and our original boat, and another boat coming down on us ... I don't know whether they're going to ram us or not ... We have *La Bayonnaise* coming up now on our port side, and we have the new boat coming up on our starboard side ... There's a big swell going ... It's just crazy as hell ... Uh, they haven't spoken to us, they haven't given any warning ... The other boat is the *Hippomay*, or something like that . . . Nigel is on the helm and both of them are coming down on us. I don't know . . . I guess that's the end of *Vega*.

La Bayonnaise started to come in tight on our port quarter, with *Hippopotame* hanging slightly back to our starboard. Gradually, *La Bayonnaise* edged in closer and came parallel to our port side. She was fifteen yards from us, the huge grey-white hull slamming up and down, the force of her displacement churning the small space of water between us into a heaving maelstrom. *Hippopotame* started crowding in on the starboard quarter. Between the striding knife-edged giants, *Vega* bounded like a frightened jackrabbit.

I looked up to the bridge of *La Bayonnaise*. There was no pity on the face of the man who clung to the railing, glaring down at me. I had looked into the faces of adversaries before, but none quite so filled with anger – and the thought shot across my mind that the man above me was probably a *patriot*, a man who had trained all his life for war against the enemies of the republic, and he would just as soon crush *Vega* as look at her. Instinctively, I knew that the man hated our guts. He was glaring down at the three of us on *Vega*'s decks with a look that I had only seen before in photographs of people in riots. It was not just *machismo* – although there was plenty of that. It was *hate*. The look on the man's face said: Look out, I'm gonna get you, but good.

I found myself locked into an eye-contact contest. Then the man on the minesweeper, obviously the commander, turned and rapped out an order. *La Bayonnaise* began to edge in – closer, closer.

There was nowhere to turn! To inch away from *La Bayonnaise* was to inch closer to *Hippopotame*, whose great blunt bow was flailing the waves just behind us to our starboard. Nigel's eyes were flicking back and forth, his head swivelling from the minesweeper to the tug, and he was doing the only thing left for us to do – to follow the basic rule of navigation, holding our course as straight as an arrow. It was the equivalent of racing full-bore in an incredible game of "chicken" along the edge of a cliff, and the slightest deviation in course would mean our end. To fall off to starboard into the wind would mean being chopped in half by the steel bow of the tug. I found myself thinking wildly of the shark I had played with a few days ago. Sharks! If we were to be smashed apart, even if we were to survive, and somehow avoid being chopped into mincemeat by the props, we were still at least bound to be bloodied, and the sharks . . . *God I hate sharks!* I had a flashing vision of being chomped, limb by limb, while French sailors stood on the decks, looking down impassively, some of them cheering like the grim-faced hardrock characters who stood now on the foredeck of *Hippopotame*, or the commander of *La Bayonnaise*.

"You crazy fuckers!" screamed Grant. "Get away! You'll kill us all!"

As if that were a signal – I was certain I saw the man's lips twitch into a grin – the commander of the minesweeper turned and yelled something to his helmsman. In response, the ship edged in closer . . . twelve yards . . . ten . . .

Nigel shouted:

"They're trying to run us down!"

Ten yards between two boats racing at eight knots is not that much more than a hair-breadth. Knowing that, and knowing the outcome of any collision between the two vessels, Nigel cursed the French furiously with every bit of his British soul, clinging to *Vega*'s tiller like a sword hilt, calling on the ghosts of everyone from Wellington to Churchill, and concentrating his whole being on that one true shot through a rapidly-closing pincer.

The heaving flank of *La Bayonnaise* crashed closer and closer, to the point where two more surges of the swell would bring *Vega* crunching against the minesweeper's hull. And now the winds that had driven us so straight were being cut off by *La Bayonnaise*'s bulk. I yelled to Nigel: "We're falling off the wind!" There was nothing – absolutely nothing – he could do. Sickeningly, we began to fall off, directly into the path of the forward-rushing steel tug. Its bow rose over us like an axe-bit, and just when it seemed we were about to be split in two,

134

Hippopotame swung violently to port, missing our stern by less than fifteen yards and shearing past the stern of *La Bayonnaise* by the same margin.

"That's insane!" gasped Nigel. No helmsman, regardless of how good he might be, could undertake that last manoeuvre with any kind of assurance of safety. At the moment *Hippopotame* had made its wild swing to port, not only had it barely missed *Vega*, it had come just as close to smashing into the stern of the minesweeper. The French had gone crazy! Undoubtedly with orders to scare the hell out of us, they'd become inflamed and were vying with one another in their recklessness. And it was clear that not one of the idiots up there in the wheelhouses of the warships had the slightest understanding of the problems of sailing. A chill ran through me. They're deliberately trying to set up an "accident", I thought.

"We've gotta break this up!" I yelled. "They don't know what the hell they're doing. Nigel, get the 'can't-manoeuvre' pennant!" We switched places at the tiller and Nigel dived below. I settled into the cockpit, taking deep breaths to steady myself.

De Grasse was now about three miles away, ahead of us, still heading toward Mururoa. *Hippopotame* and *La Bayonnaise* were churning water astern of us, and I could easily imagine that the two captains were howling at each other over their own near-collision. For a moment, *Vega* was in the clear again.

Nigel emerged from the cabin with the pennant and ran it quickly up on the port halyard. It was the international signal for "manoeuvring with difficulty", to which, technically, all responsible seamen must respond. Neither he nor I thought it would make much difference, but if this was to be a game of chicken, we desperately wanted the Frenchmen to know *Vega*'s limitations. She was a heavy-weather sailor, not built for lightning-swift changes in direction.

In the three minutes it took Nigel to find the pennant and get it up, the two warships finished their side-by-side conference. *Hippopotame*'s engine revved thunderously, smoke spewed skyward, and the tug swung out in a wide arc. The

HARASSMENT

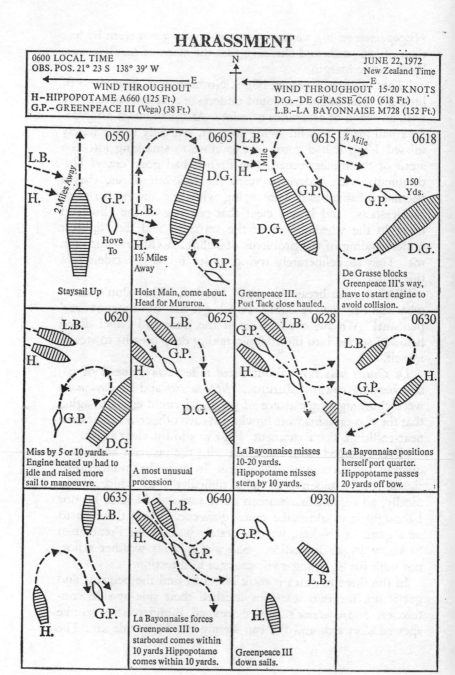

0600 LOCAL TIME
OBS. POS. 21° 23 S 138° 39' W

N

JUNE 22, 1972
New Zealand Time

WIND THROUGHOUT
H–HIPPOPOTAME A660 (125 Ft.)
G.P.– GREENPEACE III (Vega) (38 Ft.)

WIND THROUGHOUT 15-20 KNOTS
D.G.–DE GRASSE C610 (618 Ft.)
L.B.–LA BAYONNAISE M728 (152 Ft.)

0550
L.B.
H.
G.P.
2 Miles Away
Hove To
Staysail Up

0605
D.G.
L.B.
H.
1½ Miles Away
G.P.
Hoist Main, come about. Head for Mururoa.

0615
L.B.
1 Mile
H.
G.P.
D.G.
Greenpeace III. Port Tack close hauled.

0618
¾ Mile
150 Yds.
G.P.
D.G.
De Grasse blocks Greenpeace III's way, have to start engine to avoid collision.

0620
L.B.
H.
G.P.
D.G.
Miss by 5 or 10 yards. Engine heated up had to idle and raised more sail to manoeuvre.

0625
L.B.
G.P.
H.
D.G.
A most unusual procession

0628
G.P.
L.B.
H.
La Bayonnaise misses 10-20 yards. Hippopotame misses stern by 10 yards.

0630
L.B.
G.P.
H.
La Bayonnaise positions herself port quarter. Hippopotame passes 20 yards off bow.

0635
L.B.
G.P.
H.

0640
L.B.
H.
G.P.
La Bayonnaise forces Greenpeace III to starboard comes within 10 yards Hippopotame comes within 10 yards.

0930
G.P.
L.B.
H.
Greenpeace III down sails.

minesweeper also swung around, cutting its turn more tightly. There had been a change in tactics, for *La Bayonnaise* was now knifing toward us on our port quarter, while the heavy steel tug was coming around in a half-circle that was bringing it rapidly down on us on what looked to be a certain collision course.

I made no attempt to take evasive action. In a developing collision situation at sea, the rule is absolute: *Maintain course.* Any sudden change in situation can only compound the problem, and a motor vessel always – *always* has to give way to a vessel under sail. I could see no point in trying to dodge, because whatever trick the captain of the *Hippopotame* was up to now, it was his game entirely. If he was going to run us down, he would succeed on the next try if not now. If he was intent on terrorizing us with a near-miss, any sudden change in *Vega*'s movement would simply throw his calculations off, handing him the "accident" he so obviously wanted. He'd be able to say later: "I was just throwing a scare into them. I didn't intend to hit them. But they made an unexpected move, and, well, it couldn't be helped. Sorry." So I held the tiller firm. *Vega* swept forward, still on course for Mururoa. And I watched helplessly as the tug came bludgeoning in a yard-high apron of foam, its bow leaping clear of the water and crashing down, only to lift clear again, like a huge snapping jaw. It was moving now at probably fifteen, maybe eighteen knots. I had the feeling of a man in a car whose brakes won't work rushing towards a rail crossing, with a locomotive clattering down the line, and it is simply a question of which machine will reach the crossing first.

Then *Hippopotame* was rearing over us, so close I expected *Vega*'s bowsprit to shatter like a lance against the shield of its hull. Had the ship been ten yards longer, we would have ruptured against its starboard stern. Instead, we were slicing through its sizzling wake, looking up to our right, as though at the back of a hurtling caboose.

Again, the way ahead was clear. But there was to be no pause in the game. *Hippopotame* slowed only enough to pivot around sharply on our starboard, allowing *La Bayonnaise* to straighten

137

out its course on our port quarter, so that the two warships had neatly moved back into their earlier side-by-side positions on *Vega*'s stern.

Breathing harshly, Nigel yelled: "Watch out! It's the squeeze play again!" My hands were holding the tiller in what I glancingly realized was probably the famous death-grip. I knew the odds on us surviving a second mad run between two warships pounding up and down like the boots of giants trying to stomp a bug were close to negligible. There was nothing in my experience for me to cling to, for there had never been a situation like this at sea. It was against everything I had ever been taught about boats and navigation, and a part of my mind was still having trouble believing that it was really happening. *La Bayonnaise* advanced to within fifteen yards on our port, with *Hippopotame* taking the position it had before – perhaps ten yards to our starboard stern, so close now that the wheelhouse itself could not be seen over the upthrust wedge of the bow, and I knew that the man at the helm could not possibly see us. If he could see anything, it would be just the top of *Vega*'s sails, and they could easily be broken and crushed before the helmsman even realized it. The only reference-point I could find in my memory was of American movies about teenagers in souped-up cars, engines screaming, racing at eighty and ninety miles an hour within a couple of feet of each other – except that now there was the equivalent of a terrified bicycle-rider caught between them.

The face of the officer on the railing of *La Bayonnaise* was flushed now, almost lustful, as he stared, wild-eyed with excitement, down at us, snapping orders over his shoulder at another helmsman who could also only see the top of *Vega*'s sails. The orders, I knew, must be: "One point. Half a point. Half a point." I hoped to God the helmsman had steady hands, for if he so much as trembled now, that was it. The swell was running to ten feet, which brought my eye up one moment half-way to the minesweeper's deck, now down, down, so that I was level with the black line that ran along the bottom of its hull, below the bilge holes. More than sailing now, it was like shooting the rapids through a narrow white-water canyon.

Behind me, over my right shoulder, I could glimpse *Hippopotame*'s great dented bow less than ten yards away, a huge black anchor hanging like a mace, trickles of rust running out from beneath it, making me think of a bulldozer tumbling over and over down a hill toward us.

We ran like this for probably no more than five minutes, but to Nigel, Grant and myself it seemed almost as though the ordeal had had its beginnings back in our childhood, that we were frozen in time in one of the strangest hells ever devised.

Then *La Bayonnaise* seemed to jump sideways toward us. I thought for sure the top of *Vega*'s poles were going to stay upward into the top of the minesweeper's swaying hull and now there could be no doubt about it – we were only seconds from being smashed like an eggshell. Grant's scream from the foredeck was like the voice of a man pitching over a cliff:

"We're gonna crash!"

It was a reflex, like ducking. I jerked the tiller, even though it was like throwing yourself under the wheels of an oncoming train. *La Hippopotame*'s enormous grey shark jaw seemed to hang in the sky over my head and the boil of water seemed to rush toward me like death sheets. *Vega* fell off the wind, and it was exactly like falling through a void. Then, as though the moment of her fall was a signal, *Hippopotame* leapt clear to starboard, and *La Bayonnaise* sheared off to port, leaving *Vega* staggering forward into a sudden opening.

"Lower the sails," I said suddenly. Nigel and Grant understood immediately. Our only hope now was to leave the French with a situation where they would have to bear down on a stationary vessel. There was too much *machismo* in the air. I had seen it on too many of those faces looking down on us. It was blood-lust. They were crazed. The only way to break up the madness was to go limp.

The three of us were shaking. As soon as the sails were down, we slumped to the deck to try to pull ourselves together, staring dully at the warships. Still snorting smoke, *Hippopotame* made one more full-speed charge across the water toward us. No one even got up from the deck. We just stared.

The tugboat passed within twenty yards – but it was only a token last charge, a stomping of hooves. Then it banked away and came to a halt, a bow pointed toward us, almost half a mile away off our starboard bow. *La Bayonnaise* settled into a position directly ahead of us. And waited. I had the vague impression the Frenchmen were breathing hard too, as though they had all been locked in a furious running skirmish. Now we had broken contact and crawled off each to his corner, to stare across the water at each other, wondering what would happen next.

My hands still shaking so badly I had a hard time getting the machine to work, I brought the tape recorder up on deck. I lit a cigarette to calm myself, then tried to compose a report. My voice broke several times and I had to click the machine shut repeatedly before being able to continue:

I just can't believe what they've done. Uh, they at least should have had the courtesy to have spoken over the loudspeaker, which they had done before, and told us to turn back, and if we didn't turn back then they would ram us, but they just moved in and didn't say a word, and I think it was just out of our ability on the boat that we weren't totally smashed to pieces ... Anyway, I guess it's not over ... and it's still blowing about fifteen knots with a big swell. I'm sure that's their difficulty. I personally believe they'll try to board us now and tow us away. In this kind of sea, they'd probably rip out the forestay and drop the main mast and the mizzen, but *Vega* has been a good boat so far and she's really pulled through ... Oh, by the way, I've advised Nigel and Grant to contact my mother and father if anything happens. I just hope we haven't, or I haven't caused them too much worry, and I'd sure like to see Kerin, Tamra and Lisa, my kids. Maybe when they get older, they'll understand and I'm sure all the people in the world, if they get hold of this tape, will see what the bloody French are really like. I've never read anything or heard of anything like this before, to try to run down a thirty-eight foot ketch in a heavy sea with a cruiser and two minesweepers,

or a minesweeper and another boat of about the same size
. . . I just can't believe it. Just to bring you up to date, it's
seven-thirty local time, twenty-second of June, New
Zealand time . . . My God, that's two days before my birthday . . . The wind is out of the northeast and we're floating
toward Mururoa. Uh, the two boats are laying off our port
side now and we just haven't got any sails up . . . There's
no question we're all worried . . . We've decided if they
ram us, we'll cut the inflatable loose and jump in the inflatable
. . . Uh, I just would like to say a little more to my mom and
dad. I just hope they understand what I'm doing. I've done
some pretty crazy things, but I'm really against this stuff.
Vietnam, apartheid, and other things don't really excite me
too much, but atomic bombs, I just think they're ridiculous,
so Mom and Dad, please try to understand. And I want to
tell my brother how good it was to talk to him and to tell
him that, well, just how good it was to hear his voice while I
was in Rarotonga about thirty-three days ago. And to
wish my children, who I miss like hell, just to take care. And
our friends in New Zealand, we appreciate everything
you've done, and especially Ann-Marie and Mary, and,
finally, I would like to thank the crew, Nigel and Grant.
We couldn't have had a better crew. We've all stuck together
and, uh, I presume we'll all stick together now unless they
split us up . . . That's about it.

Nigel decided to take a sun sight so that if we were rammed,
we could at least prove we hadn't been inside the twelve-mile
territorial limit. The moment he appeared on deck with his
sextant, the *Hippopotame* suddenly began to move, lumbering
across the water and sliding across our bow, so close that it
blocked out the horizon, making it impossible for Nigel to
take a sight.

The action was so petty it provoked the young British
navigator into something he had not done during the entire
dangerous game of sea-going "chicken". His face went livid
and he screamed across the water at the Frenchmen: "You
bastards!" It was only a matter of time, however, before the

motion of the swells pushed the tug, for a moment, out of the way, and before it could back into position, Nigel got the sun sight he wanted. Inordinately pleased, he wrote in the log so fiercely that the pencil almost broke: Obs Pos 21° 23's 138° 30'w.

A few minutes later, a twin-engined aircraft roared out from Mururoa and made one low pass overhead. As the sound of its engines faded, I could hear a dog barking on *La Bayonnaise*.

At 0930 hours, the *Hippopotame*'s engines growled to life again. The sound affected us like the crunch of a branch in a haunted forest. Nigel and I were in the cabin, working out a series of detailed diagrams showing exactly what had transpired. Drawing on his royal navy experience, Nigel knew precisely what to do – he had done it often enough before in situations he knew were going to lead to the courts. Now we dropped what we were doing, and hurried up on deck, expecting the worst.

"It's okay," said Grant, who had remained above on watch. "That one's leaving." Indeed, the tug was heading off in the direction in which the cruiser had disappeared, toward the atoll. *La Bayonnaise* was in motion too, except that the mine-sweeper was just changing position, moving to a spot a mile and a half to the east. Then it settled down again, resuming its watchdog role.

"I think we've got a stalemate on our hands," Nigel commented. "A pawn standing off two knights and a bishop." He was trying to make light of what had happened, but I caught a new tone in his voice, something I had not heard before. This was not quite the same Nigel I'd known until that morning. There was a gritty humourless edge. Nigel had often enough been dour, and a few times angry. But this was different, almost savage.

"Are you all right?" I asked.

"Well I'm right pissed off, if that's what you mean."

I had a new depth of feeling myself. The fright and shock were wearing off. I found myself glaring across the water at *La Bayonnaise*, no trace of affection left. As near as I could think about it rationally, it came down to the realization that until now I had had an almost gentlemanly sense about the game, had been assuming that the French would treat us accordingly. But what had happened that morning was a gang-up, no more gentlemanly than a pack of street punks being turned loose on some helpless victim. I was close to trembling again, but now it was from the urge to row across the water and smash somebody's head in – in particular that arrogant sonofabitch who'd been up on the deck of the minesweeper, getting his rocks off trying to crush us.

"Right," I said, "the rules change now."

Grant had joined us. He nodded vigorously.

"I think if they throw us a tow rope, we ought to throw the bloody thing back in their bloody faces," he said.

"That's it then," I said. "Screw them. If they throw a line, we throw it back. If it's a grappling hook, we cut it. And I don't care what they do, we stay right in the fall-out zone."

By 1030 hours, we had drifted with the wind to a position about twenty-four miles off the north tip of the atoll. Slowly, like a daytime moon coming up, the balloon had risen over the horizon. Each time we had seen it before, it filled us with dread. Now the sight of it filled us with grim satisfaction. We were convinced that the French navy would not have sent three warships against us unless our presence was seriously interfering with plans for the test. If the point of the exercise had been to intimidate us, it had backfired. We were filled now with a new sense of our own strength and a new determination to hold our position. Idealism is one thing. Anger is something else.

Dimly, that night, I began to realize that the individual is anything but a powerless cipher. It was conceivable that Nigel, Grant and I, between us, really did possess the capability of holding at bay the most incredible weapon of mass destruction ever devised. At sunset, the balloon was still hovering over the horizon, as it had for days, and despite ideal conditions its hellfire had not yet bloomed across the sky. That thing out on the horizon represented a power that any earlier generation of human beings would have equated with nothing less than godhood, albeit the godhood of a fallen angel. To hold it in check for even an hour – let alone several days – lent a meaning to my life that I had never known before, had never come close to knowing. Just as an explosion had once torn a permanent rent in the fabric of my sense of myself, so now the lack of an explosion was tearing open an even larger opening. And again, there could be no going back. The change was as irrevocable as a whole new incarnation.

June 23. Ottawa. The Honourable Mark Rose, Member of Parliament for Fraser Valley West, spread his notes out on his desk and climbed to his feet.

"Mr Speaker, I should like to direct my question to the secretary of state for external affairs. Does the Canadian government plan to provide any kind of naval escort protection to the *Greenpeace III*, a vessel which is under Canadian registry, skippered by a Canadian, and reported to be in the nuclear test zone on the high seas, in order that this vessel will not be apprehended, harassed or in any other way bothered by the government of France?"

The Honourable Mitchell Sharp rose, betraying only the slightest hint of impatience.

"Mr Speaker," he said, "my information is that the *Greenpeace* is flying under the Peruvian flag, not under the Canadian flag. Some time ago, long before Mr Metcalfe sent his telegram to the prime minister yesterday, we brought to the attention of the French government the probable presence of some Canadians on the *Greenpeace* . . ."

He paused.

". . . and expressed our concern for their safety. Of course, we cannot prevent any Canadian from travelling on the high seas as he wishes, and if he chooses to go into an area of danger I do not really know what basis in law I would have to prevent him from doing so." He sat down, hoping the issue was done with. But he could tell from the swiftness with which Mark Rose got to his feet, that the issue was definitely not done with.

"Since Canada has protested this nuclear test through a note,"

Mr Rose said, "and in view of the fact that the opposition to nuclear testing is within the four corners of Canadian government policy, and since this is a Canadian vessel on the high seas that is threatened, has the minister any explanation for this appalling external affairs timidity that would embarrass the president of a banana republic?"

Catcalls. The Speaker shouted: "Order, please!"

"I rise on a question of privilege," the external affairs minister said, climbing to his feet.

More catcalls.

"Order, please," insisted the Speaker. "The minister is rising on a question of privilege."

"Mr Speaker," the minister said, "I should like to point out to the honourable gentleman that, far from being timid, this government has made very strong protests to the French government against nuclear weapons testing of all kinds."

Former prime minister John Diefenbaker rumbled: "That's not privilege, that's abuse."

"Hear! Hear!"

"*Order*, please!" said the Speaker of the House. "The honourable member will be recognized on a supplementary question, but we are obviously getting into a debate at this point . . ."

And under the rules of the game played in the Canadian House of Commons, a debate at this point was definitely not in order.

Anger we might have had and a new sense of purpose. But the following morning we found we also still had the wind and the sea and the French navy and an atomic bomb to contend with.

It seemed now as though the wind and the bomb were at odds. It was blowing at force seven and in the wrong direction, precluding any tests that day. I said into my tape recorder: "I think God says he doesn't want this thing to go off. That makes two of us."

But the wind also meant that we were back to being battered against the walls while hove-to. The waves were again walloping *Vega*'s hull and every blow vibrated through our bodies.

145

Visibility was so poor that the only way Nigel could navigate was by tossing pieces of toilet paper over the stern about ten feet apart and watching which way they were moving. We had no fresh food left at all and our eggs had all gone rotten. Out of the twenty-three days we had been hove-to around Mururoa, we had only had two days of good weather. The rest of the time had been incessant rolling and tossing, muscles stiffening at every lurch, being pushed against a wall, then pulled away as though on a leash. The brown water in the tanks was now quite impossible to drink by itself.

We raised our sails and tried to move closer to the fallout area east of the atoll. As soon as we started moving, *La Bayonnaise* came to life, throwing smoke and heaving across the scudding waves, cutting across about a mile in front of our bow, turning again about two miles away and running parallel to our course, keeping pace.

"Tonight, we'll make them work," I growled, bone-tired but still angry. Instead of pulling down the sails at dark, we kept going. About thirty miles east of Mururoa, we changed course and headed due south. The minesweeper quickly altered its own course and bore down on us at full speed. As soon as it began to close in, we changed direction again, heading east. *La Bayonnaise* turned with us, following closely on our port quarter.

"Okay, now!" I said. While Grant extinguished the masthead light and Nigel yanked down the radar reflector, I brought the boat completely about, heading in the opposite direction for about a mile and a half. We watched the lights of *La Bayonnaise* moving this way and that off our stern. When we were certain the minesweeper was confused, we came about again and headed eastward for another mile. Then we dropped the sails and hove-to. After we were settled, Nigel flashed a morse code signal, using the masthead light. It was a small revenge on the French navy and it helped to break our own tension. But the response it provoked was terrifying.

I was alone on deck when I saw the minesweeper's lights emerge out of the waves like some mutated monster. By then, I had all of *Vega*'s own lights on to make sure that the French could see us. *La Bayonnaise* was ripping through the water at what seemed an awesome speed – straight for us. I could hear the throb of engines. In the dark, the sound seemed to be magnified, and it came to my ears like a definite animal roar. Jesus no! They couldn't! They wouldn't! The minesweeper was only seventy-five yards away and still bearing directly down on us, speed unchecked.

"Nigel," I called as calmly as I could. "Better get up here and bring your knife. We might have to cut the inflatable loose."

Nigel and Grant were on the deck in seconds. In horror, the three of us watched, mesmerized, as the oncoming ship's lights rose and fell, swirling out of the dark toward us. Nigel grabbed the rope attached to the inflatable, fingering his knife nervously. My leg muscles coiled, readying for a leap. Then, a mere twenty-five yards away – the equivalent of only a couple of feet in daylight – the minesweeper swung hard over and sliced past our stern. It was clear that the war of nerves was far from over.

"Their sense of humour hasn't changed much, has it?" Nigel observed.

"No," I said shakily, "I guess it hasn't."

That night, I cracked open a large red notebook. The tapes were almost gone and I wanted to save them for an emergency. Doubts had begun to crowd into my mind again, and I found myself writing:

Well, tomorrow is my 40th birthday. I've had a full life, but should I risk Nigel's and Grant's? We had a long conversation today regarding our next step. We first decided that they will not board us but they will come alongside and say the test is tomorrow "Are you leaving?" – No – "Alright we'll give you a rope and tow you out" – our answer, we won't accept – then we would sail very close into the fallout area, about 14 miles out. This as I said has been discussed in detail, and totally agreed upon by all. I quite realize this is a different decision from that I made when we left NZ, which was that I wouldn't jeopardize the crew. Well, we're different now from then, and also the boys wouldn't listen to anything like that. Well, the die is cast. At these close quarters the blast will certainly cause harm. How badly would we be hurt at 14 miles distance? Would they still blow it off? I definitely think so. God, the boat is rolling. This weather depresses me ten times more that the mental tension of wondering, wondering. All of us are bearing up very well. Grant has great highs and lows. Nigel is very even all the time, with only slight depressions. They are a wonderful combination. Me? You'd have to ask them. Anyway, I have to decide, should I allow the fellows to go into the blast, letting detemination and ego outweigh common sense? Maybe a prayer tonight will give me an answer in the morning. Well, waves are starting to break over us. Try to get some few hours sleep.

I awoke to find that the sky had become an iron vault and the swells were so heavy that they buried both of *Vega*'s toerails. The wind made a sound that I normally associated with winters in Canada. I found, when I went to eat, that I had to force the food down. The weight of my forty years pressed down on me. I was depressed. And in my depression began to notice how much *Vega* herself was beginning to show heavy wear and tear. I had felt close to my "old girl", but now I felt that the two of us were virtually one creature. Her body was an extension of my own. Obsessively, I prowled the decks and poked in corners, taking stock of her condition.

The mizzen was just about finished. The head had been ripped out of the number one yankee, our best sail. The foot was just about chafed through from rubbing against the pull pit. Both the number one and number two genoas had numerous rips which had been repaired by Nigel. The sliders on the main track were disappearing, and we hadn't been able to get any spares in Auckland. We had chafed the jib sheet through one night when it was blowing forty knots. The new-fangled jib sheet leads had chafed the sheets terribly. Two self-steering vanes had been lost. About a thousand feet of new nylon rope had also been lost. The roller leads through which the anchor chain passed had been ripped off. The *Greenpeace III* name on the side was all but erased. The white paint on the top-sides was getting worn away just from the passage of water. The decks were cracking.

The more I prowled and poked, the worse it got. The top of the cabin had rust all over it where the forty-five gallon can of diesel oil and the five-gallon can of gas had been sitting on deck. The halyards had beaten up the mast from continual rolling. The porthole in the cockpit had been broken. The inside cabin badly needed a paint job. The carpet was soggy and tattered. The varnish was peeling. The Ham radio had punched a hole through my cabin top. The screws on my table were coming loose. The leather seats were ripped. The engine was in sad condition, and I suspected that somebody had poured salt water into the fresh water heat exchangers. The primus stove barely worked, and then only thanks to Nigel's patient daily nursing. The sailbags were all ripped. The electric system was acting as though it had a life of its own, due to all the condensation. My desk light and the masthead light only came on when they wanted. The pressure line to the stove had broken repeatedly, spilling kerosene. My bunk was soggy because a broken stanchion had ripped out a bolt from the deck, leaving a small hole through which water poured. My clothes and linen were all wet, even slightly mildewed.

Looking reluctantly into a mirror, I saw that there were dark shadows around my eyes, and while my hair was still dark, although thinning close to the point of baldness on top, the beard I had been growing since Rarotonga was more white under the chin than black. A lot more white than I had expected.

A steady rain persisted through the morning. The grey shape of *La Bayonnaise* was just visible about a mile off our starboard beam, steaming back and forth on patrol.

"Happy birthday, David," I muttered to myself, deciding to lie down and take a nap. I was tired.

June 24. Ottawa. Doug Rowland, the Honourable Member for Selkirk, was on his feet.

"Mr Speaker, my question is directed to the secretary of state for external affairs. Does the government of Canada accept

149

that the government of France, or for that matter, the government of any other nation, has the right to cordon off a section of the high seas and prevent the peaceful passage of vessels of any nation, including Canada's *Greenpeace III*?"

The Honourable Mitchell Sharp rose.

"No, Mr Speaker, we deny that right."

Mr Rowland was back on his feet quickly. "In view of the fact that the *Greenpeace III* is lawfully operating in international waters, has the government of Canada protested against France's announced intention to proceed with nuclear tests in the area, and what steps are being taken by the government of Canada to protect this Canadian vessel and its crew should such tests take place?"

Mr Sharp cleared his throat. "Mr Speaker, we have informed the French government of our view of the legal position. We expressed our concern some time ago when we first heard about the possible voyage of some Canadians into that area ... As I said yesterday, however, Canadians are free to travel anywhere they wish, and if they wish to place themselves in special hazard in this way there is nothing that I can do. I really do not know what measures I can take to prevent them from entering that area ..."

At sunrise, scattered patches of blue showed through the vault of clouds. The sea had been building up all night long and now there was a force six wind out of the southeast. I awoke with a bad feeling that the weather was going to get even worse. Then, as though to confirm my foreboding, *La Bayonnaise* began to steam away over the horizon toward Mururoa. I was convinced that the French vessel had received a weather forecast of a big storm, and was heading for shelter, leaving us to get blown over the Tuamotus. Worse, the wind had been shifting around, so it was difficult to know our position.

At 0830 hours, Nigel managed to get a quick sun sight through a hole in the clouds. We had drifted a long way to the northwest of the atoll, out of the fallout corridor. By 1300 hours, we were under sail again, taking one-and-a-half-hour turns at the helm. We figured we'd have to tack twenty miles east. It was heavy going. The wind had built up to force seven and was howling out of the southeast, as though sent from Mururoa itself in an effort to drive us away.

By nightfall, we had still not regained our position. We kept sailing. There had not been any sign of *La Bayonnaise* all day, and we were just getting used to our new-found isolation when Nigel spotted a flashing red light moving about low in the sky. As near as we could make out, it looked like a helicopter flying a search pattern.

The aircraft continued its search for close on two hours, at one point passing about a mile aft of us, hovering momentarily, then flying down along the course we had sailed during the day.

Under cover of darkness, *Vega* crept closer and closer to the atoll. I began to think we had successfully eluded the machine stalking the night sky after us, but at 2200 hours, a large plane roared overhead, banked, and made a series of passes over our masthead. We could vaguely make out the silhouette and the tiny tongues of flame flickering from the cowlings. Then a brilliant floodlight stabbed down on the sea, picking out the shadowy canyons of water and white flashes of foam on the crest of the waves. It was almost the strangest sensation I had ever experienced – being hunted by a finger of light from a rain-sleeted night sky. Then we were caught in the beam. It exploded in our eyes, dazzling us and turning *Vega*'s decks into a brief black and white movie, then was gone. Two flares tumbled slow-motion down to the sea, to our starboard. A ghostly, lurid light now illuminated us. The whole scene made me think of prisons and convicts trying to escape in the night. I half-expected the sudden wail of a siren.

The plane stayed with us for two hours, making one low pass after another, dropping flares. The roar of the engines made sleep completely impossible. It seemed clear enough that we were being pinpointed until a ship could arrive.

At 0100 hours, not one ship arrived, but two. One of them hung back about a mile and the other moved up to within one hundred yards.

"Something's up!" yelled an exhausted-looking Nigel over the wind.

The next day the Bomb came to life over Mururoa.

Dawn had been bleak, grey and miserable. With the first light, I crawled up to the cockpit and immediately recognized the two boats prowling around us like predators. *La Bayonnaise* was standing about a quarter of a mile off our port beam. *Hippopotame* was flanking us on the other side. The wind was down to force three but the sea, which had been building up for two days, was still swollen and mottled, its undulations swinging *Vega*'s masthead at least thirty feet with every roll.

There was no break in the clouds through which Nigel might get a sun sight, so he was forced to use dead reckoning. His calculations put us twenty-five to thirty miles north to northwest of the atoll, about as far as we had yet been blown from our objective.

"We've gotta get closer," I said.

Grant looked uneasily through a porthole at *La Bayonnaise*. "There's the two of them again, y'know."

"Let's see what happens."

At 0840 hours, we warily hoisted the staysail. We had no desire to move quickly, lest the two warships repeat their tactics of the last time. Slowly, *Vega* began to move toward Mururoa. Immediately, the two ships closed in to no more than one hundred yards on either side of us, their engines growling across the waves.

Vega reeked of kerosene. The stove's pressure line had broken yet again. I had also discovered that morning that the leak in my cabin had resulted in ten cartons of cigarettes – two thirds of our remaining supply – being soaked. The jib had chaffed through again. Somehow, *Vega* did not seem up to another jousting match. Neither did her crew. All three of us were puffy-eyed from a sleepless night. Our nerves were on edge.

For twenty minutes, I held the tiller firm. Steadily, the warships pressed in and I could see that even at our greatly reduced speed, the gap between us would have closed within another ten or fifteen minutes of the squeeze play.

"They don't want to let us through, do they?" said Nigel.

"To hell with it," I said. "We'll wait till the weather clears before pushing it." The thought of attempting to run the gauntlet again, only to arrive in position – even more exhausted than we already were – then being driven inexorably back by the wind, and having to make the run all over again in this miserable damned weather was simply too overwhelming. By now we had grown accustomed to the idea that the French would only blow a bomb when the wind was moving in the right direction to carry the fallout down the corridor. Right now the wind was wrong, and with all the rain, I was certain that they wouldn't try it. To push at this point seemed futile.

We hove-to. Grant started cleaning up the kerosene mess and Nigel set to work patching the torn jib. The warships came to a halt on either side of us, lolling in the swell. There were about a dozen men visible on each ship's deck. I ignored them and went below, leaving *Vega* to drift. I made a few desultory entries in my notebook:

Conjecture as usual. Why did they spend so much energy in trying to find us last night when they could have spent ten minutes this aft? Is it because they have something to hide and we might sail into it? We wonder what the fellows on the ships think as we roll back and forth, hour after hour, mast lurching. We have a few rotten eggs left, the fellows want to save them as gifts the next time the French guys come in close. Everybody way down deep thinking, wondering, and even worrying, what will happen when the wind finally changes and we start sailing for the fallout area. Shall we keep on course steady while sailing? I'm sure if we do we'll end up ramming them . . .

The wind increased to force five and the sea got worse. At 0940 hours a large aircraft, similar to the one that had buzzed us during the night, came winging out over the horizon and dropped toward us. With a reverberating roar, it swept only a hundred feet over our heads. It was a twin-engined job, with a huge blister-like bulge on its underbelly. Reflexively, we ducked. The plane surged on, banked, and swept back toward us. As though on a signal, *La Bayonnaise* and *Hippopotame* revved up their engines and began to shuttle back and forth, edging in closer and closer. The tremendous crashing sound of the aircraft was enough to start my head buzzing, and the sound of the warships, so close, revving their engines, backing up, plunging forward, swivelling, backing up, made me think of the racket at a roadside diner after all the truckers have finished their lunch and hopped back into their transports. Either this was some variation on the Chinese water torture, or else the pilot had gone slightly mad. It seemed like pure maliciousness, as though the pilot, angered at having been dragged out of bed the night before to hunt through the squalls for us, was having his revenge, aided by his buddies on the warships. The only reason I could imagine for this bizarre assault of noise was to wear us down. After seven low-flying passes right over us, the plane seemed to go completely bananas, flying in tight figures of eight directly overhead. I wondered how long it would be before our eardrums began to be damaged. The sound of the waves was completely lost. We had to shout at each other to be heard. There was only the high-pitched whine and clatter of the plane, the deep rumble of the warships' huge diesels.

"They're trying to drive us daft!" yelled Grant.

It was during that time – between 0940 hours and 1100 hours – that the French fired the triggering device, the small bomb used to activate the big bomb, a thousand feet over Mururoa, twenty-five miles away, with the wind carrying the fallout in a deadly invisible swathe whose outer fringe passed within fifteen miles of *Vega*. Pinned down in a cone of plane and warship engine noises, neither Nigel, Grant nor myself heard a thing, or if we did, we took it for another dimension in the cacophony of pistons. All we knew was that at 1100 hours, the plane suddenly banked away. *La Bayonnaise* and *Hippopotame* mysteriously pulled back to their earlier positions, a hundred yards away. And then, an hour later, the tugboat chugged away over the horizon. From the moment the aircraft left us, the relative silence that descended seemed almost oppressive. Our ears rang.

Exhausted, with only *La Bayonnaise* acting as a passive watchdog, we tried to sleep, despite the savage rolling of the boat in a wind that had risen to force six.

Lying in our bunks naked, we did not suspect that the ocean south of us was being dusted by radioactivity. And if we had been in the position we had maintained earlier, even now poisoned particles would be settling through our flesh into the fine tissue of our bones, and penetrating even further, down, down, burning holes in the infinitesimal blueprints upon which the message of life itself is written. A stormfront of death had gone out from Mururoa. A small stormfront – just the triggering device – but still enough to have made us into very old men had we been in its path.

Throughout the night, *La Bayonnaise* swung restlessly back and forth in her vigil. Dawn found us, still sunk in depression, having our dull breakfast of Weetabix and hot chocolate. The wind was gibbering like a witch, and it seemed as though ghostly fingers were thumbing the rigging. I understood perfectly why, in every previous age, men of the sea had been a superstitious lot. It was impossible to avoid moments when my hair wanted to stand on end, so definitely did the wind make sounds like ghouls crying from their graves, like weird beasts whose giant dripping heads might emerge any moment over the swells. I had once seen a painting of skeletal red-eyed men, their hair running like seaweed, on the mouldering green decks of the *Flying Dutchman*. Their flesh had been yellowish, their skulls gone soft like rotting fruit. The painting had begun to reappear vividly in my mind as the great scallops of green-blue water came surging over *Vega*'s own paint-peeling deck. Examining my body, I found several spots where the flesh had started to go soft and white, from being damp so long, and I worried that if we did not get some sunlight before long, the soft spots would break into open sores, and then I'd have the problems of infection to deal with.

Checking over our food supplies, I came to the glum conclusion that we were getting extremely low. I wondered how close we could cut our return journey. The nearest friendly port was Rarotonga, sixteen hundred miles away. If we left our departure too long, and ran into headwinds or storms along the way, the situation could quickly become desperate. Cutting it as fine as I dared, it still left us with no more than two weeks before we would have to withdraw from Mururoa. There was always the emergency alternative of Isles Gambier, four days' sailing from where we were, but it was a French colony, and with all the tapes and photographs we had on board, I knew we were bound to be arrested. Weakly, it occurred to me that compared to the thought of another month of being tossed around inside *Vega*, a French prison cell would be paradise.

That day, we saw only one plane. *La Bayonnaise* stayed close, apparently not taking a chance on losing us again. It was our sixtieth day at sea. With the coming of darkness, the sea hags howled in concert, and long white arms seemed to reach out of the sea, clawing at the halyards and rigging, rattling the spars. I could hear Grant tossing and groaning in his bunk. Nigel's eyes seemed abnormally large and red.

Unable to sleep, I crawled up onto the deck at 0430 hours. The masthead light was still on. I'd been worrying about the engines, and decided to switch the light off to conserve our failing batteries. Within five minutes, *La Bayonnaise* had moved up to within thirty yards, exactly like a big hound coming over to sniff suspiciously at its prisoners. Assured that we were still stationary, the minesweeper fell back to a quarter of a mile away. I stumbled down to my bunk.

I awoke to the usual wintry graveyard sky, with the boat stumbling like a bird with a broken wing in a force five easterly. Forcing myself not to scratch at the tender spots on my skin, I waited irritably while Nigel tried to work out an estimate of our position. Still having to use dead reckoning, he finally pointed to a spot on the chart thirty miles from the atoll. We had drifted almost that many miles eastward and were now back near the point where we had been when the first storm hit us – oh, Christ, how long ago? Three or four days after we had arrived near Mururoa. There was a horrible feeling that we had been on a treadmill for almost a full month, and were back basically where we had started from. Who the hell had said the tests would start at the beginning of June anyway?

My voice sounding mechanical in my own ears, I said: "We've gotta get back in." I could not avoid the feeling that the game was slipping by, that our position was poor, time was running out, that after all this effort, we were losing the initiative. For an hour, the three of us sat in the saloon, painfully clinging to the table, forcing our aching backs against the seats, exploring all the possibilities. If we tacked north, the French would undoubtedly follow us without interfering, but the moment we came about on a course southward for the atoll, we were bound to be blocked again, and we would wind up further from Mururoa than ever. If we tacked south from here, we would end up on the wrong side of the test site, and that would be useless. Finally, seeing no alternative, and still unable to muster the will to challenge *La Bayonnaise* to another game of chicken, we decided to remain where we were and wait another day for a wind change.

Looking out of the porthole, Nigel suddenly said: "We've got a new visitor."

The new ship was another minesweeper. Identical. Her name was *La Paimpolaise*, also ex-Canadian. The moment she arrived and took up a position half a mile away, *La Bayonnaise* flung a last cloud of black smoke into the air and moved off toward Mururoa.

"Good riddance," muttered Grant.

We spent the day reading and trying to catch snatches of sleep. Late in the afternoon, I decided that the mood on board *Vega* was going into a tail-spin from which I began to fear we might not recover. Goddamn it, we weren't finished yet! I crawled into my cabin and dug out a bottle of champagne I'd been saving. Then I marched into the saloon, popping the cork. "Gentlemen," I announced loudly, "we are now celebrating having the world's record for being hove-to in a nuclear test zone! Twenty-six days! Congratulations!" A couple of swallows of champagne and we immediately began to feel better. I even uncovered some dried peas I had left over in my

157

stores from a visit to Fiji. They tasted reasonably good. Relative to our other food, that made them seem like caviar. A couple more swallows of champagne and we began to feel warmth for our new neighbours.

"We really ought to invite them over for a drink," suggested Grant.

"Bloody right!" I agreed. "Where's our manners?"

In New Zealand and many other places, the flag meaning, "Come aboard for a drink" is white with a red cocktail glass. Since we didn't have one, we decided to convert my pillow case into a flag. It was well-worn and near its end anyway. For a cocktail glass, Nigel magnanimously donated a pair of brand new red shorts. With much chortling, we bent ourselves to the task of drawing two cocktail glasses on the shorts, cutting them out and sewing them with rusty needles to the pillow case. The operation took close to half an hour, with the boat continuing its eternal roll. Grant tried to practise a jig, to entertain our prospective guests, then lost his footing on the tilting floorboards and crashed against a wall. Nigel and I collapsed, laughing. Painstakingly, Nigel sewed nylon cord to the left edge of the pillow case.

"S'not bad," I announced, admiringly, wobbling a bit on my feet. Triumphantly, we marched up on deck and while Grant took pictures of the historic occasion, Nigel and I attached the flag to the halyard on the mainmast. Loudly singing "La Marseillaise", and with much fumbling, we hauled her proudly up into the wind. Unfortunately, it was a force five wind, and no sooner was the flag a few feet above our heads than it began to come apart.

Quickly, we lowered it. "S'gotta be perfect f'our friends on their big important ship," I said. Falling against each other by this time, we managed to find some spinnaker repair tape to reinforce the edges. This time, gustily taking turns singing "Oh Canada," "Waltzing Matilda" and "The White Cliffs of Dover", we hauled our new flag skyward. It snapped smartly in the wind.

"See!" cried Grant joyously. "They're comin' over!"

Immediately curious, the new minesweeper edged toward us.

Soon it was only thirty yards away, and a dozen stony French faces were looking down at us, several of them with binoculars. Happily, *Vega*'s besotted crew waved wine glasses in the air. All we got in return were disdainful looks. Haughtily, the mine-sweeper backed to its former position.

"Well, who the hell wants *them* f'neighbours anyway?" I demanded indignantly. It was only later that I learned the Frenchmen had mistaken the red cocktail glass symbols for a mushroom cloud, and thought the whole business was a provocation.

"Well, they *are* foreigners," sniffed Nigel in his best Oxford accent.

After the brief release of tension, I found myself back in the depth of depression by nightfall. I found I actually missed our old adversary, *La Bayonnaise*. At least its crew had seen us sailing under a variety of difficult situations. We had tested each other. And my feeling was that in any coming confrontation, the crew of *La Bayonnaise* would at least have a bit of respect for us. The new ship was a stranger, whose respect we would have to start from scratch to win. It sat out there, aloof, cold, dangerous.

The news over Radio Australia the next morning left us stunned – twice over.

Faintly, but distinctly, we heard the announcer say: "France is reported to have exploded the first nuclear device in this year's scheduled series of tests at Mururoa atoll at 11 am Monday. News of the blast leaked out in Tahiti last night although French officials are refusing to say anything about it . . ."

"That's three days ago!" Grant burst out.

"Shush!"

". . . the French government has informed Canada *that the Canadian peace vessel* Greenpeace III *sailed away from the Pacific nuclear test area June 21 and has not been seen since* . . . The message, delivered to the Canadian embassy in Paris, said French authorities did not know the whereabouts of the yacht or where it was heading when it left the vicinity of Mururoa . . . *Greenpeace III* was not intercepted and sailed away on its own initiative, the

French government said . . . In Canberra, the foreign affairs department said it received a cable from the Australian Embassy in Paris saying that the *Greenpeace III* was not in the danger area. It gave no other details . . ."

A chill ran through me then. My mind leapt from its initial shock – that the bomb had gone off – to the sinister statement that we were not in the area. Suddenly, it was as if we had become "unpersons". If the French wanted to set up a situation in which they could put *Vega* to the bottom with impunity, the obvious tactic would be to do exactly what they had done – pretend that the boat was long since gone from the area. If the statement was accepted, it meant we had no hope of protection at all.

Nigel was already pawing through his log book. "The bastards! That's when they had that bloody plane on top of us. It was a bloody camouflage, so we wouldn't know what was happening!" He slammed the book shut. "That business about us being gone, you know what that means, don't you?"

"We're set up right proper, aren't we?" Grant said, looking dazed.

"God damn it," I said. "God damn it!" And my thought was: *We're in deep trouble now*. But I kept it to myself.

We sagged back in our seats, glancing briefly at each other – as we had when the balloon first appeared – then each of us stared into space, trying to get hold of our thoughts.

"God *damn* it!" I said again.

Vividly, I remembered the plane and two warships closing in on our flanks and the noise. Well, I had to admit, that had been a pretty move. Try as I might, I couldn't remember any other sound but the combined noise of the engines. I couldn't decide whether the French were being damned sure they had *Vega* pinned down so they could go ahead with the test, or whether the entire exercise had been an attempt to make it impossible for us to know. The fact that the French government was still not admitting to the world that it had set the thing off seemed to lend weight to the idea that they simply did not want anyone to know. But that seemed almost academic now. The real problem was that statement about *Vega* having left the area. I groaned inwardly, thinking of all the people who would now turn away, simply waiting for us to show up in Rarotonga or somewhere else. No governments would be making inquiries. There would be no pressure on the French now to account for us. The phrase "lost at sea" kept reverberating through my thoughts. Sure. That would be the story: "Oh, they left over a week ago. Haven't seen hide nor hair of them. Must have been lost at sea." I got up and went to the porthole. *La Paimpolaise* was still on patrol, less than a quarter of a mile away. "You lying rotten bastards," I thought, furiously.

Only a few minutes had passed since the broadcast. Already, the chill of fear – as though we had just heard our death sentence – had faded, and in its place, I felt a hot rush of anger. That was too bloody much!

I wondered if anyone on *La Paimpolaise* had heard the broadcast, and if they did, how they could have the gall to continue to sit there, with *Vega* in full view, knowing their government had told a cowardly lie to the whole world.

There was nothing else to do for the moment, so Grant began to prepare breakfast. If nothing else, the news broadcast had shocked us out of our depression and lethargy.

"It's just the *first* test," Nigel said tentatively, beginning the long discussion we all knew was coming.

I looked at him quickly, seeing again the young man who had sat with me in the pub in Hamilton, New Zealand, and who had not said "Yes" to the proposal to sail into Mururoa, but had simply said: "I'll have to break the news to my girlfriend. I'll see you on *Vega* in the morning." I knew right away that Nigel was ready to risk an almost certain sinking in one last bid to reach the fallout zone.

When breakfast was finished with, Grant said, almost casually: "Right then, when do we get started?"

While Grant cleared the table, Nigel got out the charts and began to chew on his pencil. It was going to be difficult. With the winds we had to deal with now, we'd have to tack back and forth between the territorial limits of the atolls of Vanavana, Turéia and Mururoa. It was a major gamble – exactly the gamble we hadn't wanted to take the day before. If *La Paimpolaise* blocked us when we made our tack near the territorial limits of Vanavana – which she probably would – then we would be stuck. The wind would do the rest, driving us further west and away from the fallout zone. Moreover, we were so far to the northeast now, we would have to sail all through the day and into the night. None of us relished the thought of trying to dodge the minesweeper in the dark, but if we got through the first attempt to block us, and the other hounds weren't sent out from the atoll immediately, we might be able to slip in close in the dark. We remembered that it had taken both a helicopter and a plane to find us at night before. The odds looked lousy, any way we tried to work it. But we had our anger back.

Climbing as nonchalantly as we could onto the deck, refusing to even look in the direction of *La Paimpolaise*, we raised the sails and started north-northeast towards Vanavana on our first tack.

The minesweeper came to life within moments. Rather than simply trail along behind us, she circled repeatedly, as though making it clear that she was prepared to move in and block us the moment we tried to make a sprint for Mururoa. The sensation, as *Vega* cleaved swiftly through the waves, was not very different from the feeling of racing toward a narrow pass, knowing that there is an ambush waiting, and having no choice but to go through it.

The three of us were tense during that long tack toward Vanavana. The swells were enormous, and any shoulder-to-shoulder race with the minesweeper was bound to be disastrous. I found myself having to keep uncoiling my muscles, rubbing my shoulders to ease the knots that were gathered there. But at least we were under sail, and after the continual rolling while being hove-to, it was a pleasure simply to be plunging steadily forward.

In preparation for the confrontation with *La Paimpolaise*, we had arranged the life jackets in the cockpit. The inflatable was ready in case of a ramming. I made up a detailed list of emergency supplies, and Grant busied himself getting them all together: water can, medical gear, navigation gear, pilot lights, flares, food, blankets, camera, film, hand compass, warp for sea anchors, outboard engine and gas, pots and kettle to collect rainwater, fishing gear, spear, brandy, knives, spinnaker sail, number two genoa, spinnaker pole, logs, diary, tapes, matches, cigarettes, flashlight, batteries, portable radio, passports, and wire cutter. The large eighteen-man inflatable could easily take enough equipment for us to last ninety days. Once the supplies had been packed, we all felt better.

At 1245 hours, we braced ourselves, and brought *Vega* around, so that we were now on a one hundred and fifty degree bearing for Mururoa.

The minesweeper lunged toward us.

It swept down on our starboard quarter, its bow ploughing deep onto the eight-foot waves, throwing spray wildly as it came up. It passed our stern fifty yards away, turned and came around hard. The second pass, across our bow, was about the same distance.

A third pass. A fourth.

Steadily, *Vega* beat directly toward Mururoa.

A fifth pass. A sixth. But none of them bringing the minesweeper much closer than it had come on the first try. Not quite ready to believe it, I slowly began to realize that the ship was uncertain. Not long ago, I would have been thoroughly shaken by the sight of a one-hundred-and-fifty-foot warship sweeping within fifty yards of my boat. But after the treatment we'd got from *La Bayonnaise* and *Hippopotame*, this was close to nothing.

Vega leapt steadily forward, sails full.

After an hour, *La Paimpolaise* gave up attempting to run at us, and fell back a mile off our port beam, pacing us as we continued our drive toward the fallout zone.

We kept sailing. As the light began to fail, the minesweeper moved in closer and closer, maintaining visual contact as long as possible. When darkness came, I switched on the masthead light, but now the triumphant feeling we'd experienced during the afternoon turned into horror. *La Paimpolaise*'s great sleek bow thrashed through the sea, spitting and hissing, only about a hundred yards behind us. Several times, we had to come about on a new tack – and each time, the larger vessel seemed to be caught by surprise so that as we changed course, we found it thundering down out of the inky water almost on top of us. The darkness made everything more confusing and dangerous. We knew it would also give the French an excuse to dismiss a collision as an unfortunate accident, but, having come this far, we could think of no other course but to keep going. The irony of trying so hard to reach a place where you stood a good chance of being killed was not entirely lost on us, and the night was as fierce a trial as any we'd yet gone through. We learned to flash just about every light we had for at least five minutes before attempting a course change, to give the minesweeper plenty of warning, but each time we put the helm hard over, we knew we were taking our lives in our hands. And each time, the great ship would come down through the waves like a building collapsing almost on top of us.

The first weak flush of dawn was like yet another reprieve. At the least, the danger of an accidental collision was considerably lessened. The lights in the wheelhouse of *La Paimpolaise* revealed drawn white faces almost as exhausted-looking as our own. It had not been an easy night for the French either, I knew. But before I started feeling too sorry for them, I reminded myself that this expanse of waves and spray through which we were pounding was international water, and no minesweeper had any business out here tail-gating a yacht through the night. The French were risking nothing, except their reputations. The serious risk was to *Vega*, and we had not invited an escort.

The race turned shortly after dawn into a tag-team affair. A second ship came steaming over the horizon to take over the job of pacing us. *La Paimpolaise* fell back, like an exhausted hound, and disappeared quickly over the horizon – undoubtably to refuel. I found myself chuckling, thinking that it must be a highly degrading duty for a navy commander to play baby-sitter to a sailboat.

It had been gusting all through the night and we could keep only a small amount of sail up. The wind had blown unpredictably, from force five to force nine. But we made steady progress through the early morning. About two hours after departing, *La Paimpolaise* returned to take up her task, and the other ship withdrew.

At 1000 hours, *Vega* came about on her last tack. The wind was from the east – just right for another test – and we were aiming for a position to the northeast of Mururoa, directly in line with the fallout corridor. By dead reckoning, Nigel placed our position as roughly twenty miles from the atoll. At 1330 hours, we hove-to under clearing skies. In twenty-seven hours of sailing, tacking back and forth, we had covered one hundred and thirty miles in order to advance a mere fifty.

Our escort came up within seventy-five yards and stopped. A sea anchor was thrown off the side, but it didn't prevent the larger ship – with its high hull and aluminium superstructure – from drifting rapidly away. Repeatedly, it had to come about to maintain its position. Seated tiredly in the cockpit having soup, Nigel and I could easily make out the faces of several French crewmen wandering about on deck, watching us with a mixture of curiosity and amazement.

"We're a motley-looking lot, aren't we?" laughed Nigel. I grinned, wondering how we looked to the neat French sailors. Our beards were shaggy and untrimmed, hair uncombed. The contrast was striking.

In the afternoon, Nigel managed to get a sight. He was upset to find we were ten miles further out from Mururoa than he had estimated. With all the tacking back and forth through the night, the error was more than understandable.

"Tomorrow we'll get in closer," I said.

Collapsing into my bunk, I realized that we had left Rarotonga forty-one days before. We had not touched land since then. If I felt a weariness that was close to paralysis, I also felt a sense of triumph that soothed the pain of overworked muscles. The run past Vanavana and down to the edge of the fallout corridor had been our fourth round with the French navy. And *Vega* had taken it. We were just about back in position. The game was far from over.

I awoke reluctantly from a dream that vanished from memory the moment I opened my eyes to find myself back in the soggy rolling bunk. One glance at the peeling varnish and the condensation on the walls and I buried my face in the pillow, trying desperately to grope my way back into the dream. But it was gone, leaving only a few after-images of trees and a road. It must have been about New Zealand, I thought. I found myself becoming aware that it was Saturday morning there. I could be out driving along the Coromandel Peninsula, enjoying the smells of the land. Or out sailing quietly through the Bay of Islands. I groaned.

It took an enormous effort to get up. The last wild run had taken more out of me than I had realized. I tried to remember the previous evening, but it was a blank. Had we gone to bed immediately after supper or had we stayed up and played cards or chess? It was like the dream – gone. In fact, the whole previous day and night were dreamlike. Fleetingly, the walls around me blurred and I had a split second where I seemed to be sitting on the edge of the bunk in the middle of a boat with a transparent hull. I could see the waves, and *La Paimpolaise*, and a blue sky overhead, but *Vega* herself had vanished. And then, my head spinning, I was back to normal. No – not quite normal.

"Jesus," I whispered, rubbing my face, pressing my fingers as hard as I could against my temples. I reached for a cigarette, something I seldom did first thing in the morning.

Gingerly, I probed the whitish spots on my skin. At least they hadn't broken into sores yet. I felt my arms and thighs. Solid. Physically, I was okay. The problem was definitely energy. The thought of opening the cabin door and facing Nigel and Grant was almost overwhelming. I knew they would be watching me, watching for a sign that I was ready to quit. It was one of those things that never gets discussed. But during the last week, I had found myself having to put more and more energy into maintaining my own will to continue. Intuitively, I knew that I could go into the saloon and say, "That's it, we're going home", and there would be protestations and a long discussion with all the superficial appearances of an argument, but its outcome, I knew, would never be in doubt. I would have to go through the motions, but the resistance would be purely token. I had seen the way both Grant's and Nigel's eyes had followed every French ship that went back across the horizon, every plane as it had dwindled away, and could see that they were almost choking with the desire to be on that ship or plane themselves. Christ, it had been sixty-three days since they'd had any semblance of a normal world, with decent food and girls and contact with different people.

If we turned back now, it would be because I decided to let us turn back. So if we were going to stay, I was going to have to pull my energy back into focus, get up, open the door, and go out there without betraying a trace of my own overwhelming desire to be back in New Zealand, moving along some road through the trees . . .

Up in the cockpit, I held my face into the steady force five northeasterly, letting it clear my head. There was a strong swell, but at least the sky was blue, for the first time in I couldn't remember how long. I'd be able to get some sun on my skin and dry up those dampness sores. *La Paimpolaise* was riding about two miles off our port beam, her hull almost dazzling in the unfamiliar sunlight.

After breakfast, we turned on the radio to catch the news broadcast from Australia. And, again, it was the news that goaded us more strongly than any arguments we might have been able to muster ourselves.

The Canadian-owned nuclear protest vessel *Greenpeace III* was reported safe Friday with its crew outside the South Pacific area where France apparently detonated an experimental nuclear device this week . . . In Ottawa, Canadian external affairs minister Mitchell Sharp told reporters that the safety of the three men has been confirmed . . . His statement followed an earlier disclosure by France that *Greenpeace* left the test zone of its own accord June 21, five days before the first blast in a planned test series at Mururoa Atoll . . . Fears for the boat and its crew, unsighted for several days, mounted with a flurry of evident well-informed rumours that the atmospheric testing had begun. However, Wednesday night the French government informed the

Canadian embassy in Paris that *Greenpeace* voluntarily sailed away from the danger zone a week previously and had not been seen since ... In Paris, officials at the French foreign ministry shrugged off inquiries and said they should be referred to the defence ministry ... At the defence ministry, officials would only say that it was not prepared to say anything ... a policy described by observers as an 'absolute silence' ... As the flood of inquiries poured in, the French Cabinet held a meeting. The nuclear tests? The international protests? According to a cabinet spokesman after a meeting, the main debate centred on a plea by President Pompidou that more care should be taken by drivers and pedestrians on the roads ...

The report was followed by a brief interview with New Zealand prime minister Marshall, the man who had undoubtedly been responsible for the harassment we had experienced before being able to get out of Auckland. The tone of his voice left Nigel, Grant and me gritting our teeth.

"Well," said the prime minister, "the boys on *Greenpeace III* have sailed out, which is good. Discretion is the better part of valour."

Nigel banged his fist down on the table. "We should go over to that bloody boat" – he stabbed a finger in the direction of *La Paimpolaise* – "and demand that they broadcast a report giving our position right now, and clear up all this rot about us having left. I have never listened to such rubbish in my life!"

"Let's do it!" said Grant. "The worst they can do is say no."

"Hang on," I said. "Hang on. If we do that, it'll only confirm that we aren't getting through on our radio."

"Bloody hell!" snapped Nigel angrily. "They know damned well we're not getting through anyway. They've got to have been blocking every single one of our transmissions for at least ten days, ever since they started tagging us. We haven't had a squeak of a reply from anybody since then. They've got the equipment to do it. There's no question!"

The frustration of having to listen to lying Canadian politicians and sneering New Zealand politicians alike while sitting just over the horizon from Mururoa, unable to get the truth out to anyone, was almost unbearable. Nevertheless, I stuck to my argument that it was better not to acknowledge to the French just yet that we were not getting any transmissions through. After several minutes of arguing back and forth, we decided to let the matter ride, swallow our bile, and wait to see what developed over the next few days.

At least now there was no doubt about our immediate plans. If we were mute and unable to reply to the lies coming out of Paris, Ottawa and Wellington, we had only one way left to make a statement – and that was to sail immediately as close to Mururoa as possible. It was odd, I thought as we set about cleaning up the breakfast dishes, noticing how determinedly Nigel and Grant were moving about, but if those stupid buggers out there had only shut up, we'd probably have caved in on our own long ago. Every time they opened their mouths with another lie, they got us going all over again. We should send them a thank-you note.

We were just putting away the last of the dishes. It was 0830 hours.

The low breaking-apart sound of far-away thunder. Coming from the direction of Mururoa.

One second. Two seconds. Three seconds. Four. Five . . .

Through my bare feet, I could feel a slight tremor shivering through *Vega*'s hull.

. . . Six seconds. Seven. Eight.

And the thunder was gone, like a minor summer storm.

The three of us had frozen for the time it took to pass, and then, as though we were part of a film that had simply slowed down and sped back up to normal, we casually resumed our tasks. Two levels of thought occurred simultaneously in my mind. On the surface, the image of *La Paimpolaise* appeared, with its comforting message that no bomb could possibly have been detonated so long as the minesweeper remained beside us, and the sound itself had not been much more impressive than the artillery-like sounds we had been hearing coming from the atoll on and off for days, which we took to be the ordinary noises of a construction site. But beneath these calm surface explanations for the thunder-roll, there was a deep-sunk vibration of animal knowledge, like the instinct, more finely-tuned, that causes birds to lift into the air before an earthquake. *The Bomb had gone off.*

I was never to learn whether Nigel or Grant had unconsciously known the truth too and whether, like me, they had automatically slammed the doors of their awareness against the fact. So long had we been thinking about the Bomb, dreaming about it, bracing ourselves against the moment of its awakening – yet now that it had finally happened, the defences we had been preparing in our minds took the gut knowledge and smothered it immediately, lest it paralyse us on the spot.

We said nothing to each other.

In handwriting that was only half the size of his normal script – as though he did not even want to see it in print – Nigel wrote in the log book: "0830 Possible explosion heard."

Telling myself that I was just checking the weather, I climbed into the cockpit to look at the sky. Blue overhead with scattered plumes of white-grey cloud. A grey haze on the eastern horizon. A few whitecaps. And there was *La Paimpolaise*. Lastly, I allowed my eyes to turn in the direction of Mururoa.

There was nothing to be seen. The bottom third of the sky in the east and southeast was a solid grey mass of clouds.

The "reality" of there having been no bombburst now squarely fixed in my conscious mind, I went below again.

Yet the tempo of our movements quickened, as though in response to the secret knowledge. Within less than half an hour we were under sail, consciously unaware that the Fifth Horseman of the Apocalypse had indeed emerged from the gates of Mururoa, and that directly ahead an invisible tidal wave of irradiated particles of uranium-235 was riding the wind outward across the Pacific. *Vega* had begun the last leg of her journey.

The wind had increased slightly to force six. We fixed our attention on making a point clear to *La Paimpolaise*. During the night of our race from the other side of the atoll, the minesweeper had almost overrun us a dozen times. It was evident that the officer in charge had no knowledge about sailing and now that it was broad daylight, with good visibility, we decided it was time to give him his first lesson. We would show the French officers that *Vega* was capable of steering herself without a helmsman at the tiller, and once they had grasped that fact, the officer might get the message that they should stay further away in any night time situation because they couldn't count on there being anyone at the helm to alter *Vega*'s course.

Setting the yacht up for self-steering was an easy matter. All we had to do was balance the sails for the course we were sailing, which gave a slightly heavy helm to windward, put a shock cord on the tiller to take up the strain, and let her go on her own. It was common sailing practice. We hoped that it would impress on the commander of *La Paimpolaise* the danger of relying on our own dexterity to avoid a collision. By international rules of the sea, the responsibility for giving way lay with the motor vessel.

Within ten minutes from the time we hoisted the sails, *La Paimpolaise* had pulled up beside us, closing on our port beam. Promptly, Nigel, Grant and I abandoned the cockpit and went below, leaving whoever was in the wheelhouse of the warship to contend with the fact that there was no one at *Vega*'s tiller. No one to force into making a course change. No one to bully or terrorize. For all the French could tell, *Vega*'s crew might be in their bunks, asleep.

In fact, we were in the saloon, having coffee. Nigel perched near the main cabin porthole, keeping himself out of view, waiting to see what kind of reaction we would get from *La Paimpolaise*. With the feeling that we were back on the offensive, his mind had been hard at work lately trying to think of ways to torment our escort. The idea of leaving the helm unattended had been his latest ploy. He took pleasure now knowing the dilemma it presented to the men on the warship's bridge. He had served on British vessels not much different from this narrow beamed minesweeper and had sustained himself during some of those nights of bad weather with the knowledge that rough as it was on *Vega*, it was damned rough too on the other ship. Long and built for speed, the minesweeper was essentially designed for coastal waters. Its hull was wooden to avoid triggering a mine. For the same reason, it had no metal in its superstructure except aluminium, which made it an unusually light ship by military or commercial standards. In any kind of a wind, its high hull tended to act like an enormous sail, making it difficult to maintain a fixed position. Nigel knew that there had been no joy on board during those nights when *Vega* was hove-to. He knew also that those types of ships rolled like bastards in even a moderate sea. They had flat planing hulls that only drew six feet, making them skittish and hard to control – but, of course, that only made them more dangerous in a close situation. Knowing all this, he had been far more worried than even Grant or myself during our previous encounters with the minesweepers. And, though he was enjoying the thought of the problem we had just handed to the ship's skipper, he had lost none of his concern. He watched carefully.

It was then that he noticed *La Paimpolaise* was flying signal flags: MY2.

"Look it up, David." he said. "I can't for the life of me remember what that means."

I checked hurriedly through the international flagbook, but could find no trace of MY2. Months later, after considerable research, we discovered it meant "Do not continue present course."

"How are they doing out there?" Grant asked anxiously.

"She's getting bloody close," Nigel grunted.

La Paimpolaise had moved to within fifty yards. With the large swell that was running, that was already far too close for safety. Nigel was also keenly aware that steering mechanisms can fail at the damnedest times.

"I think we'd better get up there," Nigel finally said. Quickly the three of us scrambled up into the cockpit.

Looking across the narrow river of water streaming between us, I was astonished to see several men on the deck waving at us. At first glance, it seemed like a friendly gesture, which took me by surprise. I almost started to wave back, then realized they were just trying to get our attention. Ahead, about three or four miles off our port bow, was another ship, the most peculiar looking ship I'd ever seen – with two huge metal tusks sticking up out of the bow. To my mind it looked like a cross between a Japanese fishing trawler and a Chinese junk that was somehow sailing backwards. I leapt at that point to the conclusion that the odd vessel had some specialized and probably secret function in relation to nuclear testing and that the waves and emphatic gestures of the men on the deck of *La Paimpolaise* were intended to make *Vega* change course so her crew wouldn't get a close-up view. More "security" madness!

"Leave her on course," I said when Nigel looked at me. To hell with French security paranoia!

Her tiller lashed, *Vega* remained on course. I was filled with a sense of pride at the way she moved. My good old girl might be paint-peeling and frayed, but she had taken punishment that few sailboats could have sustained, and she still flew straight and true, and if her engine was baulky now and her electrical system had grown independent and flighty, she still took great gulps of wind and threw her bow up out of the waves, tossing spray like long tresses and when her nose went down into the embrace of a wave, it was because she loved the water on her back, and her wide beam gave her the grace in her passage of a mother of queens, beads of water on her deck glittering like diamonds. It had been so long since I'd seen her in the sun that I had all but forgotten how brilliantly the white of her sails and the low-slung cabin stood out against the sea and sky, as though she were part of the crests of the waves themselves.

The race continued for ten minutes. Deliberately, the three of us on *Vega*'s deck stood away from the lashed tiller, so that whoever was running the minesweeper would not mistake the message – *Vega* was moving with the timeless freedom of the seas, *Vega* would not change course.

Finally, we could see a sailor moving to the back of the mine-sweeper's flying bridge and pulling down the signal flags. A torrent of smoke from the vast funnel amidships indicated a speed change, and then the warship plunged forward, gathering steam. With a lunge that canted it over steeply, it swept across *Vega*'s bow and executed another tight turn so that the two vessels were suddenly hurtling past each other in opposite directions. Once aft of the yacht, the minesweeper whirled around again, churning up the sea into a soup of foam all around its hull, then began to move purposefully forward, coming up on *Vega*'s starboard quarter.

The sudden change in tactics had been unnerving.

"I don't like the look of this," said Grant. "She's coming too close."

"The silly bastard still doesn't know anything about sailing," growled Nigel, slipping the shock cord from the tiller and grasping it firmly in his hands.

The minesweeper was coming up on the leeward side. It made no sense to me. If *La Paimpolaise* wanted to force us to alter course, the ship should be coming up on the windward side, on our port beam. Once in that position, it might have been able to block the wind with its towering hull, forcing us to fall off to the starboard. But coming up this way on the starboard left *Vega* no way to fall off. It was an invitation to a collision.

Forty yards.

Christ! Could it be?

I could make out one man in a dark T-shirt clinging tensely to the railing on the foredeck. On the flying bridge, four full storeys above the water line, several officers were clustered together under a canvas awning. The ship's numbers stood out in black boldface on the hull: M729. Faucets of water were pouring from bilge holes. I could hear a heavy *clump, clump, clump* each time the bow clove the back of a wave. The minesweeper's engines revved and slowed unevenly, and there could be no doubt that it was advancing methodically, step by step, its bow swinging now this way, now that, definitely as though it was being lined up, as though it was being aimed!

Desperately, I looked for a way out. But there was no manoeuvre we could make. If we fell off the wind, we'd swing to starboard, back into the path of that great long meatchopper of a bow. If we turned to port, there'd be that moment when *Vega*'s sails would be fluttering before being able to catch the wind from the other side, and her forward speed would slacken drastically, she would falter, and in that moment, the minesweeper would be coming down on top of her deck.

174

"She's moving in!" Nigel yelled.

Frantically, Grant and I tried to wave the ship away.

"Move over, you silly bugger!" Grant bellowed, his arms in the air as though trying to push the advancing mass of wood and metal away. "Move over!"

Clump! Clump! Clump!

Thirty yards. Twenty-five. Twenty.

Now I could distinctly hear the gurgle of the bilge water, the hiss of steam spurting out amidships from overheated whining, howling engines. We were moving at a steady seven knots, but it seemed as the water swished cleanly past *Vega*'s hull and the wind-driven clouds swept so far above her sails – oh, to be able to fly, to levitate out of the path of this monster – that everything was moving far faster, that we were racing over a wide blue tarmac, and it seemed as unreal, yet every bit as real, as a childhood nightmare to have this grey leviathan coming down almost on top of us.

Twenty yards. Fifteen yards.

My camera was in my hands. It seemed the height of absurdity, like being in the path of an oncoming bull elephant and standing there taking pictures, but a part of my mind clung to the notion that they might see from up there on the minesweeper's flying bridge, and might somehow be warded off. Another part of my mind insisted over and over again: They'll veer off, they'll veer off, they're just putting us through hell, any second now they'll veer off.

Ten yards.

I had a glimpse of a man on the flying bridge waving, an officer. Waving – and laughing! *Laughing!* It was like a blow. A chill ran through me. Instinctively, I found myself taking a step backwards, another step. Then I was against *Vega*'s railing.

The ship was so close now the wheelhouse and the flying bridge had disappeared behind the upthrust wedge of the bow. It came up on a wave, blotting out a vast section of cloud and sky, and all I could see over the curving scimitar of its rim were the whipcords of antennae, a last glimpse of the radar dish.

"Hard over!" I screamed to Nigel.

Nigel jammed his whole straining body against the tiller to bring *Vega* into the wind and to port. *Vega* struggling for her life, began to hesitate – the moment we had feared. The wind was out of the main. We were losing way. The minesweeper's bow was a line as clean as the edge of a page – light played blindingly on her port side, blue shadow on the starboard. Then *Vega* was caught in the pressure from the bow wave and skidded sickeningly like an animal that has just taken a bullet to her side. The bow of the warship lifted and lifted and lifted.

And then came down.

The impact of its four thousand tons crunching into *Vega*'s flank brought a cry out of tortured wood, splinters zinged through the air, the hardwood rub rail exploded, and there was a concert of groaning and cracking from *Vega*'s twisted joints. The bow of the minesweeper buried itself in the rigging, its outline jutting against the mainsail. Staggered, my mind raced with the problem of which way to throw myself into the water to avoid the propellers. Like a dish whose edge has just been stepped on, *Vega* tilted to port under the minesweeper's enormous weight. I was flung violently to my knees and had to slap my hands down on the deck to stop myself from being flipped over the cabin. There was an instant of absolute stillness. The minesweeper wavered over us, poised to come down and split us in half. Then, coming up on the next wave, her flagstaff snagged in the rigging and caught the topping lift.

The water was boiling with foam and I realized that the French ship was backing away – with *Vega*'s rigging still tangled on its bow.

"Watch the boom!" Nigel shrieked. *Vega* was heeling over heavily to starboard as *La Paimpolaise* backpedalled furiously, about to take *Vega*'s mast with her. Either the boom or the mast was about to snap, which would catch the three of us on the deck like a giant slingshot. Instinctively, Nigel grabbed a knife and slashed at the nylon topping lift. It exploded. Suddenly free, *Vega* rolled back upright.

My whole body was shaking. Unable to form any words, I looked at the others. The blood had run from their faces and I could see that they were trembling no less violently than I was myself. *Vega*'s mainsail flopped uselessly, like a wounded wing. But the deck still felt solid beneath my bare feet.

Vega, I thought. You're still alive!

FOUR

The splitting of the atom has changed *every-thing*, save our mode of thinking, and thus we drift towards unparalleled catastrophe.

Albert Einstein

Vega had somehow survived and was still floating. The question now was how long she would remain afloat. I was certain she must have sprung her frame. The dazed expressions fading slowly from their faces, Nigel and Grant threw themselves into the task of guying the main and the mizzen with all available halyards. I scrambled down the hatch and began tearing at the floorboards, fully expecting to see water pouring in from the starboard side, where the minesweeper's bow had landed its great axe-blow. Astonishingly, the hull seemed sound. It took several minutes before I discovered that she was indeed, leaking up forward. But all things considered, it was not such a bad leak. Thank God for New Zealand pine, I thought.

Back on deck, I joined the others with the rigging. The reefed main, jib and staysail were still up. Since they were lending some support to the main mast – our biggest concern, since we were not in immediate danger of sinking – Nigel was afraid to drop them. Using our spare halyards, we guyed them fore and aft. Gingerly, we dropped the sails. The main mast seemed fairly secure.

La Paimpolaise had backed off to half a mile away, riding on the swell.

I checked the chainplates and hull fittings. The starboard chainplates for the main backstays were badly strained, and the bobstay hull fitting under the water at the bow was fractured and nearly torn through the hull. That was serious, because it was the fitting that supported all the strain for the forestay. If it gave completely, both masts were liable to collapse.

We worked non-stop for close to two hours, completely absorbed in the emergency repairs. The strange-looking vessel which had appeared just before *La Paimpolaise* began its deadly advance on us had passed by shortly after the ramming its – name did nothing for our mood. It was called *Scorpion*. Then it vanished, and we put it out of our minds.

In all, the damage was enough to leave us incapable of sailing in anything but the most gentle weather, and there had not been much weather like that since we'd arrived in the vicinity of the atoll. *Vega* was badly crippled. I could count twelve specific injuries the boat had taken – the bobstay hull fitting had lifted from its seating and was leaking, the bowsprit end fitting was twisted, the masthead fitting was severely damaged, the main boom topping lift was broken, there was hull damage on the starboard quarter, the starboard main mast backstay was too weak to support the mast, the spreaders on the mizzen mast were badly buckled, the mizzen masthead fitting was bent, and the mizzen mast itself was snapped, deck beams were fractured, the starboard chainplate was strained and the radio aerial damaged.

"Well, they've pretty much put us out of commission," said Nigel bitterly.

Although we did not know it yet, the main mast had been smashed downward splitting the hull planks around the keel this would prove later to be the most serious damage, because it would lead to a steadily-increasing rate of leakage.

It now appeared evident that *La Paimpolaise* was content with having crippled us, and was either waiting to see if we would sink or waiting for us to make some move. I decided to take the initiative.

"Come on, let's get a letter together for those bastards," I said.

Below, we wrote out a list of the damages and a demand that a dispatch be sent immediately to the Canadian government with copies to New Zealand and Australia radio stations. We were in a vulnerable situation, both in the sense that another storm might easily tear us apart, and in the sense that we were like a driver whose vehicle has just been smashed by a patrol car and we were having to lay our complaint with the very cops who had smashed into us. In the letter, to my government, we stated:

THE COLLISION

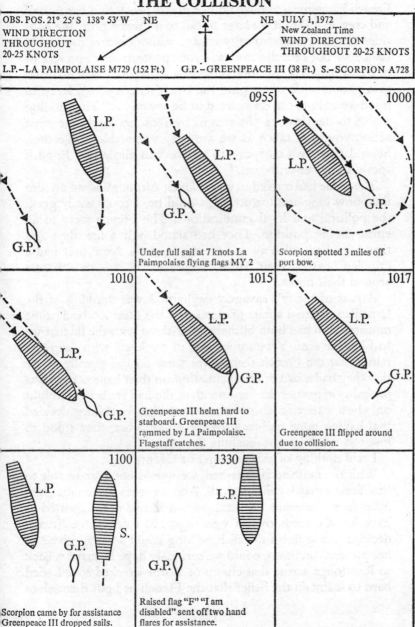

OBS. POS. 21° 25′ S 138° 53′ W   NE   N   NE   JULY 1, 1972
WIND DIRECTION   New Zealand Time
THROUGHOUT   WIND DIRECTION
20-25 KNOTS   THROUGHOUT 20-25 KNOTS

L.P. – LA PAIMPOLAISE M729 (152 Ft.)   G.P. – GREENPEACE III (38 Ft.) S. – SCORPION A728

0955
L.P.

G.P.

Under full sail at 7 knots La
Paimpolaise flying flags MY 2

1000
L.P.

G.P.

Scorpion spotted 3 miles off
port bow.

1010
L.P.

G.P.

1015
L.P.

G.P.

Greenpeace III helm hard to
starboard. Greenpeace III
rammed by La Paimpolaise.
Flagstaff catches.

1017
L.P.

G.P.

Greenpeace III flipped around
due to collision.

1100
L.P.

S.

G.P.

Scorpion came by for assistance
Greenpeace III dropped sails.

1330
L.P.

G.P.

Raised flag "F" "I am
disabled" sent off two hand
flares for assistance.

J I B — G

"Need immediate confirmation that we are safe from further French harassment and we will be given protection for myself and crew and ship if we have to sail to a French port. We consider it unsafe to attempt any voyage without escort, preferably Canadian, but French if we have your protection . . . on receipt of confirmation of this total cable we are prepared to be escorted to a port capable of slipping the boat (sixteen tons). Keep in mind we have to sail downwind or be towed . . ." Then adding a note to the French: "Inform us by 1600 hrs local time what action you have taken as we are very vulnerable to weather. Should you wish to speak to us we will allow one English speaking officer on board."

The game had moved to a new level. Although I had no idea then how long and tortuous it would be, I could easily grasp the political and legal ramifications. The French were in an embarrassing position. They had stated only a few days ago that *Vega* had sailed away over the horizon. Now they had a crippled boat on their hands. *Vega* had become an albatross around their necks.

A part of me felt savagely exultant. I was thinking of the Canadian external affairs minister and the New Zealand prime minister who had both blithely gone along with the lie that we had left the area. Yet another part of me knew with deep certainty that the French themselves were no less equally aware that they had a bad political situation on their hands. *Vega* was probably in greater danger now than she had yet been. It might only be a matter of hours before some high-level brass decided that having gone half-way toward sinking her, they stood to lose too much by not finishing the job.

I said nothing of this to Nigel or Grant.

With the radio aerial smashed, we would not even be able to broadcast a mayday distress call. And we were sixteen hundred miles from the nearest neutral port. And had been reported to have left the scene over a week ago . . . Even if the French decided not to finish us off, how long could *Vega* survive? In her present condition, could we seriously hope to make it back to Rarotonga across that chasm of storm-wrecked sea? I tried hard to maintain the belief that the French had put themselves into a stupid position, and that the great weight of international law was now moving like a tide in *Vega*'s favour. But the truth was, as I prepared for the opening gambits of the new tournament we had entered, that I felt, if anything, more afraid than I had before. At least, before, we had had the security of a tough, capable, heavy-weathersail boat beneath us. Now my queen had shattered limbs and I found myself glancing uneasily at the sky, wondering how long it would be before the winds began to howl and the waves began to throw themselves at her.

At 1300 hours, we raised the international flag "F", which means: "I am disabled, please communicate with me." As a ship in distress, we had a legal right to demand communication. I wondered, in the atmosphere of lawlessness that prevailed in the high seas around Mururoa, whether any attention would be paid to this particular right.

Moments crept by without a response from *La Paimpolaise*.

"They're gonna leave us here and let the weather finish off," said Grant, chewing nervously on his pipe.

I waited a while longer. Still no response.

"All right then," I said, "we'll knock a little louder."

I dug out a red distress flare and lit it.

We waited tensely. The warship remained distant, indifferent.

Feeling desperate, I lit a second distress flare.

And now, finally, we could see some activity on *La Paimpolaise*'s deck.

The vessel began to move slowly toward us. Two hundred yards away, it stopped, and we could see an inflatable being lowered over the side. Two men climbed into it and it began to bob over the swells toward *Vega*'s side.

As it got closer, Nigel could make out the rank of the man sitting in its bow. "Christ, that's the bloody captain!"

I didn't know whether to allow a grudging admiration for the man or to refuse to allow him on board. Captains seldom leave their ship at sea. And this particular captain had just rammed us, and had almost run us down a dozen times in the night. Technically, we had every right to bash him with a baseball bat, and how was he to know that we wouldn't do just that? Nigel looked very much like he wanted to.

I had expected the captain of *La Paimpolaise* to be arrogant and aggressive. Certainly, that was how his ship had seemed to behave. Yet the man was pale, with veins standing out beneath his dark crewcut. He looked dejected and worried. I had been allowing my indignation to build up almost to righteous wrath. The pale, nervous face in front of me – the first other human being to have come within reach since Rarotonga – produced the opposite reaction. I found myself suddenly feeling sorry for the man.

The sailor whose muscular hand controlled the outboard engine was much closer to my expectation. He looked up at us with hard suspicious eyes that said: "One move against *mon capitaine* and I'll bust your heads."

The captain's first words were: "I'm sorry, I'm sorry." As soon as he had clambered aboard, obviously uneasy on *Vega*'s cantering deck, I quickly pointed to the visible damage, and then to the place where his vessel's bow had crashed. The captain seemed genuinely upset. "Oh God! Six centimetres more . . . Oh God!"

This was not what I had expected. The French captain's movements were jerky and uncoordinated, as though he, too, had been under great strain. There was something in his face that made me think of a high-strung overbred dog. This man was definitely not the grim adversary we had been bracing ourselves to meet.

His English was quite good. After he had checked the damage on our list, shaking his head repeatedly, he asked:

"What do you wish me to do?"

"We want the collision reported and our position reported to our governments and we want to be escorted to a port for repairs, but we want to hear it confirmed on New Zealand Broadcasting Corporation or Radio Australia that we are underway."

The captain looked even more miserable. Making a vague gesture around him at *Vega*'s damages, he said:

"I do not think the admiral will permit a cable to be sent out about this."

"Well that's what we want. If a cable is not sent, we will radio a mayday and that will bring out air-sea rescue ... the New Zealand air force. You must understand, we dare not turn ourselves over to you until our governments know where we are."

The captain looked up quickly at the useless aerial dangling from the mizzen top. He made no comment, but still looked worried.

"We do not want any international problems, of course," he began.

Now I recovered my anger.

"I don't give a damn about international problems! I want to get out alive with my crew and if someone knows we're coming, then we might get there in one piece! What would you do if you'd just about been run down by three boats, buzzed by planes for hours, and then just about sunk?"

Weakly, the captain said: "I was under orders to stop you ... But I didn't mean to hit you! You ... you turned sideways toward us ..."

"My God!" I said. Then checked myself. What was the point of arguing right now? I had a brief glimpse then at the long road that lay ahead. "I've told you what we want," I finished.

The captain was silent for several seconds, clinging to *Vega*'s railing and looking out across the water at his own vessel. Then he turned to go.

The captain seemed relieved to climb back into his inflatable. His head hung dejectedly as the sailor steered them away, and it crossed my mind that there was a man who was in deep trouble. I wondered why I felt so sorry for him. Dammit, the stupid sonofabitch had almost killed us! Maybe it was the fact that it had been so long since the three of us on *Vega* had any kind of human contact outside of ourselves. I didn't know. Suddenly, I felt tired. Maybe the captain was a victim of all sorts of forces beyond his control. Maybe he was just an ambitious man whose dreams of rising had been shattered by a blunder. What the hell did it matter? If that bloody minesweeper had come ahead just a few more inches, *Vega* would be on the bottom. That much I *did* know.

187

Nigel got a sun sight that gave us a new problem to consider. We were twenty-two miles from Mururoa and the wind which had seemed determined to push us away from the atoll for so long was now nudging us directly toward it. Not much time would pass before we were carried over the twelve-mile limit and *Vega* had not strength left to tack against the wind. I began to suspect that the captain might have already thought of this and was just stalling for time. More doubts. More uncertainties.

Despair settled in again. And a new fear – that once we had been blown across the twelve-mile limit, we would simply be seized and thrown into a French prison, assuming the order didn't come down in the night to finish us off. The captain had seemed decent enough, but would he refuse an order to sink us? Could anything he said be believed?

An hour later, the captain returned and the negotiations began in earnest. First, there were two notes to be signed, one in French and one in English, saying: "I am asking help of the French Navy to make my ship *Greenpeace* fit to sail. I am freely asking to be towed into Mururoa to be mended." I refused to sign, arguing that as a disabled ship we had a right to make for any port. Had the admiral agreed to forward our messages to Canada and New Zealand and Australian radio stations? "No." I then asked if I could talk to the admiral directly. To my surprise, the captain said I could, and suggested I go with him to his ship immediately.

As we were getting ready to leave, the captain asked:
"What is our correct position?"

We stared at him, flabbergasted. The captain explained that when they were further than eighteen miles from Mururoa, they could not get a radar fix. The French Navy had apparently forgotten about the use of sextants.

For the first time in over a month, I left the decks of *Vega*.

Climbing onto the vastly-larger deck of *La Paimpolaise* was like entering a whole new world. It felt strange to be so high up and out of the water. It felt very strange to be surrounded by dozens of human beings. I found that I was self-conscious, nervous. The mostly-young French seamen around me were impassive. Some looked at me curiously. Most were stony-faced. *La Paimpolaise* itself seemed like a cross between a floating castle and a spaceship, its metal hatchways and doors seeming totally alien, the great funnel and the complex array of antennae and grids rising dizzily over my head. Following the captain into his cabin, I was shocked to find there were no portholes. We might have been far beneath the sea or somewhere outside the atmosphere of the earth. Compared to the constant motion on board *Vega*, the deck of the minesweeper was so relatively motionless that I almost stumbled. I could see now why the captain had looked, while on *Vega*, as though he were going to be seasick.

Sitting at the captain's desk, I wrote a message to the admiral on *De Grasse*, asking that it be sent collect to ZLD Auckland and NZBC Auckland. The message stated simply that there had been a collision – in the hope of getting it past the admiral, I didn't call it a ramming – that we were being taken to Mururoa for repairs, requesting that our families be advised and asking for confirmation of receipt of the message on the following day's shortwave radio broadcast. Before accepting a tow into Mururoa, where we might easily disappear forever and never be heard from again, I wanted to hear the message being acknowledged from Auckland.

The captain's name was Patrick de la Rochebrochard. While the message was being sent and we waited for a reply from the admiral, I ordered food. Two other officers joined us. I should have enjoyed the meal – wine, beef, sausages, sauerkraut, pickled beets, coffee, apples and cheese, but I found I was still too tense and the food seemed almost nauseatingly rich. Captain Rochebrochard seemed no less tense himself, but he answered my questions with surprising candour. Yes, he had been ordered by the admiral to stop us. No, no, he had no thought of killing us! If he had wanted to finish us off, he would have done it long ago. In fact, I might be interested to know that *Greenpeace III* had earlier been the subject of a discussion and there were officers who were in favour of running us down and being done with it, but the admiral would not permit it. Yes, *La Bayonnaise* had been the laughing stock of the fleet for losing us. And, yes, whenever *Vega*'s radar reflector came down, it was very, very difficult to keep track. When I asked what would happen as a result of the incident that day, the captain said simply: "I might be thrown out of the navy." And later: "Yes, that was a bomb blast you heard this morning. A small one, but a bomb nevertheless."

A feeling of failure crept over me when I heard that. We had gone through so much, but accomplished so little. By the end of the meal, I was thoroughly depressed. It was then that the admiral's reply arrived. My request to have a message sent out was refused. However, if we signed the paper saying we had freely requested permission to come into Mururoa for repairs, we would be fixed up and permitted to leave again, although we would have to turn in all our cameras at the twelve-mile limit, we would have to remain on the boat, our radio would *not* be repaired, and we would not be given any food or water.

Back at *Vega*, Captain Rochebrochard waited in the inflatable while I talked the alternatives over with Nigel and Grant. The discussion quickly stalemated. Grant wanted to go into Mururoa. Nigel's pride dictated that he wanted no help whatsoever from the French. I found myself badly torn – I was in favour of trying to make for Rarotonga unless the French agreed to send out our message. I was wary about allowing ourselves to be towed into a trap from which, for any number of different reasons we might not emerge. Yet I was also curious about the atomic test site and equally worried about our actual chances of making it in poor crippled *Vega* all the way to Rarotonga. Grant was adamant. His bones were crying out for relief from the pounding of the sea. I didn't want the French captain to see that we were divided, so I climbed back out on deck and said:

"Look, we'll let you know in the morning."

It was a long night. Eventually, we settled on a compromise. We would check the boat over in detail in the morning, and if we felt she would make it to Rarotonga, we would sail away. If not, we would accept a tow into Mururoa. When, finally, we fell into our bunks, sleep would not come easily. There were too many new creakings and groans. *Vega* was hurt and her voice rasped at us all through the night. The wind blew to force five.

In the morning, the task fell to Nigel, because of his experience, to go up the mast in the bosun's chair, a simple canvas sling. It was the condition of the mast and the masthead fitting that would finally determine our capability, or lack of it, in terms of reaching Rarotonga. Nigel's weight was a problem. He was the heaviest of the three. With the swell rolling *Vega* around, he clung desperately to the mast; if the mast cracked now, he'd be smashed on the deck. After fifteen harrowing minutes he signalled to be lowered. He was perspiring freely from the strain and tension.

"We can forget Rarotonga. We're not going anywhere!" The fitting had been badly twisted and wrenched loose. It could go at any time.

At 1015 hours, Captain Rochebrochard returned with the news that, while the admiral still refused to allow a message to be sent, he was willing to see that *Vega* was repaired free of charge and he would give that assurance in writing. Nigel, Grant and I looked at each other. It seemed hard to believe. I worried that we were being naive. Surely the French navy had legal experts on hand, and surely they were aware of the implications of such a document. It would amount to an admission of fault.

"Let's face it," said Nigel. "We really have no alternative. We either go in or we sit out here until the old girl breaks up under us. If they're playing with us, we simply have got to go along with the game."

"Okay," I said. "But we've got one last card. When we get in there, we'll bloody well stay there until they radio the fact that we've been taken in."

There was one other reason for agreeing. We had now drifted to within fifteen miles of the atoll. Before long, we would be over the twelve-mile limit, and any kind of a deal now was clearly a better bet than waiting to be grabbed for entering French territorial water without permission, however phoney the charge might be.

"I wouldn't put it past them a bit to just throw us in jail once we're inside anyway," said Nigel.

Bleakly, I wondered if there weren't any number of very

serious mistakes we were making. The fact remained that no one other than the French knew where we really were. I felt like a lamb handing itself over to the wolves. Any number of "accidents" – like the "accident" of our ramming – could be arranged in Mururoa. Vividly, I remembered the sound of the gate at Mount Eden Prison closing behind me in New Zealand. Everyone I had ever known or loved or trusted was so damned far away and my own government was either blithely accepting every word the French uttered or was actively conniving with them. I felt exhausted, and my worry wouldn't go away. Only one thing was certain: *Vega* wasn't going anywhere in the shape she was in, and that seemed to leave us very few options. Dangerous as it might be to be led into Mururoa, to face the open sea now would amount to suicide. I had more reason to fear the sea than France.

After accepting a letter from the admiral promising to undertake repairs, we prepared a letter of our own to be delivered to the admiral the moment we entered the harbour. It demanded that our respective governments be advised immediately of our presence in Mururoa. It ended: "Please be assured that we will not leave the safety of this island without confirmation that the above steps have been taken."

It was not much – another piece of paper. And I knew it meant we faced a conflict of wills once we arrived in the harbour. I wondered, briefly, how the three of us were going to fare against the admiral of a whole navy fleet with thousands of men and dozens of ships and planes under his command.

Before going to sleep, we collected all our tapes, logs, Nigel's navigational working papers, rolls of 35 millimetre films, and hid them.

I knew nothing about the man whose will I would have to challenge once we arrived in Mururoa except that his name was Christian Claverie and that he was Admiral Commandant le Groupement des Expérimentations Nucléaires and that he held a nuclear bomb in his fist.

Our first glimpse of Mururoa revealed a moonlike stretch of grey rock, perfectly flat, without a single shrub or even a blade of grass breaking through. In order to enter the lagoon, the tug which had taken us in tow had to pass ground zero itself. Until then, it had not occurred to me what a perfect name that was for the birth-place of nuclear weapons: the earth had been reduced to absolutely nothing. There was the quality of the void. Automatically, I found myself shrinking away, for it was like nothing so much as a vision of the end of the world. It came as no surprise that the first two structures we saw were concrete block houses, as though an attempt had been made to colonize a lifeless planet. Beyond the block houses we saw what looked like the wreck of a huge ship, tilted over on its side. The over-all impression was that we had arrived in a land where Armageddon was already history. Two helicopters came skittering overhead like giant mutated insects.

Once we had passed into the lagoon, we could at least see a few palm trees and patches of vegetation swathing the sand and coral. The lagoon was several miles across and clustered together along a two-mile stretch of beach were several buildings, houses and warehouses. We could see a few cars moving back and forth. The largest structure by far was the great bulk of the cruiser *De Grasse*, looking in the distance more like a factory than a ship. Beyond the cruiser were at least thirty other ships of all types and sizes: a large helicopter carrier, various warships, a number of minesweepers, passenger liners that had been converted into floating apartment blocks, research and support vessels with strange arrays of equipment. Helicopters were lofting crates and boxes. To our amazement, we could see dozens of sailboats, motorboats and small launches.

As the tugboat pulled us steadily across the lagoon it brought us past *De Grasse*, close enough so I could easily see that there were hundreds of sailors on the decks. Grant waved at them. Tentatively, not expecting any response, Nigel and I waved too. Yet several sailors did wave back. I began to feel safer. With so many witnesses, I reasoned, we would not just disappear.

My fears had been eased considerably by the smiling faces of the three seamen who had been sent from *La Paimpolaise* to ride with us. One young officer had looked at us with such open admiration that I had felt myself becoming embarrassed.

193

"We are proud to have the honour of towing you in," the officer had said. He was filled with questions about what it had been like on *Vega*, curious about every detail. It began to dawn on me that *Vega*'s presence had probably loomed large in the minds of every person at the base during the long weeks of her vigil.

"I think you are the first foreign ship ever to enter Mururoa," the officer had added.

Certainly, our entrance was causing considerable excitement. As we passed *De Grasse*, a shrill whistle blew a salute. The tugboat slowed and dozens of pleasure boats converged on us. Cameras were clicking everywhere. It turned into something very much like a parade. The tugboat in front, battered *Vega* in the centre, *La Paimpolaise* hovering almost protectively behind, and the swarm of sailboats, motorboats and launches criss-crossing and circling around us. It was a Sunday and the sun was blazing. I had the distinct impression that many of the people on the circling pleasure boats were actually delighted to see us. This was not what I had expected. I felt relieved, but also confused. Why were they so friendly? *Vega* was being dragged in, virtually in chains, wounded, like a prize of war – *and here were all these crazy Frenchmen waving and smiling!* I felt giddy. It was real dizziness, partially due, I knew, to the fact that for the first time in two months, *Vega*'s decks were not swooping and surging in a swell. The waters of the lagoon were being stirred by a brisk wind, but the effect on the motion of the boat was almost negligible.

The tug stopped, leaving *Vega* dangling at the end of her line in an oily spread of water. A launch pulled up and two photographers climbed aboard and immediately started taking pictures of the damage.

Then I spotted an official tender coming toward us, with Captain Rochebrochard on board, immaculately dressed in whites. This is where the party ends, I told myself. Earlier, I had called the captain on the walkie-talkie which one of his men had brought onto *Vega* and told him: "When we get to the lagoon I have a letter for you to deliver to the admiral." Now the captain of *La Paimpolaise* was forcing a smile as he accepted the letter. Again, I felt sorry for the man. I watched as the tender chugged away toward the command cruiser. A white speck in the distance, the captain marched smartly up the gangway, saluted, crossed the deck and disappeared inside to face the probable wrath of his commanding officer. The letter he carried with him was not going to make things easier.

In the few moments that passed before a second, smaller tug appeared to tow us to a dock, I had time to notice flowers of oil folding and unfolding in the water all around us, garbage bobbing in the shallows and the smell of sulphur fumes and creosote. Then the second tug arrived and it became evident that the French were not going to waste any time. *Vega* was pulled over to a small floating dock next to a huge grey maintenance ship, the *Garonne*. The ship's deck was lined with curious faces and a crowd had gathered on the beach. A phalanx of senior officers arrived within minutes, cordial and friendly, but businesslike. They obviously were under orders to get the repairs done as quickly as possible. I felt claustrophobic from the press of bodies clambering over the boat. I winced at all the military boots biting into *Vega*'s deck. I still felt dizzy from the lack of sea-motion. It was all quite unreal. There was a sense of being engulfed.

Nigel had estimated it would take at least ten days to complete the repairs. The French were to astound us by finishing the job in forty-eight hours, working around the clock, employing up to twenty men at a time. From the moment she arrived at the side of the dock, *Vega* became the centre of a swarm of activity, with senior officers as well as enlisted men furiously tearing her apart, then putting her back together again. They worked on her with an almost manic urgency, like a team of surgeons and nurses operating on a traffic victim whose heart is only a beat or two away from stopping.

Still groggy from the ordeal at sea and immediately absorbed in the task of explaining, mainly with diagrams and sign language, what had to be done, it did not occur to me to question the Frenchmen's strange eagerness to work. Most of them were so solicitous, courteous, polite and *normal* it was hard enough to keep in mind that, collectively, they were busy building thermonuclear devices whose sole purpose was mass destruction of human lives, let alone look for ulterior motives in their evident energy.

Hove-to in the waters outside Mururoa, it had been easy to focus my awareness on the end-product of these busy men's labours, for there was only one image in my mind: *la bombe*. Now, in the midst of what seemed like nothing much more than a medium-sized industrial port (if you could overlook the cannons and anti-aircraft guns mounted on the decks) I found it all but impossible to focus on anything but the immediate task of directing this team of bustling French repairmen. There was no balloon in sight. The no-man's land over which it had floated was somewhere on the other side of the lagoon. There was only the press of curious faces, the hustle of workmen, and the mechanics of *Vega*'s resurrection with which to contend.

We had travelled over four thousand miles of ocean to reach the heart of the fortress of the Bomb, but now that we were inside the gates, there was nothing to be seen. I was more disorientated than I knew. And if I gave any thought to the pace of activity around us, it was passed over with the vague assumption that these cheerful Frenchmen were eager to make amends or maybe they just felt guilty about what had happened. It did not occur to me until much later that their "eagerness" was solely to get off another bomb test, and for a combination of reasons, mostly political, *Vega*'s presence in the lagoon made that impossible.

My first inkling that an order had arrived from Paris to cover up the damage to *Vega* and push her back out to sea as quickly as possible so the tests could continue did not come until that afternoon.

According to the terms of the agreement we had signed in exchange for repairs in Mururoa, we were forbidden to step ashore. So we were nothing short of astonished when the captain of the *Garonne* poked his head through the hatch and said: "The admiral requests that you and your crew join him for lunch."

It was all Grant could do to avoid letting out a whoop on the spot. Nigel nodded darkly. I hesitated for only a moment, then agreed. I hadn't expected to get a chance to negotiate directly with the admiral and probably would not get another.

"If you hurry," said the captain, glancing at our sweaty, grease-stained bodies, "I'll show you where you can have a shower."

That settled the matter very quickly.

The luxury of that first fresh-water shower since Rarotonga left the three of us feeling very close to reborn. Grant was babbling excitedly, first from the joy of being clean, and second because he had never dreamed that he might some day have lunch with an admiral. Nigel was unimpressed. I was looking forward to it with no more pleasure than a board meeting. The shower had given me back some of my perspective. We weren't going to lunch, we were going to a showdown. By now the admiral would have seen the letter stating that we refused to leave unless a message was dispatched, and I knew as well as the admiral would know that such a message would reveal the fact that the French had lied earlier about *Vega*'s "departure".

An official tender pulled up beside *Vega*, bearing a very reserved and nervous-looking Captain Rochebrochard. As we climbed aboard, the captain explained that the admiral had a beach house across the lagoon about a mile away. As we motored toward it, I asked if the admiral had agreed yet to send a radio message. The captain looked away.

"No. The admiral agreed to bring you to Mururoa, repair your boat, with no communication. He told you that more than once." I started to argue. Then Grant broke in, eager to restore good feelings.

"Ah, hell, David, a deal's a deal. Let's just —"

I cut him off with a chopping motion of my hand and a furious look, but not before the French captain had seen that there was division among the protesters. I knew that our position was much weakened. I tried to compensate by hardening my voice.

"Look, captain, we have a legal right to talk to our countries and a moral right to assure our families that we're safe."

Captain Rochebrochard hardened as well. Folding his arms, he looked me in the eye. "You realize this affair has gone much further than the admiral?"

"How much further?"

"I can't say, but there are very few above the admiral."

In fact, there would only be the minister of defence and the president of France.

Soon we were alongside a concrete pier jutting out from a coral beach. In contrast to the oily harbour side of the lagoon, this section consisted of magnificent white beach, palm trees and even a few grass huts. We walked for about a hundred yards – an odd quartet. Captain Rochebrohard in his formal white uniform, ramrod shoulders, crew cut, and, of course, clean-shaven. Nigel, Grant and myself, barefoot, bearded and looking like gypsies. Ahead was a group of ten men in light-weight navy fatigues. As we approached, one of them broke away and came toward us. "That's the admiral," whispered Captain Rochebrochard.

Admiral Claverie immediately reminded me of an ageing George C. Scott. He was in his mid-fifties, solidly built and his grip was strong. He greeted us warmly, with Captain Roche-brochard acting as interpreter. The other officers closed in on us and there was a flurry of handshakes and greetings under the palm trees and it was all very very civilized. Most of the officers, attired like the admiral in casual fatigues, seemed as friendly as the others who had gone to work on *Vega*. There were at least two whose eyes were like chipped steel, from whom I received a definite impression that they would far prefer to throw the three of us in irons than stand there politely chatting. But it was the admiral who set the tone of the gather-ing, and his attitude seemed to be that of a kindly patriarch, his body more compact than those of the other officers, his move-ments just slightly more ponderous. His only ornamentation, apart from the three stars of his shoulders, was a narrow gold wedding ring. As soon as the ritual of introduction was com-pleted, he spread his arms graciously toward the lagoon and the beach and said something that the captain quickly translated:

"The admiral asks if you like our South Pacific paradise?"

I bit back the variety of comments that came to mind and mumbled that it was very nice.

"He wishes to know if you would like to go for a swim."

"No, thanks, we've just had fresh-water showers and we've had our fill of salt water for a while."

Behind wire-rim sunglasses, the admiral was eyeing us in a way that was some combination of calculation and amusement. He had smiled when the captain translated our rejection of the offer, then asked again if we wouldn't enjoy a swim. "He says the water is very clean."

It was then that I noticed a cameraman with a telescopic lens some distance away behind a palm tree. I could see the picture in the newspapers and the headlines: Protesters find no radio-activity in waters of bomb site. *Happy protesters.*

Firmly, I declined again. The nagging feeling of unreality which had been plaguing the back of my mind now found its focus. Clearly, this was to be a public relations production, complete with gracious French hosts. Well, no matter. If all this ritual had to be gone through in order to get our chance to square off with the admiral, we'd go through and that was it. Apart from having the sense not to go swimming in Mururoa lagoon for the benefit of French cameraman, I put the public relations aspect of it all aside. My main purpose was to talk to Admiral Claverie about getting a message out. In taking this attitude, I made a fatal assumption. I assumed that no one *out there* could fail to put two and two together. All they would need to know was that a small sailboat and a warship had been in a collision in international waters in the vicinity of a nuclear test. To me, the conclusion was so breathtakingly obvious that virtually nothing more need be said. Everyone knew the rules of navigation concerning vessels under sail and those driven by motors.

But the problem was, most people did *not* know that a motor-ized vessel always has to give way to a boat under sail. And in one respect, despite all my experience, I was indeed naive. I did not quite realize the press is called the "establishment press" precisely because it listens to the establishment first, and it listens to "kooks" hardly at all. In two months of isolation with Nigel and Grant, both of whom I knew to be intelligent, sensi-tive human beings, I had completely lost track of the reality that there were legions of cynical news editors sitting *out there* waiting for the slightest opportunity to write the voyage of *Greenpeace III* off as the work of kooks, radicals and frauds.

Intent on having my moment with Admiral Claverie, I thought nothing of it as we sat down to lunch under the palm trees with several litres of wine ostentatiously displayed on the table. From behind the palm trees, the cameras clicked. The three of us might have won our long and desperate struggle against the sea. We might have won a savage jousting match with French warships. But we were about to be totally clobbered on the public relations front. Although we had no inkling of it yet, the French military would be releasing a "message" soon enough. The message would be that the food and wine at Mururoa were excellent and that a good time was had by all. Only incidentally would there be a brief acknowledgement that there had been an accidental collision which was caused when the skipper of the *Greenpeace III* made a false manoeuvre and crashed into a French minesweeper which had been attempting to deliver a message. The French statement would go on to say that out of concern for the safety of the protest yacht, the admiral of the base had willingly taken it in for repairs and had treated his guests to a banquet under swaying palms. A photograph of this pleasant gathering would be released to the wire services and widely printed. And I would wonder why I got nothing but disbelieving looks when I tried to tell my story. With a brilliant flourish of a single carefully-staged photograph, the French would just about completely negate the effort of *Vega's* first journey to Mururoa.

Unaware of the dimensions of the trap into which we had stepped, Nigel, Grant and I sat down to lunch with the admiral, his chief of staff, three medical specialists on radioactive effects, a commander, and a cheerful major whose job was not clear, but whom we later concluded was the head of public relations. The meal was a delight of pizza, roast beef, fried potatoes, fresh bread, cheese and salad with bottled water and wine. Admiral Claverie had indicated that Nigel and I should sit on either side of him. As we ate, three unobtrusive photographers with telephotos snapped picture after picture.

The conversation around the table went smoothly enough.

I had asked Captain Rochebrochard to ask the admiral if we could talk privately after lunch and the admiral had nodded. That settled, I sat back to see what I could learn about the man who ruled Mururoa.

Admiral Claverie's charisma was subtle but powerful. I found myself quickly being drawn to the man as he talked freely about his own experiences at sea. "In 1937 I sail for three years alone in a sloop through French Polynesia and I am at sea ever since." His English was broken and he looked frequently to Captain Rochebrochard for help, but while he was talking directly to me, the other officers discreetly maintained a low buzz of conversation themselves so that there would be no eavesdropping.

"You could take a magnum of champagne under each arm to those nightclubs in Auckland and you had the pick of the girls and they were wonderful!" He talked on about his past with that special ability of men who are good leaders to give the impression of a very personal and special rapport. He had dark brown eyes, very piercing. I found my hopes rising. This man would understand what we had been through. He would be receptive. At least in our regard for New Zealand ladies, we had a definite common ground of agreement. The admiral talked on, relaxing, about his career, his family, his grandchildren, leaving me with the distinct feeling that I was the first person the old man had felt he could talk openly with in a long time. Then, embarrassed, he broke off and spoke to Captain Rochebrochard in French.

"The admiral says he has had much experience, but certainly none like yours. He wants you to know that your sailing here and laying off Mururoa for thirty days so close to the twelve-mile limit was a great feat of navigation and sailing."

Admiral Claverie added that he had known our whereabouts all the time. "You need not have worry."

Throughout the meal, our glasses were kept filled with wine. The admiral himself drank little and what he drank was radically cut with bottled water. I asked him about the large white ship we'd seen which had kept its distance every time we tried to approach.

"That was the US ship, *Wheeling*," the admiral said easily.

"*Wheeling?*"

"Yes, *Wheeling*. We are very friendly with them." The expression on his face then told me to drop the subject.

I asked if he understood that we had undertaken our voyage to question France's right to close off international waters.

"Yes I do and I confess it is the first constructive protest we have come up against." He paused to let the flattery set in. "I realize we have no legal right over you and no legal right to cordon off these waters, but, you see, I must put human life above human rights."

"Well," I said slowly, "I believe them to be the same thing where atomic fallout is involved."

The admiral accepted the challenge without a blink.

"But you do not have Russia at your doorstep. There has to be a third nuclear power to act as a balance between Russia and the United States." He sipped on his watered wine for a moment and his voice changed. He seemed for a moment almost to be pleading. "I would never hurt anyone, you see I'm a Catholic. We are very careful. Look, we watched over you for thirty days. We never set a bomb off until we are sure of where the fallout will go."

"But the bomb is designed to destroy human life!"

The admiral's face softened and he sat back, looking at his wine glass thoughtfully. "Yes, things could have been different and I could easily be sitting in your seat." Obviously the subject troubled him. His forehead wrinkled. He withdrew, leaving me to have to search for a less sensitive subject. Twice, before lunch was through, the admiral referred to his Catholic background. He seemed to hold it up as proof that he could not possibly be an evil man. I sensed a guilt of sorts but knew better than to start a theological debate.

After lunch, the admiral, Captain Rochebrochard and I strolled away from the others. Placing his hands on his hips and turning face-to-face, the admiral nodded to the captain to interpret. I set out my case as simply as I could. I told them that we had been able to hear BBC, Radio Australia and Radio New Zealand, yet for close to two weeks before the collision, nobody could receive our reports. I left the implication hanging that we were being jammed. The admiral's expression did not change. A lot of people would be worrying, I said, especially since the French government had stated that we had left the area twelve days ago. "This would mean that we should have arrived in Rarotonga by now. If we add the time it's going to take to finish our repairs and another ten to fifteen days to return to Rarotonga, it will be close to a month from the time the outside world was told we had already begun our return voyage."

I finished: "You have a family. So do I. And my crew have families. This must be causing them terrible worry. I believe you have a moral duty to report that we are safe in Mururoa and I'm asking you to do so as soon as possible."

There was a moment of silence. The admiral gave me a long hard look, then spoke slowly in French to the captain, who translated:

"The reports of your leaving were not my doing. But as a religious man, with a family, a good Catholic, and more important, as sailor to sailor, I give you my word that I will ask Paris for approval to report to the press that you are here in Mururoa. You have my word."

"This will be reported before we leave?"

The admiral flushed, perhaps unused to having his word questioned, perhaps because his lofty statement had made no reference to timing.

"Yes," he said, almost harshly. "I will ask Paris."

Then he shook hands, all admiral again. He offered Captain Rochebrochard as a liaison. The unobtrusive photographers clicked off several more pictures. With that, Admiral Claverie made his way off to a building set back in the trees. The captain and I rejoined the others, another round of handshakes, and then we were on our way back to *Vega*. I was left with the feeling that I had just bounced off a brick wall. When I thought back over the luncheon, I could not see that anything had been accomplished. I still had a damaged boat, the protest seemed to have been unsuccessful, and the admiral would still not authorize a radio report without the unlikely approval of politicians back in Paris. I did not realize that the officer in charge of public relations did not see futility in the banquet under the palm. From *his* point of view, it had been very productive indeed.

Back on the tender, I asked Captain Rochebrochard if he was in trouble after all. The Frenchman replied that the admiral had assumed full responsibility and it had been ordered that *Vega* be stopped that day. As the tender's engine came to life, the captain added:

"You were sailing into the fallout."

Vega was aswarm with workmen. The food and the wine had left us feeling groggy. We had not had much sleep the night before, had been up since very early, and so much seemed to have happened that all I really wanted to do was sleep. Clearly, that was impossible. We were soon back at work and the work continued until after dark under brilliant floodlights. Late in the evening we were invited on board the *Garonne* for supper and this time, at least, there were no photographers around. The supper was a rather strained affair, with several officers peppering us about details of our voyage, but whenever the subject of nuclear testing came up, the commander made it clear to the others that they should mind what they said. With *Vega* in a state of disarray, it was impossible for the three of us to sleep there, so the captain of the *Garonne* agreed to let two of us sleep in the ship's infirmary. Nigel agreed to stay on *Vega*. It was well past midnight before we got to bed, and I realized we had been up for twenty-two hours. I had a nagging feeling that events had slipped out of our control . . .

Unaccustomed to a stationary bunk, I slept poorly, tossing and turning through the night. At 0700 hours, Nigel came in, bleary-eyed. *Vega* had been banging against the float. We felt every bit as fatigued as we had before going to bed. A force six westerly was slapping rain against the porthole. Foggily, I realized that it was coming from the direction in which we hoped to go, as though the wind which had tried to push us away from Mururoa for so long had now perversely changed its mind, determined to keep us trapped in the lagoon. Also, the heavy rain was going to make it impossible for us to tighten the rigging screws and seal them, which meant that we wouldn't be able to leave for at least another day.

Vega looked dismal, lying against the float in the down-pour. Dully, we set to work cleaning up the interior. A maintenance crew arrived to do the finishing touches on the work they'd undertaken. A short while later, Captain Rochebrochard arrived in his tender to take me for a final meeting with Admiral Claverie. Throwing on my oilslicks, I stumbled into the tender. I sat sullenly in the rain as we putted across the lagoon to the great grey bulk of *De Grasse*. The vessel was crawling with crisp smartly-dressed officers. My sandals flopped wetly as we padded down a long corridor. We stopped and knocked at a hatchway. The admiral's voice replied. We went in.

The two officers spoke for several minutes in French, with the admiral nodding from time to time. I assumed the captain was bringing him up to date on the repair work. When they finished talking, they turned to me expectantly. I asked the admiral when I could expect to hear the report over the radio that we were in Mururoa. Admiral Claverie responded in French.

"The admiral will advise Radio Tahiti that you are safe in Mururoa and that you have been involved in a collision and that you will be arriving in Rarotonga in eleven days," the captain translated.

I asked when the information would be sent out, but all I got was an evasive answer.

"I have to repeat, we have no intention of leaving until this is done," I said.

When Captain Rochebrochard had interpreted the admiral nodded off-handedly. "Yes, yes, of course."

I then explained that the tightening and balancing of the rigging could only be done when it was dry, so I did not see how we could leave until at least the following day. The admiral agreed.

"Are the repairs satisfactory?" he wanted to know.

"Yes, as far as I can see."

We dickered for several minutes more over whether or not I would sign a document listing the repairs that had been done. It was in French, and I was afraid that it might amount to a total release. I didn't want to sign anything like that until I could get a proper marine survey. We finally settled on a version that was an acknowledgement of the work that had been done with me accepting responsibility for the safety of the boat and crew until we reached a port where a survey could be undertaken. It was all very businesslike.

In the end, the admiral came around from his desk and shook my hand. The unreality of the situation sunk in once again. It was as though nothing much more had happened than a routine traffic accident, and the nagging feeling of having lost the initiative came back to me. But there comes a point in every battle where one side or the other starts losing ground. The long voyage and the exhausting struggle to remain hove-to had sapped me. Since the ramming, I had not had a chance to sit back and calmly appraise the situation, or even to get a decent rest. The thought of the long voyage to Rarotonga that still lay ahead was almost more than I could bear.

Now the admiral was holding the door open for us to leave. I tried to think of something to say that would somehow break this illusion of normalcy. The admiral looked, for all the world, like a busy powerful executive who had actually done some minor customer a personal favour. In some way that I couldn't quite put my finger on, the older man had turned the situation around. He had gained the upper hand. I was now being let out the side door, back into the rain and the admiral seemed to be already dismissing the incident from his mind, preparing to get back to business – the business of building atomic bombs – as usual. I had the feeling I'd been in a revolving door from the moment we'd arrived in Mururoa. Now it had stopped, facing outward into the rain. There was only the slightest trace of a glint in Admiral Claverie's eyes. It was almost impish, almost a twinkle. Nothing in his face betrayed it – his control was far too elaborate for that. But he did not look like a man who has just lost a war.

If there was any one expression he might have uttered which would have summed up the secret look in his eye, it would have been: "Son, you've been had."

But, of course, all he said was: "Bon voyage."

Bleakly, I said: "Goodbye." And just barely managed to avoid adding: "Thanks." The admiral, I realized, had not become commander of a nuclear test site by accident.

The rain did not let up until early afternoon. As soon as it stopped, we went to work tightening *Vega*'s rigging screws. There were seventeen individual screws and the job was a bit like tuning an enormous guitar. After tightening them, we had to fill each one with lamb's fat and cover them with tape to prevent the corroding salt water from getting at them. It took us most of the afternoon to get it done.

That night, we had supper again with the officers of the *Garonne*. The atmosphere was tense. My repeated assertions that the admiral had advised me that we didn't need to move *Vega* until the next morning were being ignored. Twice, the captain of the *Garonne* had told us that he had been told by his commander that we were to leave.

I felt my energy failing rapidly. Before I quite realized what had happened, Nigel, Grant and I had all been hustled back to *Vega*, and the tender was waiting alongside with a line already attached. The other lines were being let loose. The tender's engine was revving up. We were left with no choice. We had to jump onto *Vega*. Within seconds, we were being towed out into the lagoon. The wind was still blowing hard, there was a heavy chop, and it was dark. *Vega* was yanked away, like a puppy on a leash. The tender operator either didn't know what he was doing, or was angry because he was forced to work in the dark. Whichever the case, he jerked *Vega* around furiously, and as she came around the stern of the *Garonne*, the wind began to push her down on top of the tender. Her bowsprit climbed over his stern and missed his cabin by inches. The tender suddenly speeded up to get clear and took up the slack so quickly that the towline snapped. We found ourselves being blown helplessly toward a breakwater. I grabbed the tiller while Nigel dived below to start up the engine. Near-misses were getting to be normal, and so by the time the engine started, and we were only about fifteen yards from the breakwater, I felt very close to simply shrugging. I turned *Vega* into the wind to hold her in position. The tender was pulling alongside by then, but with the wind and the chop, he had become a menace. I shouted at him: "Get the hell away!"

Using the engine, we edged up to a large steel buoy. Grant

reached desperately from the bowsprit to try to attach a heavy nylon line, but couldn't reach. Nigel suddenly grabbed the line and dived into the water. Grant tried to yell instructions back to me, but the wind and the engine noise made it impossible to hear. I was afraid of pinning Nigel between the bow and the buoy. Somehow, the young Englishman managed to get a loop around it, but smashed his head in the process, so that when he climbed gasping onto the deck, blood was streaming from his head. When the rope was fast, we could see immediately that our movement on the choppy water would soon chafe it through. Cursing furiously, Nigel threw himself back into the water, this time dragging our anchor chain.

When at last we were fastened, we stood on the deck, screaming insults at the Frenchman on the tender, then went below to clean the wound on Nigel's head. The whole operation had been completely unnecessary, except for those pigheaded sons of bitches who had virtually kicked us away from the float. The whole fiasco of Mururoa had chafed our nerves no less violently than the towline. We tried to have a rational discussion about our situation, but within moments it had broken down into an argument. Grant was exhausted and wanted to leave immediately in the morning. Nigel didn't want to budge until we had definitely heard that the message had been broadcast that we were at the atoll. "To hell with it!" Grant said. "We've done enough! Let's get the hell out of here!"

With a lump rising on his head, Nigel smashed his fist down on the table. "If they tow us out of here in the morning, I'm bloody swimming to shore!" Everything had gone from sour to rancid. We had failed, we had been manipulated, we had been spun around in circles, we had been completely rubbished and then rubbished again. When everybody had finally calmed down, we settled on a weak compromise: we would present the French with a note in the morning informing them that we were leaving under protest. We collapsed into our bunks then, sullen, tense and angry.

Floodlights on the shore swept us repeatedly, great bursts of white light that would have made sleep almost impossible under any circumstances. Now it added a nightmarish quality to my unstoppable flow of morbid thoughts. Damn, damn, we had blown it! We had done everything wrong! The images of the past few weeks jangled and clattered through my head, and it seemed like the bow of the minesweeper was coming down on us again, down on us again, down on us again, chopping us into twitching pieces, and all that effort, all that time, all that struggle had somehow been taken and spread like confetti in the wind. The admiral had looked so smug, so certain, the tests were going ahead, we were being thrown out on our ear like beggars or bums. What had happened? How had the whole thing been turned upside down? Where had we lost the initiative? I wished to God that my mind could just slow down, turn off, but the floodlight kept exploding through the porthole, and my thoughts would not stop racing.

Finally, at 0400 hours, I dragged myself to the saloon table and started trying to compose a letter to Admiral Claverie protesting our forced departure. I struggled with it for an hour, but was unable to get together a single comprehensible paragraph. My brain had never felt quite so scattered. So this is how it ends, I thought, over and over again, not with a bang but a whimper, this is how it ends, this is how it ends, not with a bang but a whimper, whimper, whimper . . . I had never felt so helpless in my life.

Nigel finally got up and I abandoned my attempt to write a note. Instead, we decided we would refuse to accept a rope from a tugboat and would motor across the lagoon to *La Paimpolaise*. Using the walkie-talkie we still had on board, we would speak to Captain Rochebrochard and if we could not get a definite answer on whether a message had been broadcast or not, we would refuse to leave Mururoa.

I woke Grant and broke the news, explaining that I was doing it because of the danger we might face on the high seas in a boat whose soundness was untested.

It was a dreary overcast morning. Through the wet dawn light we could see a tug coming toward us. Dragging ourselves up on deck we braced ourselves for one last struggle. Around the harbour and in every porthole, I could see faces watching to see what would happen. I took the helm while Nigel started the engine. As the tug approached, a man stood on deck, ready to throw a towline. I waved him off. Immediately, I could see a look of consternation on the faces of the tug crew. I slipped *Vega* into forward and eased the tension on the chain that held us to the buoy while Nigel and Grant cast off. Then we slowly motored into the wind toward *La Paimpolaise*.

The tug moved quickly toward us, then hesitated as we wormed our way past the *Garonne* and another ship. I was certain that the tug crew was calling for instructions. As we slid past *La Paimpolaise*, I called Captain Rochebrochard on the walkie-talkie.

"When are you going to radio out our position?"

The voice that squawked back at me said:

"The admiral told me last night that a news release has been sent to Radio Tahiti and you should hear it today."

"We have not heard this yet, so we will only leave under protest, and only if you enter this in your log."

"I will do so immediately."

I nodded to Nigel then and Nigel signalled at the tug to close in so we could accept a towline. While it was being made fast on our bollard, we raised our ragged Greenpeace flag, green and yellow, with the peace and ecology signs.

As we were towed past *De Grasse*, I could see her deck lined with sailors. It was only 0600 hours, but it appeared that the entire harbour was awake. There were a few tentative waves from the deck of the command cruiser, then more, until finally everyone seemed to be waving openly to us. From somewhere on the cruiser, the sound came of a bugle blowing a salute that echoed across the lagoon. An astonished expression crossed Nigel's face.

"What does it mean?" I asked.

"I don't know what it means in the French navy," he answered, obviously taken aback, "but in the British it's an honorary salute only for very high dignitaries, kings and queens and heads of state."

By then we were moving at six knots, and *De Grasse* and Mururoa were falling rapidly aft. We passed the dead flat table of ground zero. And then, to our amazement, saw that *De*

Grasse was in motion, coming out after us. The vast ship quickly caught up and passed on our port side. The crew were still crowded on the decks, waving. After *De Grasse* had passed, *La Paimpolaise* came by and blew another salute. Then came *Medoc*, a four-hundred-foot troop ship, and not only was her crew waving, they were cheering. Just as we were approaching the mouth of the reef, the last ship slipped by. It was our old foe, *Hippopotame*. Her crew did not wave.

By then, the sun had broken through the early haze, and we could see *La Paimpolaise*, waiting to escort us outward. At 0750 hours, we let the towline go, hoisted our sails and set a course for Rarotonga. Mururoa was soon a vague smudge on the great line where the sky met the sea.

The ten-day voyage to Rarotonga was much like being in orbit between moon and earth: we were falling through a void. *Vega* had the atmosphere of a small floating museum. Her crew moved listlessly about like caretakers toward the end of a long shift. There was a dull sense of recuperation, such as you might feel in a hospital. There were occasional moments when it felt good, in a clear but emptied way, to be moving across the boundless Pacific under the great axis of cloudheads, with the shadows of the rigging sweeping back and forth across the deck, small rainbows flickering in the spray that came off the tops of the waves. And to feel good for even a few moments was luxury enough. Mostly, we did not feel very good at all. The feeling of failure lay like a deep bruise in our minds. There was no point in even talking about it, no point in trying to analyse what should have been done and when. Our strength had been that we had proven ourselves to be good sailors. As politicians, we were flops. Grant was perhaps more philosophical about the whole mess. It was not long before he was back to making jokes about a raft-full of Swedish blondes appearing just ahead, although his humour was strangely blunted, as though he, too, had lost some vital part of his sense of himself. Nigel and I were of a different nature, and it was a competitive nature. That might have been the thing that most sustained us during the long vigil at Mururoa, that got us out there in the first place. But it also meant that the sense of having lost our battle was that much harder to bear.

On the long voyage outward, we had speculated by the hour what would happen when we arrived. Now, during the retreat to Rarotonga, we did not bother to speculate very much. We had a pretty good inkling of what to expect. The radio broadcast that Admiral Claverie promised had, indeed, gone out. We had picked it up first on Radio Australia and later on the New Zealand Broadcasting Corporation, and it stated simply that a faulty manœuvre on our part had led to us crashing into a mine-sweeper, and that the French had generously responded to our plea for help, and that the crew of *Greenpeace III* had joined the admiral of the nuclear fleet for wine and lunch under swaying palms. A note of humorous contempt had crept into the announcer's voice: wasn't it all such a lark?

So we knew we would be treated as bumbling fools, if not outright frauds, when we got back. There was, of course, no mention of the fact that *La Paimpolaise* had abandoned us one thousand miles out from Rarotonga, even though *Vega* was taking over a hundred gallons of water a day because of hull-fracture and cracked planks that the oh-so-generous French navy had neglected to fix. Nor did it mention that permission had been refused to re-enter Mururoa or, for that matter, to head into Tahiti for further emergency repairs. Captain Roche-brochard had simply shrugged. His orders were to leave us there, in the middle of the ocean, having to pump two hundred and fifty strokes a day just to remain afloat, and if *Vega* broke up before we reached Rarotonga, well, *c'est la vie*. And, of course, there was no reference at all to the various attempts by *La Bayonnaise*, *Hippopotame*, *De Grasse* and *La Paimpolaise* virtually to run us down in international waters in violation of every known rule of navigation. Incredibly, the French version of what happened seemed to have been generally accepted.

The attention of the media had now shifted to another protest boat which had been launched July 2 from New Zealand.

"A bit late," commented Nigel sourly.

The boat was a fifty-foot trawler and it carried a six-man crew. Its name was *Boy Roel* and its voyage had been organized by a group called Peace Media Research Project. With the best will in the world, we did not see how a small fuel-powered trawler could possibly hope to make it across the three-thousand miles of ocean to Mururoa. It sounded as though the press corps was wondering too. Two other boats, a thirty-seven-foot sloop called *Tamure* and a forty-one-foot cutter called *Magic Isle* were also frantically being prepared for protest voyages. Large demonstrations had been held against French testing, there were all the usual threats of breaks in diplomatic relations, there had been United Nations resolutions against nuclear tests, France had been wrist-slapped at the big enviromental conference in Stockholm, dock-workers in New Zealand and Australia were refusing to service French ships and planes, but, somehow, emerging from the reality of Mururoa, I could feel little enthusiasm for any of it. I had no sense of a world-wide wave of anger rising up against France. It was impossible to believe that any sort of that activity so far away was going to have any effect on the magnificently isolated fortress of Mururoa. Bitterly, I thought: If they can get away with their lies about *Vega*, they can get away with anything, including the bombs.

At that point, pumping furiously to keep our battered boat afloat as she limped toward Rarotonga, I did not have much of a grasp of the sweep of history, nor did I have much more of a perspective than a man who has been in an isolation tank for over two months, with only a brief visit to a tropical prison before being tossed back into isolation, unable to communicate even once with anybody except his captors. The total effect was to leave the three of us staring vacantly at the waves, casting the occasional glare at the radio and a frequent nervous glance at the sky for fear that a storm might engulf us before we could make it to port.

We reached Rarotonga on the fifteenth of July, 1972.

We were flat broke. I called Richard Northey of the Campaign for Nuclear Disarmament in Auckland; understandably the voice at the other end was aloof, unfriendly. Northey and his associates had seen a picture in the papers of Nigel and me chatting pleasantly with the arch nuclear warrior, Admiral Claverie, during the now-famous luncheon under the palms, and I realized immediately that in the eyes of the ban-the-bomb people, I might as well have sold out completely to the enemy. When I tried phoning Ann-Marie, it was to find that there was a chill in her voice too, and her mother, when she heard who it was, refused to speak to me any further. In desperation, I phoned Ben Metcalfe of the Greenpeace Foundation in Vancouver and explained that we needed fifteen hundred dollars.

"No problem," Metcalfe told me.

A day passed. Two days. Our only contact with the outside world was an alcoholic reporter from New Zealand who kept demanding that we give him our photographs so he could write "the big story". I was not in a mood to trust reporters any longer, so I refused. The journalist said: "I can make you or break you y'know." That sounded so close to the truth that it was all I could do to stop Nigel from throwing a punch. The reporter went to his typewriter in a sulk and wrote a story saying: "The expedition was successful in that the yacht proved a source of irritation to the French, but it seems just a trifle disappointing that a preoccupation with financial rewards should have clouded the success." He hinted broadly that I was "in it for the bread".

After three days, still penniless, I phoned my brother in Vancouver and asked him to phone Metcalfe about the money. A call came back a short time later. My brother had phoned and had been assured it was on its way. Another day passed. Still no money. I phoned Metcalfe himself, and this time I was told that, unfortunately, there was no money after all. I had been down and out before, but this was a new experience – to be trapped on an island in the middle of the South Pacific without even any money to provision the boat to leave, and being accused in the midst of it of "having a preoccupation with financial rewards", while being betrayed by the organization that had promised to "back him all the way". I had not expected a hero's welcome, but neither had I quite expected this.

There was only one thing left to do. We took our twelve-hundred-dollar Ham radio, the one which had used up so much of the batteries and had proven useless, and sold it to a local radio operator for seven hundred dollars.

The three of us sat down that night and tried to work out a rational plan of action. The truth was, none of us knew what to do.

Going directly to New Zealand seemed pointless. The picture of what was going on there was clear enough. Our credibility had been badly damaged, there was division within the anti-nuclear movement, and with the launching of *Boy Roel* and the two other boats that were being readied, this was no time to be trying to raise money to mount a legal action against France over the ramming of a sailboat in international waters. I had no doubt in my mind that I wanted to take the French military to court. The only question was how. As an initial step, I guessed that I would have to go to Canada, take my case to the Canadian government, and go from there. Nigel and Grant agreed to stay with the boat and try to get it to New Zealand as soon as I could get some money to them.

The next day, I was on a plane, heading for the home town I had not seen for fifteen years.

Vancouver had changed. Where once a heavily-tried peninsula covered with wooden houses had jutted out into a bay at least as large as Mururoa lagoon, now a vast cluster of creamy pastel apartment blocks rose against the mountains to the north. It was home to a million people, most of whom had moved there since I left. The new airport was much like every other new airport in the world. Despite the addition of extra freeways and glass skyscrapers downtown, the place still had that Sleepy Hollow quality I remembered so well. Still, it was hard at moments not to imagine that I left in one era and returned in another. The only people who were there to greet me were my mother and father and a lone female reporter, who asked a few questions, then wrote a piece that appeared on the back page of one of the local dailies. I quickly learned that the two aspects of the voyage to the French nuclear test zone which had been picked up by the local papers had been the charge of smuggling watches and that damnable lunch under the palms.

I wanted to arrange a meeting with the directors of the Greenpeace Foundation, whom I had never met, to give them a full report on what had happened during the voyage and get some legal direction from them. The only Greenpeace person I knew was Ben Metcalfe, and Metcalfe was out of town. Seeing that I was probably going to be on my own hook, I arranged a meeting with an international lawyer who was a past dean of the University of British Columbia. The lawyer shook his head, saying that it was almost impossible to sue the Government of France or its navy, nor was there much chance of successfully bringing a suit against Captain Rochebrochard. The best procedure was to present my case to the secretary of state for external affairs, the Honourable Mitchell Sharp, the very same politician who had repeatedly assured both the Canadian House of Commons and the press that, first, *Greenpeace III* was not a Canadian boat, then that it was flying a Peruvian flag, and then that boat and crew had left the test zone area long before the first bomb went off. The Honourable Mitchell Sharp had even blithely repeated the French story that we had crashed into a minesweeper. And this man, of all people in Canada, was the one to whom I would now have to appeal for help. There was no other avenue.

I had the feeling I was at the bottom of a very deep mineshaft and none of the elevators was working.

Some homing instinct had told me, however erroneously, that by coming back to Vancouver, I would at least be on familiar ground, that I would have friends and family, that people would at least know me as a native son, that there would be support and acceptance. There would be, if nothing else, the old tribal bond. I had, indeed, been going back to my tribe, only to discover that while my family was still there, and that they loved me and believed what I said, scarcely anyone else did, and the tribe was as small as the city was large. Smaller than I could have dreamed. It seemed to consist of my brother, Drew, our parents, a couple of old friends, and that was it. A small circle to draw against a hostile world.

I had no awareness then that there were thousands out there who had fastened on to what we had been doing as one of their few human hopes that the apocalypse might not arrive on their doorstep.

It had, after all, been fifteen years since I'd spent any time with my old friends. Now I discovered that fifteen years could be fifteen lifetimes. My friends had continued along the same track I had been following until the derailment caused by the explosion at Bear Valley and my eventual flight to the South Pacific. While I was not conscious of having "changed", I had in fact been living an existence since then that was at the opposite pole from the rat-race. It had put me so far outside the influence of North American business and politics that the concerns which now still obsessed my friends had long since faded into the back of my mind like a bad dream. After the first rush of shoulder-slapping and exchanges of "You sonofabitch, how are ya?" the conversations quickly slid off in directions that made them seem like another language. A socialist government had been elected in the province. This was a subject that would trigger a stream of passionate invective. I found myself not having much to contribute. From the perspective of the deep Pacific, socialism and capitalism both seemed to amount to smudges of yellowish smog on the horizon. And then, of course, there were the great issues of the day – taxes, Women's Lib, hippies, sex, money and the stock exchange. Mururoa? Yeh, well, that must have been something, all right, you old bugger, you've really been getting around, eh? Still the same old shit-disturber! And that was about it. Nuclear testing was either something happening on the other side of the planet, or it was simply a non-topic. It quickly became evident to me that anything happening outside of British Columbia was pretty much a non-topic, especially such odd subjects as rights in international waters. What the hell did that have to do with anything anyway?

I began to feel an almost breathtaking loneliness.

Repeated efforts to get Ben Metcalfe to call together the directors of the Greenpeace Foundation failed. It was not until six weeks after my return that a woman approached me in a supermarket. "Are you David McTaggart? I thought so! Why haven't you gotten hold of us?" She turned out to be one of the people who had organized the first Greenpeace expedition. It was then that I learned that not only did the Greenpeace Foundation not have a board of directors, it had collapsed as an organization altogether, its members had gone off in a variety of different directions, and none of the original organizers – who were scattered around town – had been advised that I was trying to get hold of them.

A small meeting was arranged, and although I did not know it at the time, the meeting itself was symptomatic of the division which had racked the Greenpeace Foundation from the time of its emergence as an environmental group less than two years before. Only six people showed up – three middle-aged couples, all of them expatriate Americans. They in fact represented only one of the many factions into which the organization had fragmented during its brief existence. It did not take me long to realize that these six people had no stomach for a protracted legal battle against France. When I asked them if they had any intention of making good on Metcalfe's pledge to support me all the way, the answer I got was that Greenpeace was an "action" group and they did not see the value of a long boring court case.

My only other contact with the remnants of Greenpeace came when Ben Metcalfe called to ask me to sign a contract which would allow Metcalfe to write a book about the voyage. In exchange, I would be given three thousand dollars. I said: "Shit, Ben, you gotta be kidding." And hung up. So this was the ecology movement. The opinion of my old buddies about environmentalists was beginning to have a ring to it.

The loneliness deepened.

I had had to borrow two hundred dollars from my brother to get money down to Rarotonga so that Nigel could begin the delicate business of shepherding *Vega* back to New Zealand. Grant's parents had sent him money to get home to Australia. I wanted badly to send for Ann-Marie, but I had no money for her fare, and there was another problem. It had not taken me long to discover that the freedom I had tasted in the South Seas was something I could not so easily enjoy back on the old home turf. The fact that I had been three times divorced was considered bad enough, but I was forty years old now, and neither my family nor few remaining friends were ready to accept the reality that my lady friend was twenty years my junior. A revolution in morality and sexual ethics might well be sweeping through the big cities of the industrial world, but Vancouver was not yet a big city. It was, if anything, Victorian. And at the other end, Ann-Marie's parents were no less unhappy about the idea of their daughter leaving to live on the other side of the world with a man of my age.

I felt about as alone as I had ever felt.

Taking stock of the situation, I could see that I had virtually nothing to go on. I had no money at all and since money is power, that meant simply that I was not just penniless, I was powerless. The Greenpeace Foundation, such as it was, had lost interest in me, which meant that I had no organizational muscle behind me either. None of my friends showed any particular interest in the case, no understanding of the issue, and if they displayed any feelings about it, it was largely embarrassment that I should have got involved in such a pinko hippie trip in the first place. My first tentative approach to seek action from the Canadian government had taken the form of a telegram my brother, father and I had amateurishly put together a few nights after my arrival, describing what had happened at Mururoa and ending with the plea: "Please advise me how to seek redress." It had been sent to the minister of external affairs. The answer that came back was from an aide, explaining that the minister himself was out of town. It noted that the French account of the incident was "somewhat different from yours", and vaguely promised that when the minister returned to his office in a few weeks, "we shall be communicating with you further". I could see that even if the wheel could be turned at all, there was no way it could be turned quickly. The tone of scepticism in the communication was obvious. Had I known that four and a half years of stalling on the part of the Canadian government lay ahead, I might have given up then and there. But I did not know this. All I knew was that I was at the foot of an enormous mountain. In my mind, I saw again that knowing glint in Admiral Claverie's eyes. No wonder the old man had seemed so supremely confident. He must have known all along what the chances were against me ever settling the score. The wonder was that the old fox hadn't laughed in my face.

219

And now I remembered something else, the thing my friend David Exel had said in Auckland:

The politics of this issue is a dragon with many heads. It could destroy you. The press'll cut you into little pieces. You are going to have some powerful enemies. You'll be discredited, abused and abandoned.

Maybe I should have listened.

After three disillusioning weeks in Vancouver, I badly needed to get away and do some thinking on my own. Gathering up my logs and charts and tapes and notebooks, I went with my brother's family up the coast to Buccaneer Bay, a bite in Thormanby Island, just off the coast of mainland British Columbia. There, my family had a summer camp which was like a second home to me. It had been there, as a child, that I had dreamed of sailing out across the sea. Now I was back from the faraway places and faced with a situation that none of my childhood fantasies had anticipated.

I had only been there a few days, trying to find some way to reassemble the pieces of my life, when the rumours began to fly among the summer residents that the prime minister of Canada was on his way to the bay. Looking out through the window over my desk, I saw a large white yacht – perhaps a hundred feet – gliding across the calm blue water. Several adults were watching from their cottages, but only the children made any move. Unrestrained, they piled into rowboats, dinghies and powerboats, and swarmed out to greet their famous visitor. I could see my brother's daughters among them. When they got back to land, one of the girls ran into the cabin and said with innocent directness:

"Uncle David, aren't you going to see him about *Greenpeace III*?"

Well, I asked myself, why not? I felt restrained, partially because I knew all the people around the bay, and I had no wish to disturb the festive mood that had developed, and partially because, well . . . Maybe it was a bit too much like begging. I didn't know. Glumly, I went back to my desk, sifting through the material which was the basis of my case against France, if I ever got to present the case anywhere. Each time I looked up through the window, the white yacht was sitting there.

Early the next morning, I borrowed a tar-stained dinghy and rowed slowly and self-consciously across the bay. I was barefoot, wearing only a weathered pair of jeans. I stopped about fifty yards from the yacht and circled about. Through the portholes, I could see that breakfast was being served. I waited.

Finally, two girls emerged on deck, climbed down the steps into a large rowboat, and headed for a nearby stretch of water. I followed them ashore. Then, as casually as I could, I explained that I was the skipper of the boat that had gone into French Polynesia to protest nuclear tests, and that I wondered if I could have a word with the prime minister about it. The girls explained they were leaving soon, but they would ask. They returned to the yacht.

I hung back about twenty yards, feeling more self-conscious than ever, waiting for some sign that it was all right to approach. Then Pierre Elliott Trudeau and his wife emerged on the deck, with two powerful-looking young men behind them. Trudeau, attired in yachting clothes, was much shorter than I had expected and his blue eyes had a humorous look to them that gave me the feeling that the man wasn't prepared to take anything too seriously.

It was evidently all right to proceed, so I rowed into the shade beside the yacht and sat in the dinghy holding onto the stair rail, looking up at them.

"Yes, Mr McTaggart, what can I do for you?" Trudeau asked.

As briefly as I could, I told him what had happened on the voyage, finishing with a description of the lack of cooperation I'd had from Ottawa.

"I am not very sympathetic to the Greenpeace Foundation," Trudeau said.

"I'm discussing my case, not theirs. I'm a Canadian citizen whose yacht was rammed by the French navy in international waters and all I'm requesting is the defence of my rights as an individual Canadian."

Trudeau's response was to repeat the stories that external affairs minister Mitchell Sharp had told in the House of Commons.

"Were you not, in truth, flying a Peruvian flag?" he asked.

"Absolutely not. That's completely untrue. I was flying the Canadian flag."

Trudeau's face was impassive, but he did not argue. Instead, he launched into a lengthy discussion of the international complications and problems involved in the case. I found myself being drawn in by the man's obviously extended grasp of legal complexities. Trudeau had for years been dazzling audiences with his eloquence. There could be no doubt he was a brilliant speaker. What impressed me, however, was not so much what Trudeau was saying – I sensed that beneath the easy play of ideas there was not much that touched on the substantial reality of the bow of *La Paimpolaise* crashing down – but the physical condition of the man. I knew him to be over fifty years old, yet his arms were sinewy, and there were tight well-conditioned muscles under his T-shirt. He had an aura of Napoleonic self-confidence. He was supple, thoroughly at ease and supremely certain. He made no move to invite me on board, and remained on the deck, as though on a platform, speaking down to a barefoot audience of one.

To my amazement, the discussion lasted for forty minutes. Trudeau had been something of an adventurer in his time and seemed interested – in a veiled fashion – in the voyage. But, finally, when I said:

"Look, all I want to know is whether the Canadian government is going to help me or not."

Trudeau shrugged and made an open gesture with his hands.

"Mr McTaggart, do you expect us to go to war over your boat?"

"No, naturally, I don't expect a *war* over my yacht, I just want the government to stand up for me because I'm a Canadian citizen!"

Trudeau's lower lip protruded and he shrugged again. Obviously there was nothing more to be said. The interview was over.

"Well, thanks for your time," I said.

Rowing back across the bay, I tried to sift through what the prime minister had said. It was clear that he hadn't been very well-informed about the situation and that he did not take it seriously. There had been an undercurrent of vast amusement in his bearing, a sort of "boys-will-be-boys" attitude. And while he had been surprisingly open – I would not have accused him of arrogance – there had been the air of a professor delivering a lecture to a slightly dull student.

During the entire discussion, his wife had not said a single word.

Well, I had had my chance to present my case to the head of the government of Canada. So much for the government of Canada. It could not be more clear that I could expect no help from that quarter.

The winter rains came.

Vega was almost lost in a hurricane on the last leg of her journey to New Zealand. A story appeared that Grant Davidson had been taken into hospital to be treated for possible radiation sickness; promptly my family insisted that I undergo a checkup myself. In both cases, we were pronounced fit, but it was a grim reminder that we had in fact been close to two atomic bomb blasts. When Nigel finally got the boat safely to Auckland, it was promptly pounced on by customs officials, who discovered that the generator which had been donated had been smuggled into the country a year before. Ann-Marie's parents' home had been burst into by cops claiming they were looking for more smuggled watches.

The second, third and fourth New Zealand protest vessels had all either failed to reach their objective or had been called back. *Boy Roel* was listed as missing at sea for several weeks before it drifted to safety at a South Pacific island, its engines dead. *Tamure* made it as far as Rarotonga. *Magic Isle* continued on to Tahiti after it was announced that the French had completed their 1972 test programme. The press savagely attacked the whole anti-nuclear movement in both Australia and New Zealand.

I received a series of telegrams from the Honourable Mitchell Sharp telling me first that "there is little the government can legally do to assist you in your pursuit of any claims you may have as a result of this incident", then that "it is my hope we will be in position to give you a more definite response in the near future", and, finally, that "the French authorities have not reacted in any way to your account of the incident".

My relations with my old friends were deteriorating rapidly. Their wives grew visibly nervous about them spending any time with a drop-out, especially one who was involved in such a freaky cause.

On the invitation of a friend I met briefly on the street, I stopped in one day at the Vancouver Lawn and Tennis Club, where I had won more awards than any other member. But I no longer had a membership, and no one would talk to me. For the people on the Right, I had become too damned weird. The few people I met on the Left were not much more communicative. For them, I was too damned straight. I had become more than just an outcast – I had become a pariah.

The loneliness now had become unendurable.

I retreated to Buccaneer Bay, where I found at least one person who enjoyed my company, an eighty-eight-year-old caretaker who had sailed all over the world, who could remember jumping ship in at least thirty different ports, and who had found his way into Canada by buying a drunken sailor's passport which gave him the name he now used. It was this same old man to whom I had listened as a child to stories of the sea which had stirred my imagination and implanted the urge to get out there on the waves. Now, as though I had come full circle, I was back in Buccaneer Bay, and only the old man believed my story, only the old man chuckled about it. The rest of the residents of the area shunned me, vaguely embarrassed by my presence.

To clear my mind, I sawed wood for the fireplace and went fishing. I assembled the tapes and logs into order, hoping that in the process of assembling the pieces, some direction might emerge. None did.

And the rains came down. And came down. And came down.

The outlines of the tops of the pines were shadows. The mountains vanished in mist. The ocean became a sullen sluggish slate of grey, pocked by raindrops. An enormous and seemingly endless HISSSSS filled the air. The pine-cones all went soft. Ferns staggered under the weight of the water pouring down. The mud became gumbo. The beach was cold and empty. It seemed to me at moments that I must surely have come to the end of my life. After almost six years in the South Pacific and many more than that in California, I had forgotten just how dismal the West Coast of Canada is in the winter, had forgotten that locally this fogbound Land's End is known as the raincoast, and had forgotten how the world beyond thirty or forty feet becomes a thing half-erased, with the ground giving off steam and dampness penetrating any number of layers or clothes, and a cold slippery slick covering everything except the sand, which became as hard-packed as it was cold.

It was mid-morning – or so my watch said – on one of these grey days with sleet-laced rain hissing on the bay, when I saw a burning fish boat being towed from around the shadows of the rocks. There were three boats involved – the one that was burning, the one that was towing, and a third, on the deck of which someone was standing with a water hose aiming a thin, ineffectual trickle of water into the flames. This was the most exciting thing that had happened since I left Vancouver. Quickly I jumped into the rowboat to go out to watch from up close. The three boats stopped in the middle of the bay and sat there while the fire licked at the forecastle and crept along the decks.

There did not seem to be much sense of panic. A man was standing idly on the deck of the boat that had been doing the towing, watching.

"Hey!" I yelled out of the rain. "Haven't you got a salt-water hose? Anything's better than that garden hose your friend is using."

"Oh yeh, I suppose," the man replied slowly.

It did not take me too long to figure out what I was witnessing. As the fish stocks fell along the West Coast due to

Russian and Japanese overfishing, more and more fishermen were being driven out of business. It had become not uncommon for boats to mysteriously burn or sink with the result that owners could collect hefty sums of insurance money. Neither did it take too long for the man on the boat to figure out that here was a witness who might say something unfortunate to an investigator for an insurance company. A new effort was made, using salt-water hoses, to put the fire out. I rowed back to my cabin.

As soon as the fishermen thought I was out of sight, they towed the smouldering vessel toward the shore and let it go up on the rocks. They turned off the hoses and chugged away out of the bay.

The moment they were gone, I was out of my cabin and down on the beach, trying to calculate how much equipment there was on board that could be salvaged. By this time, fire was belching skyward again. The fishermen had made sure they didn't put the fire out too much. The fire burned for close to ten hours until all that remained was a charred hulk, very little except ribs still standing above the water line.

I wasted no time. Borrowing a hack saw and ten brand-new blades from the old caretaker, I waded out into the freezing water. What I was interested in was the huge bronze propeller, with a shaft made of a very special kind of stainless steel. I didn't know how much I could get for it, but I did know I needed money desperately. The bills were starting to come in for the telegrams to the Minister for External Affairs and the food was running out.

Not waiting for the tide to go out completely, I clambered behind the boat, up to my chest in water, and started sawing at the propeller underwater. The Royal Canadian Mounted Police might arrive at any moment. I cinched ropes as tightly as I could so that when the massive object finally came loose, it would not just crash into the water where I couldn't possibly lift it.

Eight hours and all ten hacksaw blades later, it finally came loose. Then I had the job of rolling logs down the beach so I could float her free. It took another two hours to fight the thing out from between the rocks. Using an almost sinking rowboat, I got it around the corner of the bay to a beach where I cut it loose in the sand at the high tide mark and covered it up. I was shuddering so badly I could hardly stand, but at least I had my buried treasure, and, eventually, I managed to sell it for three hundred and fifty dollars.

Back in Vancouver, I used some of that money to retain a lawyer to take my case against the navy of the republic of France.

During my exile at Buccaneer Bay, I had discovered that I could not make myself forget what had happened.

If that smacked of something as simple as positive thinking, it didn't matter. Two things stood out in my mind: the bomb and my boat. The two of them had somehow become related, as though they had been wed in the fierce embrace of the warship. The violence done to my old girl had been an extension of the violence that was the bomb itself. I could no longer think of the one without thinking of the other. They were locked together. In the moment of *Vega*'s deflowering, the bomb had reached out and struck at me. The issue had ceased to be abstract. It had ceased to be a matter of concepts. It had taken tangible form. In the shudder that went through the decks, I *felt* its presence. I could not forget it.

There was something else I could not forget. For a few days there in the stormy waters around Mururao, I had known that the tests were being delayed because we stood in the path of the fallout. It was not something I could talk about with my friends, or even my family, because it was completely outside the realm of their experience. It was not something I was sure I even wanted to try to put into words. But I had known then that as surely as men possessed the power to build the bomb, they possessed the power to stop it from being built and even, ultimately, to dismantle the bombs that already existed. There was nothing inevitable about the destruction of the world. And having *known* that, for however brief a time, it was not something I could lightly put away. Perhaps it was something I could not put away at all.

It seemed infuriatingly clear: if *Vega*'s case could be forced into the courts and proven, the French would be embarrassed, and the pressure against the weapon-makers at Mururoa could do nothing but increase. Why couldn't anyone see it?

Talking to the lawyer in Vancouver gave me the first flicker of hope I'd felt since getting back to Canada. The man, Jack Cunningham, was a staunch supporter of the Liberal government in Ottawa, but he was also an expert in marine law. I could scarcely believe it. He actually understood the significance of the case. He understood the rules of navigation. He understood the relationship that is supposed to exist between vessels under sail and those driven by engines. He understood immediately that whether it was called a ramming or a collision didn't matter, the manoevres of the French vessels had breached the provisions of the International Regulations for Preventing Collisions at Sea. Rule 20 of the Regulations specifically provides that "when a power-driven vessel and a sailing vessel are proceeding in such directions as to involve risk of collision ... the power-driven vessel shall keep out of the way of the sailing vessel".

"Yes," said Jack, settling back in his chair, "there has clearly been a violation here."

For a moment, I stared. I felt a bit like Robinson Crusoe finally having seen a footprint in the sand.

"So you agree I've got a case?"

"Oh yes. A very clear case."

"Well," I said, "maybe we could point this out to the government."

At last I had a toehold.

A toehold. That was all. If getting through to Mururoa had been a long tough journey, it seemed almost simple in retrospect compared to the problems of getting through to Ottawa. But with Jack Cunningham acting now as a navigator and sheets of paper for sails, I began to learn the art of tacking with an electronic wind. While I had been more or less adrift during my first months back in Canada, in mid-October I found myself beginning to move. I was invited down to Toronto to appear on a national television show. Until then, I had not realized that so long as I remained in British Columbia, the government in Ottawa could easily afford to ignore me. The great voting blocs, the wealth and the media centres in the country were concentrated in Eastern Canada. From Vancouver, I could set nothing in motion. The parochial local press had already buried me, and federal politicians felt perfectly safe in looking the other way.

The programme was called W5 and it had one of the largest viewing audiences in the country. The reporter who interviewed me was a hard-bitten veteran named Ken Lafoli. As part of the format, Lafoli cabled external affairs minister Mitchell Sharp to ask whether he would appear on the programme. Mr Sharp declined. But the knowledge that I was about to appear on national television had a definite impact on the mandarins in Ottawa. The day before I was scheduled to appear, reporter Lafoli got a phone call from the department of external affairs asking if he had seen the wire to me advising me that the Canadian government would take action on my behalf. I had not received any such wire – it was all news to me. When the reporter pressed the external affairs aide for the date of this mysterious document, a hesitant voice replied, "October nineteenth". It just happened to be October 19 that day.

To me, the lesson was clear enough. The practice of government in Canada is based squarely on expediency, not principle. Threatened with adverse publicity, the government would move, although only one short step at a time. If it was to move another short step, it had to be prodded with an electric rod. And prodded again. And prodded again. Initially, I had felt frustration, confusion and despair in my dealing with the government. Now I felt vaguely disgusted. Later, that feeling would evolve into a thorough-going contempt. One of the Toronto television reporters made an attempt to explain to me how it works: "It's like the joke about the guy who sees the man smashing his mule on the head with a sledgehammer, and he says, 'Hey, that's no way to train a mule', and the other guy puts down his sledgehammer and looks at him and says, 'If you're gonna train a mule, you gotta get his attention first!'"

The joke proved to be not so much of an exaggeration as I first thought.

Getting back to Vancouver, I found a telegram waiting for me from the Honourable Mitchell Sharp, saying: "As you are aware, the government of Canada shares completely your concern about the testing of nuclear weapons by any state in any environment and has missed no opportunity to express this concern publicly and internationally, in particular to the French authorities . . . As for your claim against the French I have asked my officials to give careful consideration to your case to determine if some form of assistance might be possible. As you perhaps know it is necessary for an individual claimant to exhaust the available legal remedies and to show a denial of justice before a government can consider any espousal of his claim. However, we appreciate that the circumstances in your case are unusual and for this reason we are prepared to use our 'good offices' with the French government in making inquiries on your behalf . . ."

The toehold now looked as though it might have become a foothold.

But along with the wire from Ottawa, another message arrived. The marine survey on *Vega* had been completed in New Zealand. Damage was estimated at thirteen thousand dollars. If that meant nothing else, it meant I was a long way from being able to go sailing again.

My expedition to Toronto had been enlightening in more respects than one. While there, I had encountered Farley Mowat, the naturalist and author. Over several drinks, I had related my story, and the bearded writer had become increasingly excited. "Write it!" he said. "Write it! Don't worry about a publisher, I'll take care of that." It made sense, I told myself. I had already come to realize that if I was going to press my case, I needed some sort of documented account of what had happened, and I also badly needed money, not only to repair *Vega* but to cover the mounting telegraph and telephone bills, lawyers' fees and surveyors' costs.

I went back up to Buccaneer Bay, determined to write it all down. But the loneliness of the empty beaches and the endless rain had become oppressive. I wrote to Ann-Marie, asking her to join me. Paying for her fare with her own money, she flew over in early November.

The only place I could think of to take her was to a lodge on Vancouver Island owned by an old friend who approved of what I had done and couldn't have cared less about my private life. It was curious, I mused, how my circle of friends had now come down to two old pirates, one of whom, the caretaker at Buccaneer Bay, had been on the run from the law most of his life, and the other of whom, Jerry Hill, owner of the lodge to which Ann-Marie and I now retreated, had been a rum-runner in his youth, and had survived prisoner-of-war camps in the first world war by chewing on bones – as though it was only the outlaws and toughened old survivors who could relate to me any longer. Very curious. When I thought about it, I realized that I had always had an affinity with old loners, whether mountainmen or seadogs, and I guessed that there was something in the wilderness and independence that was a mirror of something inside myself. I had never liked teams, and my marriages – efforts at domestication – had collapsed repeatedly. The flinty old men who had never allowed themselves to become dependent on any person or any organization, who stood off to the side, amused, supremely indifferent to the little rules that bound the others as surely as ants to an antheap – I supposed that if I had any heroes, it would be those old outlaws, and they were so rare that it meant I did not have many heroes at all.

I had met Ann-Marie on my own at the airport. We were both nervous. It was the first time she had been outside New Zealand. Coming to "America" was a giant step in itself, and she had realized that our relationship was going to be different from the easy existence we had known when I used to take her cruising among the islands around New Zealand. That was before the shadow of Mururoa had fallen across our path. She did not know whether the experience had embittered me. She also knew that if our love went sour on the rocks of this new existence, she could not simply turn around and go home. After graduating, she had had to work to save the money for the flight. In Canada, with no work permit, she could not get work and I had no funds either.

We drove straight from the airport to a ferry and across to Vancouver Island. Our new home was a crude cabin with plank walls through which the wind blew constantly. The only source of heat was a pot-bellied stove that gave out terrific heat if we sat next to it, but did almost nothing for the rest of the cabin. We bedded down in a pile of sleeping bags and in the morning there would be ice on the water in the sink and frost on the inside of the windows. This was not the "America" she had seen in films and magazines. Every morning, Ann-Marie would find herself moving along the beach, looking for driftwood. Just to keep us warm, she would have to spend most of the day gathering wood, her breath turning into unfamiliar puffs of steam, snow falling silently on the grey water. There was, of course, no phone, and not even a typewriter. I didn't know how to type, so I wrote with a ballpoint pen in a slanting script that was often close to unreadable.

From time to time, letters with official stamps on them would arrive from members of parliament, from the external affairs department, from various lawyers, or telexes from France. We made jokes about our "office", comparing it to the offices from which the politicians were writing. Ann-Marie began to feel increasingly helpless. It seemed clear to her that we were being screwed from all sides. The French were sticking to their story that *Vega* had caused the collision, and the bureaucrats in Ottawa were dragging their heels.

In mid-November, I flew to Toronto again to appear on another national television show. The external affairs department suddenly became interested in my case again. Just four hours before I appeared on the show, I received a phone call from Ottawa advising me that the government was now going to use its "good offices" on my behalf and would even send a representative to Paris to talk the matter over with the French authorities.

While in Toronto, a journalist put me in touch with US Congressman Jonathan Bingham, who had made public statements demanding to know the extent of American involvement in the French atmospheric nuclear test programme. I told the congressman about the presence of the *Wheeling* at Mururoa during the time I had been there. The congressman acknowledged that this fitted reports he had received that US vessels and aircraft had been using the French tests to collect data and that there had been extensive coordination of activities – all of this in clear violation of the Nuclear Test Ban Treaty which the US had signed with Russia and Great Britain. I asked Congressman Bingham if there was anything more he intended to do about it.

"No," the congressman said. "I've made my statement. It's part of the public record, but I've been told to shut up."

I came back from Toronto feeling haunted. I had begun to realize that it was not just the French government I was up against, it was also the American government. And, about this time, I received a letter from the British high commission denying that England had been similarly involved, even though I had seen a plaque on the wall of the captain's quarters on board the *Garonne* while we were in Mururoa lagoon. The plaque had been a gift from the British navy ship *Sir Percivale*. It stated: "We all wish you the best of luck for your 1972 nuclear tests." The British high commission admitted that *Sir Percivale* had been in the vicinity of Mururoa, but added that its presence "did not signify British participation in any way". My innocent notion that international treaties were something to be honoured now fell away, leaving me feeling more hopeless and depressed than ever. The French, the Americans and the British were all in the nuclear bed together, with none of them admitting it even to their own people.

Ann-Marie shared my deepening hopelessness and cynicism.

Two more blows fell before Christmas. The publisher that Farley Mowat had promised wrote a letter saying that he was not interested in the manuscript. And France announced that it planned to detonate a hydrogen bomb of megaton strength at Mururoa in the summer of 1973.

It snowed heavily that Christmas, the first that Ann-Marie had spent away from home. We chopped a tree, lit it with candles, and exchanged presents. By agreement, we only bought each other presents that cost less than twenty-five cents.

It had been a bleak and frustrating winter. But as the days began to lengthen, Ann-Marie and I slowly began to notice that the new year was bringing with it some definite changes. The ripple that *Vega* had set in motion turned into a wave.

In New Zealand, the government was swept out of office to be replaced by a socialist party that had promised to fight the continuing French tests. The day after winning the election, the prime minister-elect, Norman Kirk, announced that he would send a frigate into the test zone to register New Zealand's protest. A short time later, the Australian government also fell before a socialist opposition that promised to go before the International Court of Justice to ask for an injunction restraining France from further testing in the South Pacific. At the United Nations, the General Assembly's main political committee voted 106 to 4 in favour of a call for a ban on nuclear testing in the Pacific. In Mexico, the fifty-two million member International Confederation of Free Trade Unions voted to take strike action against the French ships, planes and industries throughout the world if the tests were not cancelled. *US News and World Report* was moved to observe that opposition to the French tests was "busting out all over". Nobel Prize laureate Dr Linus Pauling was widely quoted when he reminded the world that for every ten megaton nuclear bomb exploded in the atmosphere, some fifty thousand children would be born with gross mental and physical defects. In New Zealand, there were reports that a "peace fleet" was being organized to sail into the control zone at Mururoa. And towards the end of January, six months after my return to Canada, I received a letter from the Honourable Mitchell Sharp, saying, "You will appreciate that a case of this nature, involving as it does important issues of state responsibility and liability, may well require a further period of time before we may expect a definite response."

A few days later, in the House of Commons, Mr Sharp

announced that "Canada has been leading the world in trying to bring an end to nuclear testing".

I had left Canada fifteen years before, thinking at that time that it was one of the most boring places on earth. Now I was beginning to wonder if it had not evolved, in my absence, into one of the most insidiously evil. My interest in things nuclear had naturally deepened. I found myself reading more and more about bombs, reactors and plutonium, and the more I read, the more deeply I was shaken. With the development of its sophisticated CANDU nuclear reactor, Canada had quietly become one of the background nuclear powers. Canada had sold one of its reactors to India, and soon India was to fashion her own nuclear weapon, thereby destroying the balance of terror that had at least held the world's foremost powers from each other's throats since the second world war. Canada was now busily trying to sell these nuclear reactors to such countries as Argentina, South Korea and Pakistan. Canada's type of reactor produced more plutonium than any other. In a single year, it created a residue of fifty pounds of plutonium, enough to fashion three powerful atomic bombs. And yet at the same time Canada spoke piously in the world about the need for nuclear controls. Was this really the True North Strong and Free, whose anthem I had sung in school? My dealings with Ottawa had left me with a bad taste in my mouth at the discovery that expediency was the rule, but now I began to get a broader picture. What was involved was hundreds of billions of dollars, for Canada was moving steadily into a strong position to export uranium as well as reactors, and where all this stuff might go was anybody's guess. There were already five hundred nuclear reactors operating in the world. There were plans to build at least two thousand by the end of the century...

I had gone to Mururoa partly because I was a yachtsman who felt that his rights were being violated and also partly because I knew instinctively the threat that the Bomb represented. Now I began to have a vastly heightened sense of the desperation of our times. I had assumed my enemy to be the French navy, only to learn that the United States and Britain were part of the gang. Now my awareness broadened to include all the nuclear powers, and not only the ones with the bombs and the rockets, but also the quiet ones with the reactors that produced the material out of which the bombs were fashioned. A great weight settled over my mind at the thought of the conflict that seemed to lie ahead. No – I corrected myself. It didn't lie *ahead*. It was a catastrophe that was already happening all around, taking the form of weapons tests and the construction of reactors, with background radiation levels rising like a barometer. It might as well be a state of war. The effect was the same. It wasn't that the world might be poisoned by material that had been named after the Roman god of the underworld, rather it was that the world was already being poisoned. Plutonium was deadly in microscopic quantities. Soon there would be hundreds of tons of it on the surface of the planet – stuff that had never existed on earth before.

I had no sense of myself becoming "radicalized". If I was aware of a change having been wrought by my experience at Mururoa, I still thought of it largely in personal terms. *My* boat had been rammed. *My* crew had almost been run down. *My* reputation had been thrashed. But day by day, month by month, as I learned more and more about what my government was doing, about what the other governments were doing, my personal anger expanded into a wider, more generalized sense of outrage, not at what was being done to *me*, but at what was being *done*. Little by little, I was being transformed into one of those goddamn environmentalists so detested by all my old friends. I had learned the hard way to look behind the headlines and the printed statements by politicians, to doubt, to question, to wonder what was really going on, to challenge in my mind the announcements I read, to look for the secret motive behind the public utterances. I did not think of myself as becoming "politicized" either, yet I found myself watching the shifts in power in the world with a new alertness – aware now that a change of government in France, for instance, might have a decisive effect on what happened at Mururoa, that a change of government in New Zealand meant the difference between people like myself being thrown in jail and a navy frigate being sent out the following year all flags flying to do precisely what I had done.

My new perception of the world of politics told me one thing clearly: it might be deadlier, but it was the same as both business and sports in one critical respect. If you wanted to win you had to keep pressing, keep pushing, keep sawing away. And so I wrote letter after letter, to members of parliament, to individuals, to hundreds of people. Steadily I began to accumulate stacks of filed correspondence. I kept track of every scrap of paper, every clipping, every telegram that came my way, with a growing certainty that if I could just keep up the pressure, sooner or later, something would give. Without any conscious sense of having become radical or even political, I methodically set to work. If I had no battering ram with which to break through the doors, I could at least keep sawing away, sawing away . . .

Finally, in March, the steady drop-by-drop pressure flushed a response out of the French ministre des affaires étrangères, who wrote to my lawyer:

I beg to inform you that the inquiry which I ordered into the matter allows one to conclude that the said collision was caused by a faulty manœuvre on the part of skipper McTaggart . . . At 11.10, as the sailing ship is imperturbably continuing on her course, the "Paimpolaise" very cautiously draws nearer to 15 metres, stabilizes herself at the same level on a parallel route and asks her by loud speaker to change her course. At 11.13 and while the "Paimpolaise" has stopped and has turned the helm full right to move aside, the sailing ship, which is level with the minesweeper's prow, fully alters course to throw herself under the minesweeper's bow . . . By deliberately staying in a zone which the French government had declared unsafe to navigation, Mr McTaggart could not be ignorant of the fact that he would disrupt the sea and air manoeuvres taking place there. In so doing, he was exposing himself to dangers which the French navy had, furthermore, always tried to forestall and to avoid . . . Taking into account, on the one hand, the errors on the part of the "Green Peace" in causing the collision and, on the other hand, the repairs made free of charge to the sailing ship at Mr McTaggart's request, to enable him to sail away safely, the Government deems that the damage claim which you submitted to me in your above-mentioned letter is without foundation.

Yours,
Saint-Legier

So that was it. I had viciously attacked a French minesweeper with my yacht causing thirteen thousand dollars damage to my own vessel in the process. But no matter, the republic had kindly fixed up my boat anyway, so what was the fuss?

By this time I had found a small local publisher who was willing to print the manuscript I had now almost finished. I was given fifteen hundred dollars. I sent all but two hundred immediately to Nigel in Auckland, to at least start on the repairs to *Vega*. The rest of the money went into paying some of the bills that had stacked up in Vancouver, and then I was broke again. I took a construction job in the British Columbia interior at the small city of Chilliwack and Ann-Marie got a job as assistant English teacher. At nights, I continued to write letters, relentlessly chipping away.

Then one morning I got a call from Vancouver saying that a representative of the Australian government had arrived in town and wanted to get an affidavit from me concerning what had happened in the test zone. Astonished, I drove into town immediately. Australia intended to include the affidavit as part of the case it was presenting jointly with New Zealand at the International Court of Justice in The Hague, where they were seeking an injunction against any further nuclear testing in the South Pacific.

After the waffling from Ottawa, I was vastly encouraged to find at least two governments that were actually talking sense and making some kind of a serious effort to bring the tests to a halt. The Australian representative was crisp, friendly and efficient. He wasn't sure what the chances were of the International Court ruling against the tests, and even if the ruling went against France, he wasn't sure that it would have any effect, but "we'll have a jolly good run at it".

On April 21, a hundred-foot former Baltic trader, the *Fri*, hoisted sails in Whangarei, New Zealand, and set out for Mururoa. There were thirteen people on board, representing the United States, New Zealand, England, Holland, and even including a French clergyman. The crew included four women one of whom, a twenty-three-year-old New Zealander, revealed before she left that she was pregnant. Three other sailing vessels were being fitted to join the *Fri* in the test zone. In Fiji, the general secretary of the Fijian Seamen's and Dockers' Union announced that several canoes, each carrying five people, were planning to enter the zone within a month. The Australian government declared that if France did not respond to the ruling of the International Court of Justice, it would send a navy tanker as a support craft to join the New Zealand frigate that would be entering the zone at the time of the blasts.

Ann-Marie said she could see it coming.

It had been a year since I had come to visit her in hospital and she had almost jokingly mentioned the crazy scheme to sail to Mururoa. She remembered defending the idea then and making a bit of a speech about standing up for rights and protest not being something for the young and how there were principles involved and a lot of other stuff that she said she now had the feeling might have been utter rubbish. I had taken it all far more seriously than she had expected. Her immediate reaction when I said I was going to go had been: Shit-hot! Do it! Basically, it had blown her mind. She had always thought of herself as a bit of an adventurer, keen on excitement, and it just seemed a good thing to do.

But now the whole picture had changed. She had seen too much over the past year of power and money games and the dishonesty of politicians. She had seen the barely-restrained savagery of Kiwi cops whom she had always thought of as being more or less harmless. She had seen the implacable coldness of a judge pounding his gavel and sending me off to prison on what was obviously a political set-up. And during the long period when I had vanished into the sea, she had known confusion and a feeling of guilt, as though it might just have been her fault that I'd gone. She had watched the press turn on me and tear me to pieces. She had seen the incredible ego-trips and in-fighting happening in Auckland as the other boats were being launched.

She could see that despite all the protests and the diplomatic stuff and even the threats of boycotts, the French were adamant about going ahead with blowing off even bigger bombs this year, and that made it all the more sickening that everything we had gone through last year had added up to so little, except that *Vega* was now a wreck and the government was doing everything it could to ignore us. Oh, she still had her anti-nuclear beliefs and wanted to do her bit for disarmament and the ending of testing, but she knew now that it wasn't as simple as good people getting together and letting their feelings be known, not that simple at all. Somehow, it had become a rather ugly business . . .

When I told her that I was going back in, she realized she had been expecting it for some time. What else was there to do? Her own feeling was that we had done enough and could achieve more by staying in Canada and working with the lawyers. Yet she knew that I couldn't bear the thought of the tests going ahead again and that I was pissed at the French and at my own government . . .

It was one night in April when Ann-Marie and I met with my brother Drew.

"Listen, Drew," I said, "I've decided to go back in."

Drew looked at me closely, "Ah, David, I don't know. They're going to be laying for you. I'd think about that very carefully."

"Yeh. Well, I've been thinking a lot. Did you read that thing in the paper today? The French have said it, they're just gonna ignore whatever anybody says at The Hague, they're gonna go right ahead, no matter what the decision . . . Anyway, I've been thinking and thinking and I just don't see anything else to do."

"Those guys are military freaks," Ann-Marie said. "They're all into the *macho* thing, David. They'll take it as a direct personal challenge. They'll wipe the decks with you. Look at the trouble you've caused them. First you show up and now they've got half a dozen boats down their necks and governments screaming at them all over the place, and if they're going to blame anybody for the whole mess, it's you. If you go in there, that's like handing yourself over to the firing squad."

The reaction of my brother, a psychiatrist, was to argue vehemently against it. His two main points were that the chances of my reproducing the feat of getting to Mururoa were probably low, so from a hard-nosed point of view the trip wouldn't contribute anything that it hadn't already, and would likely be an anti-climax. And, secondly, his professional opinion was that I had not recovered, either mentally or physically, from the previous year's ordeal, and I was simply in no shape to undertake another voyage.

I got up and paced the room. "Yeh, yeh, I know all that. But those guys rammed my boat and they've lied, and those bastards in Ottawa have gone along with every single bloody lie, and *nothing's happening!* Not a single goddamn thing! I'm no expert on any of this stuff, eh? But there's one thing I know and that's the only way I'm gonna get any of those bastards moving is to stick it right to them, and that's right, you're right, me going in there again is gonna make them so goddamn mad they won't be able to see straight, and that's exactly what I want."

FIVE

Roll on, thou deep and dark blue Ocean – roll!
Ten thousand fleets sweep over thee in vain;
Man marks the earth with ruin – his control
Stops with the shore.

Lord Byron
Childe Harold's Pilgrimage

Vega looked like a wounded goose.

My first glimpse of her sitting on the ways under an iron-grey sky in drizzling rain stopped me in my tracks. The once-bright paint had flaked away in great thin scabs and green slime hung from her keel and propellers. Her planks had opened in long razor-slashes, and right away I could see that she would have to be burned down to the wood, re-caulked and painted. Climbing gingerly aboard, I found that she had the mildew smell of a hulk. The engine was badly corroded and rusted, the electrical system was a mess, the mast had been driven down into the hull, springing the keel and fittings, all as a result of the previous year's collision. The air inside the cabin had the dank rotting quality of a fridge abandoned in a garbage dump. Everything squeaked when I touched it. The walls and portholes were covered with an opaque scummy slick.

I slumped into one of the cracked leather seats and heard it make a soggy squishing sound. For a few moments I did nothing but blow smoke rings into the wintry gloom. Winter. It was winter again in New Zealand. It seemed I had been living in winters for a long time. We had set out for Mururoa in what was winter in the Southern Hemisphere. Then I had gone to Vancouver and had lived through winter, and now I was back in the Southern Hemisphere just in time to experience winter again. It was 1973.

Getting out of Vancouver had been like running down a nearly endless corridor, pushing open one door only to find another closed ahead and having to push it open to find yet another beyond, and another and another. By the time I'd got off the jet and started toward the boatyard, I was almost staggering. And now here I was, and it was a bit like arriving in an oddly-shaped old shack and I could see that rather than having reached the end of a journey or even the beginning of another, I had arrived in another kind of limbo. It was going to take at least five weeks of bone-cracking work to bring this lovely old derelict back to life.

The last few weeks were like bits of coloured shrapnel in my brain. I had no idea any longer what it all added up to – some parts of it, like the look on my parents' faces when I had broken the news to them, were too painful to think about. Their eyes had widened first with alarm, then something very much like panic, and I had had to brace myself against the sudden fear that my aging father was going to have a heart attack . . . And then the news, just a day after I had talked to Nigel long-distance about two of us going back in, that Nigel himself had had a heart seizure, and the doctors said flatly that he would not be able to go . . . and all those long-drawn-out meetings with the Greenpeace people, one question after another question. I had always hated meetings with passion, but there had been no way around it, and these meetings, particularly, had been tinged with paranoia on both sides, my own left-over distrust of any promises they made, and a lingering distrust on their part. I had the definite impression there were a few people in the group who doubted the seriousness of my intention to go back in, and I knew damn well that there had been arguments when I wasn't there, with the suggestion being put forward that I was only pretending to go as a way of raising money to repair my boat. There had been nothing I could do about it. I didn't have the resources to raise the money myself, so I swallowed my anger, stayed away from as many of the meetings as possible, and concentrated on doing the necessary hot-line radio shows and making all the necessary appeals to church groups, labour groups and environmental groups. It had been a grind, an awful grind, even though there were moments and people who stood out in my mind now with exceptional clarity. It had been astonishing how quickly Greenpeace had come back to life. I hadn't realized how many people there were who in fact had always believed in what I was doing and how strongly they felt about it. It was too damn bad I hadn't met them sooner. Things might have gone differently . . .

I had been right about one thing. The moment word went out that I was sailing back into Mururoa, the mandarins in Ottawa had come to life. The flow of letters and telegrams took a quantum jump, exactly as though somebody had tossed a firecracker into a chicken coop. Through my lawyer, I was advised to "lay off" the external affairs minister on the grounds that the honourable gentleman was really moving, and that the whole business would be resolved very soon. And then, just before I left Vancouver, a message arrived that the French were willing to pay me five thousand dollars for damages to *Vega*, providing, of course, I called off this second voyage. I had been a bit punchy then, very disheartened by the news that Nigel would not be able to come with me, beginning to suspect that Drew had known what he was talking about when he said I was not "mentally or physically capable" of another trip – and then came the carrot from the French. I had at least become politicized enough to realize immediately that there was much more at work here than coincidence. Only two weeks had elapsed since the public announcement that I was going to return to Mururoa, and the French government, which up until then had been refusing to say anything except that I had rammed a minesweeper, was suddenly offering five thousand dollars, providing I called off the second trip. Perhaps more than any other single thing, that confirmed in my mind the decision to get rolling again.

Yes, things had begun to move in the chicken coop back in Ottawa. The external affairs minister was reported to have had talks with the prime minister about the possibility of Canada actually espousing my claim, and indeed, there had been much progress since the initial response to my request for assistance, when I had been told there was virtually nothing the government could do – but by far the most of that progress had been made in the short space of time since I had announced my intention to sail again.

But now I looked around at poor soggy *Vega*, and reminded

myself that the price of this move was that I was out on a limb. Much was in motion. The Canadian government was finally clumping about, flapping its wings. The French government was offering bribes. Even the Greenpeace Foundation had found its voice again. But if any of it was to be kept in motion, it all depended on whether we made it to Mururoa again.

The first year, there had been the excitement of facing the unknown to buoy me at the start of the trip. This year, there was nothing like it. I was moving toward the conclusion of a game that had already been set in motion, and whereas I had been innocent about the forces I was dealing with – I had once admitted to my friend, David Exel: "I didn't know it was going to be this heavy" – now I knew perfectly well how heavy it was. If I could maintain the pressure, Canada would be driven into an inexorable collision-course with France, and the weight of that was not something I could accurately judge. Yet I knew enough about the flow of power now to know that it was considerable. France was embarked on a quest for the unholy grail of nuclear military status, but she did not have the natural resources – specifically, the uranium – to sustain that Gaullist fantasy for long. Canada, bound to France as closely, if not more closely than she had once been bound to Britain, was one of the few countries France could expect to depend on in the future. Taking shape between Canada and France was a symbolic relationship wherein the one provided the raw material and the other fashioned its weapons. If I could succeed in driving a wedge between these two obscene lovers, then I could die content in the knowledge that I had at least broken one of the strands in the spider-web that was enveloping the earth, awaiting only the final atomic sting.

Whatever our standing in the media, my supporters, I knew, were not that strong. I had overheard an expression that went, "The environmental movement tends to fragment faster than the New Left." And I knew – Christ, I knew! – how close to the truth that was. I knew also that among them were not a few who would turn on me faster than the governments themselves. So the pressure was on. It was a pressure quite unlike anything I had experienced during the first trip to Mururoa, when I had simply thought of myself as a guy going out to protest against a bomb. I knew that the limb out onto which I had moved could be cut by any number of people, and there were any number who would be more than willing to do it.

Greenpeace and myself had raised the money to repair *Vega* for her second voyage to Mururoa, but the re-organized Greenpeace Foundation was also, on the whole, a fierce and testy ally, ready to withdraw the moment it looked like I was producing anything less than superhuman results. There were moments when I was tempted to think: with friends like this, who needs enemies? But I was also sensitive enough to realize that the Greenpeace people themselves were victims of a strange public ethic that demanded of its ecological champions nothing less than perfection. Failures were not to be tolerated. It was very much as though there were a gut understanding that the ecologists were *right*, and therefore there was too much at stake. Politicians might make multi-billion-dollar mistakes and still retain office. Maybe, after all, that didn't matter. But for somebody like me to spend money even on a motel for one night to get out of the rain, well, that was serious business. I did not need to have it spelled out for me: if I did make it to Mururoa, I would be devoured. It was not just that the forces which I had set in motion would settle as quickly as dust back into their previous statue-like positions. It was also that they would use me as an excuse for their own inadequacies, even as a way to divert attention from the deals they were quietly pulling off in the background. In all the reading I had done the previous winter, there was one thing I had learned which stood out in my head, and as a former businessman, I understood its implication perhaps better than almost any of my supporters: *Canada stood to make hundreds of billions of dollars from the sale of nuclear reactors and uranium.* To the extent that my actions threatened those deals, through the focus of public attention on the whole nuclear issue, I was indeed caught with the dragon ahead and the sharks behind. More so than ever.

In the weeks that followed I more than once questioned my own wisdom.

First, there was the rain. It beat down in volume contesting even the rains I had known in British Columbia, with squalls ripping under the canvas I had erected over *Vega* to make work possible. White-faced and drawn, a ghost of the old Nigel Ingram joined me to help put the boat back in shape, even though his doctors still insisted that it would be suicide for Nigel to move very far away from medical facilities. The moment we stepped away from the boat, we found ourselves ankle-deep in mud. The cold left our fingers numb. During this time, I had no idea who would help me to make the voyage, and I had more or less come around to the idea of trying to sail in alone.

Second, there was the remorseless pressure from Vancouver. At least once a week, I had to answer the phone and give a detailed account of progress to date.

The weeks went by – endless torrential rains, mud, and cold. Aided from time to time by various individuals, Nigel and I worked steadily on *Vega*, with something of the feeling that we were carving a statue. One square inch at a time, she began to come back to life.

The change in government had meant quite a change in attitude by the authorities. There was no harassment, and the press, jaded already with "peace boats" to Mururoa, paid hardly any attention, leaving us free to work. A second vessel, the *Bluenose*, had set out after the *Fri*, but had turned back in the face of gales and had been prevented from leaving again because her skipper had failed to clear customs. A third boat, the *Spirit of Peace*, a forty-foot sloop, had set out in mid-May, and very quietly done a terrific job; by early June she had rendezvoued with the *Fri* sixty miles from Mururoa. A fourth boat, the *Warana*, had set sail from Melbourne, Australia, and a fifth, the *Barbary*, which had once been owned by actor Errol Flynn and was now skippered by a seventy-five-year-old man, had left from Auckland.

A group of two hundred set out from London, England, to walk to Paris to protest the tests under the banner of Greenpeace. After hiking through the Belgian countryside, they were stopped at the French border. Two hundred French sympathizers appeared on the other side of the border, but the guards would not let either group cross. Camping on the fringe of the French border, the Greenpeace protesters offered flowers to the guards. Several New Zealanders and Australians among them asked for asylum in France on the grounds that their own countries were being made uninhabitable by French bomb tests. Finally, one hundred French riot police moved in and began swinging at people with clubs. The attack backfired. Within a week, several thousand French demonstrators had gathered under the Eiffel Tower to protest against *la bombe*.

In Geneva, labour union leaders from eleven Pacific Rim nations threatened to boycott dealings with France.

Prime minister Trudeau had finally responded to the deluge of letters he had been getting and wrote me a personal letter saying,

> I would like to say at the outset how much I admire your courage, determination and willingness to take personal risks in order to protest, as a matter of principle, the carrying out of an atmospheric nuclear explosion by France ... I might add that I followed the course of events last summer involving the *Greenpeace III* with interest and concern. The Canadian government made known to France its interest in and concern for your safety and that of your companions well before the tests ... It goes without saying that the Canadian government is fully in accord with you on the question of principle involved in your personal protest against these tests last year.

Well, perhaps it did not matter that the Canadian government had, in fact, been busy disclaiming that *Vega* had anything to do with Canada at the time of the tests, and it was perhaps irrelevant that there was nothing in the prime minister's letter referring to *this* year's tests. At least, it was an endorsement of sorts. And it would mean, if nothing else, that if the French chose to take rash action against the *Vega* this year, they would be attacking a boat that had, however weakly, been given a blessing by the head of the Canadian government.

On 23 June 1973, the International Court of Justice in The Hague, due to the New Zealand and Australian action, by an eight-to-six vote ruled that France should desist from further tests in the Pacific pending a further full judgement by the court. France promptly announced that it did not recognize the World Court's competence to deal with matters of national defence. By another one of those odd coincidences, Leonid Brezhnev and Richard Nixon signed a pact in Washington that day pledging to defuse the risk of nuclear war with what the Soviet Communist Party Secretary called "a truly historic ceremony". A day later, New Zealand cabinet ministers drew straws to see who would sail on the frigate HMNZS *Otago* to Mururoa. The minister of mines won the draw. The Australian navy oiler HMAS *Supply* was launched to cross the Tasman Sea and link up with the *Otago* to provide it with fuel.

The *Fri* and the *Spirit of Peace* reported being buzzed by French aircraft. In Papeete, Tahiti, five thousand marched against the Bomb.

On June 28, the 24,000-ton *Otago* steamed out of Auckland with two hundred and fifty sailors standing to attention on her decks. The national television networks treated the event as though the country had gone on a war footing. Prime minister Kirk made a speech before the vessel left, saying: "We shall do our utmost to ensure that the eyes of the world are rivetted on Mururoa and what is taking place there. This is a voyage of peaceful but serious purpose." He said he did not think the French would take the same action against protest boats – ramming them to get them out of the way – as they had the previous year. He also announced that, depending on how long the vigil lasted, the *Otago* would be replaced by HMNZS *Canterbury*. It was indeed a moment in history worth noting. It was the first time that an official naval vessel had been sent out on a peaceful protest. Non-violence had at last come to the military. And it was also the first time that any government had taken physical action against nuclear testing.

In Peru, one hundred thousand women signed a petition denouncing the French blasts.

Against this background, scarcely anyone noticed the departure of *Greenpeace III* on her final voyage to Mururoa.

The crew included Nigel Ingram, Ann-Marie Horne and Mary Lornie. Towards the end of the long five weeks it took to repair *Vega*, Nigel's doctors had decided that he had recovered enough to make a sea voyage. And the two of us had decided that if we were going to bring anyone else along, it might as well be Ann-Marie and Mary. Grant Davidson had disappeared after returning to Australia and I had not been able to contact him. We did not want to go through our experience of the previous year, and so decided we would only bring people we knew. Mary had worked hard to help us before, and more to the point, she was Nigel's girlfriend. I knew that Ann-Marie wanted badly to come. One advantage was that the four of us had gone sailing together in the days before the shadow of Mururoa fell across our paths. I knew that neither woman was frivolous or given to sea-sickness. The voyage would probably be far less physically demanding, because we would be arriving late in the season and would not face a protracted period of being hove-to. Whatever action the French would take would be over and done with quickly. And there was one other thought that surfaced: I did expect the French to be angry and possibly vengeful. The presence of women on board might help to defuse the situation. There might be some trace of gallantry – or chauvinism, whichever way you choose to see it – left in the French navy that would restrain them in the crunch that I knew was coming.

Ann-Marie was ecstatic. She flew from Vancouver immediately. For her, it was like coming out of a smogbank into the sun again. There was a clarity about the action of sailing into the test zone which seemed, compared to the winter we'd just been through, like an almost painful kind of release. It allowed her – as it allowed so many other people – to focus her feeling about the Bomb. Now she could make her own statement. Mary just as quickly accepted the offer when Nigel suggested it to her. She immediately took a leave of absence from her job.

Ann-Marie's personal statement had included inviting an

Anglican minister down to the boat the day we sailed to offer prayers, both for our safety and for an end to the "senselessness of nuclear testing". I had not sought any publicity for our departure. I wanted it to be a quiet affair, with just a few friends on hand. Compared to the crowd of three thousand who had cheered the *Fri* on its way and the national television blitz which had surrounded the departure of *Otago*, the launching of *Vega* had the atmosphere of a small wedding, complete with bowed heads and an air of solemnity.

It was not simply that I had developed a profound aversion to publicity. I had, but there was more to it. I wanted to keep my distance from the bizarre "peace flotilla" which seemed to be taking shape everywhere I looked. So far as I could count, no less than twenty-five boats had pledged themselves to sail to Mururoa that year. Of the lot, only the navy ships, the *Fri*, the *Spirit of Peace* – and later, *Vega* – were to make it. The rest were visited by every sort of disaster, real or imagined. Some kind of anti-nuclear Dunkirk might be in the making, but I suspected otherwise. The other, more distinct, possibility was that the whole undertaking might easily degenerate into a dangerous comedy of errors. One boat, the *Barbary*, set sail no less than ten times, having to come back for one reason or another every time before her skipper finally gave up. One yacht that tried to disembark from Honolulu was stopped by American authorities. A boat that was to be launched from Samoa did not get away from the dock. An American-owned boat that was to have left from Auckland also didn't get away. The yacht *Malaguena* left from Brisbane, Australia, and was last reported halfway to New Zealand, but after that there were no further reports. A forty-foot trimaran owned by a Frenchman tried to leave from Tauranga, New Zealand, but for one reason or another didn't make it. Three other yachts from Wellington, Christchurch and Peru similarly failed to get out to sea after announcing their intention to do so. Another, the *Arakiwa*, got away from Auckland but took one hundred and twenty days to make it as far as Rarotonga, a voyage which had taken *Vega* eleven days. The *Bluenose* was only out for one day before returning to port. The Fijian canoes never did make their appearance. The *Warana* made it across the Tasman Sea, but there were reports of an attempted suicide on board, and it got no further. A press boat from Fiji was launched, but it returned after only a few weeks. A forty-eight-foot yawl, the *Arwen* made it from Rarotonga to bring supplies to the *Fri* in the test zone, then returned to its home port. A Peruvian vessel with twenty men and three women, including two government officials, was reported ready to leave from Lima, but was not heard of after that. And a thirty-foot boat called the *Carmen* was launched from Tahiti, only to vanish with no further reports being published about what happened to it. A brutal natural screening process was at work, whittling the the "peace flotilla" down to almost nothing.

From the point of view of a press that had become even more cynical than usual, there was nothing much to report about one more yacht setting sail, and so *Vega*'s departure went more or less unnoticed. That was good, I thought, because it also meant that the beleaguered French navy wouldn't pay much attention either, and our goal was to slip over the cordon around Mururoa and into position before any of Admiral Claverie's men knew what was happening.

The coming and going of anti-nuclear boats had not made much news until June 18 when reports filtered back that the *Fri* had been hemmed in by French warships in the zone and then boarded and seized by commandos wearing frogman suits and armed with knives. Three times lines with grappling hooks were thrown from the warship to bite into the aging wood of the old trading boat. Three times they were cut with axes by the *Fri*'s crew while the skipper, David Moodie, fought the wheel and held his vessel on a steady course, refusing to surrender. When the commandos swarmed over the sides, several fights broke out and one *Fri* crewman threw himself in the water and tried to swim away. He was grabbed in the water, and forcibly taken, along with the rest of the crew, including the pregnant woman, onto one of the French Navy ships. With the *Fri* in tow and its crew locked up, the French took them to the island of Hao. The *Otago* had been in the area at the time, but at the request of the crew of the *Fri*, did not beome involved. The *Fri* people announced they did not want to be rescued from military vessels by another military vessel.

With the *Fri* out of the way, and the *Spirit of Peace* back in Rarotonga getting more supplies, that left only the *Otago* in the zone. The French warships kept their distance, although they remained in communication with the New Zealanders. When the first bomb blast took place, on July 21, the *Otago* was close to the twelve-mile limit around Mururoa, but well out of the path of fallout. Her crew remained below decks, surrounded by radiation-monitoring equipment, and when they did emerge on deck afterwards, they were wearing protective gear, virtually like astronauts in their spacesuits, complete with special goggles, to enable them to observe the giant pillar of smoke ascending high into the air above the atoll. It could clearly be seen on the horizon, rising through a thick layer of cloud and billowing out into a perfect mushroom. *Otago* immediately relayed back pictures of the Bomb.

An outcry broke out around the world the next day against France. Japan, Chile, Australia, New Zealand, Columbia, Bolivia and Canada all lodged protest notes. A few days later, Peru broke off diplomatic relations. At the United Nations, seventeen nations denounced the tests. In Paris, bishops of the Catholic Church took to television to call for an end to "nuclear Bonapartism". In Tahiti, the flag was lowered to half-mast.

Our plan had been to motor down the river and anchor for the night in Urquhart's Bay to make sure that everything was properly stowed. We assumed it would be our last night in sight of land. But we awoke the morning of July 11 to find a storm force gale blowing directly out of the east with a large swell running through the mouth of the bay like a stone wall thrown up to prevent our escape. That the wall kept collapsing made no difference, for when one grey wall went, within moments another would stand in its place. Again, it was hard to resist the temptation to think that the gods did not have plans of their own. It was very much as though a great breath had been loosed from Mururoa and was pinning us like flies against a wall.

The weather reports were depressing. By all accounts, the easterly which had descended upon us was part of a slow-moving front that was likely to prevail for weeks. After listening to the radio, Nigel looked up and shook his head, an expression of hopeless despair on his face. I knew that there would be little sympathy back in Vancouver and that any delay now – after the weeks of delays getting the boat ready – would be viewed as a cop-out, that was all there was to it. At this rate, we might not reach Mururoa until well after the last bomb in the 1973 test programme had been detonated. On all other fronts, there seemed to be an enormous amount of activity. Most frustrating of all were the reports from the *Fri* that the weather around Mururoa was calm and clear.

Day after day we lay at anchor in Urquhart's Bay, listening to the wind whistling through the rigging and rattling the spars, staring mutely at the huge waters building up in the river's mouth, and as each day passed and we remained within a stone's throw of New Zealand, the frustration mounted. Radio reports told us of the events that were taking place in the outside world, the launching of the *Otago*, its link-up with the Australian vessel *Supply*, the legal arguments in The Hague, the astronomical increase in opposition to *La Bombe* that was manifesting itself in country after country, the comings and goings of protest boat after protest boat – to the point where it was impossible to avoid the feeling that some great battle had been joined, and it was a battle from which the fates seemed to have excluded *Vega*.

Ann-Marie and Mary were both geared for an immediate charge out onto the ocean. Although Nigel knew full well the utter futility of trying to push against the implacable winds that now held us in check, neither of the girls quite understood it. Their restlessness was tinged by just the slightest shadow of suspicion. To keep them from brooding, I worked out a daily routine of work – sanding and repainting the interior of the boat, so that at the end of the day, everybody would be covered with dust and paint, and there would be a good deal of complaining, but it was at least focussed on the minor irritations of trying to follow the curve of a beam with a paintbrush or getting turpentine in one's hair. In the evenings, we played chess, cribbage and hearts. The four of us were so closely confined and Nigel and I were both so tense that the possibility of a romantic interlude simply did not come to the surface. Whatever the girls had expected, they found they did not have to worry about being trapped in a small space with two sex-maniacs. Sex was the last thing on either of our minds. I was preoccupied with the knowledge that every day spent in the bay was another day's worth of momentum lost in the campaign I had toiled all winter to set in motion.

The worst agony was that, having already cleared customs, we could not set foot back on the land that was so tantalizingly near at hand. We knew we were being watched from the shore, not only by reporters who were getting used to writing stories about "jinxed" protest yachts – the failure rate among the boats being launched was so high that the whole protest movement was coming close to looking like a national joke – but also by the police. There might be a new government, strongly opposed to the French tests, but it was also a government which had staked its reputation on making the voyage of its own Navy vessels the centrepiece of the international attention that was now unfolding, and the prime minister had made a public appeal to the private protest boats to pull back and "leave it to us". Clearly, the government did not want to be upstaged, so that if any of *Vega*'s crew got caught sneaking ashore, there was a very good chance of an arrest. The rules had changed, but the new rules were not really that much more helpful than the old.

In addition to working on the boat, we occupied ourselves by learning how to operate a video camera which a Canadian television network had loaned in the event that we might get some spectacular footage. We also worked out an alphabet code for use on our telegraph key. As short on money as ever, we had not been able to install any radio equipment that was much of an improvement on what we had had the previous year. Our main hope now was to be able to relay messages through the powerful transmitters of the New Zealand navy vessels in the area. In terms of any other capability, the best we had been able to do was to have a morse key added to our own transmitter. The problem with that was that none of us was a proficient operator, so we devised a code that would allow us to communicate a message by sending a single letter. From A to Z, each letter would signify a different situation, such as "sighted the French", "being boarded", or "being harassed". The French themselves would not be able to make any sense out of the single-letter messages. After working laboriously for several days on the code, we made a copy of it and I slipped ashore one night to mail it to Vancouver with the request that Greenpeace send additional copies to Auckland and Rarotonga radio stations.

When word came through over the radio that the *Fri* had been boarded and towed away, the frustration level on *Vega* approached hysteria. The weather had not improved in the least, but we decided to make an attempt to punch through the swells in the river's mouth anyway. I knew in my heart that it was impossible, but by this time, anything seemed better than spending even another hour in the bay. The swells were twenty feet and the wind was blasting in our faces. *Vega* threw her nose to the sky, crashed downward as though trying to plunge below the surface, her sails flapping helplessly, wallowing in the troughs, wrenching around violently – there was simply no way. We tried for hours to beat out from the coast, but any angle we tried left *Vega* floundering, heeling over so precariously that we were finally forced back. That evening, nursing our bruises, we heard over the radio that *Otago* had spotted the balloon rising over Mururoa. There was no consolation to be had.

It was not until June 22 that we finally heard a radio broadcast predicting that the weather was about to break and that there would be a wind shift to the southwest within twenty-four hours.

Alone among the four people on the boat, Ann-Marie still retained her basic religious convictions. Mary had been openly contemptuous when Ann-Marie had insisted on inviting a minister down to the boat to offer a prayer, and neither Nigel nor I wanted to go near the topics of God, an afterlife, or any of it. Ann-Marie had quickly learned to keep a low profile on her beliefs. Yet, all along, she said she had felt that the Lord in His infinite wisdom was not only watching over us, but steering our real course. At night, she silently prayed, and it was not a ritual prayer, it was a deliberate effort to communicate with the Father of Fathers, not to instruct Him or ask for particular favours or privileges, but to maintain a channel, as she put it.

She did not particularly feel the need to see "miracles" or signs or portents, because her own feeling was that everything was a miracle to begin with. Beyond the fact that she existed and that the universe existed, there was no need for "proof" of God's existence: the proof was in the fact that there was any reality to talk about at all. It had been her conviction all along that these voyages against the Bomb had their true source in the exercise of Divine Will, just as the creation of the Bomb in the first place was a part of some test designated to shape and re-shape human consciousness. It was for this reason that she believed we would ultimately succeed, because we were meant to succeed, and for that reason, despite the low points she had experienced during the winter, she had not argued much against the decision to return to Mururoa. The agony of the past weeks, with *Vega* seemingly rendered useless, had been endurable only because she assumed there was a purpose to it all – very much as though we were, indeed, pawns in a great game, and that the Player had not yet chosen to move us.

Now the wind changed, and it just happened to be blowing in the ideal direction to take us straight as an arrow to Mururoa. She almost wept at the news, for it seemed to her that the great hand which had stayed us for so long was now picking us up and pushing us unerringly into position and it seemed to her that a voice was whispering in her ear: "*Now!*"

At 0800 hours the next morning, we raised anchor and headed seaward into a blindingly-clear day. Amid the toothpaste explosions of whitecaps, yard-long rainbows flickered in and out of existence around *Vega*'s bow and a school of porpoises appeared, their fins cleaving the water with fine zipping sounds, bodies shooting clear like projectiles from below, their dark mysterious eyes containing a look that seemed to say: "This way! Follow me!" *Vega* rushed to keep up with them, and Ann-Marie climbed out onto the bowsprit, feeling delirious with joy and excitement. She knew full well that these strange creatures had always been known as an omen of good fortune. She didn't *need* signs, but the day seemed full of them nonetheless.

That day, three thousand miles ahead of us, the triggering device on an atomic bomb was detonated and the great pillar of smoke went up over Mururoa.

From the start, we had strong winds. Fearing that we had precious little time to reach our destination before the last bomb was triggered, Nigel and I decided to drive the old girl as hard as we could. We took two-hour watches and shared the navigational duties on alternate days. If the winds held, we knew we could maintain a course due east of Auckland, which would keep us out of the trade winds to the north that had caused so much trouble the year before, and well clear of the cold and unpredictable Roaring Forties to the south. If the winds stayed as they were, and *Vega* held up under the relentless pressure, we just might set a record.

Neither Mary nor Ann-Marie was quite ready for the hurtling caboose motion of the boat in full flight. It was all they could do for the first few days to hang on for dear life, and, indeed, pounding along at eight and sometimes nine knots, it did seem that *Vega* was smashing through the water at twice that speed. Both girls were having trouble holding their food down and their various attempts at cooking were disasters. Accustomed to a stove that stands in one spot, to tables and cupboards that do not move, they found that most of their domestic talents were useless. Ann-Marie spent five hours one day trying to make a casserole only to open the oven door at last – and have the casserole come flying out and crash upside-down on the floor. It was like riding on the back of a great beast in full gallop with no way to slow it down even for a moment.

Physically stronger than Ann-Marie, Mary adapted more quickly. A practical, efficient person who had been managing a staff of five people at the legal firm where she worked, she quickly learned to carry out her various tasks – mainly helping with the sails and keeping the boat in good shape – and then retire to her bunk to conserve energy. She read a lot, and joined in what conversations there were with ease and wit, Normally, she was gregarious and very much at ease in groups. But now there were just the four of us, and with Nigel and I alternating at the helm, there did not seem to be much point in idle chit-chat, so she adopted a role somewhere between a passenger resigned to a long journey and a crew-member. She got her work done and seldom, if ever, made mistakes. After about a week, under Nigel's guidance, she began to learn how to handle the tiller. Within a few days, she was relieving Nigel on his watch and he would gratefully retreat to his bunk. Far less adroit at giving instructions, I simply invited Ann-Marie to share my watch, and did not leave her on her own, partially because I did not think she was strong enough, and partially because I was accustomed to doing things myself. It was not long before my own energy began to flag and I wished I had taken more time to instruct Ann-Marie.

The wind held.

Within ten days, we were halfway to Mururoa, having pushed 1,330 miles. The clouds closed in over our heads like a great hatchway, then broke apart and scattered to let magnificent shafts of light sweep the water. Squalls came and went. The ocean was never the same from one hour to the next. The deep emerald of the water around New Zealand gave way to cobalt blue. Some days it was mottled and flecked, some days stippled like sand dunes, other days it took on a sulky menacing quality, and yet other days seemed to dance in ecstatic patterns as though the foam wished to re-join the clouds. And always there was the glacial drift of multi-coloured forms in the sky, so far above us that the feeling persisted that we were crawling along the bottom of a crystal-clear ocean rather than riding on the surface of one.

We had just passed the halfway point when we heard that

262

the second test had taken place at Mururoa. The French weren't saying anything, but by all reports it had been a dud. The *Otago* had already left the area and had been replaced by the *Canterbury*. Observers on the vessel said that the bomb had scarcely managed to produce a mushroom cloud at all. French authorities were not saying whether there would be any more tests or not.

Very far out now on the limb, I began to wonder whether we weren't already too late.

The wind still held.

Despite our sense of urgency, time took on a frozen quality, as though we were suspended somewhere. It could be any age, future or past. There was only the pinwheeling of the clouds and the drift of galaxies at night, the silent footfall of massive shadows gliding across the waves.

Later, Ann-Marie wrote in her diary:

Our 17th day at sea and 30th day on the boat. It is very tiring. Last night we checked our second 1,000 miles. In five days, we should reach Mururoa. Still no satisfactory contact with Radio Rarotonga. Haven't missed seeing the land. Much to look at, sea is never boring, waves, foam, phosphorescence, stars, clouds, sun, colourful sunrises and sunsets, birds, and especially albatrosses – they have a fabulous primitive feeling about them, stark silhouettes, sharp-angled wings, yellow beaks, brown spotty tums.

Did a three-and-a-half-hour watch this morning. I did a four-hour watch another time, but it was calm then. Today the helm was really heavy and I am now very tired. I shall go up soon and relieve David for an hour or so – we have two three-hour watches today and only one four-hour watch tonight, which is easier – and then prepare tea. Guess I'll have to use the potato casserole left over from last night.

Think I strained my stomach this a.m., as I don't feel well again: yesterday I felt fine – one of the few days I have.

Getting more used to always being sticky with salt. And as I grow tireder, not so hard to sleep. Legs still very bruised. Whole body always on edge, always braced, impossible to relax, ever. Hardest thing to get used to is that the boat sails on twenty-four hours a day. The motion never stops except for the odd second here and there when she sits quietly on a wave. But you know it's always only for a second. Also difficult are the strange hours. One just doesn't go to bed at night. In theory one should sleep whenever possible. But there is only one comfortable bunk and someone else always seems to have it.

A day after this entry we found ourselves penetrating an uncharted region of the South Pacific. Neither Nigel nor I had thought much about it, but I woke out of a light sleep midmorning to feel a strange new motion in the boat, something I had never felt before. Warily, I got up and climbed to the cockpit.

Nigel was at the tiller, looking uncharacteristically nervous. Behind him, I could at first see nothing but a wall of grey water, as though *Vega* had just descended from the side of a mountain. Looking around, I found myself struck speechless. It was as though *Vega* had been magically shrunk to the size of a bathtub toy.

"I swear to God they're a hundred feet," Nigel said softly.

The swells over which we were crawling must have been building up all the way from the Antarctic and it might have been that there was a radical change in the depth of the water below. Whatever the reason, the swells were literally the size of small mountain ranges. From the top of one to the top of another was the distance of at least two miles. It took *Vega* fifteen minutes to descend one of those slopes into the valley, ride across the equivalent of three football fields, and begin the long haul up the other side. Coming up over the top, we had such a vantage point that I was quite sure I could see for a hundred miles. For several seconds we would remain poised at the peak, then begin the long shallow descent into the next valley. By the time we were halfway down, the twenty-knot wind would be cut off almost entirely by the vast mass of water behind us so that *Vega* would scarcely move. After a while, we started the engine and took to motoring. As we putted across the plain at the bottom, the sky ahead and behind was obliterated by the sea at least halfway to the zenith. It was hard to shake off the feeling that the sea could not possibly have assumed such gargantuan proportions, that we must, somehow, have been miniaturized. In all his years of sailing Nigel had never seen anything remotely like it.

In the troughs there was a weird stillness – none of the normal sounds of the ocean at all except for a faint whistle of wind far above and a vague sound as though the weight of the vast moving plateaus was squeezing the sea-bed below. It was awesome in a way that no man-made thing, not even a hydrogen bomb, could ever possibly be. It gave the word "titanic" a fantastic new dimension in my mind. And it left me feeling as vulnerable as an insect crawling among turbines. So long as these languid monsters maintained their ponderous rhythm, seemingly impervious to the wind, *Vega* was in no danger. But should they begin to roll over slightly, their scale was such that *Vega* would be swamped within minutes.

The sky remained overcast all that day as we climbed one Olympian swell after the other and another and another with yet more ranges moving with no more sound that the swish of great robes away toward a horizon that seemed achingly distant. A feeling of deep humility came over us that lingered for days, even after the sea returned to normal.

We had long since lost voice contact with the outside world. Nigel had begun using the morse key, sending position reports out in hesitant dots and dashes, uncertain if they would be received and unaware that even if they were no one would know what they meant, since the Greenpeace office had mislaid our coded radio messages. For hours each day, I sat over the radio, trying to make contact with any nearby craft, speaking over and over again into a box that made sounds like a cavern full of witches and cats on heat, bizarre gibberings and squeaks that might have been messages from passing flying saucers. Then, one night I was astonished to pick up a distant conversation taking place between the *Fri* and the *Spirit of Peace*. The voices faded in and out, as though someone were shouting in a labyrinth, but I managed to figure out from what fragments I could hear that the *Fri* had been released, along with her crew, and they were, at that moment, some forty miles from Papeete, Tahiti. Her captain was reporting that she was "not seaworthy" and he was trying – so far unsuccessfully – to get permission from the French to put in at Papeete for repairs.

That didn't make any sense to me. Why would the French have released the boat and why would her skipper have accepted her back in an unseaworthy condition, putting himself in the degrading position of having to ask for assistance from the very people who had illegally seized his vessel in international water?

"The only thing I can see is that the test must be over with," said Nigel.

A mood of depression settled over the boat. It did seem like the only logical conclusion. After all the work and the pounding race across the ocean, it looked as though it had all been in vain. And at another level, I knew full well that my campaign back in Canada would cave in on itself without the impetus of a final confrontation. To arrive even a moment too late would be the same as arriving not at all.

A cross-current of conflicting emotions gripped us now. There was frustration and a bitter sense of failure, even a vague feeling of foolishness as though our whole enormous effort had been quixotic. But there was also an irresistible relief. We did not know what to expect when we arrived in the zone but we did know there would be some kind of unpleasant reaction from the French. Arriving late, we would be ignored. None of us could say for certain which feeling was the stronger – the relief or the disappointment. The edge had been taken off our gnawing anxiety but it had also been taken off our spirit. Again, we were faced with the emotional paradox of wanting so badly to get to a place which was the last place on earth we wanted to go. The irony was that we were less than two days from the cordon.

Then that night we picked up a news report saying that the French were planning to set off their big hydrogen bomb test within a matter of days. The news galvanized us. It was as

266

though we had been thrown down on a floor, only to find ourselves being flung upward against the ceiling. Ann-Marie became so excited she was shivering. Even the normally un-flappable Mary Lornie was having trouble keeping a tremor out of her voice. *Vega* seemed to be right on schedule, the timing so perfect that even I found myself slightly awe-struck. Had we got going any sooner, we would one way or another have been disposed of by now. The news report had also con-tained the sobering news that the *Canterbury* had left the area and the *Spirit of Peace* had headed for Tahiti to assist the *Fri*, which meant that out of all the boats in the peace flotilla, there was none at Mururoa to stand in the way of the final big blast. Crashing along on her own perfect orbit, *Vega* was now the only vessel within striking distance, and from the looks of it, she would be coming down on Mururoa at the very moment the hydrogen weapon was set to explode. No, we could not have planned it more perfectly. No one could have. It was almost as though we had been guided by a secret schedule known to no one else. For me, there was satisfaction to be had in the thought of the expression on Admiral Claverie's face when he learned that the persistent little boat from Canada which he had so adroitly shaken off last year was back on his doorstep, back in the path of the bomb he was constructing between visits to his confessor. From all reports, things had not been going well for the admiral this year. His bombs had been small and one at least had been a dud. Much French pride would be vested in this big hydrogen blast. They had paid a high price in terms of ill will and bad publicity throughout the world to hold their course and so their investment would be greater than it had ever been. It was possible that Admiral Claverie had much more to contend with this year than just his tortured Catholicism. I knew how little margin I had for failure myself and I wondered if the admiral's job was on the line. I doubt that the glint was still in the old man's eye.

The night after the report that the Bomb was being readied, I settled down at the radio, feeling it was imperative that we get a message out to someone who was friendly. I sought out the frequency we had heard the *Fri* using and after a few min-

267

utes of fiddling with the dials, heard the *Fri*'s skipper talking to Marine Radio in Tahiti. He was explaining that the French government would not permit him to enter port for repairs despite the fact that his vessel was taking water badly and that his crew was having to pump non-stop on a twenty-four-hour basis. Every time he stopped talking or paused, I cut in immediately.

"Calling *Fri*, calling *Fri*, this is the *Greenpeace III*, this is the *Greenpeace III*, do you read? Over."

After half a dozen tries, the voice at the other end said:

"Hello *Greenpeace III*, hello *Greenpeace III*, I copy you faintly. Over." The voice was so faint that it seemed we were on opposite sides of the galaxy, but at least it was contact.

I quickly gave our position, repeating it several times, and asking the *Fri* to relay the information to Rarotonga or Auckland.

"I'm sorry, *Greenpeace III*, I do not copy. I do not copy. Let's try again in one hour. Try again in one hour. This is the *Fri* standing by."

But an hour later, when I tried, the reception was even worse. It was to be our only contact with the other protest boat. And as for the rest of the world, no one had the faintest idea where we were.

Late that night, August 12, we crossed the cordon line.

We had covered three thousand miles in twenty-one days! When we had set out, we had expected that the best time we could reasonably hope for was at least thirty days. But the wind had stayed with us and *Vega* had moved as though catapulted. We had no champagne with which to celebrate this time, but we did have the satisfaction of knowing that the French would not be expecting anyone to have arrived so quickly all the way from New Zealand. So it was possible that we would have a slight advantage of surprise.

The news reports were full of speculation that the hydrogen test was imminent. As we moved across the forbidden zone, it was impossible to avoid a nervousness that went beyond the anxiety associated with knowing that the French could move quickly against us. I was not absolutely certain what the precise difference was between a hydrogen bomb and an ordinary atomic bomb – if "ordinary" was a word that could be used to describe any thermonuclear weapon. But I did know that it represented a quantum increase in destructive power. Having arrived so swiftly and with so little fanfare in the zone, it was conceivable that the French did not yet know that we were in the area. It was more than possible that they might assume the protest boats had all been scattered and so, at any moment, the famous man-made sun might erupt into existence directly ahead of us. It was much like approaching a dragon's lair, alert to the slightest sign of the monster coming to life. If we were to be consumed by the blast deliberately, that was one thing. To be caught in it accidentally because no one knew we were there was a cruel thought to bear.

For Nigel and me, the knowledge that we were back in the test zone had an inevitable *déjà vu* quality. For the girls, it was quite different. Ann-Marie found herself unconsciously holding her breath from time to time. It was almost impossible to sleep. But more than feeling fearful, her reaction was mainly a sense of excitement. We had arrived, and on time! Her faith had been confirmed. She did not share my glum expectations of serious trouble. She expected, at worst, that we would be arrested and towed out of the area. She was having trouble keeping her food down, but she had felt that way during much of the voyage. Compared to the unbearable anxiety of not knowing whether we would make it on time or not, the feelings she had now were close to relief. What happened now would be rather like an automatic machine reaction, as though in the process of entering the zone we had tripped a mechanism that would set certain forces in motion. She knew what this meant in terms of my case against France and she had a good idea how many headaches it would cause for the politicians and the generals, and so she felt exultant. And proud. She had always been defiant by nature. Now she felt more defiant than ever. Whatever happened, it would attract attention to the Bomb and she had learned to think of the weapons builders as rather creepy characters who worked best in dark remote places as much out of sight as possible. The glare of publicity was like a light being thrown on them and they feared the light; it blinded them, drove them back further and further into the caves.

Mary did not share our foreboding either. She had even teased Nigel a couple of times about his worry. From the way we talked, it sounded to her a bit like boys playing pirates. Mary enjoyed Nigel's company and good looks enormously, but even though she was six years younger than him, she felt that her own attitudes tended to be more mature. All of this added up to an interesting legal case, no doubt about it, and, so far as she could see, it was about the only effective action that could be taken against the tests. The rest of the diplomatic shilly-shallying obviously wasn't making a dent. She felt realistic about it. She thought the French would do to us what they did to the people on the *Fri*. They'd seize the ship and take everybody off to a place of detention until the tests were over, then send us packing. Mary rather doubted that the French would try any of that intimidation business they'd done to us the previous year because there was simply too much publicity surrounding the whole issue now.

We had raised our radar reflector to announce our arrival to the French Navy. By sunrise the next morning we were thirty-five miles from the atoll. Despite myself, I was starting to feel jittery. I suspected that it would not be long before the confrontation came.

Nigel was busying himself by reading. He was sprawled on the foredeck, looking for all the world like a slightly down-and-out but unconcerned yachtsman. Mary was washing her hair over the side. Ann-Marie was sitting beside me in the cockpit, mending my jeans. The peace of this domestic scene was suddenly broken by the drone of an aircraft.

"They're here!" Ann-Marie cried, diving for my Nikon. I scooped up the video camera. Mary peered through her soapy locks at the black shape bearing across the water toward us. The plane, a Neptune, passed two hundred feet directly overhead, its big motor shaking the air around us. It banked and returned on a trajectory that took it directly over the boat again. I followed it in the camera's range-finder as it swept away back toward Mururoa.

"Well, it won't be long," said Nigel, as casually as he could.

At noon, we spotted a ship approaching. I had been expecting events to move far more rapidly than they had the previous year, but now I felt slightly unnerved. I wasn't sure that I had expected this almost push-button swiftness of response. I didn't like the feel of it. It was too much as though we were stepping into a pre-set trap. The ship was coming at full speed. Very soon we could tell it was a minesweeper, presumably either *La Paimpolaise* or *La Bayonnaise*. As it swept by about half a mile away on our port side, I experienced a definite feeling of disappointment that it was not *La Paimpolaise*. At least if it had been Captain Rochebrochard's ship, I would have known the man we were going to have to face. But this minesweeper was p653 and her name was *La Dunkerquoise*, another Canadian gift to France. She circled around behind our stern and came up to within a quarter of a mile off our starboard quarter before stopping. I could see an inflatable being put over the side and several men jumping down into it.

Within moments they were drawing alongside. There were four men, none of whom I recognized and none of whom were smiling. One of them threw a bow rope over *Vega*'s safety rail.

We had rehearsed for this moment. I had the movie camera ready. Ann-Marie had the Nikon. Nigel had a copy of the report that the University of Auckland had given us, the same one we had used the previous year, stating our rights of innocent passage in international waters. We had sealed it in an envelope along with a covering letter stating our intention to remain in the area.

One of the men in the inflatable, a lieutenant, awkwardly got to his feet in the flopping, lurching craft and held out an envelope to Nigel. Taking it, Nigel passed over our own document. Not a word was exchanged. It had the stiff quality of a writ being served except that it was difficult to tell from anybody's expression just who was the bailiff. I noticed that the minesweeper had moved ahead and now lay directly in our path a quarter of a mile ahead. At that moment, the Neptune roared over our masthead again.

The ritual now through with, I took the bow line which was hanging limply over *Vega*'s safety rail and threw it back into the inflatable.

"You don't have permission to come aboard," I said.

Immediately, the inflatable swung away and headed back to its mother ship. I had watched the Frenchmen's faces and had seen them looking at Mary and Ann-Marie. Well they knew now we had women on board, I thought.

The inflatable was just pulling up to the minesweeper's side when an officer on deck yelled something down at the men and the rubber boat immediately spun around and came back across the water. Sensing that there might be trouble, I handed the camera to Mary and joined Nigel by the rail.

As soon as they were alongside the lieutenant leaned forward and waved the envelope we'd given him, indicating that we should take it back. Right away, I understood what was happening. The French were refusing to accept it. The fact that they had accepted a similar document the year before had worked in our favour because the Canadian government was in a position to assert that I had formally notified the French of my right to be in international waters. This year, obviously, the French navy had no intention of making the same mistake. Except for the legal implications, what followed looked like a farce. I refused to accept the envelope back, so the lieutenant reached over and laid it on the deck. I picked it up and thrust it back at him. The Frenchman immediately threw it on the deck again. The inflatable started to back away, but I scooped it up once more and threw it into the bottom of the inflatable. The officer grabbed it, then stared at me with obvious frustration. Finally, he tossed the letter into the water and the inflatable pulled away.

I had just started to open the manilla envelope the French had delivered in the first place when I noticed that Ann-Marie's face was deeply flushed.

"What's the matter?"

"I forgot to take any pictures." She was mortified.

The envelope contained three sheets of paper, the same warning as we'd received the previous year, except that an executive decision legalizing the institution of a security zone within French law had been added.

La Dunkerquoise made no further attempt to contact us so I turned my attention to the serious problem of making sure that Ann-Marie, who had never taken a single picture in her life, would be ready when the showdown came. It did not particularly matter that she hadn't got any shots this time, but later, it could well be our only hope of producing evidence in the event of a boarding. I sat with her in the cockpit for close to an hour, going over the mechanism of the camera again and again.

"The main thing, no matter what happens, is just to think of yourself as an observer. Stay detached. Don't get involved. Don't pay any attention to anything except what you see through the lens. That's all that matters. Forget the rest. Just stay detached like you aren't even here, no matter what. Just take the picture and take another picture and take another . . ."

Ann-Marie was shaken. She knew full well the importance of getting pictures but she had astonished herself by becoming so engrossed in what had been happening – even though nothing much was happening at all – that she had completely forgotten the camera in her hands. Everything depended on having proof. We had worked out a routine where her position in the event of a boarding was to stay at the bow and take pictures as long as she could, then to go below through the forward hatchway and hide the camera. A second camera, with exposed film, would be left on the saloon table. Hopefully, the French would take it for the one she had been using.

Satisfied that I had done everything I could so that Ann-Marie would be ready, I turned to the task of resuming our journey. We continued to sail directly toward Mururoa. The minesweeper made no effort to block us. Instead, it moved off to about three miles and simply dogged along behind us.

That night, the weather changed dramatically. By midnight, we were in the grip of a force seven wind that was coming out of the east, pushing us steadily away from the atoll. By morning, the wind had become a gale. Remembering that the French had set off two bombs the previous year as soon as *Vega* had been driven out of position, we determined to make every effort to stay in place in the neck of the fall-out corridor. Carrying only the smallest amount of sail, we tacked back and forth all through the day while waves broke over us. *Vega* struggled to climb the waves but as often as not the best she could do was to torpedo through their flanks and she seemed to spend as much time under the water as riding on top of it. The minesweeper crashed past us repeatedly and once it had got ahead, it would stop and wait for us to beat our way up to it and past, then would repeat the manoeuvre.

Ann-Marie wrote in her diary:

> Generally, everything is moving. Have to be always bracing oneself. Wind howling non-stop. Water slushing and crashing. One bruise after another. Everything damp today. Each time we come about, anything that is loose crashes to the other side. Mary and I aren't allowed to eat anything. I've taken a couple of sea-pills. Wonder if the cockroaches feel the heaving. It's exactly like being on a Ferris Wheel or an Octopus ride at a show – only this is twenty-four hours a day. Exhausting.

I found that I did not have anything like the reserves of strength that I had had the previous year. I knew that I would not have the stamina to withstand a prolonged period of heaving-to again nor would I be able to hold out for very long against this kind of a battering. Clinging to the tiller, I found that my thoughts were unravelling wildly in every direction, a sure sign of fatigue. I remembered how it is in the big international championship games when a badminton player has run so long and hard, using every muscle and two players both in perfect condition are so evenly-matched that the game can go on for an eternity: it becomes an endurance contest. I had been in my prime then and I had learned to watch for that moment when the other player has been going at it so long that his heart is finally not able to keep up with his will and its muscles start to give up the struggle to pump enough blood to the brain. There came a cruel moment, sooner or later, where you could see his eyes starting to glaze over, and that was the moment you had been waiting for, the moment to put all your remaining energy and strength into a final whirlwind attack. I had the feeling now, fighting *Vega*'s tiller against waves that wanted to hurl her aside, that I was close to the point where my own eyes must be starting to glaze. I half-expected the sea to surge with redoubled fury and the wind to let out a cry of triumph as they closed in to finish us off.

But the other thing I remembered from all those years was that there always came a point where you were absolutely convinced that you didn't have even a good twitch left in you, that your body had been pushed beyond all reason, and the whole exercise then became to keep going for just another second and then another couple of seconds and then another minute – and you would finally break through into some to-tally new space wherein you were capable of a performance beyond anything you ever seriously thought you could do. I was into the trough now, that point where paralysis groped for my will and my body ranted angrily against all the abuse it was taking, and this was the tunnel I knew led through to the other side . . . Or, at least, it used to. I also knew that your body inevitably does reach a point where it has peaked and its best performance lies somewhere behind, never to be matched again. This was what my brother had warned against, and it had been a good warning. I had been drawing on my reserves of energy for so long that I was no longer certain there was anything left to draw. I felt emptied, sucked dry, and it was all I could do not to call for Nigel to take the tiller from me. But something – maybe nothing more than pride – made me hang on until the end of my watch.

Toward dusk, we decided to reef the sails even further down, dropping the storm jib and leaving only the staysail and fully reefed main. To do it, Nigel and I had to climb out to the bowsprit in our safety harnesses and endure the awful sensation of the ocean breaking in all its force over us, knowing that if the harness broke, nothing could save us from being swept head over heels from the boat.

Darkness brought no relief. We had made headway, but it had been slow, and the only wonder was that we hadn't been blown back at least twenty miles. Taking hour-long watches, we continued to pound through the night, the lights of the minesweeper appearing and disappearing as huge black shapes blotted them out for minutes at a time.

The morning of August 15 brought with it a vortex of racing dark-bellied clouds and rain so heavy that the minesweeper, scarcely more than a mile away, was only a wraith-like outline. Shortly after dawn, we arrived at the point that Nigel had calculated by dead reckoning to be our objective – due west of the mouth of Mururoa lagoon. Numbly we hove-to, grateful that the wind had fallen off and we would not immediately lose all the ground we had gained at such a cost of spent energy. The rain stopped after a few hours and the clouds broke apart, as though they too were so exhausted they could no longer sustain the solid grey-black arch they had formed from horizon to horizon. Nigel was able to get a number of sun shots. Our position was fourteen miles from the atoll!

Using the bearing Nigel had calculated, I took a compass with me and climbed to the foredeck to look for signs of activity. *La Dunkerquoise* had circled us and had now stopped, about a mile and a half off our stern.

"There!" I yelled. "Right on the button! The balloon!"

I could see it just above the horizon, swinging to and fro in the wind.

Try as they might, none of the other three could make it out with the naked eye and had to resort to the binoculars. Only then did it swim into their view.

The sea was calming rapidly and the wind continued to die down. As the day wore on, all of us sensed a growing tension in the atmosphere. Planes flew in and out of the atoll. Intuitively we reacted to the sense that something was about to happen by going over our plans in detail. I went over the operation of the video camera with Mary several times and set it so all she would have to do was aim it and push the trigger. Then I went over the handling of the Nikon again with Ann-Marie.

"Taking pictures is a helluva lot more important than worrying about Nigel or me. Stay detached. Whatever you do, stay detached."

276

We cleared the decks, arranging our equipment so that nothing was in the way, and rehearsed our movements carefully. If it looked like the French were going to board us, Nigel would go below and send an SOS. All of us were feeling nervous now. The girls had lost their earlier confidence. The sight of the balloon had had its effect on them.

At 1500 hours, our nervousness turned quickly to open fear.

We had decided to motor a little closer to the atoll, with the intention of perching just one mile beyond the twelve-mile limit. As soon as we started moving, *La Dunkerquoise* came to life. The minesweeper had been about two miles away from us at the time. Now it bore down on us at full speed, looming larger and larger. It was on a collision course. Even though Nigel and I had been through the experience before, we found it was no easier to bear. For the girls it was terrifying. Ann-Marie's face went chalky. The camera seemed such a futile weapon in the face of an onrushing one-hundred-and-fifty-foot warship. Less than a hundred yards from *Vega*, the ship veered off sharply. If the intention had been to unnerve us it was a complete success. I held *Vega*'s nose toward Mururoa, but I found myself trembling slightly.

La Dunkerquoise charged again and this time did not veer off until roughly fifty yards away.

None of us said a word. I licked my lips, feeling that I was treading a high wire over an enormous pit.

One more rush by the minesweeper at us and my instincts said, okay, this is as far as we go. I brought *Vega* about and we allowed ourselves to drift. Satisfied, the minesweeper made no further attack. It had been very much as though we had been approaching private property and a great metal guard dog had reared up, snarling its disapproval.

During the day, Nigel took close to thirty sunsights, giving us five accurate positions. This close to the territorial limit, we could take no chances.

At close to 1600 hours, I spotted a small vessel about fifty feet long coming over the horizon from the direction of Mururoa. I could make out a number on its bow – 41. That was all. No name.

"What is it?" I asked, passing the binoculars to Nigel.

"It's what we used to call in the Navy a vedette. It's a high-speed cutter. I think we're going to be boarded, David."

The vedette rendezvoused with *La Dunkerquoise* about two miles away. A few minutes later, we saw the smoke from a third ship, none other than the tug that had come so close to running us down the year before – A660, *Hippopotame*. Our old enemy held a steady course toward us. As it drew near, both the minesweeper and the vedette swung into motion. The three ships began to converge purposefully on *Vega*.

"Okay, stay cool," I said, as much to myself as to the girls.

We hauled up the sails in the hope that it would be harder for the French to board a moving ship, but the wind had perversely fallen off just when we needed it. It was blowing scarcely three knots. *Vega* moved sluggishly as though she were not ready for this final race and did not want to take part. I aimed her nose southward, slightly away from Mururoa so that we would not get squeezed into a situation where we could be herded over the territorial line.

And then the three ships were virtually on top of us. The steel tug came up on our port beam and *La Dunkerquoise* crashed past about a hundred yards on our starboard, with the vedette knifing smoothly along in its wake. As it came abreast, I spotted a large commando-type inflatable being dragged behind, carrying what looked like a small crowd of men. It seemed to me that *Vega* was not moving at all. She had barely gotten up to two knots. I had the engine on, idling to warm it up.

I was half expecting the tug and the minesweeper to close in on either side, in a variation of the squeeze play they'd used before. But my main focus of attention was on the inflatable. There, clearly, was the boarding party. The vedette was probably going to pull it in close enough to prevent *Vega* from outrunning it. I waited for the moment when the rope was released. If we were to have any chance of out-manoeuvring the inflatable, it would be then. Quickly I gauged the sky. The light was failing. If we could dodge them for even an hour, it would be dark and there was a chance they would not risk a boarding party then. And if *Vega* could stay free until the next morning, any number of things could happen. The Bomb might be postponed and then the weather might worsen again. All I wanted now was to gain a few moments, and those few moments might be stretched out into hours and the hours into a day, maybe another day ...

"Okay, Nigel," I said.

The Englishman nodded and jumped down the hatchway. The radio was on and ready. He methodically began to transmit on the 2182 international distress frequency, using the Morse key: SOS, SOS, SOS, then adding our latitude and longitude, 2139 S/13906w, VEGA, SOS, SOS. I cranked the diesel up to 1600 rpm's.

The inflatable had been released and it was swinging toward us, kicking up a wash that told me it was being driven by a powerful outboard engine. *Vega* was picking up speed, but I knew right away that we had no chance at all of outracing the rubber boat, even with the engine in gear. The only manoeuvre I could see now was to come about and try to get into a position to be running past the inflatable in the opposite direction by the time it pulled up to us. I rammed the tiller hard to port. *Vega* began to respond but with agonizing slowness. *La Dunkerquoise* was passing on our starboard quarter, *Hippopotame* was closing to our port and the vedette was about a hundred yards aft, with the inflatable pulling up with chilling speed on our starboard beam.

A muscular man in shorts was crouched at the bow of the inflatable with a rope ready to throw. There were six others hanging on as the rubber boat jumped and slapped across the waves. Their mouths were hard straight lines with the face muscles set. The inflatable crashed over the last wave separating it from *Vega* and slammed heavily against the hull just a few feet from the cockpit on the starboard quarter. Three arms shot out and hands grabbed for the safety railing, while the soldier standing at the bow hurled the rope onto the deck, grabbed the railing and scrambled on board. Getting numbly to my feet, I let the tiller go and stepped across the cockpit. I could see them clearly now. Most of them were in short-sleeved khaki uniforms although two wore windbreakers and one had a peaked cloth construction hat. These were no ordinary French sailors. Their faces were contorted with savagery and I could see that they were struggling to be the first to reach me. I saw the knives sheathed at their sides and I had a brief flicker of relief that they didn't have them in their hands. Then I saw the long black truncheons.

"This is private property," I said. "You can't come aboard." And then, because I knew they intended to beat me whatever I did, I brought my arms up in a blocking motion level with the neck of the soldier who was now halfway over the railing and with all my strength I checked him hard. It was enough to stop him in his tracks and for a second we were frozen face-to-face with snarls in our throats. Then there were two others coming over the side fast and before I could make any other move, the commando in front of me had grabbed my T-shirt and jerked it over my head. I felt each of my arms being grabbed in vice-like grips so that I was pinioned.

The first truncheon came down with a weight and force unlike anything I had ever felt on the back of my head and the second came down across my shoulders and the next blow landed on the back of my neck and the next on my head again and the next on my spine and the next on my shoulder blade and the next against my kidney and I was suddenly in the air being flipped over the railing and being yanked furiously into the inflatable, unable to catch a single breath or even find a way to make a sound. Two hands grabbed my right arm and jerked it down over my left hip and two other hands had my left arm, holding me as though I were in a straightjacket unable to try to cover myself. With scarcely a pause, the truncheons were flailing again, each blow rattling my teeth so that it seemed they would be shattered and that my spine and ribs and skull would cave in any second. Back. Neck. Head. Kidneys. I writhed and thrashed but was so expertly pinned there was absolutely nothing I could do, not even duck, and that was somehow the worst part as the truncheons continued to land at random, two truncheons smashing against me at once, three landing almost simultaneously, as though they all had gone mad and were simply trying to smash me to death, stamp me out of existence like some loathsome bug. Through the wild ringing in my head, I could hear their grunts. I could not believe I was still conscious. Then, with one man still pinning each arm, I was yanked upright and jammed in a sitting position against the side of the inflatable. Something crashed into my right eye with such incredible force that it seemed to come right into the middle of my brain in an explosion so that I thought that half my head had been torn off. And then everything went black.

When I came to, I was still being held so tightly that I couldn't move and I could hear Mary and Ann-Marie screaming. Half of my head seemed to be a vast hole. Only one eye would open. The other seemed to be clamped shut. Bending my body forward, I was able to get one hand up to probe at it. With a cold shock, I realized there was nothing there, just a wet pulpy socket. I could feel hot welts rising all over my head and back. My shirt had been torn off and there was blood splashed all over my arms and chest. With one good eye, I could see *Vega* beside me, her sails flapping wildly and I could see a cluster of men in the cockpit, their truncheons rising and falling, and briefly, I glimpsed Nigel's face.

When he heard the sound of the inflatable bumping against the hull, Nigel had stopped transmitting, rushed out through the main cabin and up the companion-way onto the deck, the girl's screams echoing in his ears. He immediately recognized the two men facing him as commando types. Before he could think of anything to say or do, he was grabbed from behind and his head and shoulders were forced forward. Vividly, he saw a truncheon right above him silhouetted against the bright blue sky. He saw that it was wrapped in black tape and his mathematician's mind automatically calculated that it was a foot and a half long and one inch in diameter with a white cord at one end that fitted around the wrist of the man who was preparing to bring it down on his head.

With his head bent forward, he was looking across the starboard side of the cockpit and he could see me, gripped by two men. The area around my right eye was a mass of blood and the right side of my face was smeared and dripping red.

Then the first blow landed on the back of Nigel's head, shuddering through his whole body, and the pain of it was incalculable. The second blow landed at the top of his neck. Briefly, he lost consciousness. And awoke to find himself on the deck forward of the cockpit, being kicked in the stomach and then full in the groin and then in the ribs and then in the stomach again. As he curled up to protect his groin another kick landed on his ribs and another and another. Between the blows, his eyes kept opening, and he could see the khaki canvas boots with round pads on the ankle-bones, thick rubber toe-caps and heavy rubber-treaded soles. He lost consciousness again.

All too soon he came to, finding himself on his back under the tiller which was swinging back and forth above his head. A man with a vicious hate-filled face was poised above him with his truncheon high in the air, ready to smash down. He had a small horizontal scar that stood out sharply on his cheek just below one of his sideburns. Then Nigel heard a voice yelling:

"Ça suffice! Ça suffice!"

He saw the men stepping over him and scrambling along the port deck toward Mary and he could hear her still screaming.

Throughout the whole thing, she had kept the video camera pointed and had seen it all through the lens. She had kept her control until the truncheons started to come down on Nigel and then the first scream burst from her lips.

Ann-Marie said she was shaking and it seemed that Mary's scream was coming from far away. In her haste, she had jammed the camera.

"Stay detached!" she ordered herself. "Just get this fucking camera unjammed. Just breathe deeply and take this winder across and get the bloody thing unjammed. Oh Christ! Damn!' An age later it seemed, the mechanism clicked and when she pointed the lens in the direction of the ferocious scramble at the stern, the shutter released.

Her head was spinning. Through her mind's confusion and through Mary's screams and the jolting of the boat as *Vega* crashed blindly through the waves, almost as though in a panic, the boom swinging from side to side and the sails rippling, she saw Nigel being held by two men while a third brought the truncheon down with such force that it seem he was trying to split Nigel in half.

Through a haze, she saw two of the soldiers starting up the port deck toward Mary, who was backing away. Instinct – nothing else – told her: "Now's the time! You've got to hide the camera!" As the Frenchman grabbed for Mary and wrenched the video camera out of her hand, Ann-Marie dived for the forward hatch. She caught a last glimpse of the video camera being thrown into the water, then she had landed in the darkened interior of the forepeak and was scrambling over the buckets and ropes. It was close to pitch black in the interior because the porthole boards had been slid into place during the storm. Her hip smashed painfully against the saloon table as she squeezed by and the sound of heavy boots on the deck was terrifying. She scrambled into our cabin and locked the French-style louvred door with its single twenty-five-cent catch.

Mary's screams suddenly ceased. Silence. Ann-Marie put her hand to the door. Had she been mistaken? Should she still be up on deck filming? Rough voices coming down the hatch stopped her from making a fatal mistake. A man was yelling in the saloon. They were hunting for her.

Locked away in the darkness of the cabin, she felt her limbs becoming petrified. There was no time to remove the film. The only thing to do was to hide the whole camera. There was no time to pull out the boards and do it properly as she'd practised – that took a full three minutes. Then her mind seemed to speed up and she thought of a new way to get the camera into the hiding place, thereby solving within seconds a problem that we had not been able to solve with weeks of thinking. She jammed the camera through a cubby hole and thrust it up and away into the interior of the boat's structure.

Already, the louvred door was being rattled. She gave the camera one last shove and then huddled in the corner on the floor as if she was just hiding there, knowing that the decoy camera was sitting out in the saloon.

Within seconds, the door was wrenched open and three of

the boarding party were standing there, shouting at her in French. By then she was angry as well as terrified. Through her tears she yelled at them:

"Fuck off!"

The tall one who had clubbed Nigel reached in and grabbed her wrist and hauled her out.

"Bastard!" she screamed, slapping him across the cheek. His face twisted and his furious eyes bore down on her.

"Don't you dare," she hissed, turning her back on him quickly before he would hit her.

She climbed the companion-way ahead of them and found Mary shivering on the deck, yelling at one of the officers for a representative of the New Zealand government.

"Nigel's lying on the floor," she gasped.

Then she heard me yell:

"Don't help them!"

Ann-Marie spun around and saw me in the inflatable, still held by my captors, blood pouring out of my eye.

Nigel was lying at the bottom of the cockpit. She started to shake and feel ill. One of the Frenchmen was throwing up over the side.

I found myself in the grip of a compulsion to hurl myself backward over the side of the inflatable, taking the two men that were holding my arms into the water with me. But something told me they would just start beating me all over again. Then I passed out.

When I came to, I was still being held. I could see Nigel being lifted by two men and pushed down the hatchway. I saw another man talking fiercely to Mary and found myself yelling:

"Don't tell them anything!"

Dimly I was aware of a Frenchman emerging triumphantly from the cabin waving the camera he'd found, I had no idea at the time whether it was the decoy or the one Ann-Marie was supposed to use. I could not even remember whether I had seen her taking any pictures. It had all happened so fast. And then the inflatable was pulling away from *Vega*, one man driving and the other two still holding my arms. I must have passed out again because the next thing I knew, I was looking up at the side of the minesweeper.

Nigel reported afterwards that he had awoken to find himself being stuffed into the bunk in the main cabin. Waves of pain pulsed through his head and neck and shoulders. Slowly, the muscles in his stomach began to unknot, leaving him with an almost overwhelming desire to vomit. A deep hurt spread out from his groin. Dimly, through his nausea and pain, he could see two Frenchmen dismantling the radio and cutting the microphone away. Another, who was searching the cabin, suddenly let out a yelp of triumph and waved a 35mm camera triumphantly at him. Nigel did his best to look utterly defeated, but, in fact, it was all he could do to repress a savage laugh. They had only found the decoy.

The boarding party had now taken control of *Vega*. Even in his pain, Nigel's attention came to focus on the fact that the engine was overheating rapidly. He had been too long around boats to be able to tolerate the idea of one being abused, so he called out weakly from his bunk in French, telling them to cut the speed before the diesel blew up. His last responsibility discharged, he faded out . . .

On deck, Mary and Ann-Marie were ordered to huddle together on the port side. Both of them discovered they had bruises on their arms where they had been grabbed. Mary tried once to jump through the forward hatch to see how Nigel was, but she was headed off, grabbed by the hair, and pushed back to her spot on deck. With both Nigel and myself out of the picture, a primitive fear surfaced in both women's minds. The Frenchmen were hard-muscled and they still had a slightly glassy look in their eyes, as though some terrible lust had been unleashed in the violence. Their power now was absolute, and both women half-expected to be raped.

Vega seemed to have been driven half-crazy herself. From the moment the attack had been launched, she had run like a horse with the bit in her teeth, engine revving wildly and three sails flapping. Even after Nigel had told the boarding party how to operate the engine, they continued to run the boat with no regard to the sails. The boom crashed from side to side and the sails continued to beat like fluttering wings. Finally, it was Mary who could not stand *Vega's* torment any longer. Gingerly, she gathered in the mainsail and lashed it secure. Then she climbed back down on the deck beside Ann-Marie. Both of them had begun to shiver, whether from shock or cold or terror, they couldn't tell.

Vega had been brought about and was now heading toward Mururoa, with the minesweeper on the port side, the *Hippopotame* on the other, and the vedette trailing behind. Except for what had just happened, it would have been a comic tableau. Bitterly, Ann-Marie said she could see a picture in her mind of a tiny sailboat with huge chains around her, linked to three steel warships, and two shivering girls on the deck, with a headline that went: Great Moments In French Naval History.

Whispering, and pausing to look nervously at their captors, the girls decided that if Nigel was taken away, they would jump into the inflatable which was now being towed away behind the boat, or into the water if need be, but they agreed they would not stay on *Vega* overnight alone, surrounded by these men, with no one to protect them.

When sunset came, it was blood red and turned the sails a brilliant scarlet.

After that, it got so cold the girls were finally allowed to go below and join Nigel.

He had recovered consciousness again. There was not much that could be said because the Frenchmen were standing in the hatchway, keeping an eye on them. It was then, as she described it later that Ann-Marie noticed the strap of the hidden camera hanging out on the floor. Nigel had spotted it too, and they knew it was only a matter of time before the French finally found it. Nigel and Ann-Marie exchanged looks, then he indicated with a nod that she should put her ear to his lips.

"Pretend you've got to go to the bathroom," he whispered.

She waited a few minutes, then signalled to the nearest guard that she wanted to take a bucket and go into the side cabin. Curtly, he nodded.

Closing the louvred door, she forced her trembling hands to

take the strap and stuff it out of sight, while pretending to bang around with the pail. That done, she forced her bladder to work.

The rest of the ride into Mururoa was uneventful. Nigel stayed in the bunk in obvious pain. From time to time, Ann-Marie looked through the porthole at the lights of the minesweeper and wondered what was happening to me . . .

A part of me knew a sense of relief. We were, at least, still alive. But another part knew a deep chill for I could not tell whether my right eye still remained in my head or not. It had, in fact, been driven so far back that when I prodded it with my fingertips, there was nothing to feel. A sick horror filled me, mixed with a rage that left me sitting straight up on the sofa in the captain's quarters of *La Dunkerquoise* where they had taken me and ordered me to lie down. I had come out of the state of shock so that my body shuddered and would not stop shuddering. Blood was still coming from the eye and there were pulpy spots all over my head where the truncheons had landed.

A first-aid man had been brought in to examine me. I could tell from his expression that he was worried. He spoke to the captain in French, and again, they asked me to lie down. Again, I refused. I sat rigidly, looking out through my one good eye as though from the vantage spot of a lighthouse, throwing the beam of my glare, in which all my anger was brought to focus, on whoever came into the room. At one point, one of the men who had beaten me stepped through the doorway. My eye looked on him furiously and seemed to have acquired an almost physical force. The man stared back at me wordlessly for a moment, then a haunted expression came over him, and he backed away, closing the door behind him. I could remember seeing a film once showing a mortally-wounded deer, its flesh torn and pelt covered with blood, quite helpless and utterly at the mercy of its hunter, yet there had been some mesmerizing dignity in the way it turned its head and looked out from the shambles of its body, as though, in the process of being mutilated, the animal had risen above its tormentor and was now looking *down* at him.

The feeling I had was not so much that I was a prisoner, but

287

that, in the bloody process of seizing me, they had bound themselves to me, they had made themselves prisoners of *my* fate, and as I surveyed them now from my lonely lighthouse I did not see triumphant warriors with the power of the atom at their command. Rather, I saw a succession of nervous and troubled men who seemed eager to get me off their hands into the hands of someone else.

Rather than having cowed me by the beating up, they seemed in some definite way to have cowed themselves. The captain of the minesweeper acted like a man who has lost all his sense of authority. My first words to him had been to demand:

"Was it you or the admiral who ordered us beaten up?" The captain shrugged and looked away and muttered in broken English that it was not something he could discuss.

"We were in international waters," I rasped. "You know that as well as I do." Defensively, the captain nodded and, again, he looked away. At one point, he asked me if *Vega* had enough fuel in her tanks to make it to Mururoa.

"That's not my problem," I snapped. Despite the spots that were dancing in front of my remaining eye, despite the pain that rolled back and forth through my body, and the nausea and faintness that threatened to envelope me in mist, I held my body as rigid as a stake driven into the sofa. I was still in that position four hours later when we finally docked at Mururoa.

A commodore bustled in through the door, waving a finger angrily at me. Nine or ten other officers squeezed in behind him.

"You entered French territorial water," the commodore half-shouted. "We had every right to seize you."

I turned the beam of my eye on the officers one at a time, seeing that, except for the commodore, all they could muster by way of reaction were various expressions of horror, queasiness and disgust. Then I concentrated on the commodore.

Pointing to the captain of *La Dunkerquoise*, I said:

"He was there and he knows damn well we weren't in territorial waters. Ask him!"

The captain was unable to do anything except nod his head. An uncomfortable silence hung in the air. The commodore's bluster lost its momentum. He tried to regain it, but failed.

"Get me a decent doctor, somebody who knows something about eyes. I want a proper examination," I said.

Instructions were quickly given in French. Within moments, two men came forward and began to probe my face. One of them shook his head and addressed the commodore in polite but uneasy tones.

Finally, the commodore said:

"We will fly you immediately to hospital in Papeete."

"I'm not going anywhere until I make a phone call to Canada."

"That's not possible."

"Then stuff it. I'm not leaving."

It did not occur to me then that there was anything incongruous about a wounded man in torn clothes sitting in the midst of the officers of a navy with the power to build a hydrogen bomb and telling them to "stuff it". Whether they spoke English or French made no difference. The language of their bodies said that some astonishing and unexpected balance had been struck. None of them would come near me except the medical officers and then they approached with exaggerated caution.

I could see that every last one of them was worried, worried to their guts. And the concern was my eye. They had overdone their little act of vengeance. Otherwise, the truncheons had been expertly applied. I knew there would only be bruises and that all the French had to do was hold Nigel and me for a week and the bruises would have gone away. The French would deny that any beating up had taken place and there would presumably be no proof. But the eye – if the eye was lost, there would be proof. They were going to have one hell of a time explaining the eye, and sooner or later, they would have to let me go. Whether there was a political law, or a deeper law, at work, I did not think much about it. I simply knew that they had overdone it and now I had the power to cause them a lot of trouble. Moreover, they all knew it too.

"You *must* go to Papeete. Otherwise we cannot cure you."

"I'm not going."

"This is a medical matter now. It is not a –"

"I want to speak to Admiral Claverie."

"Oh no, he is not here right now!"

"Bullshit! I want to talk to him."

"It is not possible for you to speak with the admiral."

"Then I want to talk with my government. By phone. Before I go anywhere or anybody touches me."

"Mr McTaggart, if you do not accept medical treatment, then we can not be held to blame for what happens to your eye."

"You're goddamn right you're to blame."

"It is necessary that you have treatment immediately. You *must* go to Papeete." Whether the commodore was aware of it or not, a pleading note had crept into his voice. He still spoke harshly, as though his authority was not to be questioned, but I knew that he was speaking like that for the benefit of the other officers. Certainly it wasn't having any effect on its target.

"I want to make a phone call."

"It is not possible. I'm speaking the truth. After eight o'clock we cannot link up with the island telephone system. You cannot get a call out until tomorrow. But then it may be too late to cure your eye."

I had not yet thought much about what it would mean to be without one of my eyes. My mind did not want to go near that kind of thought. But I knew my eye must be bad. The doctors had not been faking their worry and I knew there was truth in what the commodore was saying. I had the power to bargain all night – but the cost?

In the end the commodore promised that I would be allowed to make a phone call to Canada as soon as we got to the airport in Papeete. Only then did I allow the two medical men to apply a large piece of white gauze to my eye.

Then, with a man on either side, I half-walked, was half-carried through a maze of corridors, past hatchways through which the sound of huge generators pounded in rhythm with the pounding in my head. Lights leapt out at me sparkling among the bright spots that were already dancing around my field of vision. Dimly, I saw French sailors all around, on the decks, now on the dock down which I had been led along the gangplanks. Some of their faces were chipped out of stone, others were electrified. On whichever eyes I turned my single

290

lens, they all looked quickly away. It became a side-game, trying to find one man's glance I could fasten on before it escaped. They turned from me as though I were Medusa.

Just as I was being ushered into an ambulance, one of the officers leaned toward me and said:

"You are being allowed to see your crew. They'll be here in a minute."

The dock was bleakly illuminated by a few floodlights. The vast bulks of the warships towered in the darkness. There were at least a hundred officers and men in the space between the end of the dock and the ambulance. Squinting, I could see that the Frenchmen were parting to let two pale figures through. It was Nigel and Ann-Marie, moving with a poignant child-like nervousness between the rows of uniformed men. There was an incredible tension in the air, as though the Frenchmen expected something dramatic to happen. I was stunned by the enormous exhaustion written on Nigel's face and I wished I could think of something comforting or appropriate to say to Ann-Marie.

They had been told only a few minutes before to pack a small bag with toilet articles for me. The bag had been searched several times before being handed back to them.

Ann-Marie thrust it into my hands and put her arms around me, squeezed me briefly, then stepped back.

Hurriedly, Nigel told me that they were being confined on *Vega*, that Mary was still there, and that their requests to communicate with their government had been denied. I scanned his face for some sign one way or another that photos had been taken and the film successfully hidden away. But with officers crowded all around and a hundred sets of eyes on us, Nigel did not so much as dare a wink or a nod. Rather than risk giving our secret away, I asked no questions. After only half a minute, the guards led Nigel and Ann-Marie away and the ambulance door was closed.

Although I had thought myself to be coherent, the other two said later they were left with the impression that I was either drugged or dazed. They had hardly been able to understand a word I said.

At the airport, I found myself being ushered onto a four-

291

engined plane the size of a DC–6. I had evidently been trans-
ferred from military to civilian authority because the guards
had been replaced by a single gendarme. The plane itself had
been stripped except for seats. It was obviously used for troop
transport. Now its only passengers were myself, the medical
officer and the gendarme, who jabbed a form at me advising me
that I was now officially declared an undesirable alien in French
Polynesia.

"Sign it!" the gendarme ordered.

I grabbed the piece of paper and stuffed it in my hip pocket.
"Not signing anything."

"You must sign it."

"Nothing."

Angrily, the gendarme dug the form out of my pocket and
took it back.

We lifted from Mururoa at roughly eleven in the evening. If
I had any reference-point for the flight in that all-but-empty
troop transport plane, it was the recollection of climbing on a
late-night elevated train with only a conductor and one other
half-asleep passenger for company. It was a measure, I knew, of
the problem I now represented to the French that they would
immediately launch an aircraft of this size to take an emergency
run from Mururoa. There was only the glimpse of a necklace of
lights in the midst of a tremendous darkness to tell me we were
above the atoll, then the darkness swallowed our long, empty
tube for the next three hours. Exhaustion tried to pull me down
into sleep, but I felt incredibly alert and lucid despite the leaden
feeling that crept into my limbs.

At 3 am, we landed on the outskirts of Papeete. An ambulance was waiting. Lying in the back, I had a kaleidoscopic
impression of familiar neon signs as we raced across town to a
large hospital complex. The attendants tried to get me to lie
in a stretcher when the time came to leave the ambulance, but I
refused. I had only one thought in mind – to resist everything
they offered until I could get a call out to Canada.

The hospital lobby was swarming with police and military
personnel. Several nurses and orderlies immediately closed in
around me, indicating I should follow them.

"No. It's been arranged for me to go to a phone. Where's the phone?"

"It will be arranged," a doctor said in English. "But just come with us for a moment."

I followed them down a corridor, down another corridor, and into an operating room. The gendarme and the military were stopped at the door. Now there were only nurses, technicians and doctors. I allowed them to help me onto the table. It was only then, when they removed the gauze and asked me to close my good eye and try to look up into a blinding circular light through my injured eye that I fully realized the enormity of the damage that had been done. Nothing. Absolutely nothing but blackness. Not so much as a pinprick of light could I make out.

Then I saw a nurse come through the door with a tray full of surgical instruments and needles. I surged up from the table, roughly thrusting aside the several arms that tried to force me back down. Now, perched on the side of the table, I glowered at them as I had glowered at the officers back at Mururoa.

"Please! You must lie down!"

My voice had a sandpaper quality to it now that sounded strange in my own ears, as though it were a familiar but not-quite-recognizable voice, maybe somebody I had known a long time ago.

"Oh no, absolutely not. I'm not taking any injections until I get to talk to my brother in Canada."

"It is too late for that. We must treat you now."

"No. No phone call, no injections."

One of the doctors became angry.

"You are under medical orders now. You must do as we tell you."

"The hell with you," I snarled. I half-jumped, half-fell from the operating table and pushed my way to the door. Yanking it open, I found myself face to face with the gendarme and two military police. Whether I had become such an apparition they could not resist me or they were simply on unfamiliar turf, they did not try forcibly to restrain me. I marched back down the two corridors and out into the lobby, followed by a small crowd of jabbering people. Ignoring them, I sat down in a chair by the doorway and warded them off with my half-mad furious one-eyed glare.

The supervisor of the hospital appeared and raged at me, saying that this was his hospital, that no one could come in and disrupt it like this, that there were other people to think about, and, finally, that if I did not allow them to tend to me soon, they would wash their hands of the whole affair.

"Good luck," I said.

At length, they promised to arrange the phone call – if I would only lie down in a bedroom while they were making the necessary connections. I agreed.

There was only one bed in the middle of the room. I laid in it for what seemed like an eternity, alone with my own doubts and a growing sense of panic about what was happening to my eye. Only once was I disturbed. An attractive nurse who spoke English appeared and talked to me soothingly and sympathetically.

After a few minutes she reached casually for the hypodermic which I had noticed her slipping beside the bed just out of my view.

"Forget it," I said.

"Oh now, Mr McTaggart, you'll get your phone call later. Right now, we must –"

"Forget it."

The nurse became angry, and when that didn't work, she stamped out of the room.

Dawn was starting to lighten the sky through my window blinds when one of the doctors who had been in the operating room came in and explained to me very matter-of-factly;

"The blood is going to start coagulating in your eye very shortly, if it hasn't already, and once that process has begun, you can kiss your eye goodbye. There just will not be anything we can do to save it. It is as simple as that. You can argue all you like, but those are the facts."

It had been close to fourteen hours since the beating and I had not accepted any medication at all. I knew that if the various authorities didn't give in soon, I would have to allow them to get to work.

At 7 am, they brought in a wheelchair. "Your brother is on the phone."

I did not speak to Drew for long, just long enough to dictate a passionate telegram to be sent to prime minister Trudeau, demanding my immediate release and the release of Nigel, Mary and Ann-Marie.

It was Drew who said: "Okay, David, now listen to what I'm saying. Let them treat you right away. For God's sake, don't push it any longer. I'll get things going here, the telegram, everything. We'll get you out. Now let them do what they can."

The moment I put the receiver down, I felt a wave of nausea and exhaustion pass through me. The defiance left me all at once, and all I wanted was relief from the pain, release, sleep, and for that awful bottomless blackness in my right eye to be penetrated.

I nodded weakly to the doctor. Immediately, I was wheeled into the operating room.

Nigel and the girls had awakened the morning after I was flown to Papeete to find four guards armed with machine guns standing on the jetty next to the boat. Nigel knew the three of them now faced the difficult task of finding some way to get out of Mururoa with the film showing the attack. Merely to avoid letting the French find the film was going to be tricky. Getting it out was another matter entirely.

At 10.30 in the morning, an interpreter arrived with a half-dozen Frenchmen. One was introduced as Philippe Berges, a representative of the Polynesian Government, another as the military commander of Mururoa, and the others, including one who kept taking pictures of them, were not introduced at all.

Still weak and hurting all over from the beating, Nigel mustered his most official manner and requested that all except the commander, the government representative and the interpreter leave the boat immediately. He realized it was important at the outset to establish as many precedents in their treatment as possible.

He was quickly advised that the three of them would not be taken to Papeete, as they had been told the previous night, but that they would be flown to the island of Hao, some three hundred miles away. There, they would be lodged in a school and would have "the same freedom as the ordinary people of the island".

"We want to see David McTaggart in hospital," Nigel said.

"I'm afraid that's out of the question," said Mr Berges.

"Then we want to see representatives of our governments."

"That's impossible."

"Will there be facilities to communicate with our governments in Hao?"

"I believe there are international telephone facilities at Hao, yes."

Nigel had planned to lock the boat up on their departure, but now he was told that an inventory of all its contents was required. During the night, he had already hidden the charts and logs so skilfully that he was confident it would take the French weeks to find the stuff. But as the inventory started, he found himself flanked by two gendarmes and two military men. The military men began pulling things apart and rifling through personal belongings including the women's toilet bags.

Nigel protested to the government representative. To his surprise, he was supported by the senior gendarme and the two military men were sent out of the boat. Clearly, there was a rift of some kind between the civilian police and the military – and there, perhaps, was the crack in the armour that he had been looking for. Making a point of being polite to the gendarmes, Nigel cooperated with the rest of the inventory, duly signing the pages of the official notebook on which the senior gendarme was making his entries.

His next move was to express concern about personal searches.

"Since we are being held illegally, we have no intention of being subjected to searches," he said.

"That will not happen," he was told.

Finally, at 4 pm, they were given five minutes to get ready to go to Hao. At this point, there were twenty men standing around on the jetty, including the commandos who had beaten us up the day before. No appeal to protocol was going to work. Nigel found himself having to fight the fear that was rising in him as he looked over the harsh faces of the waiting men. Mary and Ann-Marie were terrified to leave the slight security of the boat. Both of them began to cry.

The gendarmes and military men had all left the boat. Unable to think of anything else to do for the moment, Nigel slammed the hatchway shut and locked it.

"Get the film," he said to Ann-Marie. Once they left the boat they would never get another chance. Whatever they did, they had to have it with them when they were taken from Mururoa.

Forcing herself to control the trembling of her hands, Ann-Marie dug the camera out of its hiding spot and pulled loose the small plastic canister containing the exposed film.

"We can't just put it in our bags," she said in a whisper. "There's too much of a chance they'll search us anyway."

There was a banging on the door.

"Come on! Get ready to go!"

Desperately, Nigel shouted back in French:

"We're just getting some personal belongings together. Give us ten minutes and we'll lock up the boat!"

Turning to Ann-Marie, he said:

"There are precedents, you know. Have we got any of those little plastic bags? Give me the film."

Putting the canister in the bag, he went into the head. Bending over and pulling down his pants, he struggled for several minutes to try to insert the canister through his anus into his rectum. But the pain was too great. He couldn't do it.

Ann-Marie had understood immediately what he planned to try to do. The moment he stepped out of the head, she could tell from the expression on his face that he had failed.

"All right," she said, making up her mind "Give it to me."

If she was pale and walked stiffly when the three of them finally clambered out of the boat and moved down the jetty past the rows of French sailors, it was because the pain of the object in her vagina forced her to bite her teeth. She became obsessed that the slightest unusual movement would betray her, yet it was close to impossible to walk normally. She clung to Nigel, and tried to pretend that she was faint – which was close enough to the truth. Nigel put his arm around her as though to help her keep her balance. And if there were tears running from her eyes, the Frenchmen had no way of knowing they were tears not just of fright but of pain.

SIX

I stood and watched the sun so it went down
the horizon. When the sun went down the sky
turned into different kinds of colour like the
rainbows. It made me so lonely when I
watched all different colours appear in the sky
many ideas appeared in my head like I was
dreaming and floating like a leaf on the sea. I
dreamed all the things I did in the past.

I felt the cold air from the sea all around me
so I remembered that I was still standing on
the same place. I turned and looked at the sky,
the sky turned its colour and became dark so I
went home.

Alice Thel
(Polynesian native)

Twelve days later, I was on a jet descending into the galaxy of lights that was Vancouver. During a stop-over in Seattle, I had self-consciously purchased a pair of dark sunglasses so that the black eye patch I had been wearing since leaving the military hospital in Papeete was tucked in the hip pocket of my jeans. I was flanked on one side by a young consular official sent by Ottawa to arrange for my release and on the other by Dr Robert McCreery, an eye specialist who had been sent by my brother to Tahiti.

Nigel and the girls had been released from Hao several days before. The girls had been given air tickets back to New Zealand and Nigel to London. But Nigel had traded his ticket in Los Angeles and flown directly to Vancouver where he handed the film canister to my brother. Drew had, in turn, passed it to Greenpeace. Thirteen pictures had turned out, four of them showing knives on the belts of the boarding party, three showing truncheons and one clearly showing Nigel being clubbed. The two best pictures had already been picked up by the wire services and published in at least twenty countries – excluding France where it was censored and where the Naval High Command was still insisting that its men had been unarmed and had not thrown a single punch. The French Government's official position was that I had slipped on the deck and accidentally banged my eye on a cleat.

As the jet settled to a landing, a stewardess approached me and said:

"Mr McTaggart, would you please stay seated until everyone has departed?"

It was 2 am. I was tired, my eye was bothering me – I didn't argue. The consular officer said: "I've done my job.

You're back in Canadian territory." With a nod, he slipped away, mingling with the other passengers.

When they had all left, the stewardess came back. "It's okay to leave now."

Leaving the door of the plane was like stepping onto a brightly-lit stage. The lights and the flashbulbs stabbed through the glasses into the expanded iris of my right eye, blinding me. I stumbled down the ramp, vaguely aware of some kind of crowd consisting of more photographers, television cameras and reporters than I had ever seen. There, at the bottom of the ramp, were my parents, brother Drew and Nigel. Drew whispered: "There's more news people here than when the Queen arrived. They'd only let a few of them outside. The rest are waiting inside for a press conference."

I was still under sedation, my eye hurt badly, and I was dazed and tired. Half-uncomprehendingly, I was pushed and pulled into the air terminal, hugged by people I didn't know, my hand grasped and shaken dozens of times. The noise and the lights crackled in my head. When I had left this same terminal, back at the end of May, there had only been a few relatives, a couple of Greenpeace directors and a lone reporter. Dimly, I became aware that the release of the photographs showing the beating had created a storm in Canada, with demands that French trade commissions be closed and the French ambassador kicked out of the country for having told an outright lie. The prime minister had called him into his office and protested my treatment "loud and clear".

The press conference was mercifully brief. Drew came to my rescue after I had answered several dozen rapid-fire questions by announcing that I had to be taken to hospital forthwith. Then, when we emerged from the conference room into the main lobby, close to fifty Greenpeace supporters swarmed around, popping champagne bottles and singing. It was all surrealistic. They would have picked me up and carried me around had Drew not once again intervened.

I spent the next two days in hospital undergoing a battery of tests. The eye had healed to the point where I could see blurred images through it but that was all. In it's weakened condition, with the optic nerve shattered, there was a fifty-per-cent chance of me coming down with acute glaucoma. If that happened, unless I could get to a specialized medical facility within fourteen hours, I would lose sight in the eye completely. Among other things, it meant I could never go sailing again unless I was willing to risk complete blindness in one eye.

Time Magazine was to remark a few days later that the *Greenpeace III* incident had "sunk Franco-Canadian relations to the lowest point since Charles de Gaulle dropped his *Vive le Quebec Libre* clanger in 1967", a reference to the day the French general had openly encouraged Quebec separatists while on an official visit to Canada and had, as a result, been asked to leave the country. The Canadian Bar Association took the unprecedented step of inviting Nigel to describe the boarding to their annual convention and then unanimously voted to urge the government to "pursue appropriate remedies for reparations against the government of France including, if necessary, the institution of proceedings in the International Court of Justice". The Canadian government's quick response to the suggestion was to say that France had indicated it would not recognize the jurisdiction of the World Court, despite the fact that the French government had once been one of its strongest supporters.

In fact, as I was later to learn, France had been so worried about the possibility of Canada launching an action in the World Court after *Vega*'s first encounter at Mururoa that they had hastened to legitimize the 100,000 square-mile cordon in French law because until then, it had not even been legal in France. They had been braced for retaliation from Canada, and had breathed a sigh of relief when it hadn't come. I was further to learn that the International Court itself had been eagerly awaiting the case, since it would have been the first test of the law of the sea since its creation in the 1600s and might set a precedent that would apply not only to nuclear tests, but to oil and mineral rights in the sea-bed and could affect the future of "nodule" underwater mining and a variety of other emerging technologies aimed at exploiting the resources of the sea in international waters. By taking the case to The Hague, Canada could have made a substantial contribution in terms of preserving the marine environment. Instead, Canada avoided the issue. It was not until much later that I began to fully understand the reasons behind Canada's astonishing reluctance to move against France . . .

While I lay in hospital in Vancouver, my only contact from the Canadian government came in the form of a long letter which the external affairs department had elicited from a dean of the faculty of law and economic sciences at Grenoble, coming to the conclusion that I could enter a liability suit before the courts of law in France but that "his chances of success are practically non-existent". I was also advised that any such action might cost in the neighbourhood of six hundred thousand dollars and that in the view of the Canadian government my claim was not large enough to warrant it.

My lawyer, Jack Cunningham, came to visit me.

"David, what do you want to do?"

It was no easy question to answer. Already, the pattern was clear. The federal government had only sent an envoy to Tahiti after it had been embarrassed into the action by my brother and Greenpeace having sent an eye specialist. Afterwards, when asked in the House of Commons what the Canadian government had done to help me, external affairs minister Sharp had grandly stated: "We arranged to send an eye specialist to Tahiti." He had acknowledged that the seizure of *Vega* was a violation of international law. Canada had asked France for an investigation. But France was sticking to its story, despite the published photographs, that the boarding party was unarmed and that the seizure had taken place for "humanitarian reasons". At Mururoa, two more bombs had been fired and one had created a "blow-back" with radiation fanning westward across the Pacific instead of eastward along the fallout corridor. Some of the fallout had settled in Samoa. But French defence minister Robert Galley had nevertheless gone to Tahiti and announced: "France will never undertake to stop testing in the atmosphere."

What to do?

I stared at the ceiling for a long time. *Vega* had been stolen by the Republic of France and had now sat through two atomic blasts at Mururoa. Regardless of what happened to her as a result of the blasts, I knew that every day she sat in the tropical sun, her decks would be scorched and she would rapidly deteriorate. So I had no boat – and, according to the doctors, even if I had, my long-distance sailing days were over. Nigel's injuries were worse than had been expected. X-rays had revealed damage to his spine and he still suffered from appalling headaches and attacks of dizzinesss.

I had no money. The rest of my belongings were still on the boat so all I had was the clothes on my back. There had been a tremendous amount of publicity and a tremor had gone through the political establishment, but in the absence of any deter-mined drive by the Canadian government to take legal action, the ferment would die down. France would stick to its story, and the news stories would march inexorably to the back pages.

Despite all this, I had not yet lost the mood that had gripped me after the beating up – a rigid unbending defiance. I had made life as miserable as possible for my captors in the French hospital, marching down to the lobby every day with my armed guard trailing along, making everyone nervous because the official reports repeatedly stated that I was free to come and go as I liked. After a while, the guard had been replaced by a plainclothesman. But just as surely, I had remained a prisoner. Twice I had tried to escape, once with the assistance of a Frenchman and his wife. At the last minute, ten secret service-men had swarmed into the hospital to prevent my leaving. On the second occasion, when I was preparing to climb down from a balcony, it was to find three cops waiting in the shadows below. My arguments with the French hospital and military authorities had been persistent and bitter. I had been hardly less furious with the Canadian envoy when he arrived.

By now I was back in Canada and no longer face-to-face with the power that had attacked me. Instead, there was a wide grey buffer zone around me through which I could barely make out the vague shapes of Ottawa bureaucrats and politicians and reporters whose attention-span could be measured in days and weeks but certainly not in terms of the years it might take to finally pin the French down in their own courts. And then there was the stunning thought of the amount of money that would be involved.

With the Canadian government refusing to take the case to the International Court of Justice – something I couldn't do myself because actions could only be launched at that level by governments – the only course open to me was to initiate an action in the French civil courts and press the Canadian government to "espouse" my claim. Espousal is a rarely-used technique of international diplomacy wherein one government presses another to settle a grievance through the setting up of the equivalent of an arbitration board. Espousal can only be undertaken, however, when the claimant has "exhausted all local legal remedies". In other words, I would have to do everything that could possibly be done to seek redress in the French courts myself before Canada would undertake to deal with the matter on a state-to-state basis.

After being released from hospital, I retreated to Buccaneer Bay to chop wood and think.

In early September, Ann-Marie arrived from New Zealand. She had lost weight. During the time she had been held on the island of Hao, she had had nightmares every night. She was haunted by the fear that the French at Mururoa might at any time develop the exposed film in the decoy camera and realize they had been duped. Each time she heard footsteps outside the building where they were being held, she had flinched, thinking they were coming to search for the real film. Every day they remained, it seemed the chances of their ruse being discovered increased enormously. Finally, along with Mary Lornie, she was flown to Tahiti. She had been promised she would be allowed to see me on compassionate grounds, but at the hospital she was refused at the last minute because her "footsteps might disturb the other patients". Getting on the jet for New Zealand, she had been stunned by the discovery that all the other passengers were behaving quite normally and that there was nothing to indicate that the issue of French nuclear testing had so much as crossed their minds.

The bond between us had deepened. But even then, in the spectacular early autumn of the West Coast, we both knew two shadows lay across us. The first was familiar – it was the problem of how our age difference affected my family and friends. The second was something she would just have to prepare herself to deal with in time. She mentioned the previous winter and the disillusionment it had brought. It seemed that we were back to square one, except that I was now permanently maimed and that the boat was in French hands. She wanted nothing more than to forget the whole mess now before things got even worse, before I descended once more into the unclean catacomb of politics and red tape and letters and telegrams and phone calls and interviews and more red tape and more letters into which I had all but disappeared in that long awful winter we'd just been through.

I loved her as much as I had ever loved any woman. Of course it was different with each, which meant that love itself was always different. It was exquisitely good to have her with me, not to be alone. But I found myself writing in small almost guilty print in my log one night: "... it is not in *living* that one wishes to be alone, but in *doing* ...." Sometimes I felt uneasy at the thought that my feelings had become like my eyes. They were really two different organs now. They simply did not work together. One saw the world in a certain way, the other in its own. My feelings were no less uneven – aloneness might break me, but I had always worked alone and it was the only way I truly knew how to work.

The immediate problem seemed to me to be the rescuing of *Vega* from Mururoa, and after that – regardless of what Ottawa said – the idea of going to a French court had a certain ring. I did not expect to win, but I guessed that such a move on my part would put pressure on the Canadian government to act. And I realized that the name of the game was pressure ... pressure ... pressure. I was indeed back where I had been the previous winter, sawing away at the government's Achilles heel. About all that had really happened, apart from my own losses and injuries, was that the stakes had gone up. I had been told enough to know that the penalty in France for the kind of action the navy had taken, should they ever by some miracle be convicted, was nothing less than death by the guillotine for armed piracy. I was also told flatly that if I ever tried to go into France to press the case I would be taking my life in my hands. The last foreigner who had gone to France to try to lay a serious charge against the French government – a German – had disappeared.

One night I told Ann-Marie, almost defensively:

"Why should they be allowed to get away with it? The whole purpose of the government, including the navy and army and air force and everything else the citizen pays for, is first of all to protect your person, and second, to protect your property. If the Canadian government won't do either, then it might as well not exist. As for what the French did, it's the same as Italy sending a tank into Canada, running somebody's car down, pulling them out and beating them up and then hustling them off to jail in Italy, and the Canadian government just standing there, watching it happen. A thing like this happening in international waters is a lot different from somebody getting mugged on a street in Chicago. In international waters, you have rights, damn it! It's like being in your own home."

In her diary, Ann-Marie wrote:

"We have done enough. We have drawn attention to the problem. David is ageing terribly."

It was true. I was losing hair rapidly and what hair that remained was turning grey and white. To add to it, my eye was aching now most evenings, it kept causing "flashes", and reading was difficult.

Nigel left for England. Mary Lornie had gone back to work in Auckland. Beyond having filled out an affidavit, she seemed not to want to have anything more to do with the whole business, which was Ann-Marie's own feeling, although she did not say anything to me about it. Instead, because we were broke, she moved back into Vancouver and got a job as a dental assistant.

The Canadian government continued to drag its heels. When my lawyer demanded to know why the government was hesitating, he was told that the RCMP had not yet certified the original 35 mm negatives as being authentic. When the lawyer asked to know the contents of the diplomatic notes that had been exchanged between Canada and France over the matter, all I got back were letters stressing the need to maintain good political and economic relations with France "in the interests of all Canadians".

By October the lawyer – himself a lifelong supporter of the Liberal Party – was becoming so exasperated that he wrote to the director of the legal advisory division of the Department of External Affairs, saying:

> It would appear from the correspondence between us that the same pattern is developing with respect to Mr Mc-Taggart's claims this year as developed in his claim for damages arising from the ramming of his boat by *La Paimpolaise* in 1972, which is still not resolved . . . Your department has given us every evidence of the continued use of your "good offices", and public pronouncements have been made supporting his claims arising from both incidents, but whatever courses of action are being pursued on a government-to-government level, they do not appear to be producing any results . . . We have come to the reluctant conclusion that while Mr McTaggart and ourselves have been given your repeated assurances that efforts are being made on his behalf to deal with his claims, it is clear your department is actually only "going through the motions" . . . We suggest that the Canadian government could rightfully be accused of exhibiting a lack of concern for the rule of law in the world.

On November 1, the first reports appeared in the newspapers stating that French engineers had begun drilling preliminary tunnels for underground nuclear tests "to replace the annual series of atmospheric tests which have aroused vigorous objections in Asia, Australia and South America and have become a diplomatic embarrassment for France".

One of the local newspapers inserted a one-paragraph editorial, titled "Victory":

> The French are reported preparing to stage future nuclear tests underground at uninhabited Pacific atolls. This would be a considerable victory for world public opinion, and the

skipper of the Greenpeace and his supporters at home and abroad can take credit for their part in that victory.

If Dr Linus Pauling's calculation was correct that fifty thousand children would be born deformed for every ten-megaton bomb tested in the atmosphere, then there was no telling how many children had been spared by that victory. For at least one evening, I felt very good indeed.

It was only then that Ann-Marie felt it was time to tell me her feelings.

"We deserve more time together," she said. "Some peace and quiet. We haven't had a free day for a long time. You need the rest, David. And I need it too."

"Yeh, I know what you're saying, but it's not over yet. There's . . . more involved."

I did not think it made much difference whether France did truly stop testing in the atmosphere. Even presuming that they were not lying – and I had little reason to believe in the French government or military – it remained that they were still fashioning their nuclear bombs at the expense of the people of a conquered territory. It still remained that while I had no direct legal grievance that would put me into a position to go after the United States or Britain or Russia or China to affect their weapon-making in any way, I did have an avenue open to me in the case of France.

Not many individuals in the world had even that much of a chance. Quit now? It seemed that everything that had gone before had only succeeded in giving me this one real opportunity to strike at the heart of the beast. *La Bombe* might have been driven from the light of day, but it was no less alive. Rather than feeling that the battle was over, my instinct was that it had only begun.

Three days after the announcement that the tests were going to be moved underground, I got a letter from Ottawa saying that the French were willing to allow me to pick up *Vega* in Tahiti, if I promised to sail her away immediately.

The doctors said no. I definitely could not undertake such

a voyage. The danger of an attack of acute glaucoma was too great. So I asked, through Ottawa, if I could be allowed to stay on the boat in Papeete until I could arrange for a crew. That was refused. I countered then with a request to have the boat shipped to Vancouver. That too was refused. Close to a month of intense negotiation followed, at the end of which the Canadian government – stung by editorials and scores of letters – finally offered to pay the twelve-thousand-dollar cost of having *Vega* shipped on a freighter to Canada. I accepted, with the condition that Canada would try to recover the money from France. It did seem odd to many people that the French could not only get away with an act of piracy, but could then hold up the Canadian government for what amounted to ransom before releasing the vessel. It was not a great time for Canadian national pride. So many people were now thoroughly disgusted that the department of external affairs had to hire two full-time employees just to answer the steady stream of letters pouring in every day.

In early December, I returned to Tahiti. Because I had been declared an "undesirable", I had to have a special visa. The moment I arrived at the airport in Papeete, I was greeted by two secret servicemen who escorted me to a hotel and followed me everywhere after that. In the two days that remained before *Vega* was finally delivered, I discovered that the animosity that I had noted between the civil authorities and the military had not abated. Despite the shadowy presence of the secret service, I was able to renew acquaintance with several people I had met during my stay in hospital who were either sympathetic to or actively involved in the Polynesian independence movement.

The incidence of leukemia in French Polynesia had gone up considerably since the beginning of nuclear testing at Mururoa, although the French authorities kept the statistics carefully buried away. Among the Polynesians themselves there was a deep resentment against the French colonists that had its origins in the last great wave of European imperial expansion, but which had deepened by the choice of their area to test bombs after the French had been driven out of the Sahara Desert. The Tahitians' own leaders had been locked in jail any any formal political organization aimed at independence banned. But the movement still flourished behind the deceptive calm of the beaches and palms. For these people, the return of *Vega* was a symbolic event whose outcome they awaited with pleasure.

By the time the 372-foot converted liner *Medoc* pulled into the harbour at Papeete, thousands of Tahiti eyes were watching with glee. Aware that there were many on the island who viewed the return of *Vega* as a moral defeat for the French, the military authorities waited until dusk before entering the bay. There was just enough light to make out the white patch on the foredeck which was *Vega*, looking like a toy on the deck of the great steel navy ship.

In the pre-dawn light of December 12, a floating crane moved like a robot swan across the bay, its great neck swinging over the deck of the *Medoc*, picking up tiny *Vega* like a duckling and lowering her into the water. Two tugs moved into place and pulled her across the bay to the naval yard. In order to get into the yard to get my boat, I had to be escorted by the chief of police, himself no admirer of the French navy. I was slightly shaken by the barely-restrained fury of the navy officers and I was quite certain that, but for the protection of the civil police, they would have as soon beaten me up again as looked at me.

It gave me some sense of the mood that existed then at Mururoa, in the wake of the announcement that the tests would be moved underground, and the tensions that must now exist between the navy brass and the politicians back in Paris who had been the ones to bear the brunt of the embarrassment of having been exposed on the international stage as complete liars in the matter of the beating. I needed nothing more than the surly pride-wounded expressions on the faces of these men from Mururoa to know that heads had rolled and that resentment ran deep.

Vega was tied up beside another familiar French warship, the *Garonne*, next to which she had sat during the repairs at Mururoa back in '72. She looked tired and sorry for herself. The decks were blistered, as I had feared, the paint had begun to peel, the radio had been torn apart, and there could be no doubt she had suffered from her long imprisonment.

The engine was not working, so she had to be towed across the bay to where the other private yachts were moored. At this point, the French navy gave me a last spectacular display of incompetence. A lieutenant De La Motte was in charge of the delivery operation. Once the boat had been dragged into position for the anchors to be dropped, I tried to explain that the lieutenant's crew was doing it all wrong. He had two tugboats and nine sailors under his command. "Look," he snarled, "we are in the navy and we know what we are doing!" I stood back. By this time a crowd, including several newsmen and photographers, had gathered on the wharf to watch the unfolding of this great chapter in the history of France's command of the seas. With two tugs and nine men, it took the lieutenant three full hours to set a single anchor properly. By this time there were howls of laughter coming from the wharf When the lieutenant finally handed me the form to sign, discharging the French navy of my boat, the young officer's face was purple with rage and humiliation.

The next day, I arranged for *Vega*'s return to Vancouver on the deck of a freighter, then headed to the airport, still accompanied by the secret service men. As I prepared to board the plane, one of them said: "I have been advised to tell you never to set foot in French Polynesia again." I took one long last look, briefly thinking of the honeymoon I had spent there, the hotels I had been involved with during my construction days, the long days I had spent with my artist friend at Moorea, and all the people I had come to know. So now I was cast out forever from beautiful Tahiti, where my crime had been to be a victim of piracy! I knew that, short of the independence movement succeeding in overthrowing its French masters, it was undoubtedly true that I would never be allowed to wander these beaches again. And they represented a large chunk of the South Pacific I had always wanted so badly to roam freely.

I left feeling depressed, and more than a little uneasy about the thought of going to France and venturing into the streets of Paris, knowing that my victory at Mururoa had left me with more enemies than I could count. Briefly, to test the water, I had mentioned to one secret serviceman that I might, in fact, be going to the French courts. The man had scowled and then shrugged. "You will not be welcome in France," was his only comment. I said nothing more.

Back in Vancouver, I concentrated my energy on trying to get the Canadian government to espouse the case. If it failed, I would have no other choice than to go to France, and I sensed now that such a course of action, quite apart from the seemingly insurmountable legal obstacles, represented a definite physical danger, possibly greater than sailing to Mururoa itself. I had talked with several Greenpeace people who had been involved in earlier attempts to "raise consciousness" about the bomb in Paris, and while one had been mildly beaten up, another had been arrested, taken immediately by train to the border, and told to leave. Others, including Britons, New Zealanders and Australians, who had tried to "meddle in French affairs", had found themselves caught in club-swinging mêlées with gendarmes coming down on them from every side. My experience in Tahiti had taught me much. And the people I had met there had taught me more. Whatever France's official status as a democracy, the day-to-day reality for anyone trying to buck the government was something that was much closer to a police state.

A few small donations were trickling in from individuals who agreed with what I was doing. Several organizations, including labour groups, conservation bodies and people like the World Federalists, had sent me cheques that occasionally went up to a hundred dollars, but these were rare, and most were far smaller. The Greenpeace Foundation was still not interested in a legal action and was turning its attention to the possibility of another boat to Mururoa in 1974, so there was little help forthcoming from that quarter. Even with Ann-Marie working and me taking odd jobs, we were barely able to stay ahead of the bills that were steadily accumulating from legal expenses, phone calls, telegrams, treatments to my eye – which continued to hurt and was still not functioning properly.

When *Vega* arrived back in Vancouver, I took her up to

Buccaneer Bay where I had arranged for a mortgage against the boat to buy a small cabin. At least we had a place to live. Methodically, I set to work restoring the old girl, already aware that if I was going to press my claim I would need money, and the only possibility I had of raising the kind of money even approaching what I needed would be through the sale of the boat. The thought filled me with bitterness. Sometimes, alone on the boat, painting or scraping, I would put my tools down and stare across the water at the dim outlines of the mountains of Vancouver Island, and seriously ask myself if it was worth it. At least I had my boat, the boat I had wanted all my life. I had a small cabin on what was one of the most beautiful coastlines in the world, despite its dismal winter rains. And I had Ann-Marie, as beautiful and intelligent a woman as any man could hope to know. I retained all of my business experience, and had already formulated several ideas for developing some local properties which would put me back on my feet. I still had my health and one good eye. The tests at Mururoa were to be moved underground . . . *Why bother?*

No matter how hard I thought about it, there was no single answer. The thought of the French getting away with what they had done filled me with a feeling that could only be described as outrage – in fact, I had finished the last part of my long manuscript, and after having been edited to the bone it had been issued by a small local publisher under the title *Outrage, The Ordeal of Greenpeace III*. It was far too expensive but had sold reasonably well, although not anywhere near well enough to generate the kind of funds I required, and had been given excellent reviews throughout Canada. It summed up my feeling all right. But was outrage itself enough to justify the enormous expenditure of energy and time and money that would be required to push my case through.

In those moments of self-questioning, my mind threw out dozens upon dozens of answers. There were principles involved. There were profound issues of law involved. There were political realities involved. There were vast environmental factors at stake. The question at times seemed to come down to something so huge that I could barely grasp it. Although self-consciousness prevented me from discussing it openly with anyone, my sense of the issue was nothing less than the question of human survival. I knew that individuals aren't supposed to think in those terms, that history is supposed to be directed by swarms and masses and tides that take centuries to accumulate their momentum. But I could not shake off the thought that a single well-directed shot at the heart of the political and legal mechanism which was itself the force behind the machines which were being built to destroy the earth was worth more than everything my own life could add up to. I thought, too, of my own lost children and what hope they had of living out their time without being blasted or poisoned. And, inevitably, I wondered whether the whole tortuous business couldn't be reduced to something as simple as guilt for not having been able to fulfil my role as a father.

Angrily then, I would go back to work. There did not seem to be any way to make sense out of what my life had become and the choices I now faced. There were moments when I felt it was all quite unfair – that no man's brain had ever been designed to cope with the ultimate kinds of questions that humanity now faced about its future survival on the planet. Amid the depressions and the confusion, there were other moments, however, when I felt a rush of excitement. Few men had the opportunity that I now possessed – to set a precedent in international law which could apply at least one brake against the otherwise apparently unstoppable gallop toward some kind of nuclear holocaust. I had always felt strong, but in the face of a responsibility on this scale, I suspected that my strength was something in the order of a fly setting off to stop the charge of a herd of elephants.

It remained that I could not shake myself free. I wondered if, in fact, there could be any freedom anywhere at such a time in history. Or whether there had ever been any freedom at all.

I still possessed enough self-discipline to know that wallowing in my own doubts and fantasies and fears would not get me anywhere. And so, between long sessions of working on *Vega*'s ravaged hull, I travelled down the coast into Vancouver to consult with my lawyer and the many new friends I had acquired in the environmental movement, the press and else-where, and continued to nag the government.

One of my new friends, a New Zealander who was teaching international law at the University of British Columbia, came up with the suggestion one day of writing to Jean-Jacques Servan-Schreiber, the French intellectual and publisher of *L'Express*, who had vigorously opposed the nuclear test pro-gramme and the whole concept of a *force de frappe*.

With my friend's help, I drafted a letter to Servan-Schreiber, explaining the situation, asking for his advice and any recom-mendations he might make about a French lawyer who could take the case. To my delight, a reply came back within two weeks, naming a possible sympathetic lawyer. I wrote immedi-ately to the lawyer.

While waiting for an answer to that letter, I finally got what I thought of at the time as my big break in Canada. A closed-door meeting of the Cabinet was held and a decision reached to espouse my case. At the time, it seemed that the wheel had finally turned. It did not matter that a senior external affairs official admitted to a reporter that the action had only been undertaken because the Canadian government was getting so much "bad publicity" over the issue and that, yes, there was an election coming up. I had learned not to expect too much in the way of idealism from the bureaucracy.

Beyond the statement that Canada would espouse my case, nothing much happened. By April, I was beginning to get worried. My lawyer warned that time was running out and that within two months we would have passed the transcription period for the collision in 1972. I wrote to Ottawa, and got a reply back smoothly advising me to relax. According to the legal experts at external affairs, a thirty-year limitation period applied. Another month passed. Then I got an urgent call from Vancouver warning me that the mandarins had once again either been completely ignorant of the actual law or else they had been trying to throw me off the track. In fact, the two-year limitation period applied and if I did not act within a month, my chance to go to court would have passed forever.

The last thing I wanted to do was go to Paris. I had since

317

looked into the matter more closely and had learned that the German who had tried to sue the French government, over a bad beating up he had received during a demonstration, had been shot. I said nothing about this to Ann-Marie and she did not argue against me going, except with her eyes. I had consulted just about everyone I could find, looking for specific guidance, but it remained that no one could tell me exactly what the procedure was for a foreigner trying to seek redress against France in a French court. There appeared to be no precedent. I knew that the only way I would ever find out would be by going to Paris myself.

A local television programme made an appeal, Ann-Marie loaned me the rest of the money I needed and on the last day of May, 1974, I took off from Vancouver with a briefcase full of files and affidavits and photographs.

I had been to Paris often enough not to feel overwhelmed by the size of the city itself, bu talways, in the past, I had had money and the support of one large corporation or another behind me. Now I found myself close to broke, wandering the streets in search of a cheap single room.

Nostalgia swept over me. I could remember the Racing Club of France where, sixteen years before, I had played in the French National Badminton Championships. And nine years before, I had negotiated a multi-million-dollar contract over bottles of expensive wine for the construction of a hotel. Now I was an undesirable alien whose presence was viewed as a political affront to both the government and the military. All I could afford was a twenty-franc room. It was dirty and windowless, not much more than a grey cell. The coarse sheets made me itch. The noises kept me awake. My nerves were on edge.

I had not received a reply from the lawyer who had been suggested by Servan-Schreiber and I had no idea how to get in touch with him. All that I could do was to go to the offices of *L'Express*. I only got as far as Servan-Schreiber's secretary but she, at least, directed me to a man named Brice Lelonde, president of the environmental group, Friends of the Earth. Brice had sailed on the *Fri* into Mururoa. It was Brice who rescued me from the labyrinth, found me a small apartment in the St Germain-des-Prés area on the left bank, complete with a telephone and a hotplate. I at least now had a tiny beach-head from which to launch my one-man invasion of France.

I had arrived in France at a time when the spent energies of the 1968 uprising had begun to come together again in a series of formal political alliances which were pitting the Left against the Right in what looked to be a major battle for control of the country. President Georges Pompidou had just died and with the near-collapse of the old Gaullist front, the election which was in the works looked to be the closest fight of the century. The Left, which had been shattered in the wake of the abortive revolution, had re-grouped itself around socialist François Mitterrand and the Right was still trying to choose between Valéry Giscard d'Estaing or Jacques Chaban-Delmas. My contact, Jean-Jacques Servan-Schreiber, was jockeying for position in the midst of the tug-of-war. The issue of testing at Mururoa and the whole question of a French nuclear deterrent had emerged for the first time as a factor in the outcome of an election. The socialist candidate had taken the position that he would cancel the programme. The candidates on the Right promised to carry on with the tests.

It was in this context that Brice Lelonde saw my case as having political significance in France. Anything that made the government and the military look bad was good: it was as simple as that. Brice himself had been deeply involved in the 1968 uprising. Now in his late twenties, he spoke of that period with a mixture of remorse and nostalgia. "We were so close," he said. "We could have won but we lost our nerve at the end. That was all. We were betrayed by the Communists, of course, but we could have won." It did not take me long to realize that environmental groups in France differed substantially from their sister organizations in North America, whose goal appeared to be the modest one of effecting changes in government policy toward ecology. In France, the primary objective was the overthrow of the government. All else followed from there. I was now in the company not so much of environmentalists but of revolutionaries. Their mood was hard-edged, unequivocal. Many of them had had their bones broken in demonstrations and had seen their friends languish in prison and yet others shot down in the streets. By then, I had moved a long way from my initial innocent impulse to "do something" to protect the illegal cordoning-off of a slab of international waters. I liked the hard-nosed flavour of these French activists. They meant business. After the relaxed setting of Vancouver, where even the eco-freaks had waffled away from my decision to carry the case through, it was a relief to encounter people who saw what I was doing in steely, no-nonsense terms.

Brice immediately set up an interview with the lawyer who had been recommended to me. Another young lawyer, Thierry Garby-Lacrouts, was invited to attend as an interpreter. Thierry's English was poor, which made the interview long and painful. At the end of it, the older lawyer made it clear he did not want to handle the case. Instead, he suggested, why didn't I ask Thierry to take it? My initial reaction was to reject the idea. I had long ago learned that, in medical matters, you wanted a young doctor who was up to date on all the latest drugs and treatments, but in law – which seldom changed – what you wanted was an old lawyer. Thierry was in his mid-twenties, inexperienced.

Yet when we talked it over, he was more than willing to take the case on. And he was willing to do it for free. We stood in the sun on bustling Avenue Georges Mandel. Thierry had heard my story by then and he seemed to grasp the issue. What he lacked in experience, I judged, he might make up in energy and if it was going to be a protracted battle, it might well be energy that counted in the end.

Thierry was a dapper pipe-smoking intellectual who favoured turtle-neck sweaters. He was not particularly aggressive nor did he project himself strongly. Yet his intensity appealed to me and perhaps, best of all, he was fascinated from the beginning by the case. He saw it not only as important, but possibly as the most important case that had yet developed in terms of the law of the sea. The more we discussed it, the more fascinated Thierry became. I sensed, behind the broken English, an intellect that reminded me somewhat of Nigel. Perhaps it was just the European quality. Whatever it was, I realized that in

320

this young Frenchman I had a passionate ally who might be poor and untried but who, nevertheless, might be able to stand up to the rigors of attempting to run the gauntlet of the courts with little or no money behind him.

The month that I spent in Paris saw the near-defeat of the government. In the dying weeks of the election campaign, with the socialist Mitterrand locked in a bitter neck-and-neck contest with Valéry Giscard d'Estaing, representing the Gaullist-allied Independent Republicans, the issue of nuclear testing came increasingly to the forefront. In France, the clamour of the election reverberated against the background of a new bomb-test season that featured the detonation of India's first atomic blast, using material from a Canadian-made CANDU reactor. Three weeks later, France resumed her atmospheric tests at Mururoa, followed two hours afterwards by a Chinese bomb estimated to be fifty times the size of the one dropped on Hiroshima. Britain got back into the act with a bomb test in Nevada. The United States followed with another. The Japanese government reported an increase in the level of radioactive fallout five thousand times higher than normal. The British Atomic Energy Commission duly acknowledged that the fallout levels over England had tripled. Pakistan announced that it would begin developing nuclear energy to counter the threat from India. Several newspapers carried reports to the effect that Israel had made a secret deal with France and had embarked on a crash programme to develop a bomb. Egypt's foreign minister promptly replied with the declaration that Egypt would soon have the same capability. From my vantage point in France, it looked like a baseball game being played in hell.

I had been warned by officials of the Canadian embassy to avoid any public comments which might lead to me being kicked out of the country. But before I quite realized what had happened, I had been caught up in the vortex of French politics. In the final days of the election, Jean-Jacques Servan-Schreiber had thrown his support to Giscard d'Estaing, despite their difference of opinion over nuclear testing. The election saw Giscard d'Estaing defeating his socialist opponent by a margin so narrow that many felt Servan-Schreiber's move might have been the factor that made the difference. As soon as the new government was formed, he was appointed to the position of minister of administrative reforms. A few days later, several angry environmentalists marched down to his office at *L'Express* to upbraid him for his "defection" from the cause. Among them were Brice Lelonde and Thierry. They brought me along with them. Servan-Schreiber defended himself by saying that it was better to have a voice in the government than not at all and that he would continue to oppose nuclear tests. After the meeting, Thierry had the idea of testing the new minister's sincerity by asking him to endorse a letter Thierry had planned to send to the president, the prime minister and the minister of war, explaining my case and asking for them to intervene on my behalf. Servan-Schreiber agreed and the letters went out – never to be answered – with his endorsement.

The new president had been forced in the last stages of the election campaign to soften the resistance to further tests at Mururoa by promising that the current series would be the last in the atmosphere. He announced, as a further step, that one of the planned summer's tests would be cancelled outright. Two days after the meeting which I had attended, Servan-Schreiber called a press conference denouncing the tests. It was the same day that Thierry's letters, with Servan-Schreiber's endorsement, arrived on the desks of the new president, prime minister and minister of war.

The next day, Servan-Schreiber was fired.

The reason that he was fired was not that he had opposed the nuclear tests, for he had been doing that for years. The reason was that he had "abused his position" by supporting a foreign national against the government of which he had become a member.

While the reports were being shouted from the news-stands that Servan-Schreiber had been toppled from power, Thierry was making his way to the courts to serve a writ against the government of France, claiming twenty-one thousand dollars' damages for the ramming and boarding of *Vega*.

* * * *

Arriving back in Vancouver, I found that another election had come and gone and heads had rolled in Canada too. Pierre Elliott Trudeau and his Liberal Party had been re-elected, but by a vastly reduced margin. The parallels with the situation in France were numerous and might have made students of the deeper currents of history more than curious. Trudeau's margin of success had not been much greater than Giscard d'Estaing's. Shortly after the election, the political veteran Mitchell Sharp, was removed from his position as secretary of state for external affairs. Observers around Parliament Hill were quick to point out that his mis-handling of the *Greenpeace III* incident was a definite factor in his ouster. The chief legal adviser for the department, whose advice had consistently proven wrong, had also disappeared. One further casualty was the man in charge of my case at the Canadian embassy in Paris. There was a certain grim satisfaction in all this, but it was short-lived.

I tried testing the mood of the new minister for external affairs, Allan MacEachen, by writing to him and asking the by-now perennial question: what was the Canadian government going to do about living up to its promise to espouse my case? The answer that came back seemed to bubble with the enthusiasm of a new minister determined not to make the same mistakes as his predecessor, but the spaces between the lines proved to be as empty as the promises. Mr MacEachen was eager to take action, oh absolutely! But the small snag now was that the French government had indicated that it was unwilling to enter into serious state-to-state negotiations until the current series of tests – the last in the atmosphere – were completed. The reasoning behind this, Mr MacEachen noted, was that France naturally did not wish to set a "precedent", but once the atmospheric tests were over with, and there could be no danger of a precedent being set, then the business of redress to me for damages could begin in earnest. I did not feel particularly swayed by the argument, but I also knew that the real precedent that I wanted to establish lay half-hidden in the details of the writ that Thierry had served on the French government, and it concerned itself not simply with the issue of the cordon around Mururoa but with the far deeper and fundamental issue of freedom of the seas and the effect this would have on all future attempts by any nation to undertake, not only atmospheric nuclear tests, by any other technological measure which might affect the marine environment. It was, at its heart, not simply a question of freedom of the seas but of protection of the seas. I knew, also, that the Canadian government needed only the slightest seemingly logical rationalization to delay and delay, and in this last argument from France they had what they needed. The only lever I had ever had to get Ottawa moving had been the press, and at the moment, the press had lost interest in Mururoa. There was little I could say now that I hadn't already said a hundred times. So, reluctantly, I agreed to let events run their course.

Only a week later, France announced the end of her 1974 test programme and the official end of atmospheric testing. I waited to hear from the new minister of external affairs, but I was not to receive another letter from my government for nearly six months. With the election behind them the Liberals, possessed a mandate that could carry them in office for four more years. In that time, they could be confident that the affair of the *Greenpeace III* would have receded in the public's mind and that they no longer had to worry about adverse political effects. The great electoral engine had shifted into gear, producing the promise of espousal – which meant, at least, action – in time for the voters to cast their ballots, but as soon as election was over and a few wrists had been slapped, the engine shifted contentedly back into neutral, leaving nothing more than a vague after-image that "something was being done".

During September, October and November, I found myself in a vacuum, with the energy that had sustained me this far being channelled increasingly into the task of immediate survival. I found, also, that as the interest of people around me waned, it became harder and harder to retain either my outrage or my determination to see the thing through. It had been well over a year since I had returned from the hospital in Papeete, and when I added up what had been accomplished in that time – despite the hundreds of letters I had written and the hundreds more I had received – it did not seem like very much. Morosely, I looked over the half-dozen files I had accumulated and the two-dozen scrapbooks with the clippings I had underlined and the notes I had made on the side, and while it represented a considerable feat of organization and self-discipline, I was not sure what if anything else it represented. The files might make a contemporary historian weep with joy. I had everything in there, including more confidential letters from various government officials and lawyers than I chose to count. All the contradictions in what the governments of France and Canada – and for that matter, New Zealand, Australia, Great Britain and the United States – had said with regard to nuclear power and the law of the sea since 1972 were there for anyone to see, but scarcely anyone would trouble to look.

The Greenpeace Foundation had fragmented once again and had only managed half-heartedly to support a ketch owned by a young German which had set out from Australia to sail to Mururoa. It had been delayed by storms in the Tasman Sea, and by the time it finally got away from New Zealand, it was late in the season. It did reach Mururoa, but not until a week after the last atmospheric bomb had been tested. The skipper had to content himself with taking water samples to be checked for radioactive debris. Two other protest vessels had been launched – one containing a Frenchman and his family who set out from Mexico but were driven back by storms, and another, organized by an American church group, which left the dock in Hawaii, but had to return when the engine blew up. Neither Australia nor New Zealand tried to send navy ships into the area again, on the grounds that their point had been made and now they would concentrate on pursuing their case against France in the World Court at The Hague. The *Fri* had been diverted from any attempt to sail to Mururoa again by lack of money and a general dilapidated condition. Instead, the old Baltic trader was sent off on a "peace voyage" through the South Pacific, delivering seeds to various islands and stopping in at ports to "raise consciousness" about things ecological and nuclear. The *Spirit of Peace*, which had reached the test zone several times the year before, remained at her wharf in New Zealand.

It looked very much as if my voyages had occurred in the dim and distant past and events had swept by. Certainly, that was the way the great majority of people I talked to seemed to see the whole matter. I had the feeling I was viewed as being eccentric for even thinking of continuing to pursue the case. "Don't flog a dead megamachine," quipped one of my friends in the environmental movement in Vancouver.

The work on *Vega* had been left unfinished when I went to Paris. Now, when I prepared to get back to it, I could not even afford the necessary paint. I approached the manager of a paint company to explain the problem and promised if they would let me have the paint, I would pay them within three or four months. The manager's eyes twinkled.

"Load your old truck up," he said. "We supported you all along. The paint is our donation."

By late autumn, *Vega* sparkled. With calloused hands, I took her sailing along the coast for a few days. The ecstasy was almost painful. It did not matter that I had sailed the old girl some thirty thousand miles in five and a half years. It was still a new experience. It re-kindled in me all the old longings I had had to sail and sail and sail, free, uncommitted, letting the wind set the direction and speed, and the old girl running as she had been created to run. God, to be away from the grey plagues of the bureaucracies and the endless petty manoeuvrings of the politicians! The smog, the highways, the automatons that clung to their ideas of individuality in the midst of the assembly lines and treadmills. Ann-Marie had come along and for at least two days we re-captured the bliss we had known – it seemed so incredibly long ago – in the water around New Zealand.

December proved to be the darkest month yet. The winter rains had arrived again and debts had accumulated. I was finally forced to the conclusion that the only way I would ever be able to push the case through was to make a substantial chunk of money and the only way I knew to do that was through the development of land. And the only way I could raise the money to get the land was through the sale of *Vega*. Since the day I had left my life in California behind, I had known no other "home" than the boat. I was not by nature a sentimental man, but the day I finally sold the old girl, it was all I could do to stop from breaking down and crying. If I had acquired a new sense of myself in the years since I had abandoned my business existence, and with it, my former wives and children and almost all of my friends, that new sense had evolved out of the mobility and security *Vega* had given me. It was hard to think of myself now without thinking of the boat. Every bit of my pride and workmanship and love of order had gone into her. She was an exceptional craft. There were few, if any, like her. I knew too that she had kept me alive through situations where few boats could have done the same. In a sense, she possessed me as much as I possessed her, as though she did indeed possess a life of her own. I had tended for a long time to think of her more as a creature than an object. When the day came that I signed the ownership papers over, I felt like both betrayer and executioner. I felt nothing less than a sense of amputation. It was strange. At the beginning of our struggle together, there had been a bomb and there had been one small boat. Now the bomb no longer existed in the sky over Mururoa and the boat was gone from my hands. It was very much as though I had passed from one world into another – as though a whole age had come and gone.

With the money from the sale of *Vega*, I bought a slice of waterfront property at Secret Cove, close to Buccaneer Bay. It was heavily-treed, rocky and very close to being not much more than a cliff face. I gambled that if I could drive a road down from the main highway to the water's edge, it would make an excellent marina, or, if nothing else, once a road had been driven through, the value of the property would at least double. I could not afford to hire expensive equipment such as compressors, so I would have to do it myself with a helper.

Day after day, in cold pouring rain, I clambered over the granite rocks and through the black oozing muck, using a heavy gas-driven hand drill to bore holes into which I would pack sticks of dynamite, then carefully cake the hole with mud, leaving a long fuse. The next effort involved rolling huge Euclid truck tyres down through the bush and stacking them up on top of the place where the dynamite waited. On top of the tyres I would pile branches – so that when the rock finally blew, the shrapnel would be smothered as much as possible and would not go flying in every direction. It was muscle-ripping dangerous work. And the road I was trying to drive through solid rock had to be at least a quarter of a mile long, zig-zagging steeply down to the water.

When it got too dark to work, I would shamble home, covered with mud, to the small cabin I had rented nearby, and start work all over again doing batiks. As a young man, I had painted a lot and learned to do batik-work. It was a side of my nature I had not cultivated because, in my own mind, I had seen my limitations early and had decided not to waste time trying to become something – a great artist – I could never be. Yet my batik-work was good enough for a show at Vancouver Arts Club to be arranged, and I eventually sold them for one hundred and twenty dollars each. I told myself as I laboured late into the night, that it was strictly a commercial proposition, like working on the roadway. I even made the frames myself to reduce the costs. It was during this period, when I was working seven days a week, trying to get the roadway built in six months that Ann-Marie again broached the subject of whether or not to continue with the court case.

In her mind, it served no purpose except perhaps some inexplicable desire for revenge, a sort of "getting even" thing which she did not particularly like and which she certainly did not appreciate. She said she understood why I thought I had to finish it off, and even why it might be important. But, as before, she had not been able to keep up with the flow of paperwork and so she had steadily lost track of the exact point at which I had arrived.

She had quit her job as a dental assistant, and moved up to Secret Cove to help me. The two of us lived in the small cabin, and while it was not quite so poorly insulated or as poorly heated as the cabin in which we had spent the previous winter, it was not all that much better. There was still the austere grey presence of the immense northwest coast winter with its league upon league of rain, the forests blurring into nothingness, and the silent beaches where the only companionship was the

328

rhythm of the grey waves on the sand against a background of grey misty shapes of pines and firs.

Damn it, why couldn't we just leave it all and go off and be happy?

On December 21, the International Court of Justice decided to drop the cases of New Zealand and Australia against France over the issue of nuclear testing on the grounds that since France had stopped testing, the questions which had been raised – and accepted – were no longer valid. It might have been that the World Court was worried about having lost France's support. It might have been that the jurists simply had no appetite for a major struggle over that particular issue at that particular moment in history. It might also, more likely, have been that partisan political and national goals had driven deep wedges into the structure of the court itself. Whatever the reason, the combined cases were thrown out and that left only one case in the world that still addressed itself to the fundamental issues involved – who owned the sea and who could do what they wanted with it? And that was my case in Paris.

Rather than having the effect of finishing-off what remained of my feeling that something could be done, the failure of the International Court of Justice hardened my determination to keep pressing. I was left more and more with the feeling that you could not rely on governments to do the job. Just as the task of physically blockading the bombs by parking yourself in the path of the fallout could not be trusted to navies which diplomatically took up positions well outside of the fallout corridor, so it seemed that the business of pressing charges that might stem the tests forever could be left to neither governments nor even the only international court ever created. Where I had the French was on their home ground and there was now obviously no other place to get them.

Still, with neither Ann-Marie's support nor the support of the government of Canada nor the Greenpeace Foundation nor anything much more than token support from any other group, it was hard to sustain any real belief in what I was doing.

My own self doubts had grown ot the point where they had

almost succeeded in engulfing me completely. I had not heard from Thierry and it was hard to have any confidence at all that things were moving in Paris. The moments of doubt had expanded into hours and sometimes whole sleepless nights. It went against every instinct or reflex I possessed to seriously think of quitting, yet each week that passed without any visible sign of activity from either Paris or Ottawa left me with the feeling that I was sinking slowly but inexorably into quicksand. Then one day in early January I found a letter in my mailbox that swept the doubt from my mind and gave me back the sense of outrage and anger that I had come so very close to losing.

It was addressed to me simply care of Vancouver. It contained a seventy-dollar money order which I realized had originally been sent in the form of cash. Somebody at the post office had gone to a lot of trouble to trace me and had even taken the unusual step of changing the money from cash to a money order to make sure it got to its intended recipient. The handwriting was clumsy and it was signed: "A Concerned Woman in her middle 40s".

It said:

Find $70 enclosed in cash. I have saved the money, dollar by dollar, I am so ashamed of our government for giving you so little or no assistance in your great cause. My father was gassed in the first world war in France. I had a brother killed at Dieppe, France, in 1942. This money is in their memory. They thought they were fighting for a cause. Maybe they were better off not to have lived when you see the terrible nuclear problem. Their hearts would have been broken. Use this money in any way you see fit. You have my complete faith and confidence. Good luck.

That stirred something in me. Perhaps, if nothing else, it gave me a perspective which had been all but buried in the heaps of diplomatic notes and the "rational" excuse for political expediency. All right, Concerned Woman in your middle 40s, I thought, to the memory of your father and brother then! I marched straight back to my cabin and wrote a letter to prime minister Trudeau angrily demanding that he live up to his

330

promise. At the end, I enclosed a copy of the letter the woman had sent. Then I wrote another letter to Thierry in Paris and forwarded the seventy dollars to him immediately.

Two days later, a telegram arrived advising me to come to Paris right away. A court date had been set for April 8 and there was a lot of work to do in order to be ready.

I stood in the rain that afternoon looking at the rough rubble of the road I had almost completed down to the water's edge. If I were to stay and finish it and build the marina, I would be well on my way back to financial independence, with my children's security guaranteed. To leave it now meant serious complications. Even with the sale of *Vega*, I had to borrow a lot of money. It left me with a deadline. I had gambled everything on being able to complete the work and generate a profit before the time came to make the first annual payment on the loan. To drop it now, with the work unfinished, and plough my remaining available funds into the court case meant that in all likelihood I would find myself a year hence without even the property I had gained at the cost of giving up the boat. My children would be left with nothing. And Ann-Marie would probably have left me.

I had not forgotten the middle-aged woman's letter. It was odd that a complete stranger could have introduced a thought that came close to offsetting the thoughts of all my own personal losses. Dimly sensing that what I really wanted to see was at least one instance of justice to atone, however insignificantly, for all the injustices of wars and broken trusts and forgotten loyalties, I told myself again: All right, for the father who was gassed and the brother who died at Dieppe!

The next day I made arrangements to return to Paris.

A beaming Thierry Garby-Lacrouts was waiting for me at Charles de Gaulle airport. He was excited and pleased with what he had been able to get done. His English had also improved. But he was disillusioned about the Canadian government.

"David," he said, as we were driving into the city, "I must tell you that I was very impressed at first, you know, with all those letters you have from your prime minister. Over here, it is simply not heard of to have a letter from the top man and so also because I am very naive I think of your country like Sweden, you know, one of the real democracies. But I have had no cooperation at all from your embassy. They have done nothing. They get very unhappy when I call. They are just like all the rest."

The period that followed was one of unrelieved work. According to French law, all the evidence on both sides had to be submitted before the trial. And that meant at least eighty pages of documents which first of all had to be written out by hand as Thierry struggled to learn the exact details from me and then translated – again by hand – into French and, finally, back into English so that I could gauge their accuracy. Despite the promise by the Canadian government that its "good offices" could be used, the embassy refused to help with the translations at all. Instead, Thierry managed to find a young woman who was willing to undertake the task in her free time. Ironically, she was a daughter of a nuclear engineer who was passionately in favour of nuclear energy and *La Bombe*. A further irony was the fact that Thierry's tiny apartment, where we did most of our work, was only two blocks from the house where Hugo Grotius had lived in the early 1600s when he was commissioned to write a law of the sea to bring an end to piracy.

That particular work played the most significant part in the case. It had been written at a time when the maritime European powers were destroying each other's fleets as fast as they could build new ones and piracy was so rampant that shipping was coming close to a standstill. Realizing that they were hurting themselves as much as each other, the maritime nations decided to appoint a neutral observer to write a law of the sea that would dictate everyone's behaviour on the ocean. Describing the sea as something "which cannot be held nor enclosed, being itself the possessor rather than the possessed", young Hugo Grotius sat in his Paris flat and wrote a law that was to stand unchallenged right up into the twentieth century. Two blocks from where he had laboured, Thierry and I now scribbled furiously as we assembled the first test case of the validity of that ancient law. This, too, did something for my sense of perspective.

332

Over the Easter weekend we locked ourselves up in Thierry's apartment and worked in up to seventeen-hour stretches to complete the documentation. For the moment, at least, I found life more to my liking. I had always preferred to do one thing at a time, and now the one thing was to be ready for court. Thierry, for his part, found the experience to be one of the most stimulating and exciting things he had ever done. Until then, he had been pecking at the case in the evenings and at weekends, digging through hundreds of old law books in the search for a precedent. As search after search led into blind alleys, it sank in on him that he was handling a case that was truly the first of its kind, despite the nearly four centuries that the law of the seas had stood.

As far as Thierry could dig, he could find no defence that the navy could muster. The law governing the behaviour of motorized vessels in relation to ships under sail could not be more clear and the photographs left no doubt whatsoever. The laws in relation to armed piracy were no less immutable. His only concern was to try to anticipate the multitude of minor technicalities which the French Defence Ministry could be expected to employ to wriggle off the hook. The problem, for Thierry, came down to putting together a case that would reduce the complexities of nationality, French law versus international law and the issue of cordons down to a straightforward question of any individual's right to travel on the sea without being molested. At the beginning, he had run into so many contradictory opinions by lawyers, diplomats and professors that he had despaired of finding a way to present it to the courts without becoming completely bogged down in the many diversions of power that existed under French law. After searching and puzzling and thinking for months, he had finally seen the case precisely. As he described it:

A light came into my mind. I saw a way to side-step the international law complexities by making the case simple and taking it to a civil court. There I would argue that all these acts – the ramming, the boarding, the beating up – were acts of violence on the high seas against a person's body and property and that all this was illegal under France's laws of protection of individual freedom. I saw how I could demonstrate this. You know, I was really very excited, almost drunk.

On March 11, we stepped through the high wrought-iron gates of the Tribunal de Grande Instance, a vast grey stone edifice overlooking the Seine, just a block from Notre Dame. Our footsteps echoing in the great arched hallways, with their stone pillars, we passed the room where Marie Antoinette had been detained before being taken to the guillotine. The room of the Tribunal itself was enormous, with dark wooden panelling and guilded ceilings.

This first appearance was simply to submit our written evidence. There were several other black-gowned lawyers and a smattering of reporters sitting on the wooden benches. The Tribunal itself consisted of three judges and a "procurer" – whose duty was to advise the judges of the opinion of the French government.

I felt very little emotion. Thierry had already taken me to the ancient chamber once before so that I would not feel intimidated when the time came for the trial. At this stage, it was more like going to the post office to pick up your mail than facing-off against the Navy. Essentially, all that Thiery was doing was submitting our evidence and picking up a copy of the defence lawyer's evidence so that each lawyer and the judges would have a chance to study the arguments before the actual trial.

We waited till an official announced:

"McTaggart versus France."

Thierry rose and walked up to the high curving bench, joined by another lawyer, the assistant of the one who had been appointed by the government. The two stood and talked with the judges. I saw Thierry hand over our neatly-packaged bundle of documents. It was impossible to tell anything from the implacable expressions of the judges themselves but I suddenly noticed that the conversation had heated up. Some kind of argument was taking place and the senior judge, the one sitting in the middle, was addressing himself harshly either to Thierry or to the other lawyer. Then Thierry whipped open

334

his briefcase and produced an envelope which he handed to the judge. A moment passed while the old man read it, then he addressed himself firmly to the other lawyer, who looked distinctly uncomfortable. The next thing I knew, Thierry was walking stiffly back toward me, and my hopes crashed. Something had gone wrong. Thierry did not have the packet of evidence from the government we had come for.

But once we were back in the hallway, Thierry excitedly rushed to tell me what had happened: the lawyer for the military had tried to have the case delayed by claiming that the evidence had still not been submitted to his firm by the Defence Department. Quick to see an opening, Thierry had put on his most righteous tone of voice, saying that the military authorities had had a year to prepare and certainly he and his client were prepared to proceed. Then he had remembered the last letter I had received from prime minister Trudeau, who, in defence of his own lack of action, had written that "representations have been made by our embassy on your behalf on six separate occasions, not only to French foreign ministry legal and political advisers but also to officials in the office of the prime minister of France... Unfortunately, the French defence ministry's apparent continuing opposition to settlement has, so far, frustrated our expectations. We therefore contacted the office of the prime minister of France to see whether its officials could act as mediators in what appears to us to be a French inter-departmental dispute . . ."

"If the prime minister of Canada is unable to elicit the necessary material from the defence ministry," Thierry had argued, "it cannot be left to my client and myself to have this responsibility."

The senior judge had looked up from the letter and said sternly to the other lawyer:

"You can keep the Canadian government waiting, and you can keep the French government waiting, but you cannot keep the court waiting." He ordered that the evidence be submitted by March 21 so that the trial could proceed on April 8.

Thierry was elated. "There is hope, my friend! There is hope."

I found myself once again being intensely questioned by reporters. Besides the international wire services, the *Herald Tribune* and *Time* Magazine, there were several representatives from various Canadian news agencies whose editors back home had grown curious about this bizarre spectacle of a lone Canadian marching into a Paris courtroom to lay charges against the French navy. It brought to mind recollections that prime minister Trudeau had promised to "espouse" that case, hadn't he? How long ago had that been? The answer was that it had been over a year and a half. Intrigued, the editors began to wonder why, a year and a half after the Canadian government had announced it would more or less "take over", that I was still having to go into a French court alone, with no assistance, financial or otherwise, from the government. The more they studied the situation, the more intriguing it became. Particularly intriguing was the fact that among all the damages I was claiming was one item for twelve thousand dollars, the money which the Canadian government had paid to have *Vega* shipped back from Tahiti. It seemed rather absurd that I should be suing France to get money back for the government of Canada. Indignant editorials soon began to appear in newspapers across Canada, and, once again, the phones began ringing, this time between Paris and Ottawa.

Among the reporters were a few who were more than mildly intrigued. They knew that by no stretch of the imagination could the Canadian government be described as lion-like, but the over-all pattern of behaviour in response to my situation smacked of something more than timidity or even cowardice. If Canada was bending so far backwards to avoid any kind of confrontation with France, there had to be a reason. After questioning me at length, a few of those reporters started sending discreet inquiries back to associates in Ottawa, and without the government being aware of it, an intense journalistic investigation began behind the scenes in Canada, checking into the backgrounds of prominent figures, probing for an explanation . . .

Life had once again become extremely hectic. I found myself on the phone for hours each day, arguing with diplomats, firing letters back and forth. During all this time, I was living on three dollars a day.

On March 25, we returned to the Tribunal de Grande Instance, and this time the defence ministry's evidence had been submitted. We went straight back to Thierry's apartment, threw off our jackets and went to work poring through a series of confidential documents which constituted the navy's defence of its actions. We had scarcely begun the enormous job of translating the material when we came across a report stamped "Confidential" from Admiral Claverie to the director of the Centre of Nuclear Testing and general of the French air force. The report was dated 23 August, 1973 – just eight days after the boarding. I had been surprised many times in the past few years but never more surprised than I was now.

The first paragraph of Admiral Claverie's letter to the general said: "After having been assured by you that no measure of retaliation would be feared by the Canadian government against our Air France and COTAM and their stops in Montreal, I decided this boarding on 15th of August in the beginning of the afternoon . . ."

COTAM was the name for French military flights and it suddenly clicked in my mind that, having been forbidden to land military aircraft either in Australia, New Zealand or the United States, France's only possible landing spot between her own soil and the South Pacific was Canada, obviously Montreal.

But that was almost beside the point. What the admiral was saying was that the general had assured him that somebody had made contact with the Canadian government before the boarding and had been given assurances that there would be no reprisals from Canada. That meant there had been a deal – collusion between two governments to allow France to act against a Canadian citizen with impunity. It meant that the Canadian government had been an accomplice in the breaking of both international and Canadian law by, in effect, authorizing the violation of the rights of one of the citizens it existed to protect.

"Thierry, am I crazy or does this mean what I think it means?"

337

The young lawyer read the paragraph over several times, shaking his head and letting out low whistles. Finally he looked up.

"This case should not be tried in France," he said. "It should be tried in Canada. If your laws are anything like ours, this is high treason."

All the delays and the inexplicable reluctance to act. Now it made sense. No wonder the Canadian government didn't want to put too much pressure on France. France might come back and say, "Look, you guys, you were in on the deal." Within hours, I was on the phone and sending telexes back to sympathetic politicians in Ottawa trying to get them to put questions to the government in the House of Commons. Within days, confronted in Parliament, the government began a series of carefully-worded denials – so carefully-worded that eyebrows were raised in the press gallery. The new parliamentary secretary to the minister for external affairs said, lamely: "Those exchanges which did take place between French and Canadian government officials immediately prior to the 1973 boarding of the *Greenpeace III* expressed the Canadian government's concern for the safety of Mr McTaggart." So there had, indeed, been high-level communication between the two governments just before Admiral Claverie received the assurance that there would be no retaliation from Canada. One member of parliament asked the acting prime minister, who happened to be Mitchell Sharp, the former external affairs minister, to table all documents exchanged in the affair. Mr Sharp answered that he would take the request "under consideration", but, as events were to develop, the documents were never released. Another MP asked for a public inquiry. But it was never to be held either. All I was left with was an admission by my own government that conversations had taken place with French officials about *Vega*'s presence at Mururoa and that, afterwards, a French general advised Admiral Claverie not to worry about Canada's "retaliating" and at that point the admiral had unleashed his goon squad. Looking over the terse denials of any conspiracy, several reporters remarked that the answers were ambiguous, whereas

338

Admiral Claverie had been very specific. He had named Air France COTAM and Montreal as being the precise concerns of the French military. There was nothing ambiguous about that at all. When I asked for permission to see the records of the meeting that had taken place between Canada and France "immediately" before the boarding, I was refused. The department of external affairs informed me that release of the records would "raise questions of both international practice and good judgement" and that a request to the French government to allow publication of their side of the exchanges might be "counter productive" and damage relations with France.

Whether Canada's complicity in the boarding had been explicit or implicit seemed to me beside the matter. What was foremost in my mind now was the question of *why*. Why would my own government do such a thing and run all the risks of ultimate exposure? The answer – or at least part of the answer – was not long in coming. The reporters who had already grown suspicious and begun to conduct their own investigations were more than ever intrigued by the revelation of Admiral Claverie's letter. Piece by piece they had started to put together a picture of a great web linking Canada and France, stretching from Northern Quebec to Mururoa. I had often enough heard vague references to pending uranium deals between France and Canada, but now, with the assistance of several journalists, I began to see the parts that had been in shadow before.

The Canadian government had that year allotted three million dollars for an exploration consortium to pursue fresh uranium resources. The consortium included Eldorado Nuclear Ltd, which was owned by the Canadian government. A feasibility study had been completed on a special uranium enrichment plant to be built at James Bay. It was expected to cost between two and eight billion dollars, and France would be a major partner in the development. France's interest was to guarantee a stable supply of enriched uranium to fuel a huge programme of nuclear power station construction. The major companies involved in the scheme all had strong ties to prime minister Trudeau's Liberal Party. They included Brinco, the British Newfoundland Company, which held mineral rights in Labrador

and had been pushing the uranium enrichment programme
for years, proposing that the plant be built on the north
shore of the St Lawrence River near Sept Iles. On the
board of directors of Brinco was Liberal senator Maurice
Bouget, a former speaker of the senate, and two Frenchmen,
Edmund de Rothschild of the famous banking family and
Dominique Tabard de Grieges, who was chairman of the Suez
Finance and Real Estate Company of Canada. Another director
of Brinco was Paul Demarais, president of Power Corporation,
which was often linked with the federal Liberals. Interlocking
directorships pulled Brinco together with a company called
Brascan, on whose board of directors my old adversary, the
former external affairs minister, Mitchell Sharp, had served
until his election. Another multinational corporation involved
in the uranium enrichment plan was the mammoth Canadian
Pacific Investments on whose board the Canadian defence
minister, James Richardson, had sat and who still owned fifty
thousand shares in the company.

It was just a glimpse, but it revealed the stark reality that
my appeals to my government on the basis of violation of
individual rights had been more than drowned by the rumblings
coming from the board rooms and by the drone of great
machines. The lucrative deals being worked out behind closed
doors had been known to the higher ups in the government all
along, and I could now see why they had not been eager to rush
to my support, why, in fact, they had been eager to smother
the issues I had raised as quickly and thoroughly as possible.
With billions of dollars at stake, what were "rights" anyway? I
had not thought much before about the impact that the emergence of multinational corporations might have on me as an
individual, but now I could see at least one critical way in which
they affected me. As governments came more and more to
depend on the incredible wealth generated by the multinat-
ionals, their concern was bound to shift from protection of the
individual citizen to protection of the vast continent-spanning
mechanisms upon which all that wealth depended. If Canada
had been eager to come to anyone's rescue, it had been to the
rescue of corporations that joined the country to another

country for mutual profit, rather than to the rescue of a citizen who had put himself squarely in the path of the grinding gears. Borders no longer really mattered and neither did nationality. There were Frenchmen – such as de Rothschild – who had more say in what the Canadian government did than a mere citizen could ever possibly hope to have. It meant that the will of governments was coming to merge and that their respective citizens could never again be certain by which government they were truly ruled. I had thought for a long time that the "enemy" was France, and now I knew that the "enemy" had just as much been Canada. The two, in fact, were obscenely joined.

Moreover, since France was still not a signatory to the Test Ban Treaty, there was no guarantee that the enriched uranium supplied by Canada would not be used to manufacture plutonium which would in turn be used to fuel the bombs that were now being tested under the tortured coral in the South Pacific. It was not just that all of Canada's pious utterings about its desire to see nuclear testing come to an end had been drivel, because Canada had had the power at any moment to bring the tests to a halt by refusing French military aircraft any landing privileges on Canadian soil. More than that, it was that Canada was even willing to provide the material for the bombs themselves, if there were enough bucks involved. The country I had quietly loved and respected for almost all my life now seemed to me to be nothing much more than a whore, and worse than a whore, for it pretended to be a nun while spreading disease in every direction.

I had a new sense of myself, as though I had awakened one morning on another planet. The old familiar world which I had known was gone. My perception of the world now had a razor quality to it, and it was not just the influence of the cynical hard-nosed Frenchmen in whose company I found myself. It was, in large part, because the suspicions I had felt for close to two years now had been borne out, more than borne out. I felt almost embarrassed at times about how innocent I had been. When I recalled how Admiral Claverie's expression had told me at the end of my first forced visit to Mururoa, "You've been *had*, boy!" I laughed. I had, in fact, been *had* a thousand times over and the old admiral was only one of the foxes who had run circles around me.

How could I have been so naive?

The day finally came – April 8 – when the case was to be heard.

It happened to be two days after the thirtieth anniversary of the dropping of the Bomb on Hiroshima where 200,000 people had died.

I did not realize how exhausted and tense I had become until I could eat neither breakfast nor lunch. For me, that was unheard-of. Ann-Marie had arrived only a few days before, and while it had been a joy to see her, her arrival had also revealed to me the extent of my tension. We had slept together the night before the trial but I had not once during the night felt the urge to make love. Instead, I was possessed by a sense of loss. It reminded me of the night before I had first set out for Mururoa. I felt very much the same – exhausted from endless hassles, an endless sense of being on the edge of an abyss after treading my way through a seemingly endless quagmire. The phone had not stopped ringing for several days. Political bushfires were burning in Canada. And in Paris itself there was a ripple of excitement. There had been no other case like this. An attempt by one of the Frenchmen who had been on board the *Fri* to mount a case had been thrown aside by the courts with scarcely a shrug. The fact that I had even got as far as a trial – with the added handicap of being a foreigner – was an event in itself.

The trial was set for 2 pm. At 11.30 we set out from my room on the seventh floor of the old building which housed the offices of Friends of the Earth. It was a good long walk along the Seine to the courthouse. It stood out as one of the longest, most beautiful walks I had ever taken. On one side was Ann-Marie, decked out in a stylish French raincoat which had been loaned to her by Lison d'Caunes, a twenty-six-year-old Frenchwoman who was involved with Friends of the Earth and was well known as a women's rights speaker throughout the country. Walking along with them, Lison carried a tape recorder hidden under her coat which she intended to smuggle into court so they would have a record of what was actually said, in case the authorities decided to change their story later.

342

For me there was a warmth in that long walk that could not be explained by the spring air or the sunshine. None of us said very much, but I felt a definite buoyancy that seemed to emanate from the two women. It was not a light-headedness, despite the fact that I could not push any food down. Rather, it was as though Ann-Marie and Lison were sending out impulses that held me up and made the walk almost ethereal.

I had agreed not to meet with Thierry until we entered the courtroom. Thierry had said simply: "Look, my friend, I am nervous enough and you are even more nervous than I, so I'll see you in court, okay?"

Now, walking along the Seine, unable to resist humming snatches of "April in Paris", I felt briefly blessed. Tense I was and apprehensive and exhausted, but out of precisely those feelings had come an almost eerie clarity that I guessed some might call psychedelic. Ann-Marie and Lison were both so beautiful that they seemed to glide along beside me like guardian angels.

It was 1975, I realized with a shock. Four springtimes had come and gone since I had set out for Mururoa to penetrate the heart of a bomb. I wondered if I was yet truly any closer to my objective than when I had started. When I came around a curve along the riverbank and saw the domes of the court rearing above Place du Pont Neuf on the island, it gave me almost the same heart-pounding sensation as I had experienced when first I had glimpsed the balloon over the atoll. Could these two events really be related? They were, I knew, but my mind felt tired and did not want to think hard enough to try to bridge the gap that existed between the bomb site and the courthouse, nor did I want to think much about the shadowy figures who had appeared along the way or the manner in which my view of the world had been forced, step by step, to change until now the life I lived and the world I lived it in seemed to have been transformed.

There was a curious preponderance of women in the courtroom, which I could not explain but which did something to ease the almost unbearable sensation of panic that was welling up in me. In all, there were roughly one hundred people squeezed together on the benches, including a hard-core of a dozen heavy-duty journalists, some of whom had been flown in from England and Canada especially for the trial. There were also a large number of French lawyers whose interest had been excited. The hallways and the courtroom itself were swarming with police. The trial had been given an unusual amount of attention in the French press in the last couple of days, and the authorities were obviously worried about the possibility of a demonstration. It could easily have been arranged by then, but I had wanted to keep the issue nose-to-nose in the theatre of the courtroom itself.

And finally there was Thierry.

When the court officer called, "McTaggart versus France", Thierry stood up slowly and took a few hesitant steps forward from the front row of benches, clearing his throat. The three judges were impassive. The procurer – seated at a high bench to the right – looked gnome-like and vaguely malevolent. It was the procurer, more than the judges, who left me feeling we had moved far out of our depth. For in the person of the procurer, the government was listening to every word, watching every move. As for the stout, ageing defence lawyer, Jean Gallot, I sensed a vast scorn and amusement radiating from the man, as though the proceedings which had now begun were little more than a charade. Well, they might prove to be, but for the moment there was no sense that we were involved in a game. It was all too real. And I knew that everything depended on what Thierry now said, for under French law there was no cross-examination of witnesses. Everything hinges on one presentation by each lawyer.

I had a sensation for a moment that Thierry would not be able to summon his voice. And when he did find it, it was coming out so high-pitched that it echoed unconvincingly in the huge chamber. Most distressing of all, I was not sure the judges could hear him properly against the numerous background noises – chairs being scraped against the floor, murmuring voices, coughing, papers being rustled, doors squeaking open and shut, footsteps, whispers.

"Mr President, sir," Thierry began, addressing himself to the senior judge.

344

He knew his material intimately. He had gone over every detail so many times that it was vividly imprinted on his mind. The problem now was to take this entire mental construction which had been assembled in his head and let it unfold.

He had decided to tell it in the form of a story, to describe me as a businessman, a sportsman – to get away from any bias the judges might have against political radicals – and to move on from there in a simple narrative, detailing the sequence of events, saving the arguments about protection of individual rights under French law until the very end.

He was talking too slowly, leaving too many pauses. But it was essential at the beginning to lay the framework clearly. He did not want to have the judges fast asleep by the time he neared the critical part of his presentation, but neither did he dare leave anything out, for he would never get a second chance.

He spoke, in all, for an hour and a half. It took a while, before his nervousness finally left him and he began to warm to the subject which he had come to know so thoroughly. A few times I had a flash of panic when I suspected that he had perhaps been labouring a given point or going into too much detail or, worse, when I sensed that he might have left out some key link in the chain of events. But, to my relief, the noises in the courtroom had faded away into an almost complete silence. While one of the judges managed to retain a completely detached expression, the other two were now following Thierry's words with an intensity rare in French courts, where judges are trained to remain as wooden and aloof as possible. The procurer was following the argument no less carefully.

As he began to talk about the actual ramming and the boarding, an air of authority surfaced, stemming from the long months he had spent going over and over the details. And as he became more animated, the silence in the courtroom became complete. Several more lawyers had slipped through the door and now everyone was hanging on his every word. His hands started to move, striking at each other to indicate the minesweeper crashing into *Vega*. Brandishing the photographs, he approached the judges to indicate exactly what he meant.

Although the one remained slouched in his chair, looking quite unimpressed, the other two leaned forward to peer through these windows onto the event itself. Even the procurer got up from his bench and crossed the floor to study them. When Thierry came to the part describing the beating up, he flourished the pictures Ann-Marie had taken.

The defence lawyer, Jean Gallot, finally got to his feet to shuffle over and have a quick glance. Vigorously, he shook his head and muttered: "I cannot see anything." Thierry then produced a rubber truncheon of the same type used to beat Nigel and me. It had been stolen from the French by the *Fri* crew members.

One of the judges sniffed: "The military authorities use white truncheons, not black."

"But this was not their usual activity," Thierry countered quickly.

Coming to the centrepiece of his argument, he said: "The issue in this case is whether the seas are free. It is not one of French politics."

At last Thierry had said all he could say. He had managed to describe what had happened, and had succeeded in keeping the legalities of the issue on the simple track he had chosen. Whether the approach would work or not remained to be seen, but he had done well, as well as he could, what he had hoped to do. He retreated to his seat.

Jean Gallot now rose. A short, pear-shaped man in his late fifties, he surveyed the judges and the procurer, then cast an amused look at Thierry. "My friend," he said, "you are so young. You should not take so long." Radiating a sense of superiority, he then turned back to the judges and began in a rambling, conversational tone of voice. His defence, as it turned out, was to take exactly as long as Thierry's appeal.

For the first ten minutes, he did not address himself particularly to the case. Instead, he derided Thierry's idealism and painted a picture of me as a kind of ageing hippie troublemaker who lived rather well in a comfortable apartment and was doing all this for amusement.

He had only been speaking for a short time when I suddenly

realized that the older lawyer was confused and did not seem to know very much about the case at all. Gallot was far off the track. It was not long before the man was displaying such a lack of knowledge, not only about the case, but about boats themselves, that he was actually defending several of the points that Thierry had made! The spectators, who had been glowering sourly at Gallot during the first part of his presentation, now burst into laughter when they recognized his mistake. At one point, the government's defender tried to insist that the photographs themselves showed that I had rammed the minesweeper, despite the fact that *Vega* had been hit from the stern and the photos showed her sails taking her away from the warship.

Finally unable to restrain himself any longer, one of the judges cut in:

"A yacht cannot sail backwards!"

More laughter.

Plainly worried, the older lawyer quickly retreated to safer ground. It was concern for my safety that had motivated the navy, he argued. And, besides, the boarding was a legitimate act under French law and was not a violation of international maritime procedure. Finally, mustering his main argument, he referred to several previous judgements and drew from them the conclusion that both the ramming and the boarding were "exceptional cases" and that, as these military acts resulted from government policy decision under the heading of national defence, they could not, in fact, be discussed or challenged.

Thierry leaned over at that point and whispered to Ann-Marie and me:

"Those examples are from the Algerian war. They have never been evoked in peacetime before. If they accept that, it is an open door to let the army do whatever it wants . . ."

The defence lawyer went on to contradict himself several more times. He was interrupted repeatedly by the judges, who now seemed definitely annoyed. He wound up his defence quickly, quoting several professors on issues that Thierry said were not in any way relevant, and, from the tone of their questioning, neither did the judges. Abruptly, Jean Gallot sat down.

I could scarcely believe that this was the best that the government could muster. I knew that if the decision were to be made by the judges then and there, the outcome was obvious. At this point, Thierry had the right to "answer" the other lawyer, but he chose to ignore the whole confused argument and rest his case.

But now the moment came that we had dreaded.

The procurer – the voicebox of the government – climbed from his bench in the silence and strode over to the three judges, speaking to them in a whisper that no one else could hear. There had only been one part of Gallot's rambling defence that could possibly have any weight, and it was not a legal argument at all. It was purely political. He had stated that the Tribunal de Grande Instance was not the appropriate court for the hearing. It was presumably on this issue that the procurer was now addressing himself to the judges.

When he had finished his whispered conversation and returned to his bench, the senior judge announced:

"The procurer has asked for a postponement before he can give his opinion. This case is therefore postponed until May 13." And he banged down his gavel.

Five weeks!

Thirteen days after the hearing I received a letter from my prime minister saying that the Canadian government would definitely espouse the case. The bad press had had its effect once again. The letter was cleverly written, including such lines as a reference to doubts "which have led my advisers to believe that it is in your interest to delay espousal until following the outcome of your own action". It ended: "On receipt of your further request for espousal, I undertake to you that it will take place without delay."

I made note of the date of the letter – 10 April 1975 – for I had come to grow suspicious every time that phrase "without delay" came up in a communication from the government. I recalled that it had been a year and a half since the prime minister had promised to espouse my case, and here he was – *after* the court case had started – still waiting for a "further request" before he would proceed. I couldn't begin to count the number of times Thierry and I had tried to get the government to espouse *before* we were forced into court on our own. Neither could I count the number of times I had been told, by various government officials, not to bother preparing the case because the government would be taking care of everything. After all that, it remained that the government had not been flushed into any kind of action at all until the embarrassment of my having gone it on my own finally forced them into it. On top of what I had learned from Admiral Claverie's confidential letter and what the reporters had discovered about uranium deals between Canada and France, this was the final bit of chicanery. The Canadian government was wily. First they had refused to act until the court case came up, and then they refused to act until the court case was over. Not bad! I had to admire their style.

The period of time that elapsed before the French government procurer gave his opinion to the courts passed neither quickly nor slowly for me. I felt as if I was wandering around in a daze. Ann Marie and I had become involved in the lives of our French friends, but we were both so broke that we were essentially dependent on the others, an experience which neither one of us particularly enjoyed. My disillusionment had turned into an almost fanatical desire to win. I had decided, on the basis of what had happened so far, that my most effective weapon in terms of prodding the government to respond, was to get as many people as possible to write letters to Ottawa. By this time, the files I had so meticulously kept were almost knee-high. I still had copies of every letter that had ever been sent and dupes of all my replies. Each day, I sat down and wrote at least ten personal requests to individuals to write to the government and ask their friends to do the same. I was to cling to this strategy for several months, generating thousands of letters to members of parliament, the prime minister and the external affairs department. Postage had, in fact, become my single biggest item of expense. I was spending up to six dollars a day on stamps and evelopes, and my resources were dwindling steadily. Often, even though I had not asked for it, donations would come back as well as the promise of letters. I would take the donated money and transfer it immediately into yet more stamps and envelopes, and get up the next morning to start scratching more letters by hand. I had no idea what the breaking-point would be for the government, but I was back – as so often before – to the technique of steadily chipping away.

Ann-Marie watched all this going on with a feeling of numbness. It seemed that her life had settled into a pattern which she was afraid might not end for years, if ever. It had been just the same the first winter we had spent together in Canada. The second winter had provided more of the same. And now, here we were in Paris, and life was essentially no different. My mind was perpetually whirring away on its own private track, thinking, thinking, thinking. It was not that she would describe me as "obsessed", but if it was not obsession, it was something awfully near to it. Here in Paris there was less chance than ever to express her view that we should just pack it in and salvage what there was to salvage of our lives. And, for a time, it looked like I might be on the verge of finally settling the issue once and for all. That was all that kept her going. Once the judges had come down with their decision, *then* we would either know it had been worth it or know for sure the whole approach was futile. She said she could not remain with me much beyond that point. For what she wanted was a whole man, not one who only had a half-awareness of the time we spent together. The incessant churning of my mind hardly ever ceased, except in the actual moments when we were making love. I could not even rest for more than a few minutes afterwards before my brain slipped back into the by now so familiar track.

On May 13 we returned to court.

There was nothing we were allowed to say. Neither was it a day for the judges to speak. The only additional dimension which was to be added to the trial that day was the "opinion" of the procurer. Of course, it was not his opinion to any degree at all. Thierry had already explained the mechanism. The procurer delivered the viewpoint of the government. The judges themselves had all worked for the government on their way to

350

the bench, and now that they were on the bench, they were salaried by the government, and the government's voice was the voice they listened to. When the procurer rose to speak, everyone knew – or thought they knew – that whatever he said by way of "opinion" would mysteriously surface later as being exactly parallel to what the "opinion" of the judges would be.

The procurer gave a lengthy speech. I could follow a little of it, but all I had to do was watch Thierry to see how it was going. At the end, Thierry said simply:

"Well, he has told the court that it is not competent to judge any part of the case and the only thing they can do is throw it out."

That was enough for Ann-Marie.

A little more than two weeks later, she left.

The parting was so traumatic I could not even pull together the necessary self-control to go down to the airport with her. We had discussed it over and over again. I was still not convinced that the game had been played out or that I had necessarily lost. For her part, she had heard all the long conversations with Thierry. If we lost in the civil court, there were other courts we could move to. If we wanted, we could always appeal. There seemed to be a hundred small doorways that were at least slightly ajar, although none of them could necessarily be opened enough to let us through. The eyes of the French government guarded each one like a camera mounted on the ceiling. It was all so 1984-ish that she wanted to weep. And still, I could not – or would not – let go. It was something I would either have to work right through, or get beyond, or win or lose so decisively that there could be no coming back, and she said she was not sure that she would know or love the man who might struggle out of the wreckage of a total defeat. It was as though I had gone too far now to find my way back, and the only thing she could do was to leave me to follow my course. On the boat it had been easy, when our goals had been so clearly defined, and in retrospect, so simple. But here in Paris, everything was so confused that it was impossible to know the direction you sought that you might ask for the energy and will to sustain you. In the end, it had simply been too much. So she went back to Vancouver, and from there, when she had earned the money, she retreated to New Zealand.

On June 17, I walked tiredly and only semi-consciously into court. I could tell there were a hell of a lot of reporters around. But Thierry had not been able to make it because he was wrapped up in another case, and the legal firm he had been working for was by this time upset about the amount of time he had been spending on this non-paying case. I fully expected to hear that the case had been dismissed. There did not seem to be any other conclusion to expect. From the time that Ann-Marie had left, I had functioned like an automaton, writing letter after letter after letter, taking odd jobs painting boats and trying to keep my mind blank about the future until I knew for sure that the avenue we had pursued was absolutely closed.

I had been warned by Thierry that the judgement, when it came, would be read so fast – it was something like a tradition – that I would have no chance of understanding it. I had gone to the courtroom with one of the newsmen I had got to know, a seasoned veteran of more wars and scandals than I could remember.

The first indication I had that anything unusual had happened was when I realized that several of the journalists were suddenly leaving the room in a rush. And that the senior judge himself was not in his usual confident mood. In fact, the old man's hands were visibly trembling, and it wasn't until much later that I fully appreciated the enormity of what had transpired in that courtroom. The judge's hands might well have trembled, for, despite the "opinion" of the procurer, which meant despite the ubiquitous and awesomely-powerful French government, the court had not been able to come to the conclusion that the case should be dismissed. The judge did, indeed, agree that the civil court was "not competent" to deal with the charges arising out of the boarding – including the critical charge of armed piracy. But the judges were not willing to agree that the charges involved in the ramming itself could be discarded. Setting the piracy charges aside, the judges ruled that the French naval vessel *La Paimpolaise* had created a "dangerous situation" at sea and had been guilty of deliberately ramming the *Greenpeace III*. The judges even went so far as to order the government to pay out two thousand francs, about five hundred dollars, to have an independent marine surveyor look over the boat so that full damages could be paid.

The newsman whom I had entered the court with had an incredulous expression on his face. I nudged him and whispered: "What's happening?"

"You've won!" he said, before turning to run for a telephone.

I wanted to scream after him! "Goddamn it, what do you mean I've *won*? They threw out the piracy charge, didn't they?" But, before I knew it, I was engulfed by French supporters and newsmen alike.

The press conference that followed was crazy. Thierry was late, which put all the journalists on edge, since they had their deadlines to face. And I refused to say anything until Thierry had arrived. I still did not fully understand what had happened. We had apparently won part of the case but lost the rest. Why was everyone so excited? The people from Friends of the Earth all wanted to head off somewhere and get drunk. To them, it was a major breakthrough. To the press it was a moral victory as well as a partial legal victory. The thrust of everyone's excitement seemed to centre around the fact that victories of that magnitude just did not happen in France, and that I had somehow managed to drive a wedge between the French courts and the government. Whatever the victory meant in terms of international law – and there it was significant because at least part of the centuries-old law of the sea had survived its first test – it meant much more to the assembled Frenchmen. The ramifications for the government from actually having lost the case in the eyes of their own judiciary were enormous. The previously-untouchable military czars had finally been stung! They were no longer invulnerable. Once cracks had begun to appear in their armour, it gave hope that the cracks might open into wounds and that the whole elaborate interlocking structure of the military-industrial-government complex might really someday fall apart. Whether any of this was true or not, it created an atmosphere of euphoria.

I alone was unhappy.

When Thierry finally appeared to set down what the legal alternatives were from there, the reporters turned to me for my comments.

"Well, all they've given me is a carrot," I said. Clearly, in my own mind, I could see that the serious part of the case had been dusted aside, and the less-important matter of the ramming had been allowed to go through. I knew from watching that for the senior judge it had been an act of heroism to even rule that much against the formidable power of the state. I understood, too, that it was a "moral victory" that would have a large impact back in Canada and elsewhere, and that it would cause the French government, and particularly, the military, no end of embarrassment. But I saw no less clearly that it left me in a situation where I could gracefully bow out – accept my laurels – and leave the guts of the matter unresolved. They had still got away with piracy. And they had got away with it by claiming an "exceptional case", which left them with a *carte blanche* to go ahead and bash the hell out of anyone any time they felt like it, in international waters as well as at home. The ruling on the ramming dodged the question of the legal cordon entirely. It simply followed the known laws of navigation anywhere. And so no precedent had been set which would settle, once and for all, the question of who owned the sea and whether anyone could do what they like with it.

I knew, too, that if I bowed out now, that would be the end of it. It would be so easy to say, "Okay, I've won, thank you very much, goodbye."

It was tougher to hang on at that moment than it had been at any other time. In the midst of the celebration that followed the press conference, I sat there, grinning and laughing, as the situation demanded, but remaining within myself feeling completely sour.

"Yeh, well you might call it a carrot, David," said one of the journalists after a few drinks, "but isn't it also at least half a loaf?"

Yeh, I thought, that's right. A carrot or half a loaf, what does it matter?

354

"It's just round one," I said.

After a few more drinks, amid the shouts of laughter and singing, I said again: "Just round one."

But despite the feeling that I had been "had" one more time, I could see the course that now lay open and the entrances to the courtrooms took shape in my mind like trapdoors, one after the other after the other. We could appeal, we could shift from one court to another. Nothing less than a labyrinth remained. Having got through one court, where would we find ourselves except in another? The government could keep retreating forever, throwing crumbs on the floor as it vanished behind yet another door. How long could I pursue it? It felt good, to be sure, to have the French navy running before me as though a film was being played backwards and it was really little *Vega* charging across the waves with the warships crashing frantically to escape over the horizon. That had a good taste. I could savour it. But the victory – moral or otherwise – did not taste like real meat. It was somehow substantially phoney. How could I have been "right" about what happened in 1972 and not be "right" about what happened even more violently the next year? Was the law real or was it totally phoney? Had I accomplished anything or nothing at all? What the hell did it mean that, yes, I had been rammed and that was wrong, but the court was "not competent" to decide on whether I had been boarded and beaten up? The evidence in one case had been no less solid than in the other. If the court was competent to tell the difference between lies and truth on the basis of one set of photographs and all the other data, why on earth was it not competent to decide in the second case? To me, it was all bullshit. It felt schizophrenic. It took almost everyone off the hook. It flinched away from the truth. It proved almost nothing. Or, if it proved anything, it proved that what passed for justice was at the very best, only half a loaf.

I had several months in which to decide whether or not to appeal and there was still the question of the Canadian government's long-delayed, often-promised espousal, and the effect it might or might not have on any further action in the courts.

Instead of anything having been clearly settled, the fame had taken a quantum jump to a new order of complexity.

For a while I basked in the thought that at least the damages to *Vega* would be paid. But I still had a few lessons to learn.

The first sign that the French government was not going immediately to respond to the orders of the court came when Thierry phoned up the lawyer who had represented the government to ask when the money would be delivered to pay for the surveyor. The other lawyer had "not heard anything about that" from the ministry of defence.

Well, when would he hear?

He had "no idea".

The two men were not on good terms by then and the conversation ended abruptly, leaving Thierry with the distinct impression that the older lawyer was not particularly concerned by the thought that the government might actually refuse to obey. French jurisprudence had surely not fallen on such hard times that the government could openly defy a court order. Or had it?

Thierry was left with no course of action except to return to the court and file a complaint with the judges.

Weeks passed. Thierry phoned the lawyer again. He had still "not been advised".

A deadline of August 31 had been set by the courts. The deadline came and went and still nothing was heard from the ministry of defence. By this time, Thierry had contacted the surveyor, whose response was that he would not proceed until he was paid. When Thierry telephoned the government lawyer again, he was told:

"No, we're not paying."

I was dumbfounded and then doubly dumbfounded when I learned that there was no such thing as contempt of court procedure under French law. Our only hope now was public opinion and a written appeal to the president of the court. In France, public opinion was impossible to mobilize because, as the reporters themselves admitted, they had been told to lay off the story. It was worth their jobs to publish anything about it. There had been a flurry of stories before the trial, but after the trial itself, nothing except a one-paragraph report in one of the official government organs mentioning an "ambiguous ruling" against the navy.

The story that France was ignoring a ruling by one of its own courts went out on the international wire services and was published in the United States, Britain, Australia, New Zealand and Canada. But in France, our only chance was that the judges themselves might be able to bring pressure to bear. Thierry's repeated letter to the president of the court finally moved the judge to get on the phone himself to the government lawyer and protest that the government's refusal to pay was "scandalous".

It was not until well into September that the lawyer himself finally handed over the two thousand francs while the defence ministry maintained a stony sulking silence.

A day was finally set when Thierry and I were to sit down with the surveyor with a copy of Harry Pope's survey report listing the damages to the boat. The list was long and technical and I knew we were in for a gruelling session. The moment we stepped into the room where the session would take place I knew it would be even more gruelling than expected. There were six men present, all of them in black suits and shiny shoes. Most of them were from the ministry of defence and it was impossible at first, to tell which one was the surveyor himself. When he was finally introduced, my heart sank. On his lapel, the man wore a French veteran's insignia.

Thierry had no sooner begun to go through the list of damages with him than he started to cross out items from the list.

"What's he doing?" I demanded.

"There is nothing I can do," Thierry shrugged helplessly. "He is the surveyor and he just says 'no' to these items."

"But he hasn't even seen the bloody boat!"

"I know, but –"

Grimly, I took over the negotiations. I had not learned to speak French, so I painstakingly drew pictures illustrating each particular item, its function, the nature of the damage, and the way it had happened. The surveyor grunted and nodded repeatedly but as often as not, when I got to the end of my illustrations, the Frenchman simply shook his head and crossed another item off the list. It was a long tussle. I fought him all the way down the list, but, incredibly, the surveyor ignored me fully half the time, so that when we were finished, I could see that my damages had been whittled down to a fraction of what they had really been. I suspected that when the time came for France to pay – if, indeed, it ever did – that the damages acknowledged by the government would probably amount to no more than the five thousand dollars they had offered to pay me before I set out for Mururoa the second time, despite Harry Pope's carefully itemized survey that put the damages to *Vega* at twelve thousand dollars.

By the time we emerged from the meeting, I was so frustrated and angry I could not bring myself to speak for several blocks and Thierry looked stricken.

Finally, I said:

"That's it, man. I think I've just about had it, to hell with French law."

I went down the next day to the New Zealand embassy and filed an application to immigrate.

During the months of waiting for the ministry of defence to pay out the money for what had turned out to be a complete farce of a survey, I had maintained a steady correspondence with Ann-Marie. I had never disagreed with her impulse to turn her back on the whole mess and neither had she lost any of her feeling for me because I had chosen to carry on. From the time she had got back to New Zealand, she had started writing me letters and I wrote long letters back. With the distance of the whole planet between us, it became possible to bring everything out into the open. She pleaded with me to join her.

I was by this time so disgusted with my own country that I had no desire to return there. The place was rotten to its core, as far as I could see. And I missed Ann-Marie unrelentingly.

I had no intention of giving up the case but my feeling now was that since it was clear the number of roadblocks that could be thrown in my path were endless, the best course of action was to get everything set up for an appeal and then head down to New Zealand and try to put a new life together.

I would sell my property in British Columbia and salvage what I could out of that. It might just be enough to get me started again. At her end, Ann-Marie had arranged through her father for me to have a job when I arrived, so that there would be no problem with immigration.

There had been a note of urgency in her last few letters. An election was coming up and the socialist party which had been swept into office in the wake of the first voyage to Mururoa was in a shaky shape. The prime minister who had launched the navy vessels against the French tests had died and it looked very much as though the same old Conservatives who had done everything they could to prevent me getting away from the dock were about to get back into power. How eager they would be to have me as a citizen was a moot point.

The employees at the New Zealand Embassy were friendly enough until they saw my name written down on the application form. Suddenly, they became very nervous.

There were delays. And more delays. Then the election came and the Conservatives were back in office.

Until then, the bureaucratic mechanism into which my application had disappeared had been proceeding normally enough. Then, shortly after the new government got in, a letter arrived telling me flatly that my application had been rejected.

I was not welcome in New Zealand.

I had never been one to spend much time brooding. Yet there was a special shock in the discovery that the country whose skies were now free of fallout because of what I had helped do should reject me as though I were a leper. Politics. My God, I had not realized how thoroughly the fabric of my life had become saturated with it. And while I had known that real life seldom offered up fairy tale endings, there was a quality of poetic cruelty to New Zealand's decision to slam the door in my face that went beyond anything I had ever read.

I did brood for a short time. The door to New Zealand had closed, leaving Ann-Marie and me with literally a world between us. All the islands and atolls of French Polynesia were locked against me and there was hardly any chance that my "undesirable alien" status would ever change. Canada had

grown wormy and unpleasant in my mind and I had little sense
of myself any longer as a "Canadian".

Oddly, France itself was beginning to look good.

During the periods when I had been taking jobs painting
boats in the southern part of the country, I had come to realize
that once you got out of Paris, it was a magnificent, different
world. It was not just the countryside I had come to love, but
the villages and small ports and the people I met. I liked their
style.

It had taken a while, but I had begun to adopt the French
way of life. At first, I had plunged into my work early in the
morning after a heavy breakfast, and was always astonished to
find that the French themselves were bubbling with energy and
wit by the time I was ready to fall into bed. Slowly, I had shifted
my methods of operation, adopting the French style of starting
slowly with nothing much more than a coffee and easing into
my work during the morning, taking part in a leisurely lunch,
and then going at it full-bore until perhaps seven or eight, with
much of the rest of the evening devoted to a dinner that came
one course at a time, rather than being thrown together into a
messy pile on a single plate.

I liked their manners, too. There was none of the social
aggressiveness which was the rule in the United States and
Canada. I would find myself invited casually to dinner "some-
time". Upon arriving, there might be several people present
and they might have been invited simply to meet me, but often
I would not realize that till weeks later. Everything would be
arranged with fantastic precision, but from there it would be
left to whatever natural flow developed.

It was through one such apparently casual gathering that I
was introduced to a man who suggested, when everyone else
had discreetly moved out of earshot, that I might like to meet
a couple of the sailors who had been at Mururoa and who were
willing to talk to me about what they had witnessed. My immediate impulse was to want to talk to them about the possibility of them appearing in court on my behalf. I agreed quickly
to a meeting.

There were to be two meetings, one in Paris itself, and the

other in a small town in the south. One man had been an officer at Mururoa during 1972 and 1973. The other had been a radio technician. The officer had been intimately involved in the discussions that had preceded the arrival of *Vega* and the technician had been directly involved in the monitoring and surveillance. The preparations for these meetings reminded me of nothing so much as a spy movie. On the first occasion, I had been directed to a certain restaurant, and then left there for an hour past the agreed time while hidden observers waited to see if I had been followed. Then my contact appeared and quickly whisked me away, down back alleys and narrow lanes until I had no idea where I was, and into yet another restaurant, to a table hidden in a corner where the officer was waiting nervously. His nervousness was genuine. For him to be caught telling me what had gone on behind the scenes at Mururoa would mean a long prison term. He was willing enough to talk, with the clear understanding that his identity would never be revealed, but there was absolutely no way he could appear in court. To testify against the military would put him in breach of every known French security regulation. I learned much from the officer, including the fact that *Vega's* presence in the cordon area both years had created enormous problems. Repeatedly, the commanders had been forced to postpone the tests themselves, and each postponement had cost them millions of dollars. The testing of an atomic bomb was no casual matter. Weeks of waiting for exactly the right winds were involved, and then, when the winds were finally right, the presence of that small boat directly in the path of the fallout had forced them to hold back repeatedly. Yes, there had been discussions about sinking *Vega* to get her out of the way. And, yes, the balloon had been hoisted at one point, with all the fantastic cost involved, just to try to scare us away. There was one other piece of information which I found more than mildly interesting: when *Vega* had arrived in the zone in 1973, she had succeeded in arriving on the very day that a test was scheduled. The wind conditions had been generally unstable for quite a while. *Vega's* arrival on the first perfect day they had had in all that time had driven Admiral Claverie and his officers into a rage, precipitating the swift onslaught by the boarding party. Even then, it took another day to get Nigel and the girls out of the way, and by that time the wind conditions had changed. In their frustration the officers had unleashed the bomb against the advice of the meteorologists and that was the bomb that had suffered "blowback", spreading fallout over Samoa.

I had learned, too, that the military authorities were growing steadily more furious every week. It was bad enough that they had been forced to make tests underground, bad enough that they had been humiliated in one of their own courts, but what bothered them most was that the underground tests were not going well. They did not provide the same easy flow of data which could be accumulated by atmospheric tests. And worse, the series of tests they had just conducted at Fagataufa had had the effect of blowing the atoll almost to pieces. They were going to have to switch the following year to Mururoa, and once the coral of Mururoa had been demolished from within, where were they going to go? To compound it all, schisms had opened between the military and several top-level politicians, including the president of France, who were furious over the loss of international prestige which the ramming, the boarding, the beating up and the court case had caused, and who blamed it all on the ineptitude of the navy. Finally, there was the serious long-term problem of the fact that, with its declarations that it would ultimately espouse my case, the Canadian government – if it followed through – would be locked in a collision course with France that sooner or later would have to be resolved, and which the French knew could finally lead to a break in relations with a country that looked to be one of their surest sources of the fuel for their whole nuclear power programme.

A similar meeting a few weeks later with the young radio technician gave me all the details of the methods which had been used to monitor *Vega*, block her transmissions and broadcast phoney responses – all of it in violation of every existing rule governing the uses of radios at sea. But like the officer, the technician did not dare repeat what he had said in public.

The knowledge that the voyages had been effective and that the court case continued to be effective gave me back the will to carry on with as much vigour as ever. In Paris, I continued to crank out roughly ten letters a day. One other thing happened to revitalize the sense of outrage which had come close to turning into a simple feeling of hopelessness: among the letters which I was receiving every day from individuals in Canada were several containing copies of letters from the external affairs department, claiming that the government had "paid" me the twelve thousand dollars which had been used to cover the costs of bringing *Vega* from Tahiti to Vancouver. It had in no sense been a payment to me. It had, if anything, been ransom money paid to get the boat back from France, and it was still a part of the full damages I was trying to prosecute for. The information that the Canadian government was defending its inaction by claiming that I had been "paid" twelve thousand dollars infuriated me. From this and other letters containing news clippings from back home, I got the distinct impression that the government was manoeuvring more desperately than ever to get off the hook. The headlines which had appeared after my partial victory in court had emphasized the "victory" aspect leaving many people in Canada with the impression that the issue was somehow over and done with, that I had been vindicated and there was nothing much more to it. Perhaps sensing that this was the mood in the country, the tone of the letters going out from external affairs to the people who were still writing in changed subtly, implying that my victory had been due primarily to the "good offices" of the Canadian government and the unflagging support which it had given me, to say nothing of the twelve thousand dollars I had been "paid".

My correspondence with Ann-Marie continued but in the face of the fact that I could not go back to New Zealand, there was less and less to say. And then one day a letter came saying that she had met a man ...

Living on my own, dependent on the small donations that trickled in from Canada, my life had become austere. The survival skills that I had learned so long ago in the mountains of British Columbia and the years of sailing served me well. I knew better than to let my physical situation deteriorate, so I kept my small room immaculate, washed all my own clothes by hand in the sink, and did my own cooking. I had learned where to shop for good, cheap food.

My new-found love of France grew by the week as I came to know more and more people and to extend the web of relationships of which I was now firmly a part. There was a sadness in it all, however, because I knew that, much as I would like to I could never settle in France. I was listed as an "undesirable alien" there as much as in French Polynesia. Simply in order to get into the country in the first place, I had had to threaten the French consulate in Vancouver with the prospect of the newsmen and television stations being alerted to be on hand when I arrived at Charles de Gaulle airport so that they could record me being refused entry to the country while attempting to bring my case to the courts. With Franco-Canadian relations already so low, neither the consulate nor anyone in Ottawa wanted that kind of publicity, so a tacit agreement had been worked out to allow me to move back and forth across the border. But the moment my case was finished, my status as an undesirable alien would immediately be put into effect.

And then, I wondered, where would I go?

I was rapidly becoming a man with no country, or at least a man with no country that I wanted or that wanted me.

I spent Christmas alone in Paris, so broke that day that all I had to eat was rice. My friends had all taken vacations in the countryside. It was grey and foggy. I sat in my room, listening to the carols being sung, and missed Ann-Marie so badly that I thought I would burst. In the afternoon, I went for a long walk, my head twisting rudderlessly as it sought to point me in some direction that would make sense. My time in France, I knew, was limited. And beyond that, regardless of the outcome of my case, there did not seem to be any place to go. I had tried to shore up my crumbling business plans back home but without me there to carry out the work, they were falling steadily apart and the time was not that far ahead when I would be left with no property, no assets at all. I was now forty-three years old.

On January 18, 1976, we launched our appeal.

According to everyone I had talked to, including Thierry,

there was virtually no chance of winning. The government's procurer could be expected to give the opinion he had given before – that the boarding party and armed piracy charges were outside of the jurisdiction of the civil court, and there was little reason to hope that the judges would find any grounds to disagree. It was a necessary step, though, because the decision of the Court of Appeal would automatically be examined by the Supreme Court, whose job it was to consider the legal validity of the judgement. In its examination, the Supreme Court would be forced to rule one way or the other on the Catch-22 that had been invoked by the government as an umbrella to justify its actions.

The French Supreme Court had never been called upon to examine the meaning of "exceptional case" before. The government had used that particular justification some one hundred times in the past to have cases thrown out of the civil courts, but in all but five of the instances, it had been done while the country was at war. If my appeal was rejected, and at the next stage the Supreme Court upheld the rejection, then the rulings would become fixed in French law. The government from then on would have the legal power to do what it wanted in international water. The dilemma for France would be that such a ruling would fly in the face of the 1958 Geneva Convention which had upheld the law of the sea and it would put the republic in the position of an outlaw whose own internal laws were in open conflict with the laws by which all other nations had agreed to allow themselves to be governed. The impact on France's relations with other countries could not be foreseen except for the certainty that it would leave the country in an embarrassing and untenable position. It would also mean that France herself would have difficulty protesting against any other foreign activity near her own shores or for that matter, against any action taken by foreign governments against her own citizens.

Yet for the Supreme Court to overturn the "exceptional cases" ruling would strip the government of one of its more cherished methods of enforcing the will of the military. It was not just that the navy would have to pay damages, or even that certain officers within the navy would theoretically find themselves facing the possibility of the guillotine. Worse, they would lose forever, under their own laws, the right to test nuclear weapons in the atmosphere or even to fish or drill for oil in waters which did not belong to them.

My "insignificant" little case against the navy had now set a legal mechanism in operation which threatened to have a decisive influence one way or another not only on France's nuclear programme but on the outcome of the international struggle which was emerging over the whole question of exploitation of the resources of the sea. It could set a precedent in world law which would ultimately apply as much to fishing rights and oil-drilling and underwater mining as to nuclear testing.

No one in Paris could guess what the outcome of the case might be. It was generally agreed that the appeal would be rejected, but beyond the appeal, at the Supreme Court stage, the government would finally have run out of room to manoeuvre. The judges themselves might be perfectly willing to rule whichever way the government ordered, but what would the government's order be? To rule against me would put them in the position of having created a law which completely contradicted international law and which could be used by other countries against them. A ruling in my favour would have the unthinkable effect not only of humiliating the military but also of removing one of their most effective techniques for disposing of troublemakers.

To add to France's woes, the Canadian government finally responded to my long campaign to make Ottawa act. In the last week of March, a representative of the Canadian embassy in Paris formally presented a Note to the French foreign ministry announcing Canada's espousal of my case. Until then, the step of espousal had only been taken by Canada in cases where socialist countries in Eastern Europe had nationalized property which had been owned by people who were Canadian citizens. With that step, Canada had moved into the game as a player in its own right. France now not only faced me in the courts but also now faced an opponent more or less its own size in the larger theatre of international diplomatic relations. With the delivery of the Note, the espousal of my claims against France had become part of official Canadian policy. It meant that if the claims were not settled, Canada would be forced steadily to escalate the pressure on France. In the end, there would either be a settlement or Canada would ultimately have to sever relations or employ economic sanctions, which might easily jeopardize France's hopes for getting the uranium it so badly wanted or might even lead to loss of its military flight privileges in Canadian airports.

On June 13, Thierry and I stepped back into the courtroom to hear the verdict on our appeal. To the end, I had preserved a small stubborn belief that the court just might find the courage to rule in my favour. But the court did not. It accepted the position of the government that the boarding had been an "exceptional case" and that France's rules of conduct during wartime could be applied equally in a time of peace, regardless of whether France was acting on her own territory or in international waters.

It was only at the end of the reading of the lengthy verdict that the government procurer, Jacques Simon, paused and then added something that sent the reporters rushing to their typewriters. He spoke clearly and deliberately.

"It should not be denied that McTaggart may have helped to persuade the French government to decide to choose underground tests in place of atmospheric tests," he said. "It is very possible that McTaggart's attitude, reinforced by the reactions of certain countries and certain groups, caused the government of France to think again."

Thierry could not quite believe it. The procurer, after all, spoke for no one other than the government itself. For the French government to give me credit – after all that had happened – struck Thierry as being almost beyond belief. The only explanation that made any sense was that the government had used the occasion to "stick it" to the military and that the rumoured rift between the politicians and the top echelon of the ministry of defence had widened enormously. I knew that there was a power struggle of considerable proportions going on between the generals and the politicians over the whole

367

future of France's military direction, with the politicians fearing that the burden of trying to create and maintain a nuclear force was costing them dearly not only in terms of money but also votes. And the generals were known to be desperately worried that they were rapidly running out of options in terms of test sites.

I could see that I had been handed one more carrot. As before, when the court had ruled that I had indeed been rammed, I knew I could gracefully bow out. The alternative was to push on through to the Supreme Court, but to do that was going to require large amounts of money. Thierry was not qualified under French law to speak in the Supreme Court. There were only a handful of lawyers so qualified and none of them was willing, as Thierry had been, to waive his fee.

A few days after the hearing, I went for a very long walk by myself through Paris, out into the suburbs, to give my mind a chance to unravel.

In a couple of days, it would be my birthday again and I would be forty-four years old. I no longer had a boat. I had used up all the resources which might have gone into providing economic security for my children. My business arrangements back in British Columbia had collapsed. Ann-Marie was lost to me forever. One way or another, I would soon be thrown out of France, the only country left where I felt at all at home. I had changed too much, perhaps become too cynical, for any of my old friends to have anything to say to me. My right eye might go at any time. My hair had almost entirely left the top of my head and what remained was now predominantly silver. My shoulders, I knew, had become stooped and the tremendous health I had once enjoyed was ebbing rapidly. I still felt the sting of having been barred from New Zealand and from French Polynesia so that the South Pacific I had always loved was now essentially closed to me. I had in theory lost my case in the French Court as I could not afford to appeal. Ironically, to my own government I was a nuisance they wished would go away. But back in Canada the headlines had proclaimed: FRENCH CREDIT MCTAGGART FOR TEST END.

I knew exactly the extent of the achievement. *La Bombe* had been driven underground. With the launching of *Vega*, a series of processes had been set in motion which had had quite fantastic results. Canada and France were now locked in a diplomatic duel which might yet have the decisive effect of destroying the roots of at least one nation's nuclear ambitions, and who could tell what long-term effects that might have on other nations? The wheels of justice had not been made to move easily, but they were at last in creaking motion, leaving the French navy facing an inevitable no-win situation in the courts. If the contest had been outrageously unequal at the beginning, it had now progressed to the point where one tiny pawn against all the queens and bishops and castles and knights had created a stalemate. At that level, I knew I had never played a game so well as the one that had begun when first I decided to sail against all odds to Mururoa atoll.

Epilogue

It was not until the summer of 1977 that Canada was exposed, along with France, for having set up a price-fixing cartel to drive up the world prices of raw uranium.

By then, it had also been learned that Atomic Energy of Canada Ltd, the government's marketing arm for the Canadian-made CANDU nuclear reactor, had paid out nearly 18 million dollars in fees to "agents" in connection with the sale of reactors to both Argentina and South Korea. One of these agents was strongly linked with Mafia-style graft that swirled around the old Peronist regime in Argentina. His contacts extended beyond that into La Cosa, a multiple-racketeering outfit with tentacles into large-scale smuggling, illegal gambling, prostitution, extortion and fraud.

The timing of the setting-up of the uranium price-fixing cartel was most interesting. Representatives from Canada, four other uranium-producing countries and their major mining firms had gathered quietly in Paris in February, 1972, to divide up the world market for the metal and set standard floor prices for its sale. That was roughly a month before I arrived at my own decision to sail to Mururoa, when I was still innocent enough to think that my government might support me because, after all, it was supposed to be opposed to nuclear proliferation.

The reluctance of the Canadian government to stand behind me against French piracy stemmed, in no small part, from the fact that behind the scenes Canada and France had slipped into bed together in a cartel arrangement which saw the price of uranium jump some 700 per cent between 1972 and 1975 from $9.50 a pound to $41.50 a pound.

The revelations about the cartel did not emerge from either Canada or France. They only became public when released by a

US congressional inquiry, which also noted that the Canadian government had forced Gulf Minerals Canada, a subsidiary of Gulf Oil Corp. of the US to participate in the cartel, thereby violating American antitrust legislation. It was also revealed that the Liberal Party of Canada was once again deeply involved at the big money level. The president of Uranium Canada Ltd at the time the cartel was set up was Jack Austin, who was later appointed by the Liberals to the Canadian senate. In Canada – the "True North Strong and Free" – price-fixing and patronage went hand in hand, even though the politicians tried to write it all off as plain good business.

They had a harder time, however, trying to dismiss the charges of payoffs and bribes around the sale of CANDU reactors. In November 1976, the auditor-general reported that Atomic Energy of Canada Ltd had paid some 15.4 million dollars to United Development Inc. of Tel Aviv, a worldwide sales corporation headed by Shaul Eisenberg, and 2.4 million dollars to a firm called Intercontinental General Trading Establishment of Liechtenstein. More than 10 million dollars of this money was never "adequately accounted for" – which implied that the payments had gone to Argentinian and South Korean officials in the form of bribes to persuade them to purchase CANDU reactors. It was in 1972 – again, the year of my first voyage to Mururoa – that Canada signed on Eisenberg and United Development as exclusive agents to sell CANDU to South Korea and at the same time joined in a partnership with Italimpianti, a state-owned Italian engineering firm based in Genoa, to sell the Canadian reactor to Argentina. Within the year, Canada had sold its first two reactors abroad. But along the way, it had shelled out a lot of money to such characters as Camillo Crociani, one of the top officers of Italimpianti, who at the time of this writing is on the run because police want to talk to him about his part in Italy's Lockheed scandal, as well as Argentina's former economics minister Jose Ber Gelbard and former defence minister Adolfo Mario Savino, both now living in exile. According to reports out of Buenos Aires, Savino was a representative of Italimpianti during his term in office and Gelbard had been a top contender for the leadership of a massive criminal syndicate in Argentina which used its grip on government to push what its members call La Cosa, meaning "the thing", as in Cosa Nostra.

Against this background – coupled with what I have already learned about Canada's complicity with French military officials in the seizing of *Vega* and the partnerships that already existed between Canada and France concerning the development of uranium enrichment plants – it is no longer surprising that prime minister Pierre Trudeau and his cabinet ministers chose to ignore, as much as possible, the affair of the *Greenpeace III*. At the time of this writing, they have still not taken any concrete action to espouse my claim, nor has any Canadian external affairs minister done anything more than have private discussions with his French counterpart, discussions which have led nowhere.

In September, 1976, the Canadian government went to amazing new lengths to keep all this dirty linen from being aired. Bypassing Parliament entirely, Pierre Trudeau's federal cabinet met behind locked doors to pass an order in council forbidding the release of any information concerning its many under-the-table uranium deals. The penalty for disclosure of any documents – or even for the crime of "failing to guard against unauthorized release" of documents concerning uranium negotiations between 1971 and 1975 – was set at two year's imprisonment or $5000 fine. No previous Canadian government had ever gone to such lengths to cover its tracks.

This "gag law" on uranium information was challenged in the Ontario Supreme Court by six conservative party members of parliament, including the current leader of the opposition, Joe Clark. But as late as October 1977, apart from a few minor revisions, the order in council stood intact, and public discussion of the matter in Canada was – by law – limited to material already made public. It is a crime now in my country to talk about the government's crimes.